The Story of
the British Light
Aeroplane

Perfection of line: the Percival Mew Gull

THE STORY OF
THE BRITISH LIGHT
AEROPLANE

<<-<< ◈ >>->>

TERENCE BOUGHTON

JOHN MURRAY

To my understanding parents
for happy memories
of the Brooklands days

Contents

Illustrations

SKETCH MAPS IN TEXT

ACKNOWLEDGEMENTS

I make grateful acknowledgment to the following for supplying illustration material:

Flight International: frontispiece, plates, 1, 2, 3, 4, 7, 8, 9, 10, 11, 12, 13, 14, 15, 18, 19, 21, 22, 23, 27, 29, 30, 36, 39, 40, 52, 54, 61; figures 1, 2, 5. Radio Times Hulton Picture Library: plates 5, 6, 16, 17, 25, 32, 33, 41, 46. *The Aeroplane and Commercial Aviation News*: plates 20, 24, 26, 35, 37, 38, 42, 43, 50, 51, 55, 56, 57, 62, 63. Fox Photos Ltd: plates 44, 45, 49, 53, 58, 60. The de Havilland Aircraft Co: plates 28, 34. Mr C. H. Latimer-Needham: plate 31; figure 6. Hon. Mrs Victor Bruce: plate 47. Roy Bell Photo: plate 48. Mr G. H. Miles: plate 59. Topix (Thomson Newspapers): plate 64. Cheltenham Newspaper Co Ltd: plate 65. *Jane's All the World's Aircraft*: figures 3, 4, 7, 8. Sketch maps drawn by Mr Denys R. Baker.

Preface

For most people nowadays the word 'aeroplane' conjures up two pictures only: a military weapon whose destructive power is a constant threat to us all, and a fast, luxurious and world-wide means of transport. The immense complexity of modern aircraft, the gigantic capital investment which they represent, the trend of airline publicity and the Official Secrets Act all conspire to keep the ordinary man firmly in his humble role of spectator, fare-paying passenger and taxpayer. He is not invited to take an interest in what happens in the pilot's cabin; he is flown, but he does not fly himself. To the millions who travel by air but are not professionally concerned with aviation, and even to the great majority of those who are so concerned, the idea of making a solo flight round their local aerodrome is almost as remote as that of making a journey into space.

This picture of aviation is incomplete. Amateur flying in Britain has a small but enthusiastic following and an honourable history. Almost forty years ago, when commercial air travel had itself hardly begun, this country played a leading part in the development of small and simple aeroplanes as personal vehicles, and through the medium of State-subsidised flying clubs these little machines provided a cheap way into the air for tens of thousands of people. Some of the pilots who learned to fly in this way later used light aeroplanes for long-distance flights across the world, and by their example aroused public interest in aviation and showed the way which commercial air transport was to follow. The war of 1939–45 set back the development of personal flying for a number of years and only recently have there been definite signs of its recovery.

I have attempted here to bring together various aspects of the story of the British light aeroplane movement from its beginnings to the present day. Although most of the present work deals with the 1920s and 1930s, a final chapter briefly describes such post-war progress as there has been and may be helpful to those wishing to take up flying for pleasure or business.

In the days before 1939 the amateur and professional, military and civil, aspects of flying were far more inextricably mixed than they are today, and this gave the period much of its charm. Since hard and fast distinctions would therefore be out of place, I have deliberately refrained from binding myself to any rigid definition of what constitutes a light aeroplane. I have tried only to keep within a general framework of personal flight, and have omitted whatever does not seem to fit into this framework, however important it may be from the standpoint of general aviation history.

It would be very difficult to write a book of this kind without extensive help from those who were directly concerned with the events described, and this help I have had in generous measure. I should particularly like to express my gratitude to the following, all of whom have given me their time and contributed reminiscences, lent material of various kinds or made helpful suggestions: Mr L. E. Baynes; Mr J. H. Blake, librarian of the Royal Aero Club; Captain H. S. Broad, M.B.E., A.F.C.; Mr P. W. S. Bulman, C.B.E., M.C., A.F.C.; W/Cdr J. C. Cantrill, R.A.F.O.; Mr Francis Chichester; Sir Alan J. Cobham, K.B.E., A.F.C.; Dr N. A. de Bruyne; Mr Geoffrey Dorman; Mr Alan Goodfellow; Mr N. H. Jones; Mr Marcus Langley; Mr C. H. Latimer-Needham; Mr G. H. Miles; Mr H. J. Penrose, O.B.E.; Capt. E. W. Percival; Mr W. S. Shackleton; Mr F. H. Smith, librarian of the Royal Aeronautical Society; Miss E. Southern of the Association of British Aero Clubs and Centres; Captain A. G. Store, M.V.O., O.B.E.; Mr O. J. Tapper.

Of the above, Messrs Bulman, Dorman, Goodfellow, Miles and Percival were good enough to read parts of the text and point out various errors; I must take the blame for any which remain.

For the general framework of the book and most of the facts and dates I am indebted to the files of *Flight*, *The Aeroplane*, *The Times*, the *Daily Mail*, and *Popular Flying*; to the *Air Annual of the British Empire*, the *Journal of the Royal Aeronautical Society*, the *Royal Aero Club Gazette*, the *de Havilland Gazette*, *Jane's All the World's Aircraft*; and to Mr A. J. Jackson's *British Civil Aircraft 1919–59*, as well as to the books listed in the bibliography. I have also drawn on two official publications, the annual *Report of the Progress of British Civil Aviation* and the *Civil Aviation Statistical and Technical Review*, for which due acknowledgement is made to Her Majesty's Stationery Office.

More particularly I wish to acknowledge kind permission to quote the following extracts: on p. 1, from *The Story of the Aeroplane*, by Claude Grahame-White (The Bodley Head Ltd); on pp. 3–4, 29–30, from *Flight* (Associated Iliffe Press Ltd); on pp. 25, 42, 62–3, from *The Aeroplane* (Temple Press Ltd); on p. 34, from the London *Daily Mail* (Associated Newspapers Ltd); on pp. 80, 94–5, 134, from *The Times*; on p. 124, from *The Tatler and Bystander*; on p. 128, from *First Flights*, by Major Oliver Stewart (Routledge & Kegan Paul Ltd).

Finally, I should like to thank my publishers for the great pains taken in getting the raw first work of an author into a respectable shape for publication; my friend Mr L. A. Ward, for reading the proofs and helping in various other ways; and finally my wife, for doing some of the more tiresome work of tabulation and for her encouragement over the period of nearly three years since the book was begun. T. B. A. B.

⊷ I ⊷

Beginnings

We see a country house in a well-wooded park. A man in a big coat, wearing a fur cap, steps through some doors upon a terrace, crosses a lawn and walks towards what appears to be an elongated motor-car garage. Two women, warmly clad, are with him. The doors of the building are opened. Out glides, under the persuasion of a leather-clad chauffeur and two assistants, another and still lighter type of the slim-winged bird. There are seats below it. Out upon a drive, at the side of the mansion, the machine is wheeled. The man and the two women take their seats, the women with unconcerned laughter. They muffle themselves snugly with rugs. There is again the unmistakeable whir of powerful machinery. At the front of the machine a propeller flickers with immense speed until it is lost to sight. The aerial chauffeur steps nimbly upon a seat at the rear. It speeds across country, swiftly and surely, passing over hill and dale until another fine country-house looms in sight below. Then it dips—dips down sharply. It touches ground and rolls up another drive. It pauses at a fine portal. Out down the steps runs a merry party. The three visitors, breathless and exhilarated, are escorted into the oak-panelled hall. Tea is served! An afternoon call by aeroplane is now an accomplished fact.

This quotation, taken from a book published in the year 1911, is a prophecy of events supposed to take place nine years later. The author was the famous aviation pioneer Claude Grahame-White, and in his book— *The Story of the Aeroplane*—a detailed description of the contemporary state of aeronautics is followed by an expression of his belief in the potentialities of aircraft not only in the commercial and military fields but as an ordinary mode of personal transport. At the time when the book was written, the art of practical flying was still extremely young, but the achievements of the aeroplane and its very rapid development from year to year were such as to encourage a wealth of speculation as to its undoubtedly promising future, so that although to most of the thousands who flocked to Hendon in those days flying was as yet hardly more than an elaborate kind of vaudeville turn the more reflective members of the public, sharing Grahame-White's optimism, could draw an obvious parallel between the progress of the aeroplane and that of the motor-car. The latter, after being a subject for ridicule in its earliest days not so long

before, was already commonplace as a private vehicle for the relatively
well-to-do, and year by year technical progress and the pressure of commercial competition were working together to bring its ownership within
reach of a wider section of the population. The aeroplane, by comparison,
was still something of a curiosity, but what could seem more natural than
that in due course it should follow the same path and become a reliable
personal vehicle, less convenient certainly than the motor-car for short
journeys but immensely superior over long distances by reason of its speed
and indifference to geographical obstacles? One of the most outstanding
of such obstacles to British eyes—the English Channel—had only recently
been overcome for the first time by the little monoplane of Louis Blériot,
and after that historic day in July 1909 the phrase had become current
that 'Britain was no longer an island'. These words had in most ears a
sinister military ring, but they had also the more innocent meaning that for
the private aeroplane owner of the future, setting casually out on holiday
or business with his friends and luggage safely stowed on board, the tedium
of the boat-train and the Channel steamer would be a thing of the past.

Aviation has progressed so rapidly from its early beginnings to the
present day that most forecasts which seemed absurdly extravagant at the
time of their making have only been proved by the passage of time to
have been excessively conservative. The prophecy just quoted, however,
cannot have seemed a particularly rash one to the reader of 1911, for by
the time *The Story of the Aeroplane* appeared in the bookshops, private
flying and touring by air was already an accomplished fact. The brief and
golden early years of British aviation which began with the first uncertain
flight of Cody's British Army Aeroplane No. 1 at Farnborough in October
1908 and ended with the outbreak of war less than six years later were a
period when the personal, the sporting and the spectacular aspects of flying
took precedence over all others. The frail aeroplanes of the day, 'light' in
every sense of the word, were extremely well adapted by reason of their
very low landing speeds as personal vehicles for leisurely cross-country
journeys, able to come down in any convenient meadow or open space for
their pilots and passengers to visit friends, take on petrol, ask the way, or
even keep a business appointment. It is true that unreliability of engines,
shortcomings in stability and control and extreme sensitivity to rough
weather severely limited their usefulness for these purposes by comparison
with that of the motor-car, but the inevitable march of technical progress
could safely be left to deal with all such difficulties within a decade or so,
and in the meantime the more enterprising aviators were impatiently setting out to show that the aeroplane, fragile and uncertain though it still
was, could in favourable conditions be made to rival the car for the purpose of individual transport.

1. The ancestor of the light aeroplane: the Santos Dumont Demoiselle
2. The Blackburn Sidecar on show in Harrods, 1919

3.   The Avro Baby
4.   The Austin Whippet, showing wing-folding

A typical demonstration of this sort was the week-end tour of Mr Graham Gilmour and Mr E. C. Gordon England on a Bristol biplane in April 1911, said to have been the first journey of its kind ever to have been undertaken by aeroplane in England. Setting out early one Saturday morning from the British and Colonial Aircraft Company's flying school on Salisbury Plain, and navigating after the fashion of the time 'by Bradshaw', they immediately lost themselves by following the wrong railway and ended up in the grounds of a large country house where they were invited to breakfast. From there, proceeding on their way, they pursued a leisurely course round the West Country, landing as their fancy took them in order to visit friends, give joy-rides and perform exhibition flights for the benefit of the local populace. An invitation to dinner on the Sunday evening was their undoing, for the dashing Gilmour, boldly attempting to land on his host's lawn since the adjoining parkland was obstructed by trees, overshot the smooth turf and carried away an iron fence with slight damage to his machine. In spite of its abrupt and unfortunate end, this tour was a striking example of the use of the air for ordinary private travel and on his return journey by road Gilmour managed to show that motoring, too, was not without its hazards in 1911, for he contrived to turn his car upside down in a ditch and had to spend a most uncomfortable night in it until help arrived in the morning.

Grahame-White himself was inclined to specialise in performances intended to impress upon the public the possibilities of the aeroplane as an everyday means of transport. His gallant failure to beat the French pilot Louis Paulhan in the race from London to Manchester for the prize of £10,000 offered by the *Daily Mail* first brought his name before the public, and the dramatic story of how he tried to steal a march on his opponent by taking off at night in the light of car head-lamps—an extraordinary feat in 1910—only to be cheated of victory by engine trouble, is well-known to every student of the early days of flying. In the following year he made a journey by air to open an exhibition, and his account of it in *Flight* (22 April 1911) gives a good idea of the leisurely nature of cross-country flying at that time. His intention of covering the 115 miles between Hendon and the model village of Bournville, near Birmingham, in seven hours was frustrated by the weather, and after a start at 5.45 a.m. he was forced down by mist at Fenny Stratford, damaging his rudder.

> Before the mist had lifted, however, the wind had begun to assert itself and he therefore determined to remain a bit longer on *terra firma*. Not until 4.15 did he attempt to re-start, when he got well away, taking the route past Bletchley and Towcester, where great greetings were shouted to him from the racecourse visitors. He was soon after passing Dunchurch, and when in sight of Coventry he thought it would be safer to take in more petrol, for which purpose he descended for a few minutes. Resuming his journey, upon

reaching the outskirts of Birmingham he again came down at Sparkhill in a football field for information as to the direction of Bournville.

Without further difficulty he was then able to steer direct over the four last miles to his destination where, as already noted, he arrived in fine form at 6.35, alighting, in spite of the awkward surroundings of houses and trees, in perfect style.

One could continue indefinitely to quote examples of practical air travelling in the early days of aviation, such as Gustav Hamel's non-stop flight from Dover to Cologne in early 1913, Gordon Bell's journey in a stiff wind from Paris to Whitstable, and the adventures of that enterprising music-hall juggler, Mr T. Elder Hearn, who bought a two-seater Blériot in which to tour the provinces, learned to fly it in France and at once set off alone in it bound for Liverpool, arriving there safe and sound after numerous adventures in spite of the fact that his total flying experience on leaving Paris was less than ten hours. This book, however, is not intended to be a history of aviation before 1914, and the reader who wishes to pursue these fascinating topics further is recommended to spend an afternoon in a library with a stack of early volumes of *Flight* at his elbow, unless indeed he has been bequeathed a set of these rare treasures by an aeronautically minded uncle, in which case he will know them by heart already. For the present purpose enough has been said to make the point originally stated that private flying and air touring, cheerfully and inextricably mixed with aeronautical experiments of every kind from the severely practical to the frankly eccentric, were already flourishing strongly in that rich and active period. Restrictions on flying were in those days practically non-existent apart from a few prohibited areas round places of military importance, and the individual aviator enjoyed a freedom from official obstruction (whether well-meaning or hostile) such as he has never since known and is most unlikely to know again. It has been estimated that in the period 1910–12 there were something like 250 privately-owned aeroplanes in Great Britain, and by 1913 the flying schools at Brooklands, Hendon, Eastbourne, Salisbury Plain and elsewhere were turning out newly-qualified pilots at the rate of nearly one a day.

The light aeroplane as a distinct species could hardly yet be said to exist, for by 1914 the art of aircraft design had only just begun to reach the stage at which the functions of different types of machine could be sharply differentiated. When the archetype of all light aeroplanes, the famous de Havilland Moth, first appeared in 1925, it formed a striking contrast with the large commercial transport machines and high-performance military fighters of its day, but in the years before the Great War aircraft in these last categories had not yet come into being. With a few rare exceptions such as the huge four-engined Sikorski designs of 1913, all aeroplanes were

'light' in the sense that they were small, of low weight and wing-loading*
and equipped with engines (such as the famous 50-h.p. Gnôme rotary)
whose power output was in most cases less than that of the A.D.C. Cirrus
which, when fitted to the Moth, first made world-wide personal flying a
practical proposition. Consequently the pilot who had just taken his certificate and who sought to buy an aeroplane for private and sporting purposes
had a most extensive field from which to choose, at a wide variety of prices.
One of the most practical and popular single-seater monoplanes of 1909,
for instance—the Channel-conquering Blériot XI with 25-h.p. Anzani
engine—cost £480, the Voisin biplane with E.N.V. engine £780, and the
graceful Antoinette £1,000. These prices were comparable with those of
the good-quality motor-car of the day, for at the Motor Show at Olympia
a few years later the 16/80 h.p. Wolseley with torpedo phaeton body could
be purchased for £460, the 25/30 h.p. Argyll for £750, and the chassis
alone of the powerful 60-h.p. 6-cylinder Napier cost £1,095. Thus there
was nothing to prevent the young man of means who could afford a good
car from owning an aeroplane and a cheaper car in its stead, though the
running costs of both might in some cases defeat him. It was not every
prospective motorist, however, who was prepared to pay the price asked
for a full-sized car, and to attract a wider market some manufacturers
specialised in the lower-priced *voiturette*, a typical example of which was
the 8-h.p. Alldays and Onions two-seater which sold complete with hood,
screen and side and tail lamps for only £138 10s. In just the same way the
inevitable process of simplifying and cheapening the aeroplane had been
set in motion by enterprising designers and manufacturers almost as
soon as practical aviation began, and it is to their products that we must
turn to seek the true ancestors of the popular light aeroplane of the
1920s.

The most interesting and original of these ancestors, fairly deserving
the title of the world's first light aeroplane, was undoubtedly the little
Demoiselle designed by the Brazilian pioneer of airships and aeroplanes
Alberto Santos Dumont, which was developed as early as 1907 but not
shown in its final form until it appeared on the Clement-Bayard stand at
the Paris Aero Show of 1909. It was claimed at the time that the Demoiselle
—'le Santos No. 20'—was the smallest aeroplane in existence, and Santos
Dumont's object, like that of Henri Mignet with his Pou du Ciel a quarter
of a century later, was to achieve simplicity and cheapness by a drastic
reduction of size and of the number of parts, especially aerofoil surfaces
such as wings, tail unit and controls. The weight of the complete machine

* The wing-loading of an aeroplane, defined as the weight divided by the wing area, is
one of the fundamental properties at the disposal of the designer. In general a high wing-loading
means a high minimum speed, but the latter can be reduced by the use of 'high-lift' devices
such as the trailing-edge flap.

in flying condition with the pilot on board was only 530 lbs. The mono-plane wing, whose span was 18 ft, was arranged so that it could be warped* for lateral control, and the tail consisted of a single cruciform unit which was universally jointed so that it could be moved to perform the functions of both elevator and rudder. The pilot's controls were somewhat original, for the wing-warping was operated by a lever strapped to his back so that he could balance the machine laterally by leaning to one side or the other, while the movement of the tail in the 'elevator' sense was controlled by a lever held in the right hand and in the 'rudder' sense by a wheel turned by the left hand. The pilot himself was seated in an extraordinarily uncom-fortable position in the open-work bamboo fuselage beneath the wing and behind the tractor propeller, which was driven by a 2-cylinder engine of 30 h.p.; in this way not only was he exposed to all the elements but their natural fury was accentuated for him by the blast of the slipstream, in which he was totally immersed (Plate 1).

The Demoiselle was priced at £300, but Santos Dumont generously made a free gift of all rights in the design to the world at large and ex-pressed the hope that individuals would be able to have their own machines built for them for the sum of 6,000–7,000 francs, equivalent to about £260. Several firms, among them Oylers Limited and Mann and Overton in England, took advantage of this offer and constructed for sale their own versions of the Santos Dumont design, and the Clement-Bayard concern went so far as to produce a wingless ground trainer on which purchasers could familiarise themselves with the controls before venturing into the air. The Demoiselle had a certain success on its own account and in-fluenced the design of a number of other machines, notably those of the British pioneer Mr Robert Blackburn, and even if it did not cause quite the revolution in flying for which its designer hoped it was a bold early attempt to offer the public simplicity and cheapness and attract the ordi-nary man into the air.

At the other end of the scale was the wealthy private owner who did not himself wish to handle the controls but preferred to employ a pro-fessional aerial chauffeur, and he too was being catered for as early as 1911. In the latter part of that year the Blériot company built to the special order of M. Henri Deutsch de la Meurthe a remarkable personal aeroplane known as the Berline and illustrated in the aeronautical press under the heading 'The First Aerocar'. The owner was comfortably accommodated in a totally-enclosed cabin with a side-entrance door and mica windows in front and to either side, and could communicate his orders to the pilot,

---

* Lateral control by wing warping, or twisting the whole wing structure to increase lift on one side and decrease it on the other, was much used in the relatively flimsy aeroplanes of the early days of aviation, but was almost entirely superseded by the modern system of hinged flaps or ailerons by the beginning of the Great War.

who was very much less comfortably mounted on an outside seat in front, by means of an arrangement of speaking-tubes such as was in those days fitted in taxis. An additional outside seat was provided for the use of a mechanic, or possibly a footman, and the general plan of the machine was very similar to that of the stately chauffeur-driven cars of the time; in both cases streamlining came nowhere in comparison with the demands of spacious interior comfort, and the box-like fuselage of the Berline must have guaranteed an extraordinarily low maximum flying speed. The front-elevator arrangement was employed and the 100-h.p. Gnôme engine driving a pusher propeller was situated with its fuel tanks above and to the rear of the body, 'a disposition' as *Flight* commented, 'which, we must admit, savours a little too much of the Sword of Damocles to be to our liking'.

Conduite intérieure, or the enclosing of pilot as well as passengers, first made its appearance in England in the year 1912. In that summer was first seen the two-seater Avro with 60-h.p. Green engine, constructed for the Military Trials held on Salisbury Plain in August and flown in those trials by Lieutenant Wilfred Parke, R.N. This machine carried both its occupants in tandem in a narrow cabin with celluloid windows and, although relatively unsuccessful in the trials, it could well have begun an era of cabin comfort for the private owner had not events (in particular the Great War) dictated that the open cockpit should continue, for pilots of small aeroplanes at any rate, until the coming of the Desoutter and the Puss Moth in 1929.

We shall make no attempt to be exhaustive in this brief sketch of a few of the distant forbears of the Moth and the Avian, but one more type may be mentioned which was built to sell at a low price by attention to simplicity in design. This was the Grahame-White Popular pusher biplane, a small two-seater designed by Mr J. D. North and placed on the market early in 1913. Pilot and passenger sat in an open nacelle with a 3-cylinder Anzani engine of only 35 h.p. mounted at the rear. The performance was naturally somewhat modest, with a cruising speed of 50 m.p.h. and an endurance of four hours, but the simple construction made it possible to sell the Popular for less than £400.

All these pleasant developments of aviation as a personal and individual means of transport would, one may safely conjecture, have led to a flourishing private flying movement by the year 1920, amply fulfilling the prophecy with which this chapter began, had world affairs allowed the natural progress of the aeroplane to take a peaceful course; but the writing was already upon the wall. Governments were beginning to interest themselves in the warlike possibilities of the new art, and the Aero Show of 1913, the first in England for two years, had begun to take on a distinctly military flavour. The aeroplane, born into an unhappy century, was already at the end of its short age of innocence. Soon the fourth of August 1914 came to terminate the carefree days of international private and sporting flying, and subsequent events turned the aeroplane into a weapon whose effectiveness increased year by year under the forced draught of military necessity. As a result—to change the metaphor—the growth of the aeronautical tree was accelerated yet violently distorted. The emphasis was on performance—top speed, rate of climb, ceiling and load-carrying power—at the expense of economy and even safety; and the improvements in performance which war demanded were achieved almost entirely by increases in engine power rather than by refinement of aerodynamic design. Lines of aeronautical research which did not seem likely to yield an immediate practical result were ruthlessly abandoned, and development was throughout channelled along severely conventional lines with little scope permitted to radical ideas. Much progress was certainly made during the war years, but whether its direction was the best one for the benefit of aviation as a whole is open to dispute and there can be no doubt that the war dealt the aeroplane considered purely as a vehicle for personal flying a blow from which it took many years to recover. Thus the aircraft which were available in vast numbers for conversion to peaceable uses at the time of the Armistice, though greatly different and in many ways better than those which had been at the disposal of the Royal Flying Corps in 1914, could hardly have been less suitable either for the private owner or for the commercial services which were almost at once put into operation.

Naturally, the very small low-powered aeroplane of the class of the Demoiselle was of little interest for military purposes and disappeared almost completely during the war years. The training of military and naval pilots was mostly carried out at first on such machines as the Maurice Farman Longhorn and Shorthorn, and later on the celebrated Avro 504 biplane fitted with rotary engines of up to 100 h.p.; once trained, pilots would pass to the squadrons to fly the more powerful types used in active service. In 1916, however, there was built at the experimental station on the Isle of Grain, near Sheerness, a tiny single-seater which is of interest not only in itself but because its designer, Captain W. H. Sayers, was later to play a prominent part in the search for a practical 'motor-cycle of the air' which began at the Itford and Lympne competitions of 1922 and 1923. This little machine, the Grain Kitten, was an experiment in the construction of a very small and light biplane of scout type which would be suitable for carrying on shipboard. The engine was a 40-h.p. A.B.C. which provided a top speed of 80 m.p.h., and the designer later recalled that he was officially reproved for estimating that the structure weight would be only 25% of an estimated total loaded weight of 550 lbs. Stressing calculations were accordingly carried out for a figure of 650 lbs, but in practice the loaded weight came out at only 499 lbs. As was to be discovered in the Lympne competitions of later years, such very light construction and the careful attention to detail design which it demanded, proved to be exceedingly costly in manufacturing time and therefore in money.

When the war ended the emphasis was all upon the wonderful new possibilities of air transport, and the expressions 'civil aviation' and 'commercial aviation' were virtually interchangeable since private civil flying was practically non-existent. The years 1919 and 1920 were noteworthy for their long-distance flights—the Atlantic crossing of Alcock and Brown, the dramatic rescue of Hawker and Mackenzie Grieve from the same ocean, the first flight from England to Australia by Ross and Keith Smith, the laborious journey of Parer and McIntosh over the same route, and the first flight to the Cape by van Ryneveld and Brand. At home, civil flying began again at Easter 1919, and the newly-formed air transport companies —Aircraft Transport and Travel and Handley Page Transport—began a hard struggle for existence using hastily-converted military machines. The cessation of large military orders almost overnight brought many of the war-time manufacturers to the edge of ruin, and some did not survive the post-war slump. The vast majority of the pilots and pilots-in-training on the strength of the Royal Air Force, well over twenty thousand in number, had regretfully to close their log-books for the last time and turn to face the chill realities of making a living in a world in which civilian flying jobs were hard to come by. One or two, reluctant to go back to a desk, risked all and sank their savings or gratuities in the purchase of a 'disposals' aeroplane—usually the ubiquitous Avro 504—with which to tour the country meadows and summer beaches and seek a precarious living satisfying the public demand for joy-riding.

This demand was indeed tremendous—A. V. Roe and Company themselves carried over 30,000 passengers from seaside resorts during the first summer of peace—but it was not paralleled by a similar enthusiasm for learning to fly. One reason for this must have been war-weariness and a quite reasonable tendency to see the aeroplane as a weapon associated with thrills, danger and dare-devil feats, well enough for a half-guinea 'flip' when one was in holiday mood but scarcely a practical everyday vehicle for the sober family man. Even more to the point, however, was the simple fact that learning to fly in the years just after the war was an extremely expensive pastime. The Air Navigation Regulations of 1919 had prepared a framework for private flying by specifying two distinct categories of pilot's licence, the 'A' or private licence, and the 'B' which entitled the holder to fly commercially or 'for hire or reward'. The former was, and remained for the next two decades, a most elementary qualification requiring no more than three hours' solo flying and the passing of simple flying tests, yet a course at one of the post-war flying schools leading to the 'A' licence could not be had for less than £100, and £150 was a common figure. At the de Havilland School at Stag Lane in 1923 the hourly rate for dual instruction on the D.H.6 machine was £6, and for solo flying a charge of £5 an hour was made to which was added a further £3 for insurance against damage to the machine and to third parties. More advanced instruction on the Renault-Avro cost £7 an hour and on the D.H.9 £8 an hour.

In view of these charges, which must of course be more than trebled to convert them into present-day terms, it is hardly surprising that however many members of the ordinary public may have nursed a secret desire to fly for pleasure (and the number is unlikely to have been large), very few indeed came forward to try and gratify it. Learning to fly an aeroplane in 1921 or 1922 was in fact comparable in cost in real terms to learning to fly a helicopter today, and the effect on public demand was the same in both cases, namely that practically no one was interested unless he was concerned to take up aviation as a profession. The schools were kept in existence largely by contracts to train pilots for the R.A.F. Reserve, a scheme introduced in the summer of 1923 at Bristol, Coventry, Glasgow and Stag Lane. With a few exceptions which will be noted the amateur pilot scarcely existed, the number of 'A' licences issued was small, and private flying was almost at a standstill. The pre-war Aerial Derby was revived for a few years and eventually supplanted by the race for the Cup presented by King George V, first flown in 1922, but most of the entries for these early events were machines of war-time type or powerful, specially-built racing aircraft such as the Gloucestershire Aircraft Company's Mars I, or Bamel, with 450-h.p. Napier Lion engine. Attempts to popularise flying, such as the formation of the London Flying Club at Hendon in 1919 to offer the amenities of a luxurious country club combined with facilities for aviation, met with little success. Early in 1920 a deputation from the Royal Aero Club, which was anxious to provide flying facilities for its members, called upon the Under-Secretary of State for Air and boldly requested an aerodrome with shed accommodation, six Avro biplanes with spares, two airships and six spherical balloons each of 60,000 cubic feet capacity, the whole to be on loan with the Club paying running expenses and upkeep. This ambitious demand was not met, but instead an aeroplane hire scheme was brought into being with three Avros, two Armstrong-Whitworths and a B.E.2E., all presented by the Aircraft Disposal Company, and these machines were made available to members (but not of course to the general public) at a charge of £3 an hour.

There were, to be sure, a very few rare individuals who were eccentric enough to own their own aeroplanes, and these could be divided into a number of classes: there was the war-time pilot who happened to be extremely well-to-do and could therefore afford to indulge his fancy to continue flying; the occasional forward-looking business man who felt that the time saved by personal air travel outweighed the cost, noise, discomfort and frequent inconvenience; and the poor but enthusiastic amateur who managed to scrape together the low first cost of a 'disposals' machine but usually found that the running expenses forced him to an early re-sale. The earliest and one of the most persistent of private owners was Dr E. D. Whitehead Reid, who while serving with the Royal Air Force at Heliopolis during the war had managed to learn to fly in his spare time. On leaving the Service Dr Reid immediately bought an S.E.5 single-seater scout for £30, and later added to it a Renault-Avro and a D.H.6, keeping his machines at the aerodrome of Bekesbourne near Canterbury with a full-time mechanic to maintain them in good order. He continued to own aeroplanes and to take an active part in the private flying movement until his death in a flying accident in 1930, and occasionally visited by air such of his patients as were conveniently situated near a suitable open space.

Another early private owner was the well-known pre-war pilot Mr F. P. Raynham, who had for some years been associated with the firm of Martin and Handasyde (Martinsyde). He had crashed in one of their aircraft in Newfoundland in 1919 while taking off in an attempt to cross the Atlantic, shortly before this feat was successfully performed by Alcock and Brown. In view of this association it was not surprising that he should own a Martinsyde F.6 biplane, built specially for him and fitted with a 200-h.p. Wolseley Viper engine shortly before the collapse of the Martinsyde company in 1921. In this aeroplane in September 1922 he participated in the first race for the King's Cup, in later years to become an annual proving ground for the British light aeroplane, and took second place to F. L. Barnard on a D.H.4A; it was one of Mr Raynham's unlucky characteristics that he nearly always came in second.

In 1921 the infant de Havilland Aircraft Company, like most aviation concerns in that year of slump, was badly in need of orders; it was rescued from its difficulties by Mr A. S. Butler, a young man of means, who ordered from them a specially-built private aeroplane at a price of some £3,000, made a substantial investment in the company and subsequently became its chairman. The three-seater biplane built for him—the D.H.37 —was the first of a very long line of private aircraft to come out of the de Havilland factory at Stag Lane, though with its 275-h.p. Rolls-Royce

Falcon engine and 80-gallon fuel capacity it can hardly qualify for the title of light aeroplane and must have been an extraordinarily uneconomical means of transport. *Sylvia*, as this machine was named, became a familiar sight at home aerodromes, in air races and on the Continent, where its owner flew it regularly on business tours. Before this, Mr Butler had owned a Bristol Tourer, an early civil conversion of the famous Bristol Fighter in which a concession to economy, though an extremely slight one, had been made by substituting a 240-h.p. Siddeley Puma engine for the original Falcon.

For the more enterprising who wanted to fly and could not afford to buy an aeroplane, there was always the alternative of building their own. The amateur constructor, who in the early days dominated the aeronautical scene, has never been entirely absent from it since, and though his ideas are sometimes misguided his enthusiasm has usually the same refreshing and single-minded quality as that of the amateur boat-builder. For the most part, however, the amateur designs of the early post-war years met with little success. Mr F. Harold Lowe of Newcastle-upon-Tyne, a young man of twenty who had taught himself to fly, completed his seventh design, the H.L. Marlburian, in 1921; it was a braced monoplane carrying pilot and passenger side by side and fitted with a Gnôme rotary engine of 50 h.p. Unfortunately, its existence was very brief, for it suffered the common fate of crashing while being flown by its designer in the autumn of 1922. At Hale in Cheshire at about the same time, Mr J. F. Leeming was busy with a series of gliders culminating in one named the L.P.W. or Leeming-Prince-Wood (after its three constructors); it was eventually fitted with a motor-cycle engine of inadequate power which just enabled it to bound into the air though not to sustain itself in flight. This pioneering effort led to the formation of the post-war Lancashire Aero Club and Mr Leeming became its chairman.

A particularly ambitious project was the cantilever monoplane designed by Colonel J. L. Travers and Major A. Q. Cooper and built by the latter with the aid of a full-time mechanic in a shed in his garden at Hutton, Essex. It was of very advanced form for its time and most carefully built, the construction occupying two years; the fuselage and centre-section were built in one piece with the necessary double curvature in this region achieved by the use of the clinker-planking technique used in boat-building. The pilot sat in the fuselage and seats for two passengers were provided in the wing-roots, the very thick wing-section employed being of sufficient depth to accommodate them. The wings, built up on four spars, were covered with a plywood skin which was designed to carry some of the loads. In its empty state the machine weighed some 1,300 lbs with 90-h.p Rolls-Royce Hawk engine, and this was brought up to 1,800 lbs when fully loaded with the three occupants and 17 gallons of petrol. The first flight took place in 1923, but unhappily the enterprise ended in tragedy, for in February of the following year Colonel Travers was killed when the machine dived into the ground after taking off from Croydon. Observers stated that before crashing it was seen to oscillate in flight, and this was attributed to longitudinal instability associated with 'blanketing' of the tail surfaces by the thick wing-roots.

It was clear to the established manufacturers in the early years after the Armistice that there could be little future for private flying and air-craft ownership with the extravagantly large engines which were a legacy of the war, and quite soon after 1918 a number of small low-powered machines were constructed. These developments were premature, how-ever, since the market for such aircraft hardly yet existed, and few passed beyond the stage of a single prototype or of extremely limited production. A type which deserved well but came to nothing as far as sales were con-cerned was the Bristol three-seater Taxiplane, in general size and dimen-sions very similar to the popular biplanes of the Moth era and fitted with the extremely reliable 3-cylinder Bristol Lucifer radial engine of 100 h.p. Much thought was put into the design of this machine to make it a con-venient vehicle for the owner-pilot; the two passengers sat side by side in the large rear cockpit, which was entered through a wide door, a luggage compartment was provided behind them, and the engine mounting was ingeniously arranged so that the engine could be swung round sideways for easy maintenance. Although this three-seater machine was a com-mercial failure, a subsequent two-seater trainer version had a long and useful life in some numbers with the Reserve Flying School at Filton.

Similar biplanes of more or less conventional type included the Boulton and Paul P.9 with 90-h.p. R.A.F. engine, designed by Mr J. D. North, and the docile Centaur IV of the Central Aircraft Company, originally to have been a private owner's machine with side-by-side seat-ing, but in fact produced as a three-seater for joy-riding and instructional work at its manufacturer's flying school at Northolt. It was also rumoured at the time that a small two-seater triplane, of only 17-ft span and costing £250, would emerge from the Central Aircraft Company's factory, but this curiosity does not seem ever to have seen the light of day. Probably the most unusual small two-seater of the time in appearance was the Black-burn Sidecar monoplane (Plate 2) of 1919, which was provided, optimistic-ally enough, with an A.B.C. Gnat engine of 40 h.p. to propel through the air its portly fuselage containing two people sitting side by side behind microscopic windscreens. (It is not surprising to learn that the purchaser of the sole Sidecar which was built promptly removed the Gnat engine and substituted a 100-h.p. Anzani.) The side-by-side arrangement was characteristic of Blackburn light aeroplanes between the wars, being continued into the later Bluebird and B.2, and enabled these machines to be displayed in showrooms with the ticket 'Honeymoon Model', whereas the tandem cockpit arrangement of their rivals such as the Moth and Avian compelled their newly-married owners, in the words of Henri Mignet, to depart for their destination 'murmuring words of love to a rubber tube'.

There were also several small single-seaters intended for economical personal transport and for sporting purposes. Two such machines were shown at the Paris Aero Show of 1919: the tiny Bristol Babe biplane, priced at £400 with the 2-cylinder 40-h.p. Siddeley Ounce and possessing something of the rakish lines of a war-time scout, and the B.A.T. Crow, an unsuccessful attempt by the British Aerial Transport Company of Willesden to resuscitate the Santos Dumont Demoiselle using an A.B.C. engine. There was also the Grahame-White Bantam, built at Hendon in 1919 to the design of M. Boudot and capable of 100 m.p.h. on the power of its Le Rhône rotary; and, in view of the importance of the de Havilland company in the later development of the light aeroplane, it is perhaps of interest to mention the projected D.H.20 Sporting Type of the same year, even though this first tentative step upon a long road never proceeded beyond the drawing board. There is no doubt, however, that by far the most successful of the single-seaters built at this time were the Whippet biplane designed by Mr John Kenworthy and made by the Austin Motor Company (which had been engaged on aircraft manufacture during the war) and the celebrated Avro Baby.

The Whippet (Plate 4), a small biplane with a span of 21 ft 6 ins and an empty weight of only 500 lbs, was a praiseworthy attempt at an easily maintained private owner's aircraft. To simplify rigging problems for the owner-pilot, the designer had substituted for the conventional wire bracing of the wings a pair of diagonal steel tubes on either side which, acting both in tension and compression, fulfilled the function of flying and landing wires. The fuselage was built up of steel tubing and the 5-cylinder Anzani radial engine of 45 h.p. gave the little machine a top speed in the region of 85 m.p.h. Although only three Whippets were built, they were comparatively long-lasting. The one owned by Flight Lieutenant Soden of the Royal Air Force was a familiar sight at aviation meetings throughout the twenties and served him as a week-end touring vehicle for a number of years, even though its utility for this purpose was somewhat limited by its almost complete lack of luggage room, and another Whippet had an active life of eight years or so in the hands of Mr A. J. Greenshields, an Englishman living in the Argentine who took it out to that country with him in 1920.

The Avro Baby (Plate 3), originally called the Popular, was a little bi-plane of conventional wooden construction fitted with an old-fashioned but well-tried engine, the water-cooled 4-cylinder Green which had been extensively used in the early days of flying—in fact the engine fitted to the first Baby, built and flown in 1919, was the identical one which had been used in Mr A. V. Roe's triplane of 1910. It was a heavy unit, weighing 193 lbs (excluding the radiator and water) for the modest output of 35 h.p., but its excellent reliability contributed much to the success of the little machine. Eight Babies in all were built, and their experiences and achievements were various. They had considerable success in the early post-war air races, which included the winning of the handicap section of the Aerial Derby of 1919; the famous G-EAUM, a two-seater version, was a familiar competitor in air races over the next decade and was event-ually brought up to date by the substitution of the more powerful Cirrus engine in 1926. One Baby was purchased by the Soviet Government, and a Russian pilot came to the Avro factory to collect it, ultimately reaching Moscow after various political difficulties in connection with his flight across Germany. Another, fitted with floats, was specially prepared for Sir Ernest Shackleton's Antarctic expedition of 1922 by the fitting of an air-cooled rotary engine in place of the water-cooled Green and the incorpora-tion of special rigging arrangements, using struts instead of wires, to allow of easy maintenance and erection with gloved hands; it did not in fact reach Antarctica, but was sold instead to Mr Sidney Cotton's Aerial Sur-vey Company for use in Newfoundland.

The Baby's most notable flights were made by an Australian pilot who ✕ was to play a leading part in the development of the light aeroplane and the demonstration of its possibilities for long-distance flying. This was Mr H. J. L. Hinkler, a Queenslander with a lifelong interest in flying, whose Christian name of Herbert was universally abbreviated to Bert. After ex-perimenting with gliders in his youth, he had arrived in London in the fateful year 1914 in search of a career in aviation. His immediate problems were quickly solved for him by the outbreak of war, and after service with the Royal Naval Air Service he was commissioned in the Royal Air Force and flew as a pilot on the Austrian front. When the war ended he was greatly attracted by the prize of £10,000 offered by the Commonwealth Government for the first flight between England and Australia and decided to attempt the journey in a Sopwith Dove, the two-seater version of the wartime Pup; but he was prevented from doing so by the Air Ministry on the grounds that the range of his machine was inadequate for the long stretch, then sparsely provided with aerodromes, between Calcutta and Darwin. In December 1919 the prize fell to the brothers Ross and Keith Smith in their Vickers Vimy, but Hinkler, now a test pilot with A. V. Roe and Company, still cherished the ambition to fly home alone and saw in the little Avro Baby another means of doing so at moderate cost. He set out from Croydon in one of these machines almost unannounced on 31 May 1920 with the declared intention of making a leisurely journey to Australia, and nine hours later landed at Turin after a non-stop flight of over 500 miles. This feat, anticipating by many years the long-distance flights in light aeroplanes which began in the late 1920s, attracted practically no attention at the time, and after continuing to Rome Hinkler was forced to abandon his plan since he could not obtain official permission to cross the Syrian Desert in so small a machine. Had he not been stopped in this way, it seems very likely that his flight would have been successful, taking into account the extraordinary untiring pertinacity which he later showed to be one of his chief characteristics.

In the following year, 1921, Hinkler travelled to Australia by sea, taking with him an Avro Baby for exhibition at the Sydney Royal Show; it attracted a great deal of interest among the country visitors, who saw in it considerable possibilities as a vehicle for use over the long distances of the outback. After some flights round Sydney to establish the performance and fuel consumption under Australian conditions, Hinkler flew the machine directly back to his native town of Bundaberg in Queensland, a journey of 800 miles which remained for many years the longest ever carried out non-stop in so small an aeroplane. He made no special arrangements for a landing place at his destination, and in a lecture some years later he described the casual manner of his arrival:

> On reaching Bundaberg I found that the small allotment known as the Foundry Green had not been built on during my long absence, and fortunately I had the whole space of approximately three acres to myself. On landing, without dismounting, I ruddered round and taxied along the street, finally pulling up at the front door. From the time the machine left the shelter of the Mascot hangar until its return about three weeks later, it was exposed to all the elements, the best protection it had during that period being that offered by a friendly gum tree.

Hinkler's next appearance in Bundaberg was to be a marked contrast to this lonely descent out of the blue at his mother's front door.

But in 1921, the day of the long-distance solo pilot, whose vehicle was to be principally the light aeroplane, had not yet dawned. The public was little interested in the doings of small aeroplanes; it was ready enough to applaud the successes of Alcock and Brown or the exciting rescue of Hawker, but it classified them with the feats of Ball and McCudden over the Western Front a few years earlier as the performances of highly-trained and eagle-eyed supermen, impossible for the ordinary man to dream of emulating. It was not very long, though, before events in a defeated but aeronautically irrepressible Germany began to revive interest in a more personal and individual branch of aviation which had largely been neglected in England since the days of the early pioneers. The craze for gliding which infected this country in 1922 was initially short-lived, but its effects were long-lasting, and the meeting on Itford Hill in that year led on directly to the light aeroplanes of the late 1920s and helped to make flying a normal affair for the ordinary man and woman.

Itford

1922

South of Lewes the Sussex Ouse flows to the sea at Newhaven along a valley which forms one of several breaks in the long line of the Downs. This valley is broad at first but narrows on its way southward until, a mile or two short of Newhaven, it is barely half-a-mile wide, and through this gap run two roads, the winding river and the railway—at the period with which this chapter deals not yet called the Southern Railway but still the old Brighton and South Coast line. The steep slope rising to the east of the gap is Itford Hill, a favourite haunt of archaeologists, forming the western extremity of a long ridge more than five hundred feet above sea level which extends three miles to its highest point at Firle Beacon and then turns south-east for a further two miles before falling gently away to the Cuckmere River. The north side of this ridge is steep and the chalk is deeply indented with a series of cup-shaped valleys; to the south, however, the contours are more gradual, and a succession of hummocks and depressions slowly diminishing in amplitude stretches away for four or five miles to the coast at Seaford. This is excellent soaring country, as the seagulls demonstrate when they hover in the breeze above its slopes and hollows, and it was here that in the third week of October 1922 a crowd of several thousand people assembled in a cold north-east wind to witness the first gliding competition ever to be held in Britain, with a substantial prize offered by the *Daily Mail*. This meeting, though extremely successful, was not the beginning of a revival of gliding as a sport in this country; instead it led directly to the motor-glider competitions at Lympne in the following year and thereafter to the development of the light aeroplane as a distinct type, while pure gliding disappeared entirely from the British aviation scene throughout the rest of the twenties, began afresh in 1930 and then flourished along independent lines of growth beyond the scope of this book.

It will be appreciated by the reader with some knowledge of the history of human flight that the glider, though something of a novelty to the British public in 1922, was in fact an old tool of the early experimenters. That

5.   Mr F. P. Raynham's glider being launched at Itford Hill, 1922
6.   Captain F. Warren Merriam and glider

7. One of the two de Havilland gliders at Itford
8. The Cain flying bicycle

remarkable Yorkshire baronet Sir George Cayley, a pioneer whose achievements have only recently come to be valued at their true worth, carried out tests with a model glider similar in all essential respects to the aeroplanes of today in the year before Trafalgar, and it has now been established that he built a man-carrying machine before his death in 1857. By the end of the nineteenth century a number of European pioneers, notably Lilienthal in Germany and Pilcher in England, had flown extensively in gliders of their own construction, and there had been similar successes in America with the machines of Montgomery and Chanute, leading to the careful and painstaking experiments of the Wrights with the biplane gliders on which they learned the principles of control as a preliminary to their first powered flight in 1903. With the arrival of the practical aeroplane there was a shift of interest away from motorless flight, although it continued sporadically in the years up to the Great War. Orville Wright himself carried out a gliding flight of ten minutes' duration in 1911 with Colonel Alec Ogilvie as passenger, and this remained a world record for ten years. Two or three years earlier the remarkable bird-like gliders of José Weiss, an Alsatian who became a naturalised Englishman, flew successfully at Amberley Mount in Sussex carrying the courageous Mr E. C. Gordon England, who had volunteered to be launched over a precipice in these machines as observer and human ballast without means of controlling the path of his flight. The aerodynamic design of these gliders—some of which were tailless—was far in advance of that of most aeroplanes of the time, but apart from Mr Frederick Handley Page, who embodied Weiss's principles in his early monoplanes, few constructors seem to have been greatly influenced by them.

The real development of gliding on scientific lines, however, took place in Germany just after the Great War and was in some sense a result of the severe limitations placed by the Treaty of Versailles upon the construction of powered aeroplanes in that country, which was at the time pre-eminent in the field of aerodynamic theory. Motorless flight provided at one and the same time a natural outlet for the German aeronautical scientist and a cheap sport for the young student with little money. Soon there arose a friendly rivalry between the various Technical High Schools in the arts of designing, building and flying gliders, and from the dedicated zeal of their students stemmed the almost religious tradition of hard work and plain living coupled with a strongly intellectual approach which has always been characteristic of the sport. The great natural soaring ground of the Wasserkuppe in the Rhön mountains of northern Bavaria had been used for gliding experiments before 1914, and it was here that the first of the German post-war meetings was held in 1920. They were thenceforth repeated annually, and the meeting of 1922 attracted 53 entries of a great

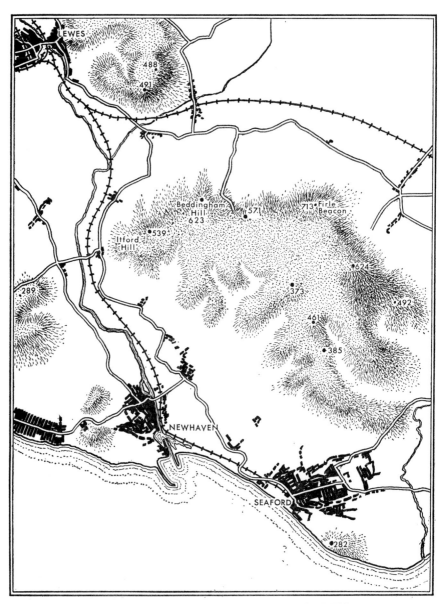

Site of *Daily Mail* Gliding Competition at Itford Hill 1922

variety of types, the most successful being the Hannover Vampyr on which Martens and Hentzen set up a series of endurance records culminating in the latter's flight of 3 hrs 10 mins. In the same year growing interest in France led to the holding of a competition at the Puy de Combegrasse in the Auvergne, which was well attended though no flights comparable with those made in Germany were recorded.

The Continental meetings were fully reported in the British technical and non-technical press, and the public, interested by a development of aviation that seemed fresh and new after its long warlike associations, seized upon gliding as the topic of the moment. The *Daily Mail*, ever ready to make the most of a momentary popular enthusiasm, had also a long tradition of supporting aviation by generous monetary prizes, dating from Lord Northcliffe's first meeting with the Wright brothers. Accordingly, on 23 August 1922, it announced in headlines its offer of the sum of £1,000 as a prize open to the world for the longest glide exceeding 30 minutes' duration, to be terminated by a landing within 800 yards of the point of departure—measured, presumably, in a more or less horizontal direction. In the same issue of the paper Mr Harry Harper, its air correspondent, painted a prophetic picture of the future of aerial sport in an article entitled 'When We All Go Air-Sailing', and thereafter scarcely a day passed without a news item, article or photograph concerning the new pastime. Next year, it was hinted, a further and even more munificent award would be made for a contest 'of a very testing character'.

The summer was nearing its end, and there was no time to waste if the competition was to take place before the coming of shorter and colder days made the whole enterprise too unattractive to both pilots and spectators. The work of organising the meeting fell upon the Royal Aero Club as the body responsible for sporting aviation in the United Kingdom, and the Club's energetic secretary, Commander Harold Perrin, immediately set to work with his newly-formed Gliding Committee to search for a suitable site, negotiate with landowners and draw up a set of official rules. A tour of inspection began only a few days after the announcement of the competition and the advantages of the Itford Hill site—though perhaps less apparent to north-country or Scottish glider-builders than to Londoners —eventually proved decisive, so that its selection was made public on 25 September, the competition being scheduled for the week of 16–21 October. The rules were short and simple. To qualify for the prize a flight had to begin between sunrise and sunset on one of the days in the chosen week, but no stipulation was made as to when it should end, probably because few people imagined that the minimum duration of half-an-hour would be reached, let alone surpassed. To prevent the affair from shading off imperceptibly into a ballooning contest the use of any gas lighter than air was rigorously excluded, but there was no objection to the employment of such motive power as the occupants of a glider might be able to provide by their own personal exertions. The way was thus open for the muscle-powered flying machine which has been so dear to the hearts of inventors throughout the ages; nor, as will be seen, were the organisers so narrow-minded as to place obstacles in the way of those wishing to embody in their designs another ancient dream—the obtaining of mechanical power for nothing by the application of the principle of perpetual motion.

A measure of the popular interest in gliding at this time was the surprisingly large entry list of thirty-five machines. Only six weeks was available for construction from the date of the first announcement to the start of the competition; but the building and flying of a glider was at this time completely free of the expenses and delays imposed by official regulations, and was not in itself a very long task, especially with large supplies of war-surplus aircraft material available at low prices. Furthermore there was no entrance fee, and this must have encouraged the entry of a number of machines which had little or no hope of being ready in time, or indeed of flying at all. Many of the entrants, dazzled by the prospect of winning £1,000, can have had little idea of the problems involved in staying in the air for five minutes, let alone half-an-hour, and in the event only thirteen of the gliders entered flew with any degree of success and many of the others never reached Itford at all.

Among the first to arrive at the great tent hangars on the north-west slopes of the hill above Asham Farm was Mr E. C. Gordon England himself, returning to gliding with a little monoplane of his own design built by his brother's firm at Walton-on-Thames, and with him was another well-known pilot of pre-war days, Mr F. P. Raynham. The latter's glider (Plate 5) had been constructed for the competition by Mr G. H. Handasyde, who having severed his connection with Martinsyde, Ltd, had now established himself in aircraft manufacture on his own account. It was a clean-looking monoplane which is chiefly noteworthy for its curious and awkward control system; in the haste of its building there had been no time to provide the conventional link-up of the ailerons to the control column and they were therefore operated by the pilot's left hand pulling directly on the cable, which passed across in front of him and was provided with a padded loop as a handgrip. The elevator and rudder were controlled in the usual manner with the right hand and the feet respectively.

In spite of Germany's leading position in gliding at this time there were no entries from that country, for she had not yet been readmitted to the Fédération Aéronautique Internationale, the body responsible for international sporting aviation. In any case it is unlikely that German pilots

would have competed in view of their country's current financial difficulties and of the resentment engendered by the restrictive activities of the
Inter-Allied Aeronautical Commission, which appeared to be doing all it
could to stifle German aircraft development. However, a specimen of
advanced German design appeared in the competition in the shape of the
Aachen monoplane entered by Mr J. Jeyes of Northampton, an English
student at Aachen who had unsuccessfully attended the Rhön meeting
with it in the previous August. This machine, designed under the direction
of the celebrated aeronautical scientist Theodore von Kármàn, was of the
type with which Dr Klemperer had won the 1921 Rhön competition, and
was of extremely refined aerodynamic form with a thick gull-like wing and
an undercarriage consisting of skids carried at the extremities of streamlined 'trouser legs'. Also, the influence of the famous Hannover Vampyr
could be traced in the design of two British-built entries, the C.W.S.
glider of Mr F. T. Courtney, Squadron Leader M. E. A. Wright and Captain W. H. Sayers—said to have been designed in 19 hours and built in
19 days—and the machine built on the Isle of Wight by Captain F. Warren
Merriam (Plate 6), a pilot of great experience who had obtained his certificate at the Bristol school at Brooklands in 1912 and had subsequently
become its chief instructor.

The Dutch designer and pilot Mr Anthony Fokker was still unpopular
with some sections of the British public owing to the association of his
name with some of the most successful aircraft used against the Allies by
Germany in the war. Mr Fokker had gone to Germany as an aircraft
designer and had taken German nationality for political reasons, but he
was now a Dutchman again and had become interested in gliding. After
flying two biplane gliders of his own design at the Wasserkuppe—one a
single-seater and one a two-seater—he had brought them to England and
had given a demonstration on the South Downs, preceded by a film show,
in connection with the opening of the Peacehaven Hotel. From here it was
only a short journey to Itford, and on Sunday, 15 October, the elaborate
Fokker equipage arrived at Asham Farm. Mr Fokker's organisation was
extremely thorough, and for moving his gliders about the hill he had an
ingenious arrangement for fastening them on top of his Cadillac touring
car, which with its powerful engine and rear-wheel chains was able to
travel over almost any kind of surface. He was also a business man with a
keen awareness of the value of publicity, and it was said with some justice
that his two-seater glider would never begin a flight before being adequately photographed, for which reason it soon acquired the nickname
of 'the camera-driven Fokker'.

The de Havilland Company began their long association with light
aircraft by building two identical gliders for the competition, one, *Sibylla*

(Plate 7), entered by themselves and flown by their test pilot Captain H. S. Broad and the other, *Margon*, entered and flown by Mr E. D. C. Herne, whose alarming encounters with lightning when flying the machines of the Daimler Airway had brought him fame in the popular press. The D.H. machines were monoplanes of high aspect ratio* and large span (50 ft) with the wings braced above and below with ordinary round piano wire. A conventional wheel undercarriage was fitted for first trials on an aerodrome but this was replaced by skids for use on the hill, and a modification to the lateral control system of one machine was made during the meeting.

The list of more serious entries was completed by the graceful Dewoitine of G. Barbot, the monoplane glider *Phi-Phi* entered and flown by Captain Rex Stocken and built by the Aircraft Disposal Company, the Peyret tandem—the only other French entry—and the home-made hybrid of Squadron Leader A. Gray and Flying Officer W. J. Buchanan. The last two machines were considered of little account by the experts.

The idea of human flight has always held a strong attraction for the eccentric inventor, whose enthusiasm is matched by his total unconcern for the past history of success and failure and by his ignorance of fundamental physical principles. Although such people are always in our midst, most of them work on in obscurity until—to the great joy of the connoisseur of mechanical absurdities—they are brought into the limelight by the prospect of fame and financial reward. The Itford meeting, with its promise of wealth for a small outlay on wood, wire and fabric, brought forth a splendid crop of weird machines, mostly totally impractical yet each the embodiment of some latter-day pioneer's dreams of revolutionising the art of navigating the already conquered ocean of air. It is sad to record that after all the thought and effort which must have gone into the making of these craft, not one of them was observed to lift its designer higher than he could have jumped with his own legs, and they returned whence they came, some for hopeful modification and further trials, others to decay in toolsheds or eke out their days as chicken-houses or garden trellis-work.

* This quantity is a measure of the slenderness of a wing seen in plan view, and is defined as the ratio of the span to the mean chord. The name is derived from the definition, since the span is the dimension seen in frontal aspect and the chord that seen in lateral aspect. An equivalent definition is the ratio of the square of the span to the wing area. The component of wing drag known as 'induced drag' is a necessary consequence of the fact that a wing obtains its lift by driving air downward, and cannot be eliminated entirely with a real wing of finite span; it can however be minimised by making the aspect ratio as large as possible, since in this case a wing of given area acts on the greatest possible volume of air per second and so obtains its lift in the most efficient way.

   Reduction of induced drag in this way is especially important for gliders, which need to be designed for the lowest possible rate of sink in still air in order that they may be sustained by an equally low rate of rise of the air through which they fly. For the same reason also, wings of high aspect ratio have been provided (whether by natural selection or by a celestial Chief Designer) for soaring birds such as the albatross.

Perhaps the most bizarre of all the designs entered was the 'sail biplane' of Mr J. J. O'Freddy of Sheerness, which appears to have been in fact a tandem monoplane* on top of which was fitted a complete set of sails comprising jib, mainsail and mizzen. The designer of this extraordinary apparatus presented himself to the officials of the Royal Aero Club shortly before the competition and surprised them by announcing that he was not quite sure whether to bring it to Itford from Sheerness by car or to sail it over. No more was heard of him until about midday on the first day of the meeting, when a telegram arrived at Itford for Commander Perrin stating that the glider had left Sheerness at 9.25 and had crashed on a hill near Maidstone at 9.38. How Mr O'Freddy had managed to sail 15 miles in 13 minutes and land on a hill higher than his starting place was never satisfactorily explained, and it seems most likely that the telegram, if not the 'sail biplane' itself, was an elaborate practical joke†.

It is a pleasant fantasy to imagine the little aerial boat scudding along above the North Downs, but in sober fact its sails, like those fitted to certain of the early free balloons, could never have been anything but totally ineffective, since an aircraft out of contact with the ground is carried freely with the wind and cannot experience the reactive force which the water exerts upon the keel and hull of a sailing-boat.

An entry which actually arrived on the hill, though it never attempted to fly, was the biplane of Mr P. W. Kingwell, propelled by a mechanism which had been designed with a magnificent disregard for the law of conservation of energy. The structure before assembly consisted of a large number of aluminium tubes to which wings were presumably to be attached, but the wings, as *The Aeroplane* remarked:

> are of little interest compared with the power plant, which seems to go several points better than mere perpetual motion in that it not only gives power for nothing but actually increases it when it has got it. To make it lighter it has its ironwork painted with aluminium.
>
> The apparatus contains a wonderful kind of blower arrangement something like a cross between a Blackman fan and the spiral intake pipes of a Jupiter engine. On the same spindle as this is what would be an ordinary airscrew but for the fact that it is made of aluminium sheet and does not conform to any known aerofoil section. The theory is that the wind blows into the fan arrangement and makes it spin round and as a result the airscrew itself turns and provides the necessary power to drive the aeroplane. Viewed as a mechanical proposition it seems to be several hundred per cent better than standing in a clothes basket and lifting oneself by the handles.

The idea of the ornithopter, or flapping-wing machine, is as old as

---

* A machine with two monoplane wings one behind the other is generally called a tandem monoplane and not a biplane, the latter term being reserved for the arrangement with superposed wings.

† Nevertheless, a photograph of a model was published in the *Daily Mail* (5 October 1922).

time, and although long ago discarded by orthodox aeronautical engineers *
it has always been a favourite dream of inventors who are unable to see that
it is on about the same plane of practicability as a motor-car with mechanical legs. The Itford competition attracted at least five machines with man-
powered flapping wings; it is impossible to be sure of the exact number
since the means of propulsion of some of the entries which failed to appear
is obscure. That constructed by Mr H. E. Waite of Morecambe, Lancashire, was an enormous machine of 54 ft span, only the wing-tips of which
could be moved for propulsive purposes by the pilot. It was usually referred to as 'the Bride' because of its curious tail, which was made of fabric
and trailed loosely behind, requiring the support of 'bridesmaids' when
the apparatus was being moved on the ground. The other aircraft in this
class were of more modest size but it can be recorded with some confidence
that they were equally unsuccessful as flying machines.

Most people who are likely to read this book know that a scheme for a
helicopter was devised by Leonardo da Vinci, and with the coming of the
aero-engine in the early days of the twentieth century it was not long
before a man-carrying machine was made to rise from the ground. This
took place in fact in 1907, but formidable difficulties of stability and control meant that the helicopter was not to become a practical proposition
for many years, and it cannot be said that the man-powered example
entered for the competition by the British Helicopter Company contributed a greal deal to its advancement. The foremost of the two occupants
of this machine was responsible for forward propulsion by means of a
tractor propeller, while his companion behind provided direct lift by
driving a 'vertical cone propeller'. There was nothing particularly new in
this fairly obvious arrangement, for it had been embodied in an apparatus
known as the 'Pterophore' suggested—but not put to practical test—by the
French mathematician Paucton in 1768. It is fairly easy to show that the
task of sustaining the weight of two men by direct lift in this manner would
have been beyond Hercules, but as a device for providing strenuous
exercise without incurring the risks of actual flight the British Helicopter
Company's machine must have been unequalled.

Only slightly more practical were the pedal-gliders of Messrs A. H.
Knott and G. W. Cain (Plate 8). The former machine was equipped with
a pedal-driven propeller which could scarcely have maintained it in level
flight but which might possibly have prolonged its inevitable descent somewhat, while the latter was no more than an ordinary bicycle with wings and
a tail attached—an idea which has probably occurred to every schoolboy

---

* The ornithopter has recently been resurrected in connection with a competition for man-
powered flight, but even if it is successful in this role it is likely to remain a curiosity outside the
main stream of aeronautical development.

with aeronautical interests at some time in his career. On the last day of the meeting its designer mounted into the saddle and dashed gallantly down the hill, but apart from a brief bounce over an ant-hill he merely confirmed the opinion of the pessimist with a taste for the unnecessarily obvious pun who said that he did not think that Mr Cain would be able to fly. It was just as well since his winged bicycle had only the most rudimentary controls for use in the air.

Those who had arrived on the hill by the Saturday and Sunday spent their time carrying out test flights which were sometimes followed by repairs and modifications to control surfaces and other parts—the most common alteration being a hasty increase of rudder size when the original surface was found to be ineffective at the low speeds used. Jeyes' Aachen glider suffered slight damage on the Saturday when one of the R.A.F. mechanics who had come from Uxbridge to help with the handling of the machines failed to let go in time and became entangled in the launching ropes. The following day M. Barbot was unfortunate enough to touch the left wing-tip of the Dewoitine on the ground while trying to take off across wind to avoid the crowd, and the machine turned on its back with the pilot's head in a gorse bush. The damage to M. Barbot was superficial but his glider was wrecked beyond hope of repair and he was forced to withdraw from the meeting before it had even begun.

On the Monday the wind was only a little north of east—a quarter in which it remained for the whole week—and Itford Hill itself, which faced west, was thus useless for soaring, so after a few short flights in the morning by Raynham, Jeyes and the two de Havilland machines, the crowd and the competitors began the long trek eastward along the ridge towards Firle Beacon. Mr Fokker arrived here in his Cadillac just after lunch, and having enticed Mr Paul Bewsher of the *Daily Mail* on board his two-seater as passenger and made his habitual pause for being thoroughly photographed he was launched into the air at 2.30 for a seven-minute flight. Shortly after this Raynham achieved 11 mins 23 secs, landing in a field below the hill; and then the wind died and many of the spectators, seeing the short autumn daylight beginning to fade, set out on the long walk back to Itford. Those who stayed, however, saw the best flight of the day, for at sunset the wind increased again and Mr Fokker took the air once more, this time alone in his two-seater with ballast in place of a passenger, and cruised about the hill for 37 mins and 6 secs. This flight was nearly three times as long as his best at the Wasserkuppe, and seemed to dispose of the current superstition that the great extent of the Rhön mountains gave the wind which blew upon them mysterious lifting properties which could not be found on smaller ranges.

Tuesday was chiefly marked by the establishment of a British endurance record by Mr Raynham in the Handasyde, whose unconventional controls did not hinder him from staying aloft for nearly two hours. On the following day the wind became more violent and Mr Gordon England carried out a short and exciting flight at the end of which he landed backwards for the first time in his flying career and found his air speed indicator registering 40 m.p.h. when he came to rest. This was followed by a spectacular crash when Jeyes, attempting to turn near the hill, struck the ground with a wing-tip. The wing broke right off and tumbled down the slope separately from the rest of the machine, which landed upside down with the pilot inside, quite unhurt. After this it was decided to abandon gliding for the time being, and someone devised the even more hazardous sport of racing down the hill on the six-wheeled trolleys which were used (in conjunction with a balloon winch) for hauling various items of equipment up the hill, but this too was given up after a collision with a gate involving a few bruises and broken ribs.

The wild night which followed put an end to the hopes of Mr E. T. Prosser, a pre-war pilot who had laboriously erected his large biplane glider inside one of the tent hangars only to find that it was impossible to get it out. The problem of whether to dismantle the tent or the glider was solved for him by the wind, which blew down the tent in the night and completely wrecked his machine. The continuation of the gale on Thursday made this a day for repairs and modifications, and finishing touches were put to the Courtney-Wright-Sayers machine and to the Peyret, neither of which had yet flown. The only glide of the day was the brief but spectacular one of Mr Herne, whose D.H. glider had been converted from aileron control to wing warping in a search for better rolling power. He was catapulted off on a test flight and at about 20 ft the wings began to warp ever more vigorously and then folded up completely, letting the fuselage down with a bump on a more or less even keel. Had the machine been launched over the steep part of the hill the consequences would have been serious, but as it was the pilot emerged shaken, surprised, but intact.

After the violence of the previous two days Friday was almost windless and little could be achieved beyond a few glides into the valley. On Saturday, however, the brisk north-east breeze returned and flying began again from Firle, where Mr Gordon England was blown into the ground by a gust and became the only real casualty of the meeting with a painful double fracture of the ankle which put him into hospital for some time. Shortly after this accident the Fokker two-seater went off carrying Mr Gordon

Olley and a passenger, and in spite of the fierce turbulence, which made control difficult at times, managed to establish a world record for a passenger-carrying glider with a flight of 49 minutes.

By lunch time, with only a brief October afternoon remaining, it seemed most unlikely that Raynham's claim to the *Daily Mail* prize could be challenged, and it was with only mild interest that the crowd on Firle watched the approach of a new machine which was being wheeled along the ridge and identified it as the Peyret. This was a curious-looking aircraft with two identical pairs of wings in tandem, one at the front and one at the rear of its fuselage. Each wing was provided with a full-span control surface, and a differential mechanism using bevel gearing enabled these surfaces to be operated either asymmetrically as ailerons or symmetrically as elevators from a conventional control column. When the pilot, Alexis Maneyrol, climbed on board and was catapulted off the Beacon at about 2.30 p.m. it soon became obvious that the little machine was by no means a freak, for the splendid manoeuvrability afforded by its unorthodox controls enabled its pilot to make the most of the limited region of rising air near the crest of the ridge and he was soon flying strongly at a good height above the summit.

After Raynham had unsuccessfully tried to challenge Maneyrol another new machine appeared on the hill—the home-made hybrid of Squadron Leader Gray, which consisted of the fuselage of a war-surplus Bristol Fighter to which the upper wing of a Fokker D.VII biplane had been attached. Each of these 'disposals' items had cost the builder five shillings and his total expenditure on the whole machine, including dope, amounted to 18s. 6d. The *Brokker*, as it was called, was heavy because it was considerably over-strength and therefore at the first attempt it failed to get away, but at the second it rose strongly against the wind and soon joined the Peyret in its steady beating along the hill. The afternoon wore on with the two gliders showing no sign of coming down until darkness compelled them to do so, and there was excited speculation as to the possibility of Raynham's time being exceeded. Then, according to *Flight*'s representative on the Beacon:

> Suddenly a great cheer went up, when Maneyrol had reached Raynham's time of 1 hour 53 minutes. The Frenchman waved acknowledgement and proceeded in an attempt to beat the German duration record. The two machines were by now mere silhouettes in the sky, and as the minutes went they got dimmer and dimmer. Finally it was decided to make arrangements for lighting up the top of the ridge with motor-car lamps, and a space was cleared for the two machines to land on. When cheering and hooting of motor horns announced that the German record had been equalled Maneyrol came down low and shouted that he would land in a few minutes. He stayed up another 20 minutes or so, and finally he and Squadron Leader

Gray made perfect landings on the summit of the ridge about 100 yards from their starting point.

Maneyrol had thus won the *Daily Mail* prize with a fine flight of 3 hrs 21 mins 7 secs, a world's record which was especially meritorious in that it was his first flight on the hill and only his second in the Peyret. He must also have suffered considerably from cold and lack of food, since he was dressed only in ordinary clothes and had had to forgo his lunch in the bustle of final preparations. Since the efficiency of his machine as a glider cannot have been very high, his success must be attributed largely to his own skill in making the best use of its powerful controls.

The excellent flights of the last day of the meeting set the seal on a week of flying which had turned out far more successful than its organisers had thought possible, and it was generally agreed by those who had grown up with aviation that for the first time since the war the carefree and un-selfish spirit of the old flying meetings had returned. There seemed no reason why the rediscovered sport of gliding should not go on from strength to strength.

Shortly after Itford Mr Gordon Selfridge offered a prize of a thousand guineas for a distance-flight of 50 miles in a glider, to be carried out any-where in the British Isles during 1923, with half the sum to be paid for a flight of 25 miles if the full distance was not achieved. A gliding club was set up at Andover by a band of R.A.F. officers of the Staff College, who set to work rebuilding the glider in which Mr Gordon England had crashed, and in the Isle of Wight Mr F. Warren Merriam, after converting his machine into a two-seater for instructional purposes, founded his own school of gliding, which offered a complete course in the art for the sum of £25. Even the films reflected the current craze, and at Torquay Mr Fred Raynham doubled for the hero of *The Hawk* by being shot over a cliff in his Handasyde (which had been suitably waterproofed) to the rescue of the heroine, who was rather improbably being abducted by the villain in his private submarine.

Yet in spite of all this activity gliding died out temporarily in Great Britain after 1922. The Selfridge prize, though offered again in 1924, was not won nor even seriously competed for, and eight years were to elapse before another meeting on the same Itford ridge led to a rapid renaissance of the sport and to its permanent establishment in this country. In this brief interval the British light aeroplane was conceived, born and brought to an astonishingly rapid maturity. By the middle of 1930, when Herr Robert Kronfeld's celebrated glide of 75 miles from Itford to Havant showed England the sporting possibilities of motorless flying, many of the world-wide exploits of the Moth, the Avian and the Bluebird were already old history, so that only those flights remarkable for speed or 'human interest' could still be sure of headlines; while at a score or so of club aerodromes men and women of all ages were taking to the air as naturally as they might have taken to the waters of the Solent on a summer's afternoon, and nearly three hundred small private aeroplanes were offering their owners a means of transport as reliable, fast and convenient as any then available. To see how these remarkable developments came about it is necessary to turn from the short-lived gliders of 1922 to the 'motor gliders' of 1923.

ⵉ 3 ⵊ

The Motor Glider
Competitions

1923

It was natural that the successful revival of gliding in England, France and Germany should cause the minds of designers in those countries to turn to the idea of fitting their machines with small economical engines, adequate to sustain them in level flight or to provide a modest rate of climb. The art of gliding had not yet progressed beyond the technique of hill-soaring in a wind, and although the duration of flights carried out by this method was in theory limitless so long as the wind blew and the pilot remained equal to the task of flying to and fro along the slope, there was as yet no question of using the glider as a vehicle for journeys across country. But the aerodynamic efficiency of the best gliders of the day was superior to that of contemporary military or commercial aeroplanes, and their light weight and low flying speed meant that they could be maintained in level flight by the application of a relatively small amount of power, perhaps 3 or 4 h.p. in contrast to the hundreds of horsepower of most larger machines. Clearly the vehicle so produced—called in France the *moto-aviette* or *avionnette*—was capable of interesting development, first, as a cheap sporting vehicle which would render its pilot independent of the soaring slope and the wind, and second, as an apparatus for research directed at the improvement of the efficiency of the commercial aeroplane. The extent to which such improvement was possible was indicated in a paper by Mr Frederick Handley Page and Mr W. P. Savage, read before the International Air Congress in September 1923. 'The aerodynamical qualities of machines', the authors stated, 'can be greatly improved with the existing knowledge that we have. At the present time the small machines termed motor gliders have as high a lift resistance ratio* as 17, whereas the existing commercial aircraft rarely exceeds half this value'.

* Now generally called lift-to-drag ratio, or L/D.

They went on to illustrate the immense effect upon the economics of air transport which would result from an increase of efficiency of this magnitude. Developments on the sporting side were foreshadowed by Lieutenant-Colonel Alec Ogilvie in a lecture on 'Gliders and their Value to Aeronautical Progress' given at the Third Air Conference in London in February of the same year. After summarising the history of gliding and powered flying Colonel Ogilvie went on to predict the appearance of small sporting aeroplanes of 15–20 h.p., capable of horizontal flight with 5 h.p. and having a fuel consumption of 100 m.p.g.

This prediction was not far from fulfilment. In Germany Herr F. Budig had already fitted a 4-h.p. B.M.W. motor-cycle engine to the biplane glider which he had constructed for the Rhön meeting of 1921, and had found this adequate for level flight following a catapult launch. Another well-known glider designer, Herr Klemperer of Aachen, was building a little high-wing monoplane with a side-valve vee-twin Mabeco motor-cycle engine of 8 h.p., and this machine was successfully flown by its designer in the summer of 1923. The Wissenschaftliche Gesellschaft für Luftfahrt had organised a competition for the design of a 20-h.p. engine suitable for very light aeroplanes, offering a first prize of 400,000 marks, an impressive sum which by early 1923 was equivalent to rather less than £3 sterling owing to inflation. The restrictions of the Treaty of Versailles had also led German designers to concentrate upon small single-seater and two-seater aeroplanes with engine power in the range 20–60 h.p., and some of these, such as the Heinkel, Udet and Albatros machines, were of the low-wing cantilever monoplane type, anticipating the trend of design of the 1930s.

Enthusiasm for the *avionnette* ran high in France too, and 1923 saw intense activity there on the part of both professional and amateur constructors. Among many other designs there appeared a small monoplane with a 10-h.p. Anzani cycle-car engine, built by M. Henri Mignet and bearing some resemblance to the Pou du Ciel with which this most famous of all aviation amateurs was to arouse such world-wide interest twelve years later. The *Petit Parisien* offered a prize of 100,000 fr. for the longest flight by a machine not exceeding 250 kg. loaded weight and carrying 20 kg. of fuel and oil, and this was carried off by Coupet with a flight of 310 km. on a Farman monoplane with 1,000 c.c. Salmson engine. On the evening of 6 May 1923 Barbot performed a double crossing of the Channel in a Dewoitine and thereby won the prize of 25,000 fr. offered by *Le Monde* for this feat in an aeroplane with an engine of not more than 1,500 c.c. capacity. The flight was not especially remarkable in terms of distance, and the Channel had already been crossed by air many thousands of times, but it caught the imagination of the British public, in whose minds memories of the golden days of Blériot had perhaps been re-awakened. Most of the British press, inaccurate as usual in flying matters, reported that the journey had been made in a glider—which would indeed have been an astonishing feat in 1923.

English designers were quite as active in the field of motor gliders as their French and German counterparts, and several small single-seaters were under construction when in April 1923 the movement received the stimulus of monetary prizes. The Duke of Sutherland, who had recently taken office as Under-Secretary of State for Air under Mr Bonar Law, came forward with an offer of £500 for a competition between low-powered aeroplanes, the details of which were to be decided by the Royal Aero Club in consultation with the Duke's representative General Bagnall-Wild, Director of Research at the Air Ministry. Two weeks after the announcement of this offer the *Daily Mail*, which in addition to subsidising the Itford meeting had already given away nearly £40,000 in aviation prizes and so was inclined to regard this branch of human activity as its own special preserve, published the following statement:

> For the encouragement of flying with small motor-power the *Daily Mail* offers a prize of £1,000 open to the whole world.
>
> The Duke of Sutherland, Under-Secretary of State for Air, offers a second prize of £500 restricted to British competitors flying British machines.
>
> Both prizes will be competed for in September at a locality in England yet to be selected under the competition rules of the Royal Aero Club.

Some exception was taken to this attempt to relegate the Duke's prize to second place—Mr C. G. Grey, editor of *The Aeroplane* and no lover of the *Daily Mail*, stigmatised it as 'gross harmsworthiness'—but eventually it was settled that the two prizes should stand independently without any question of precedence, and apart from the proviso as to the country of origin of the machines and the nationality of the competitors, the rules for both prizes were the same. Following French practice, the main emphasis was to be upon fuel economy. The competing machines were to be fitted with engines not exceeding 750 c.c. capacity, though the pilot was at liberty to contribute to the motive power by his own exertions if he was able to do so, and the winner would be the competitor who covered the greatest distance round a triangular course on an allowance of one gallon of petrol, a surplus being allowed so that the pilot could regain his starting place. There was also to be a transport test, which had to be satisfactorily passed before the distance flights were attempted; in this the machines had to have their wings folded or dismantled within a limited time so that they could be manhandled over a one-mile course which included a stretch of road and a gateway 10 ft wide, the object being to establish that

9.   The curious Gnosspelius Gull with twin pusher propellers at Lympne, 1923
10.   The prize-winning English Electric Wren

11. Mr W. S. Shackleton's A.N.E.C. monoplane, which tied for first prize with the Wren. (Photographed at Brooklands)

12. The first de Havilland light aeroplane: the D.H.53

they could easily be removed from a field after a forced landing and that they could be kept in an ordinary shed or garage.

There was some criticism of the policy of awarding the whole of the £1,500 prize money for the single quality of low fuel consumption per mile, and later other prizes were given which helped to make the competition a less specialised one. The Abdulla Company gave £500 as a prize for the highest speed attained over two laps of the course without restriction on fuel consumption, and the sum of £150 was offered by each of two bodies representing the motor trade—the Society of Motor Manufacturers and Traders and the British Cycle and Motor Cycle Manufacturers' and Traders' Union—to be awarded for the greatest number of circuits of the course completed during the competition by a British machine and pilot, provided that a minimum distance of 400 miles was covered and that no alterations were made to the aeroplane or its engine. This was in effect a reliability trial, and was sometimes referred to as the Snakes and Ladders Competition, since the failure of any major mechanical part meant that the competitor had to begin all over again. Later, Sir Charles Wakefield added a prize of £200 for the greatest height attained and the Duke of Sutherland, with members of the Royal Aero Club, gave £100 for a landing competition, so that altogether the prize list had sufficient variety to induce pilots to fly in all weather conditions.

The meeting was officially styled 'The Motor Glider Competitions', which (many people argued) was a contradiction in terms since a glider with a motor was no longer a glider but an aeroplane. The expression 'motor glider' seems to have been due to the *Daily Mail*, which curiously enough had been at pains to explain to its readers at the time of the Itford trials that a glider was 'an engineless aeroplane'. Although it was in some ways descriptive of certain of the machines entered, the phrase did not long survive; it was officially abandoned by the Royal Aero Club in 1924, and thereafter the expression 'light aeroplane' came into use to describe the aeronautical counterpart of the light car of the period.

The site chosen for the competitions, which were to be held throughout the week beginning on Monday 8 October, was the aerodrome of Lympne in Kent, and the triangular course was arranged to run partly along a range of hills, although the geography of the range was such that little assistance in the way of hill lift could be looked for. The situation of the aerodrome itself on top of a ridge with the land falling away to the south towards the sea meant that pilots could expect to meet some vertical currents in its vicinity in a wind of any strength, and these would be favourable or unfavourable according to wind direction. The scene was thus set for a most interesting week of flying, with something of the fascinating uncertainty of the early pre-war meetings, in spite of the immense advances in the art and science of design which had taken place in the previous decade. Aviation in Europe, after all, was only fifteen years old; the war had given it an artificial stimulus in a certain direction, but in other ways its development had been almost halted. Now many of the best minds in British aviation were studying the neglected problems of the low-powered aeroplane, and cheap flying for the ordinary man seemed only just round the corner.

When the Duke of Sutherland's prize offer was announced at least three machines suitable for the competition were already in an advanced stage of construction. Towards the end of 1922 the English Electric Company of Preston, Lancashire, had put forward a proposal to the Air Ministry for a small single-seater aeroplane fitted with a motor-cycle engine, as an experiment in flying with very low power. A contract was placed, and early in April 1923 the first Wren, built to the design of Mr W. O. Manning, was ready for flight. It was an exceptionally clean little machine owing to its fully cantilever wing without external bracing and to its unusual buried undercarriage, which consisted simply of a pair of pneumatic-tyred wheels protruding through slots in the underside of the fuselage. The pilot sat in a cut-out in the leading edge of the wing, and immediately in front of him was a faired structure carrying the engine and fuel tank, the rear of which was conveniently placed to act as an instrument panel. The Wren's first test flight on Lytham sands showed that it was capable of flying strongly with an A.B.C. motor-cycle engine of only 398 c.c. capacity, and it was later found to be able to fly level with only $3\frac{1}{2}$ h.p., so that at its fully loaded weight of 420 lbs with pilot it achieved the remarkable power loading of 120 lbs per horsepower. Two Wrens were built for the Lympne trials (Plate 10) and the type was offered to the public at the low price of £350, but the time was not yet ripe for extensive private ownership and there were no purchasers.

At about the same time another low-powered single-seater of very different appearance was taking shape at the works of Short Brothers at Rochester, in Kent. Major O. T. Gnosspelius, a pioneer of the seaplane, had been conducting experiments on a series of models by swinging them on a pendulum apparatus of his own devising, which took the place of the more conventional wind tunnel. As a result of these experiments he had designed a light monoplane of somewhat birdlike form, with a propulsive arrangement resembling that of the original Wright biplane of 1903, namely a centrally mounted engine driving two pusher propellers through chains. This had the advantage that the centre of gravity of the whole engine and propeller assembly was close to that of the airframe, so that the machine could be converted into a glider without upsetting the trim by simply removing the complete power unit. The Gnosspelius Gull (Plate 9), as it was later named, made its first flight at Lympne on 26 May 1923, the pilot being Mr J. Lankester Parker. Some difficulty was experienced in take-off and landing owing to the very shallow ground angle, and this was later rectified by fitting larger wheels. Although the full power of the 698 c.c. engine could not be used because the propellers limited its rotational speed to a figure well below the maximum permissible, the machine attained about 70 m.p.h. in level flight and climbed at about 400 ft/min.

The third design which originated before the competition rules were made known was Mr W. S. Shackleton's A.N.E.C. (Plate 11), built at the works of the Air Navigation and Engineering Company at Addlestone, Surrey. This was also a monoplane and had several interesting structural and aerodynamic features, among them a wing of semi-cantilever type braced by a pair of short struts on each side and having a single stiff spar of patented triangular box construction. The pilot sat in a hammock seat in the fuselage below the wing with a view to each side through cut-outs in the fuselage, and there was a hole in the wing to provide an upward view, over which a transparent cover was fitted when flying in order to give a smooth top surface to the wing. The construction of the large wheels was unorthodox, being of wood covered with plywood, and they were provided with a circumferential leather strip in place of the usual pneumatic tyre.

It had been known for some time that Captain Geoffrey de Havilland was taking an interest in light aeroplane design, but it was not until September 1923 that details of the D.H.53 single-seater (Plate 12) were published in the technical press with the announcement that two of these little machines would fly at Lympne. Captain de Havilland had his own very definite ideas of what a light aeroplane should be, and had made no effort to reach the ultimate in either economy or speed; instead he had designed a robust little low-wing monoplane with unmistakable de Havilland lines which was intended to be a practical aircraft for the owner-pilot. The method of construction followed current de Havilland practice, with a plywood box fuselage and fabric-covered wings of normal two-spar type, and differentially geared ailerons were fitted on the patented de Havilland principle, which eliminated adverse yawing on entering a turn. The engine chosen was the 750 c.c. Douglas, and the unpleasant exhaust note characteristic of 2-cylinder engines was muted by the use of a long exhaust pipe discharging below the fuselage. With this engine the speed range was about 30–70 m.p.h.

The designer who wished to succeed in both the economy and the speed contests had a difficult problem before him, since the technical requirements conflicted to such an extent that two distinct aeroplanes were really needed, one for each purpose. However, an ingenious alternative to this somewhat expensive solution was the scheme adopted by Mr Harold Bolas, the chief designer of George Parnall and Company of Bristol, namely to design a machine primarily for economy and provide in addition a spare set of wings of smaller area and a spare engine of higher power, both of which would be specially fitted for the attack on the speed prize. The two versions of a single basic type thus obtained were entered in the competitions as two distinct machines, the Pixie I and II, and were strut-braced low-wing monoplanes in the same general category as the D.H.53. The 'economy' and 'speed' wings were of the same geometrical family, but the latter were derived from the former by reducing all the spanwise dimensions in a constant proportion so that the wing area was almost halved, and the Pixie I was fitted with a 500 c.c. Douglas engine which was replaced by a 750 c.c. unit of the same make when the machine was converted into the Pixie II. A third variation on the basic theme, envisaged by the designer but not actually flown in the competitions, was to have had the large wings and the large engine for an attack on the altitude prize.

Mr A. V. Roe, whose celebrated Type 504 biplane was at this time at the height of its career, adopted the policy of building two very different types of machine for Lympne, and his own personal design, the Type 560 monoplane (Plate 13), was of advanced appearance with a thick tapered cantilever wing of biconvex section. The other Avro entry, the Type 558 biplane (Plate 14) designed by the company's chief designer Mr Roy Chad-wick, owed much in its general lines to the 504; the wings were of high aspect ratio and widely separated for maximum efficiency, and great use was made of quick-release fittings to enable the wing structure to be quickly dismantled in the transport test. The undercarriage was of the buried type as on the Wren, consisting simply of a pair of 22-in. bicycle wheels sprung by rubber cord, and this arrangement gave the machine an odd appearance when resting on the ground, rather like a conventional biplane whose undercarriage had collapsed.

Two other manufacturers favoured the biplane and built examples for the competition which have a special interest, since they represent their makers' only excursion in history into the field of the light aeroplane. Mr H. P. Folland, chief engineer of the Gloucestershire Aircraft Company*, designed a tiny biplane of only 18 ft span, which received the name of Gannet. It was of conventional wooden construction, and since its wings could quickly be folded to give an overall width of only 6 ft 6 ins it easily met the requirements of the transport test. The general appearance was extremely neat, and it was unfortunate that cooling trouble with its

* Later the Gloster Aircraft Company.

specially-designed Carden two-stroke engine, which had had little time for development, prevented it from taking part in the competitions. The Vickers Viget, designed by Mr Rex Pierson, was larger than the Gannet but of equally conventional construction in most respects; much use was

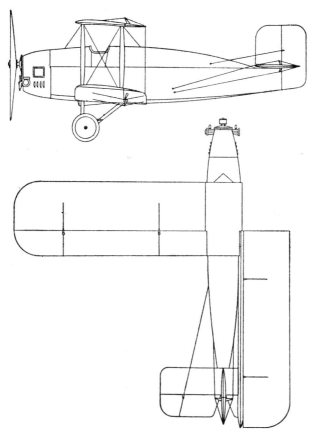

1. The Vickers Viget single-seater, built for the 1923
Lympne trials

made of duralumin throughout for detail fittings, the wings were arranged to fold and the 750 c.c. Douglas engine was neatly cowled in with a chain drive to the large propeller (Figure 1).

In addition to their own design which has already been described, the Air Navigation and Engineering Company also built a small monoplane for Mr F. P. Raynham to the design of Mr Handasyde. This was in many respects similar to the Handasyde glider which Mr Raynham had flown at Itford, though with a more conventional control system, and there were echoes of Itford also in the three entries designed by Captain W. H. Sayers and built by Handley Page Limited. All were monoplanes, and one closely resembled the Courtney-Wright-Sayers or C.W.S. glider of the previous year. The second, which was the only one to perform in the trials, was similar to the first in general outline, but in the interests of extracting the maximum performance out of the 398 c.c. engine—the same as that fitted to the Wren—the cockpit was completely enclosed and the unfortunate pilot was left with only two small holes to look through. These holes were so positioned that his outlook must have been extremely restricted in any direction but upwards and sideways. The third Handley Page machine was by far the most technically interesting of the three, since it embodied the patented Handley Page wing slots as well as slotted ailerons and camber-changing flaps, and the designer had taken full advantage of these high-lift devices by giving his machine the highest wing loading in the competition (8 lbs/sq. ft). It is likely that with its Blackburne* engine it would have been very fast, but it could not be made ready in time to compete.

Finally the Aero Club of the Royal Aircraft Establishment at Farnborough, whose members had already successfully built and flown the Zephyr pusher biplane of their own design, had by now completed the construction of a second machine, which was entered for the competitions. This was a cantilever high-wing monoplane named the Hurricane, with a thick tapered wing, a deep fuselage of triangular cross-section and a special Douglas engine of 600 c.c. driving the propeller through a 2:1 reduction gear.

The entry list for the competitions closed on 1 October with the satisfactory total of twenty-seven machines, counting the Pixie separately in each of its two guises. The twenty-three British aeroplanes consisted of two Gnosspelius Gulls, two Wrens, two Avro biplanes and one monoplane, two D.H.53s, two A.N.E.C.s, three Sayers-Handley Page machines, two Pixies, the Gannet, Viget, Handasyde and Hurricane, and the Falcon, Kingwell and Salmon monoplanes. The last three were not ready in time and so did not compete, although Mr P. W. Kingwell, whose glider based on the principle of perpetual motion had been the sensation of Itford the year before, laboured in vain throughout the whole week of the meeting to finish his tandem-winged machine, which was to be more conventionally propelled by an A.B.C. motor-cycle engine. To complete the list there were four foreign entries—two French Peyrets of the type which had been most successful at the Vauville meeting in August, and two Belgian Poncelets. So far as the British entries were concerned, the Air Ministry had agreed to waive the requirement for a certificate of airworthiness for the

---

* The makers of this engine, Burney and Blackburne Ltd, were unconnected with the Blackburn aircraft firm.

duration of the meeting and for flights to and from Lympne, provided that the machines were examined by officials before taking part as a check on general design and workmanship. The foreign entries were not subject to this scrutiny.

Although the competition flying did not begin until the Monday, the aerodrome was a scene of busy activity over the preceding weekend. It had been agreed that any entrant who was ready to do so might carry out the qualifying tests over the weekend in order to be able to start flying immediately on Monday morning, and, contrary to the usual tradition in events of this kind, quite a number of machines were ready in time to take advantage of the concession. There were no failures in the transport test since the time allowance for any necessary dismantling, transporting and re-erecting was fairly generous, but equally this denied any credit to those designers who had incorporated wing-folding arrangements or special quick-release fittings. Owing to an unfortunate oversight the tailplanes of the D.H.53s were found to be wider than the rules allowed and they had to be speedily modified by cropping the tips, apparently without detriment to their excellent flying qualities. By Sunday night fifteen of the British entries had passed the tests and were ready to begin flying on the morrow.

Monday morning dawned windless and misty, with patches of low cloud on the hills round the course. Lots had been drawn for the order of starting, and shortly after 7 a.m. Flight Lieutenant Longton was skimming over the grass in No. 4 Wren and turning on to his first lap in the economy competition. He continued his slow progress round the course for 2 hrs 40 mins and landed having completed seven laps on just over a gallon of petrol. When Professor A. M. Low, the official measurer, had performed the necessary calculations Longton was declared to have established a consumption figure of 80·3 m.p.g., and on a subsequent flight he raised this to 85·9. But the Wrens were not to have matters all their own way, for later J. H. James on one of the A.N.E.C.s covered the same distance on less than a gallon and must therefore have exceeded 90 m.p.g., though by the rules he was deemed to have used a whole gallon so that the officially recorded figure was 87·5.

When a wind arose some competitors decided to put off their economy tests until conditions were more favourable and to concentrate instead on accumulating distance towards the Motor Trade prizes. Among these were Captains Geoffrey de Havilland and Hubert Broad taking turns on one of the D.H.53s (No. 8, *Humming Bird*), Major Hemming on the other (No. 12, officially *Sylvia II* but more often referred to as the *Hemming Bird*), and Bert Hinkler on the Avro monoplane. By Monday evening Hemming was in the lead with 24 laps (300 miles) completed without any trouble from machine or engine.

Not all were so fortunate. The Douglas engine in the Viget suffered a broken rocker arm, a fault to which this engine was curiously susceptible during the competitions, and Captain Cockerell was faced with a forced landing in difficult country near Brabourne, some six miles from the aerodrome. This he managed successfully, and as there was nothing he could do in the way of an immediate repair he gave a convincing demonstration of the usefulness of folding wings by walking back to Lympne along the road pushing the machine before him. According to *The Aeroplane*:

> It is said that in one place he stopped at a 'rest house' for refreshment in his arduous labour and when he came out he found a number of people waiting who asked him when the performance was going to start. On asking what they meant he was informed that they were under the impression that the object that he was pushing was a Punch and Judy Show.

Poor weather on Tuesday led most competitors to continue lapping for the distance prize. Major Hemming was unfortunate enough to break his crankshaft, thereby losing his lead to Hinkler on the Avro monoplane, who by the evening had completed 46 laps (575 miles). One of the A.N.E.C.s was out of the running having cracked a cylinder, but James and Piercy took turns at flying the other machine, No. 17, and were close behind the Avro with 42 laps. There was no catching Hinkler, however, for with the persistence characteristic of him the little Australian continued to go round and round the circuit in the gusty wind the next day, and would have carried on above the fog which later covered the course had he not been brought down by the frantic signals of Mr A. V. Roe. By the end of the week he had worn out all opposition and was an easy winner of the £300 reliability prize with 80 laps of the course—one thousand miles' flying with no trouble of any kind either from the aircraft or from his Blackburne engine.

On the Thursday Longton set off again in the Wren in an attempt to beat the A.N.E.C.'s economy figure, but only succeeded in equalling it, although he had achieved an unofficial 90·5 m.p.g. over five laps on the previous day. The extremely low speed of the Wren made its fuel consumption particularly sensitive to wind strength, and in ideal calm conditions Longton might well have done a great deal better, as indeed might the A.N.E.C., which on a favourable day at Brooklands before the meeting had actually achieved 127 miles to the gallon over a measured course; but now the weather remained unsettled and no one managed to improve on the 87·5 m.p.g. of Longton and James, so that the Sutherland and *Daily Mail* prizes were eventually divided between them.

The Pixie had not been outstandingly successful in the economy role, and over Wednesday night it underwent its metamorphosis, emerging the following morning with the small wings, larger engine and new number to compete for the speed prize. Captain Norman Macmillan flew the necessary two laps at an average speed of 76·1 m.p.h., though it was estimated that his speed on the straight was little short of 100 m.p.h. During a further attempt on the Saturday he completed one lap at over 80 m.p.h. but half way round the second lap his engine began to give trouble and he was forced to land in a field. On the same day James on the A.N.E.C. came within 2 m.p.h. of the Pixie's figure—a remarkable feat for the machine which had tied for the economy prizes—but by the end of the meeting Macmillan's figure was unbeaten and he was awarded the Abdulla prize of £500.

The weather was unsuitable for any flights to high altitude for most of the week. Flying Officer Hamersley had taken the Douglas-engined Avro biplane up to 6,300 ft on the Monday, but this figure was not improved upon for several days and when Friday's gale made all flying impossible it began to seem that the blue skies needed for going to great heights would not reappear before the meeting closed. Saturday morning, however, turned out clear, bright and windy, and the air was soon full of machines. Maneyrol set off for altitude on one of the Peyrets with which he had climbed to over 12,000 ft at Vauville, and returned with his barograph showing 10,000 ft, the true figure after correction being 9,400. Shortly after he had landed Hamersley came in on the Avro biplane and was found to have reached 13,000 ft, but Piercey on the A.N.E.C., who landed almost immediately after him, raised the figure to 13,600 ft. Maneyrol immediately set off on a second attempt. At the conclusion of his flight he was gliding in to land when at about 100 ft a download on the wings, due either to a gust or to a manoeuvre, caused them to collapse downwards and the machine dived into the ground killing its pilot. The Peyret was very lightly built, and the wing bracing consisted of a pair of slender tubes on either side which were normally in tension. Apparently these tubes were satisfactory for normal flight but were inadequate to bear the compressive load induced in them by the temporary reversal of the lift forces on the wings.

Towards the end of the day Piercey and Hamersley set out for altitude again and the former carried off Sir Charles Wakefield's prize with a climb to 14,400 ft. Hamersley succeeded in getting the Avro biplane up to a height only slightly below this (13,850 ft) and was awarded as a consolation prize the £100 offered for the landing competition, which could not be held owing to the gusty wind.

Thus the main honours in the competitions had gone to the Wren, the A.N.E.C.—which had certainly put up the best all-round performance—

the Avro machines and the Pixie. The D.H.53s, which were generally regarded as the best example of a practical private owner's type, and whose stoutness had been brilliantly demonstrated by Captain Broad in an exhibition of loops and rolls, had won no prizes; nor had the Gnosspelius Gulls, which were plagued with engine trouble, possibly because their Blackburne engines lacked the cooling slipstream provided by the tractor installations. The Gannet, a promising little machine in appearance, had had no chance to display its merits owing to the recalcitrance of its two-stroke engine. Raynham's Handasyde had shown promise in the economy competition with a consumption of 65.7 m.p.g. but was outclassed by the Wren and A.N.E.C. The R.A.E. entry, the Hurricane, despite its speedy appearance, had proved most disappointing; the engine did not give its full power and the setting of the wing on the fuselage was such that the machine flew tail down, so that the drag of the triangular-section fuselage seriously retarded it. Engine trouble also spoiled the performance of the A.B.C.-engined Sayers-Handley Page, which might otherwise have made a good showing in the economy competition. The French and Belgian entries were not especially successful, being to some extent handicapped by the rule which limited the engine capacity.

It had been a week of typically disagreeable English weather which had prevented the pure economy machines such as the Wren from doing their best, but the flying in gales, rain and fog demonstrated that even such extremely light aeroplanes as these were far from being the fair-weather vehicles that many had believed them to be. It is true that they were all in the hands of experienced pilots, but given the necessary skill the little machines seemed capable of standing up to weather which would have deterred the military and civil types of the day. The motor-cycle engines used, performing a task for which they had never been designed, had given reasonable service, and on the occasions when they had failed the resulting forced landings had all been carried out without incident, thus effectively demonstrating the safety of aeroplanes of very low wing loadings with landing speeds in the region of 25–35 m.p.h. A relatively modest prize list had stimulated British aviation to a remarkable extent, and an auspicious beginning had been made to an era in which the British light aeroplane was to lead the world in achievement and in technical merit.

On the social side the meeting had been equally successful. As at Itford, some of the cheerful, unselfish spirit of the early days of aviation seemed to have returned. Here were many of the great figures of the old flying years before 1914, some of whom were destined to be greater still in the times to come, gathered together in not too serious competition with one another and with the less celebrated in order to make the aeroplane, so recently a weapon of war, into a vehicle for the use and enjoyment of the ordinary man. It was a meeting of enthusiasts, of men who were in aviation not for the material rewards it offered—these were few in 1923—but simply because its unique blend of subtle theory and practical engineering, of mental agility and physical skill, of eccentricity and adventure, made it the one life they really cared about. In the evenings, when the flying was over for the day and the hangar doors were closed, the meeting continued within the walls of the Imperial Hotel in Hythe; countless discussions, arguments, experiments and practical jokes lasted well into the night. The accident to Maneyrol cast a shadow over the final day and the banquet planned for that evening was cancelled, but there is no doubt that in happier circumstances it would have been an occasion to remember.

A fortnight after the end of the Motor Glider Competitions a demonstration and race meeting for light aeroplanes was held at the London Aerodrome at Hendon. The event had received little publicity, and the attendance was not to be compared with that of the great Hendon meetings of pre-war days, but those who went had a good opportunity of seeing nine of the little machines which had competed at Lympne flying in a stiff and gusty wind. The two D.H.53s appeared with their Douglas engines replaced by the inverted Blackburnes which had performed so well in the A.N.E.C. and (in upright form) in the Avro monoplane. The last-named machine was there, flown once again by Hinkler, fitted with a pair of smaller wings which Mr A. V. Roe had prepared for Lympne but which he had not been allowed to use since he had failed to adopt the stratagem of submitting two separate entries. Hamersley was also present and flew his successful high-altitude Avro biplane, whose thin wings could be seen flexing in an alarming manner in the turbulent air; and to complete the list there were both A.N.E.C.s, Raynham's Handasyde, the Viget and the Parnall Pixie II.

The starting and landing competitions, which had been postponed from Lympne, had once again to be cancelled, and after an impressive display of exhibition flying by the D.H.53 in the hands of Captain Broad and by Piercey and Cockerell in the A.N.E.C. and Viget respectively, the meeting proceeded with an exciting series of pylon races for prizes of £50 presented by Sir Charles Wakefield. In the first race one of the de Havilland machines managed to defeat the handicappers but the speed event, as might have been expected, was won easily by Captain Macmillan on the Pixie.

The year closed with a fine flight on the Blackburne-engined D.H.53. The pilot was Mr A. J. Cobham of the de Havilland Hire Service, whose name was already becoming known to the public for his air-taxi journeys round Europe and North Africa. Arrangements had been made to show the D.H.53 at the Brussels Automobile Exhibition, and it was equipped with a compass and an extra fuel tank to enable it to reach Brussels in a single flight. The tank fed petrol to the engine by air pressure which was supplied by the pilot's lungs through a rubber tube. Cobham set off from Stag Lane on the foggy morning of 8 December, calling at Croydon to clear Customs and later landing at Lympne to await an improvement in the weather. His arrival there in conditions of 200 yards' visibility was a striking demonstration of navigational skill and of the usefulness of a vehicle which could safely be motored round trees and along hedges at a mere 40 m.p.h. Shortly after noon, having replaced the small quantity of petrol which had been used for the journey from Stag Lane, Cobham decided that conditions were more reasonable and set off across the Channel, but he was soon forced down to 200 ft above the water by low cloud and heavy rain. After $2\frac{3}{4}$ hrs in the air his fuel supply was nearly exhausted, so instead of continuing to the main Brussels aerodrome at Haren he landed at the old aerodrome north-west of the city and had the machine towed into the exhibition by road. The return journey was a failure, for a stiff headwind reduced the D.H.53's speed almost to nothing, and after having the mortifying experience of being overtaken by a goods train Cobham landed at Ghent and made arrangements for the machine to be sent home by boat from Ostend.

The de Havilland company publicly made much of this flight, laying stress upon the fact that the total cost of fuel and oil had been no more than 7s. 6d., but privately they resolved that no practical light aeroplane should have a cruising speed of less than 80 m.p.h., and this resolve was later carried into practice in the famous Moth. However, the D.H.53 went into production and a small batch of machines was built for the Royal Air Force and continued in Service use for some years. Apart from its use as a vehicle for the recreation of pilots who were normally engaged on flying larger machines or on administrative duties, it was chosen for experiments in the operation of aeroplanes from airships, and in 1925 one was successfully released from and reattached to the R33 in flight. Some D.H.53s were also supplied to Australia, and as late as 1937 surplus parts of ex-Service machines were being used in the construction of small amateur-built aircraft, so that it can fairly be claimed that the Motor Glider Competitions, apart from their value as a stimulus to further progress, did in fact beget one quite successful light aeroplane.

⤛ 4 ⤜

The Two-Seater Competitions

1924

The Motor Glider Competitions had shown that a practical sporting machine powered by a small motor-cycle engine could be built and made to fly successfully and economically, and the results taken together with Cobham's flight to Brussels had silenced the critics who had said that such an aircraft would be unable to leave the ground in other than the most carefully chosen weather conditions—even if its usefulness as a cross-country vehicle was rather limited in strong head-winds because of its low cruising speed. Nevertheless, attractive though these little single-seaters were, it was clear that they could only be regarded as a first step along the road to the popularisation of flying as a sport. The Air Ministry was already considering ways in which flying clubs could be established all over the country with a measure of State assistance so that the ordinary man and woman might learn to fly at moderate expense, and the first need of these clubs would be a reliable two-seater machine since the system of instruction using dual controls was now universal.* The single-seater was also somewhat limited in its appeal to the prospective private owner, being open to the objection, frequently voiced by Mr C. G. Grey, that a young man who could afford to buy one would quickly attract the attention of the opposite sex and would therefore soon be demanding an attachment for his machine analogous to the solo motor-cyclist's pillion seat or 'flapper bracket'. There were, in fact, one or two proposals at this time—stimulated perhaps by the ingenious Pixie—for machines which could be converted from single-seaters into two-seaters by the use of interchangeable wings, engines and other parts, but none of these ever reached the stage of practical testing.

* It is interesting to note, however, that solo training *ab initio*, as practised in the early days of flying, was revived in the 1930s using a 'motor glider'—the Kronfeld Drone.

The success of the Lympne meeting suggested that the best way to obtain a good economical two-seater design was to hold another competition on the same lines. This time, however, the main prizes were to come not from the *Daily Mail* but from official sources. After a short interval to allow the technical staff of the Air Ministry to ponder upon the performances of the motor gliders, an announcement was made early in 1924 to the effect that the Air Council would present the sum of £3,000 for a two-seater competition to be held in the latter part of the year, to be eligible for which the machines and their engines were to be of all-British design and construction, capable of being flown from either seat and subject to a limitation of engine capacity of 1,100 c.c.—this figure being chosen on the grounds that an engine of 1,100 c.c. in new and well-tuned competition trim would be equivalent to one of 1,500 c.c. capacity in average normal use.

This offer was a fairly substantial one in terms of the current cost of building a light aeroplane and it was later supplemented by other prizes: a further £500 from the Duke of Sutherland, £300 from the Motor Trade organisations and £100 from Captain C. B. Wilson. The entrant who was successful enough to return home with a reasonable proportion of the prize money in his pocket could therefore more than cover his expenses, and would have before him the additional prospect that a machine which did well in the competitions might be ordered in quantity for the proposed flying clubs, though the Air Ministry was careful not to commit itself to any promises or bind itself to the adoption of any particular design.

The competition rules were not published until early in March, some two months after the original announcement, since with a considerable amount of public money at stake they had to be drawn up with some care by the Royal Aero Club and to receive the approval of the Air Ministry. After the experience of 1923 it was generally agreed that to place the main emphasis on economy, as had then been done, would be a mistake since with a low-powered machine fuel costs are only a small proportion of the total cost of operation and the limitation on engine capacity could safely be left to ensure that fuel consumption was kept within reasonable bounds. What was needed in its place was a simple criterion of efficiency, and that chosen was one of the most fundamental of an aeroplane's properties, the ratio of maximum to minimum speed.* This ratio was expressed in terms of the range of speed as a fraction of the minimum speed, i.e.

$$\frac{V_{max} - V_{min}}{V_{min}}$$

* The practical importance of this ratio is obvious. The chief virtue of the aeroplane is its ability to travel at speeds which are impossibly high for surface transport, but it must also have

and marks were awarded in proportion to this quantity provided that a certain minimum figure was attained. In order to penalise a machine with either a uselessly low top speed or a minimum speed too high for safety in the hands of the average amateur pilot, it was further required that these speeds should not fall below 60 miles an hour or above 45 miles an hour respectively. The speeds were to be determined in separate tests, and an element of reliability testing was introduced into the measurement of maximum speed by the stipulation that this figure was to be established in two successive flights of about 75 miles each, with an interval between them during which no work would be allowed to be done on the aircraft other than the replenishment of fuel and oil. As a further check on reliability it was laid down that a competitor would not become eligible for any prize until he had completed a minimum of ten hours' flying during the competitions.

Additional marks were to be awarded for take-off and landing performance over a barrier, officially known as 'getting off' and 'pulling up'. For the take-off tests the pilot was to be allowed to choose his own starting-point from which to begin his take-off run in order to clear the 25-ft 'barrier', which would not be a dangerously substantial one, and he would receive one mark for every yard by which his shortest successful run was less than 450 yards (Plate 15). Similarly he would be expected to land over a tape stretched at a height of 6 ft above the ground, and the distance from this tape to the nearest point of the aircraft would be measured after it had come to rest, with one mark for every yard by which this distance was less than 150 yards. These tests were obviously as much a measure of piloting skill as of the capabilities of the aeroplane.

The competitor with the highest aggregate of marks on the foregoing basis would receive the Air Council's first prize of £2,000, with the remaining £1,000 forming a second prize. The Duke of Sutherland's £500 and the £100 given by Captain Wilson were similarly to become the first and second prizes in the getting-off and pulling-up tests and the Motor Trade prize was to go, as it had done the year before, to the entrant of the machine which completed the greatest distance during the week.

At the Itford and Lympne meetings of the previous two years there

---

the ability to land reasonably slowly and pull up in a conveniently short distance. In the earliest days of flying with grossly under-powered machines, flight was only possible over an extremely limited range of speed and the ratio of maximum to minimum speed was near unity. With later developments a ratio of 2·5 : 1 or 3 : 1 became normal, 4 : 1 excellent and 5 : 1 exceptional, and over a wide range of aeroplane types these figures remain true today.

It should be pointed out that the quantity $(V_{max} - V_{min})/V_{min}$ is a measure of the ratio of maximum to minimum speed, being equivalent to

$$\frac{V_{max}}{V_{min}} - 1.$$

had been no specified time at which competing machines had to be completed, and it had been open to any competitor to proceed with the building or modification of his aeroplane or glider and to fly it at any time up to the last minute of the last day. This practice was now to be discouraged. The 1924 rules demanded that all competing aircraft should be presented to the officials in a fully erected and airworthy state on the Saturday morning preceding the opening of the meeting, and that subsequent replacements of parts would only be permitted according to a laid-down schedule, which included airscrews, sparking plugs, valves, tyres, and other minor parts. Replacements outside this schedule involved disqualification. After presentation the machines were required to undergo a transport test similar to that specified for the previous year's meeting and to follow this by flights demonstrating the efficacy of their dual control. It was compulsory for all competitors to complete these eliminating tests by the end of flying on the Sunday, and any competitor who had not done so would be barred from the main event of the following week. It turned out that the strict application of this rule by the stewards of the meeting removed from the lists many of the more interesting entries and came very near to bringing the entire competition to a standstill.

The emphasis placed upon fuel economy in 1923 had led to a predominance of the monoplane in the interests of low drag, but now there was a trend back towards the biplane in order to secure satisfactory performance in the take-off and landing tests, and the majority of the machines entered in 1924 were biplanes. Since a good speed range could earn a competitor a useful number of marks, most designers went to the trouble of embodying in their aeroplanes a mechanism by means of which the ailerons could be drooped symmetrically to act as camber-changing flaps and lower the minimum speed; in the normal flying condition they were raised so that top speed was unaffected. Although the principle of the landing flap had been known since the early days of flying, its use had hitherto mostly been confined to experimental machines. In the absence of the third Sayers-Handley Page machine no example of the device had appeared at Lympne in 1923, and its wide use in 1924 was a development considerably ahead of its time.

Among the biplanes the Avro Avis (Plate 16) was in effect a two-seater version of the Type 558, with the same span as its predecessor (though increased wing area) and many of its structural features. Mr. A. V. Roe had added a beautifully-made worm gear for depressing the lower ailerons as flaps, and to avoid a repetition of his difficulties with the officials the year before he was careful to enter the single Avis twice to enable either the Blackburne engine or the new Bristol Cherub to be fitted. Similarly the Vickers Vagabond was really a two-seater Viget, though it had an

13. The Type 560 Avro monoplane at Lympne
14. Mr A. V. Roe inspects the engine of his Type 558 biplane

15. The 'getting off' tests in the two-seater trials at Lympne
16. Lympne 1924: the Avis folded for the eliminating tests

unusual feature in the tail-trimming arrangement; instead of the tailplane incidence being adjustable relative to the fuselage in the normal manner, the whole rear fuselage was hinged immediately behind the rear cockpit and its inclination to the front part of the machine could be varied by rotating a handwheel situated between the two seats. The value of this arrangement in the air is open to question, but it may be argued that winding the tail fully up after landing would set the wings at a large incidence and so provide extra drag for pulling up; at all events Mr Pierson did not consider it necessary to use the ailerons as landing flaps.

The Supermarine Sparrow (Figure 2), a distinctive wooden biplane with upper wings of decidedly larger span and area than the lower, was the work of the company's new chief designer Mr R. J. Mitchell, later to become the designer of the Spitfire. The H. G. Hawker Engineering Company of Kingston entered two biplanes to the design of Mr Sydney Camm,

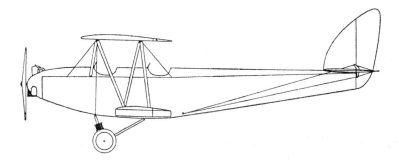

2. The Supermarine Sparrow, built for the 1924 Lympne trials and converted to a monoplane in 1926

which were identical except for their engines and were given the type name of Cygnet. Mr Camm paid close attention to weight-saving throughout; all unnecessary material had been pared away regardless of labour costs, and the result of such painstaking workmanship was that the Cygnets were capable of carrying a disposable load (pilot, passenger, fuel and oil) only slightly less than their own empty weight. Far less elegant in design and construction was the only amateur-built entry, the two-seater biplane of the Cranwell Light Aeroplane Club; work on it had begun long before the competition rules were announced and it had originally been intended as a cheap and simple machine for instructional use, so its designer, Flight Lieutenant Nicholas Comper, had made no attempt to seek a high top speed. With its broad fuselage seating pilot and passenger side by side the C.L.A.2 was barely capable of reaching the minimum of 60 m.p.h. specified by the rules. Such refinements as folding wings were also lacking, and in order to pass the transport test the wings had to be dismantled and

hung on the sides of the fuselage. Side-by-side seating was also a feature
of the Blackburn Aeroplane and Motor Company's Bluebird, but this
biplane, whose sturdy lines had much in common with the Blackburn
torpedo-carrying naval aircraft of the day, was not ready in time to
compete.

The Westland Aircraft Works of Yeovil, instead of choosing between
biplane and monoplane, built one of each type to the same specification.
The biplane, named the Wood Pigeon, was of fairly conventional appear-

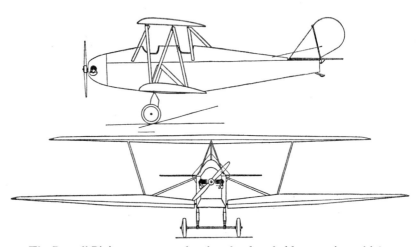

3. The Parnall Pixie two-seater, showing the detachable top wing which was
intended to improve take-off and landing performance

ance with single-bay folding wings which divided on the centre-line instead of being hinged to a fixed centre-section, and many of its features
were shared with the Widgeon, a parasol monoplane with a wing of the
'double lozenge' plan form characteristic of Westland design. This wing
arrangement, with its narrow chord at the root, ensured an exceptionally
good view for the occupants of the two tandem cockpits. The two-seater
version of the Parnall Pixie was very similar in design and construction to
the single-seater Pixie I, but once again the ingenious Mr Bolas had provided a novelty in the form of a detachable upper wing which could quickly
be fitted or removed so that the machine could be flown either as a monoplane or as a biplane. This upper wing, of smaller span and area than the
lower, was quite frankly intended as a device for getting marks in the take-
off and landing competitions by increasing wing area, and not as a permanent fixture. In its monoplane form the two-seater became the Pixie III
and as a biplane the Pixie IIIA (Figure 3).

Turning to the monoplanes, Mr Shackleton's successful A.N.E.C.
single-seater formed the basis for a two-seater competition machine on

broadly similar lines, with an extra 5 ft on the span, an additional cockpit below the trailing edge of the wing and the Blackburne engine replaced by one of the 1,100 c.c. Anzani vee-twins which were built specially for the competitions. After designing this aeroplane for the Air Navigation and Engineering Company Mr Shackleton moved to Scotland and became chief designer to the revived aircraft section of William Beardmore and Company at Dalmuir, near Glasgow, and since his first task on taking up

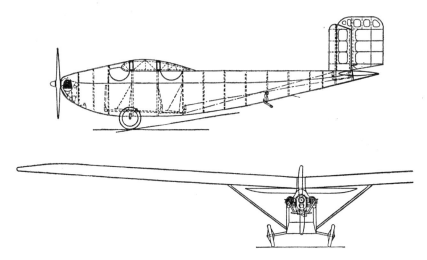

4. The winner of the Two-Seater Competitions: Mr W. S. Shackleton's design, the Beardmore Wee Bee

his new post was to design an entry for Lympne he was in the unusual position of being responsible for two machines entered by different firms. Naturally many of the successful ideas which he had incorporated in the two A.N.E.C. machines were carried over into the Beardmore design, which was called the W.B. XXIV or Wee Bee I, and all three were similar in general appearance. The Wee Bee was planned with the closest attention to the elimination of unnecessary drag, so that the lift-to-drag ratio reached the excellent maximum of 16·8, and with the direct-drive Cherub engine the estimated top speed (confirmed later by trials) was 86 m.p.h. (Figure 4).

The two remaining monoplane types afforded an interesting comparison of structural techniques in metal. The Short Satellite (Plate 17), whose clean cantilever wing and fuselage of stressed-skin construction were many years in advance of their time, followed naturally on from an all-metal biplane—the Silver Streak—built on this principle and exhibited by Short Brothers at the Aero Show at Olympia in 1920. Although the Satellite's wing and tail unit were conventionally fabric-covered, the shapely fuselage of elliptical cross-section was produced entirely out of single-curvature duralumin sheet riveted to formers and stiffened with stringers running longitudinally.* The fuselages of the two Bristol Brownies, on the other hand, were built up out of round steel tubes in the form of wire-braced girders and covered with fabric, and while the wings of the machine bearing the competition number 1 were of orthodox wooden construction, those of No. 2 were entirely of metal. On a weight basis the wooden-winged Brownie appears to have had a slight advantage since its wing area was 3% greater than that of the steel-winged version for the same empty weight. Both Brownies had the interesting feature of automatic variable camber, arranged by spring-loading the ailerons in the downward direction with rubber cord so that at low airspeeds both surfaces would droop and act as flaps.†

The names of several of the firms which had built single-seaters in the previous year were missing from the 1924 list, in particular those of Handley Page, Handasyde and Gloucestershire, and the R.A.E. Aero Club, whose Hurricane had been something of a failure with the 600 c.c. Douglas engine, had been content to modify it for purely racing purposes to take the Cherub. The success of the Wren stimulated the English Electric Company to develop a two-seater version, and drawings of this aeroplane were prepared, but an unexpected setback in their flying-boat programme caused the project to be shelved. By far the most significant absentee, however, was the de Havilland Aircraft Company. Captain de Havilland and his technical staff, after carefully considering the rules, had come to the conclusion that the engine size specified would be inadequate for a two-seater machine, and had decided to pursue a different line of development according to their own ideas. This decision was fully justified by events and turned out to be of the most far-reaching importance in the history of the light aeroplane.

When the eliminating trials began at Lympne on Saturday and Sunday, 27 and 28 September 1924, few people expected that they would present any great difficulty. The transport test was if anything rather simpler than that of the previous year, and the brief demonstration of dual control by two short flights round the triangular circuit with the pilot flying from each cockpit in turn did not seem unduly arduous. Yet for one reason or

---

* The Satellite was not the only light aircraft to be built by Short Brothers embodying their stressed-skin structural methods, for in the same year they produced the Cockle, an extremely unusual light flying-boat with a duralumin hull and two 698 c.c. Blackburne engines. This machine was a single-seater and was built not for competition purposes but to the special order of Mr Lebbaeus Hordern, a wealthy Australian aviation enthusiast. It was never delivered to him, however, and ended its days in the hands of the Air Ministry.

† Such a system was tested by the de Havilland company on one of their D.H.50 aeroplanes in the same year (1924).

another, of the fifteen machines actually present on the aerodrome on the week-end in question only eight were admitted to the competitions on the Monday morning.

There were no failures in the transport test; the time allowance of two hours was generous even for the Cranwell, whose wings had to be removed, and the aeroplanes equipped with folding wings took only a few minutes to pass through the ten-foot 'shed'. To be sure, the width restriction gave a little difficulty in a few cases, and Mr Rex Pierson's practice of designing for a folded width of exactly the maximum figure allowed by the rules with no allowance for errors caused a few anxious moments with the Vagabond, but in the end all passed safely through. The trouble began when it came to flying, and here some though by no means all of the eliminations could be attributed to the engines. Perhaps the most heart-breaking failure was that of the Supermarine Sparrow, in which Mr Biard set off on the Saturday afternoon for the first of his two laps. The engine spluttered immediately he was clear of the ground and he descended into a field just outside the aerodrome. The trouble was diagnosed as oiled plugs, and the Supermarine party worked for most of the night on the engine in an attempt to cut down the oil consumption. On the Sunday morning all was ready and the pilot successfully completed his first circuit of the course, changed seats and set off again on the second circuit. Just before he completed it, one of the connecting rods of the Blackburne smashed its way through the crankcase and Biard was faced with yet another of the nineteen forced landings which he is said to have made up to the start of the meeting. The only hope of avoiding elimination lay in fitting a spare engine to the machine and then flying the second circuit before the day's flying closed at 6 p.m. All set to work in desperate haste, among them Commander Bird, the managing director of the Supermarine Works, and when after an oily struggle the new engine was ready to run at 5 p.m. there still seemed a good chance for the Sparrow. Unfortunately, one cylinder began to overheat owing to a tight piston, and although this too was hurriedly dismantled and rectified the work was finished too late for the qualifying circuit to be completed and the Supermarine entry was out of the competition.

The Vickers Vagabond never got into the air at all over the week-end. Its engine set up tremendous vibration owing to a serious lack of rigidity in its mounting, and this could only be cured by making up a modified mounting in a local workshop on the Monday, after which the machine flew successfully *hors concours* but was not of course eligible for any prizes. The Avis had similar troubles, and although Hinkler succeeded in flying it on a small throttle opening he was never able to open up the engine sufficiently to attempt a flight round the course.

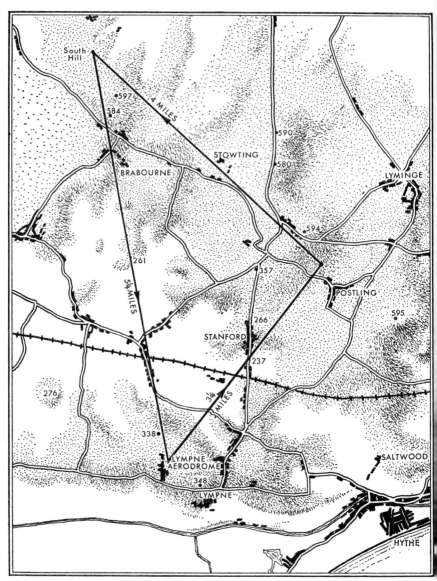

Triangular course used for the Light Aeroplane Trials of 1923 and 1924

A strong north-east wind was blowing on the Saturday afternoon. Mr Winstanley took off in the Widgeon, rounded the first turn at Postling and then ran into the downcurrent in the lee of the range of hills running along the next leg of the course. In spite of all his efforts to maintain height the machine sank so low that a wing-tip touched the ground and the resulting cartwheel hopelessly smashed the fuselage and undercarriage, though the pilot was unhurt. The Widgeon was eliminated. Curiously enough the other Westland entry, the Wood Pigeon, was blown down to the ground at the same spot later in the evening, but the pilot (Mr Gaskell) managed to land without damage, so the machine was brought back to the aerodrome on the following day and successfully completed its qualifying flights.

Mr Campbell had just taken off in the wooden-winged Brownie (No. 1) and was turning over the sheds when his port wing suddenly developed a violent flutter. All who were watching expected to see the wing break, but instead the flutter stopped as quickly as it had begun and the pilot was able to make a hurried landing. The phenomenon was thought to be due to the rubber cord springing on the ailerons, and doubts were expressed as to the safety of the steel-winged machine, but these were dispelled by its designer, Captain Barnwell, who took it into the air and executed a series of steeply banked turns with no trace of any oscillation. This demonstration convinced the officials, who allowed the No. 2 machine to continue its tests, but the trouble with No. 1 could not be satisfactorily investigated on the spot and it was therefore withdrawn from the competition.

Both the Satellite and the A.N.E.C. II had great difficulty in flying with the full competition load of 340 lbs, which did not include fuel. Mr Lankester Parker succeeded in getting the Satellite off the ground, but the climb was hopelessly inadequate and he wisely did not attempt to fly round the course. Mr J. H. James's first attempt with the A.N.E.C. was foiled by a broken valve in the Anzani, but even when this had been repaired the engine did not run perfectly and after a very brief hop half-an-hour before the official closing time he was forced to abandon all hope of prizes. The only other elimination was due to a technicality of the rules rather than to any performance difficulties. Mr Harold Bolas had entered three of his Pixies but in fact there were only two actual aeroplanes, Nos. 17 and 18 being respectively the monoplane and biplane versions of a single machine. When proceedings began on the Saturday morning the officials ruled that all machines should be presented to them for the transport tests at one and the same moment, and Mr Bolas was faced with the impossible task of creating two biplanes and a monoplane simultaneously out of two basic airframes. After conferring with his pilots he decided to run both machines as biplanes and No. 17 therefore disappeared from the list as an official entity, although its ghost (in the form of No. 18 without its top wing) was later seen performing loops and rolls in the hands of Flight Lieutenant Haig.

The only machines left in the competition on Monday morning were therefore the Beardmore and steel-winged Bristol monoplanes, and the two Hawker, two Parnall, Cranwell and Westland biplanes. Five of these had Bristol Cherub engines, the exceptions being the Hawkers with the A.B.C. and British Anzani and one of the Parnalls with the Blackburne.

The first two days of the meeting were somewhat disappointing. On the Monday afternoon Piercey set off in the Wee Bee and completed his two sets of five laps, averaging 70·1 miles an hour with his engine prudently kept down to 400 r.p.m. below its maximum speed, but this was the only complete set of laps to be performed on this day and many of the other competitors were haunted by engine trouble of one kind or another. Both the Hawkers were forced down, Longton having to land on the ridge with a split petrol tank and Raynham being compelled to come in after a single lap with a faulty ball-race which necessitated a change of engine. Both Pixies too made forced landings, No. 19 with a seized piston and No. 18, in which Mr Bolas was flying as Flight Lieutenant Haig's passenger, after a connecting rod had come through the Cherub's crankcase. Since no spare geared Cherub was available, Haig's machine was out of the competition, and so with the aid of his wife he proceeded to install an ungeared engine and prepare the machine as a monoplane for the forthcoming Grosvenor Cup Race. By Tuesday evening it began to appear that the few machines which had managed to evade elimination would steadily be whittled away until the meeting came to a standstill for lack of competitors.

But matters took on a more cheerful aspect the next morning, when the steady drizzle of Tuesday gave place to a perfect windless and cloudless day. Conditions were ideal for the slow-speed test and the getting-off and pulling-up competition, and officials were soon busy placing flags to mark the course. The slow-speed course was 500 yds long and 25 yds wide, and pilots were required to fly along it as slowly as they could, or dared, without touching the ground or rising above 20 ft, two runs being made in each direction so that the effect of wind, if any, could be eliminated by averaging the speeds. The test was a somewhat alarming one to the experienced observer, since it involved flying the aeroplanes on the point of the stall at a dangerously low altitude, but in spite of a number of involuntary contacts with the ground no machine suffered damage except Squadron Leader Douglas's Pixie, which touched a flag pole with a wing-tip. The Cranwell was not easy to fly slowly owing to its poor acceleration near the stall, and onlookers learned with some amusement that its first slow run was 2 m.p.h. faster than its average round the high-speed course. At the end of this run, which was down-wind, Comper found himself quite unable to climb and was faced with a landing in a field straight ahead, which he made successfully.

After lunch and an intermission for a race between three squadron teams of Service machines, preparations were made for the take-off and landing competitions. For the former an imaginary barrier was defined by an observer situated on top of a tall ladder and sighting across the top of a pair of tall poles; the individual pilot then chose the point from which to start his run in order to clear the barrier. Landings were made over a stretched tape and the distance taken to come to rest after crossing the tape was measured. These competitions and the slow-speed tests continued intermittently over the next two days as the various pilots strove to add a few marks to their aggregate by paring a yard or two off their previous best performance at take-off and landing or by covering the course at a slightly lower speed.

The fine calm weather continued on Thursday and Friday and encouraged competitors to carry on round the high-speed course. Raynham on the A.B.C. Hawker completed his first set of five laps and had reached the fourth lap of his second set when he was forced to land on the aerodrome with damage to his rocker-arm brackets which made it necessary for new cylinder-heads to be fitted. This replacement, being outside the permitted schedule, meant that his previous attempts were set at naught and that he had to begin all over again with only two days of the competition left to run. The other Hawker suffered a magneto failure and Longton was forced down out in the country, where he carried out a repair and flew back to the aerodrome, only to be bedevilled by a succession of valve failures on the Friday; his misfortunes were such that on this day he completed his fifteenth lap of the course without having satisfied the requirement of ten consecutive laps in two sets of five. Comper on the Cranwell had been extremely lucky in the matter of engine reliability, but on the Friday he too had valve trouble and was compelled to spend the whole morning on repairs—valuable time which the slow biplane could ill afford to waste, since it still had some four hours' flying to do to draw level with the Wee Bee in terms of distance for the Motor Trade prize.

As at Itford, the drama of the meeting was reserved for the last day. The interest turned upon the fact that although the greatest proportion of the total marks was awarded for the speed range figure, no marks towards this figure could be counted until the ten laps of the high-speed course had been completed in the prescribed manner, and engine unreliability was such that by the Saturday only Piercey on the Wee Bee and Uwins on the Brownie had succeeded in doing this. Any competitor who completed his ten laps on Saturday, therefore, and who had reasonable marks in the other tests, might turn out to be an eleventh-hour winner of the Air

Ministry's £2,000. In fact there were only two pilots who were really in the running for the high-speed figure—Piercey, who in spite of a doubtful big-end was lapping at nearly 80 m.p.h. in an attempt to better his original figure, and Raynham on the Hawker, a slower machine than the Beardmore yet one whose performance in the other tests had been good enough to give him the prize if only he could stay the ten laps. Raynham's team-mate Longton was still cursed with valve trouble and was some way short of the minimum of ten hours, and Comper on the Cranwell, having little hope of success at high-speed work, was steadily lapping for the distance prize as Hinkler had done the year before. The Brownie was not far behind, and Uwins, resting on his high-speed figure of 65·19 m.p.h., was concentrating on adding to his total by improving his take-off and landing figures.

All depended, then, upon whether Piercey and Raynham could stay the course. When the Wee Bee set off on its last lap after a fast run—having averaged over 79 m.p.h. in the first set of five—it seemed that Piercey was a certain winner, but as the minutes passed and he did not reappear it became obvious that he had been forced down. Later it was learned that the big-end which had been showing signs of incipient failure all the week had at last given up the ghost when the machine was only some two miles from the finish. Meanwhile Raynham continued his regular lapping, watched anxiously by the Beardmore team and every knowledgeable eye. He completed his eighth lap and was seen banking round the Postling turn and flying along the ridge, rapidly overhauling the indefatigable Cranwell as both machines closed on the second turning point on South Hill. There was only fifteen miles to go, and all believed that Raynham's traditional ill-luck had turned at last, but as the two biplanes approached the turn together the Hawker was seen suddenly to swing away to the eastward in search of a field. The evil spirit which had brought down Piercey within sight of the finish had now turned its attention to Raynham and caused his engine to break a rocker arm on his last lap but one. Had the fracture held off for another quarter of an hour the Cygnet would have crossed the line at Lympne and won the first prize, but instead Raynham, as at Itford two years before, had had the cup dashed from his lips in the last hours of the meeting.

There being no other contestants the Air Council's £2,000 therefore went, after all, to Piercey on the Wee Bee, who had completed the high speed course at a speed well below the maximum of which his efficient little machine was capable but who had the distinction of being one of the only two competitors to do so. The other was Uwins on the Bristol Brownie, who received the second prize, and who had improved on his getting-off and pulling-up figures to such good effect that he also won the

£500 offered by the Duke of Sutherland for the best performance in these tests. The Cranwell biplane had pursued its stately way round the course sixty-one times (762·5 miles) taking nearly 18 hours to do so, and for this achievement the little band of R.A.F. officers and men who had given up so much of their leisure to build it received £300 from the Motor Traders; a result which gave general satisfaction, noisily expressed with the help of the Imperial Hotel's spoons when the prizes were presented at the final dinner on Saturday evening. Finally there was a small consolation for the unlucky Raynham in that he received Captain Wilson's second prize of £100 for the take-off and landing competitions.

Most of the competing machines, as well as the D.H.53, Viget, Hurricane and Pixie II of the year before, were entered for the race for the Grosvenor Challenge Cup on the Saturday afternoon, and the long tale of engine failures during the week led to the facetious suggestion that the race should be run under the rules of the Gordon Bennett balloon race, according to which the competitor travelling the furthest distance from the starting point should be declared the winner. Although this suggestion was not adopted, the organisers prudently altered the course from the originally proposed out-and-home run to Manston in Kent to eight laps of the high-speed course, so enabling the pilots to remain in sight of the familiar fields which had welcomed so many of them in time of trouble over the past week. In fact, only five of the fourteen starters failed to complete the course, one of them being the R.A.E. Aero Club's Hurricane, which was forced down during the last lap but one after achieving a brilliant 80 m.p.h. with its new Cherub engine. The winner of the race, which was on a handicap basis, was Hinkler on the Avis, and the Avro team were thus to some extent compensated for the misfortunes which had kept them out of the competitions.

The main impression left by the Two-Seater Competitions was one of engine unreliability, but it would not be fair to lay all the blame on the engine manufacturers. The limit of 1,100 c.c. imposed by the rules meant that the engines were heavily taxed when pulling fully loaded two-seater machines, and many were being run at speeds well above their makers' recommended figures. Moreover the smaller units of the previous year's tests had spent much of their time at low power outputs in the economy competition, whereas the main feature of the two-seater trials had been the establishment of a high-speed figure involving two hours or so at full throttle. The Bristol Cherub, which was the only engine to have passed the Air Ministry's type test and to have a certificate of airworthiness, had performed most satisfactorily in the Brownie and Cranwell, and even the Wee Bee's dramatic big-end failure was due to a choked oil pipe and not to any shortcomings in general design. The difficulties with the Cherubs in the

Vagabond and Avis could be attributed to lack of rigidity of the mount-
ings, and once this was overcome both machines performed satisfactorily.
The average fuel consumption of all the Cherub-engined aeroplanes in the
competition was calculated to be 33·5 m.p.g., a satisfactory figure considering that a useful load twice that of the previous year was being carried.

The makers of the Blackburne radial had had almost no time for testing the engine before it was delivered to the aeroplane builders, and they
could therefore hardly be blamed for failing to discover its fault of excessive oil consumption, which had resulted in the elimination of the Sparrow. The A.B.C. Scorpion, which was fitted only to Raynham's Cygnet,
had suffered mainly from the same trouble as the Douglas in the previous
year—breakage of the rocker brackets—and this was probably attributable
to the use of over-strong valve springs. Perhaps the least satisfactory of the
1924 engines was the Anzani, which had repeatedly let down its pilot
(Longton) with broken valves.

On the aircraft side the Air Council's prize offer had brought forth a
crop of designs quite as richly varied as those of the year before, though
the inflexibility of the rules had prevented many of them from competing.
Mr Shackleton's winning Wee Bee was a remarkably clean little machine
with the same all-round capabilities as his A.N.E.C. single-seater; the
structurally efficient Hawker biplanes had shown to advantage in take-off
and landing and evidently had a good speed range (though no official
figure for top speed was recorded); the Pixies had displayed good low-
speed characteristics; and the Brownie, though slower than the Wee Bee,
had run it close on aggregate marking because of its superior take-off and
landing figures, in which individual piloting skill must have played a considerable part. The Wood Pigeon did not distinguish itself and appeared
to be rather over-burdened by its full competition load; it was unfortunate
that the crash of its stable companion the Widgeon prevented an interesting comparison being made between a biplane and a monoplane built to
the same specification.

Finally, the extra cost and complication of two-seater machines and the
increased stringency of the rules seem to have discouraged the amateur
builder and so to have brought about a total absence of the more eccentric
entries and to have reduced the number of serious amateur designs to
one—the Cranwell. The efforts of Flight Lieutenant Comper and his col-
leagues in thus challenging the whole aircraft industry single-handed were
most meritorious, and *The Aeroplane* was moved to comment:

> It is the nearest approach in England to the display of a private, as opposed
> to a trade effort in the sporting and experimental side of flying on lines
> which have been so successfully encouraged in Germany, and if the Air
> Ministry is really sincere in its desire to encourage Light Aeroplane Clubs

it will go out of its way to give a little extra encouragement to those who are ready to follow the Cranwell example.

The Cranwell had been built cheaply because its builders were comparatively poor men, and was nearer to the still distant ideal of a 'motorcycle of the air' costing £150 or £200 than were the majority of the professionally built machines. Some of these were reputed to have cost over £1,000 to build, and even when all allowances were made for the extra cost of a single prototype relative to that of a production machine it was evident that many of the competing aeroplanes were far too lightly and elegantly made to be suitable for cheap manufacture in quantity for the clubs and the private owner. Taking into account the engine difficulties already discussed, the position was that no combination of aeroplane and engine was yet in sight which could be relied upon for the daily hack-work of flying training in the hands of inexperienced pilots. This was the view of the Air Ministry, who issued a statement a few days after the end of the competitions regretting that none of the types demonstrated could receive official recommendation and warning prospective club members that some delay was inevitable before their ambitions could be realised. It was generally believed that another competition would be required in 1925, with revision of the rules governing engine size, and as winter drew on the officials of the Air Ministry entered into discussions with the Royal Aero Club and the manufacturers to determine what form these rules should take.

⤙ 5 ⤚

Lympne

1925 and 1926

The framing of a new set of competition rules turned out to be a long process. It was not until April 1925 that a decision could be announced, and in that month the Royal Aero Club stated that in future events all restrictions on engine capacity or horse-power would be abandoned in favour of a simple limit of 170 lbs on engine weight, inclusive of all accessories such as carburettor, magneto, manifolds and airscrew hub. The choice of this figure was based on the idea that an engine with the reasonable specific weight of 3 lbs/h.p. would thereby develop some 60 h.p., which it was now thought would be a much more satisfactory value for a two-seater machine than the 30 h.p. or so to which the capacity limitation of 1,100 c.c. had restricted the two-seaters of the previous year. It was of course open to engine designers to aim at more efficient (and expensive) units developing 80 or even 100 h.p., or equally to choose a low output coupled with cheapness and robustness.

The new rule provided the engine manufacturer with a clear objective, but as a means of encouraging the design of practical light aeroplanes it was open to some criticism. For instance, it could be argued that it did nothing at all to ensure that the cost of manufacture of the aeroplane itself was kept down to a moderate figure, and avoid the difficulty noted in the previous year's trials that most of the designs were 'too light to be cheap'. In fairness to the makers of the rules, however, it must be said that any formula involving cost would probably have been unworkable owing to the great difficulty of its estimation, for while in theory there can be no two significantly different answers to the measurement of a physical quantity such as weight, length or speed, there would inevitably have been a large element of guesswork in arriving at a selling price from inspection of a prototype. Various alternative suggestions were put forward in the technical press, but none appeared to have any overwhelming advantage over the simple weight limitation, and this was therefore allowed to stand. Since the development of a new engine is a long and costly process, it was at once obvious that no fully proven engine designed to the new rule could possibly appear on any starting line during the remaining eight months of the year, and the only practical course was to postpone the next Air Ministry competition until the summer of 1926 and to confine the proposed light aeroplane meeting in August 1925 to racing and performance measurement on existing types.

In the meantime, however, Captain de Havilland's two-seater aeroplane, which he had named the Moth, had made its first flight and was proving extremely successful. Its engine, the Cirrus, was an ingenious adaptation of a larger design and weighed considerably more than 170 lbs, but already appeared to be quite strikingly reliable. The idea of the aerial motor-cycle was still strong, and there were many who felt that the Moth was something between the true light aeroplane and the bigger commercial or military machine, but its practicality as a means of getting about the country and of giving flying instruction was becoming daily more evident. Official interest in the promotion of further development of light aeroplanes by means of prizes therefore began to wane, and eventually the Air Ministry decided to abandon their original intention of supporting the competition of 1926. Their decision was made easier by the fact that in June 1925 the *Daily Mail* came forward once more with the handsome sum of £5,000 to be added to any official prize-money that there might be, and the Air Ministry's withdrawal involved no change in the organisation of the competition, which was already planned on the lines of the contemporary German *Rundflug* as a series of out-and-home flights radiating from a fixed centre to different outlying towns on each successive day.

The August Bank Holiday race-meeting at Lympne attracted many entries. With the exception of the Moth, the Dutch Pander monoplane and the new product of the Cranwell Light Aeroplane Club, all the machines present could be divided into two classes: on the one hand the light aeroplanes which had been seen in the previous two competitions—many of them fitted with new engines or otherwise modified—and on the other a motley collection of types dating back in some instances to the distant days of the war and mostly entered by private owners, rare individuals whose total was at this time still to be reckoned in single figures. In the first category came the single-seater A.N.E.C. with wings cut down in span and a much improved Anzani engine, two D.H.53s—one of them with the Blackburne Badger engine which had been developed from the motor-cycle unit of 1923—the Wee Bee, Avis, Brownie, Pixie II and III, Cygnet, Satellite and R.A.E. Hurricane. The privately owned machines, none of which were light aeroplanes by the definition of the time, included Flight Lieutenant Soden's long-lived Austin Whippet, the venerable B.E.2E of Mr

R. L. Preston (which was unable to take part owing to difficulties over its Certificate of Airworthiness), the Renault-engined wartime S.E.5 scout of the earliest of post-war private owners, Dr Whitehead Reid, the Sopwith Gnu two-seater biplane of 1919 and the unique Sopwith Scooter of the same period which had been built by the late Mr H. G. Hawker in his spare time out of the fuselage of a Camel biplane scout to which had been added a wire-braced parasol monoplane wing.

Much interest was created by Comper's new C.L.A.3 parasol monoplane. The C.L.A.2 biplane of 1924 had been wrecked by a Service pilot while being tested at Martlesham Heath, but the Air Ministry had undertaken to compensate the Club for their loss. This, together with their £300 prize money had enabled the Cranwell Club to embark upon the construction of a special racing aeroplane. The C.L.A.3, unlike its broad-beamed predecessor, was designed to have the minimum possible cross-sectional area of fuselage, and to this end the designer had seated the pilot on the floor of the shapely fuselage and had neatly enclosed the Cherub engine in a large cowling of beaten light alloy. Access to the cockpit was difficult since it was situated immediately below the wing centre-section, but once installed the pilot had a good view in all directions except upward. Like the C.L.A.2, the machine was entirely built of wood.

Bank Holiday Saturday and Monday were largely devoted to racing, but the Sunday, for reasons which will presumably be clear to those well versed in the theory of the British Sabbath, had to be restricted to unofficial races and to the establishment of certified height and speed performances by the Royal Aero Club. Evidently the week-end aviators attracted to themselves no ecclesiastical ill-will, for on the Monday Flight Lieutenant Haig and his passenger, descending involuntarily in their Pixie III near the same village of Brabourne from which Captain Cockerell had stoutly wheeled back his Viget two years before, unexpectedly found themselves being shown round the church and were invited to join a tea-party at the vicarage.

Although there were a few forced landings, the meeting was remarkable for the greatly improved reliability of the engines and for the success of the amateur constructors. Flight Lieutenant Chick, flying the R.A.E. Hurricane, won the Light Aeroplane Holiday Handicap on the Saturday and the Private Owners' Race and Grosvenor Cup on the Monday, taking back to Farnborough a useful £300 in prize money. Comper brought his new design home first in a scratch race for light single-seaters, and the next day established its speed as 87 m.p.h. over a 3-km course—a figure which he hoped to improve to nearly 100 m.p.h. by careful attention to fairing. Another association of R.A.F. officers, the Seven Light Aeroplane Club based at Eastchurch, were less fortunate with their A.B.C.-engined

17. The Short Satellite at Lympne
18. The first Avro Avian at Lympne, 1926, showing its pilot, Mr H. J. L. ('Bert') Hinkler, walking towards the propeller

19. The Hawker Cygnet biplane, winner of the 1926 Lympne trials
20. The graceful A.N.E.C. IV, built for the 1926 Lympne trials

D.H.53, which was forced down with engine trouble in the Light Aeroplane Holiday Handicap and considerably damaged. The two Moths present were excluded from much of the racing by the rule limiting engine weight, which was applied to this meeting as well as to the competitions of the following year, but Mr Alan Cobham, flying the prototype G-EBKT, won an unofficial race on the Sunday against Captain Hubert Broad on G-EBKU. During the International Handicap the next day, however, the sudden failure of his engine caused him to descend at rather short notice into the only suitable field, where the ripe corn caught the axle of his undercarriage and tipped the Moth onto its back.

The courses chosen for the 1926 competitions were all centred once more on Lympne aerodrome, and to stimulate a certain amount of public interest many of the turning-points were chosen to be at popular seaside resorts, which in the week of the meeting—12–17 September—would still be fairly full of visitors. The total distance to be covered in six days of flying was almost 2,000 miles, made up as shown in the following table:

Day	Course	No. of times covered	Total day's mileage
1st	Lympne–Brighton–Lympne	3	312
2nd	Lympne–Eastbourne—Lympne–Hastings–Lympne	3	366
3rd	Lympne–Dover–Manston–North Foreland–Reculver Towers–Lympne	6	396
4th	As 1st day		312
5th	As 3rd day		396
6th	Lympne–Croydon–Lympne	2	212
			1,994

The preliminary tests, to be held on Friday and Saturday, 10 and 11 September, were familiar: the dismantling and erecting test and the dual-control demonstration were retained, and in addition there was to be a getting-off test with a fixed run of 300 yds allowed for the surmounting of two barriers 25 ft high and 25 yds apart (the object being to discourage an exaggerated pull-up followed by a loss of height), and a landing test in which machines had to be brought to rest in 125 yds after crossing a barrier 6 ft high. These tests were to be completed with full competition load by the close of flying on Saturday, following the presentation of the machines to the officials of the meeting on the Friday morning. The competition itself was to take place between the hours of 8 a.m. and 8 p.m. on each of the next six days, and the sheds would be locked from 9 o'clock each evening until 7 o'clock the following morning to prevent any work being done on the aircraft throughout the night.

The award of the prize-money, divided into a first prize of £3,000, a second prize of £1,500 and a third prize of £500, was this time to be on the basis of a figure of merit in which fuel economy was allied to load carried and distance flown. Subject to a minimum average speed of 50 m.p.h. over any stage of the course and to a minimum useful load of 340 lbs—equivalent to the weight of two people—the competitors were to be assessed according to the formula

$$\frac{(\text{Pounds of useful load carried}) \times (\text{miles flown})}{(\text{Pounds of fuel consumed})}$$

which can readily be converted into ton-miles per gallon by assuming a suitable figure for the weight of a gallon of petrol.*

This basis of marking left the designer a certain amount of room for manoeuvre, since a reasonably efficient engine of the maximum weight allowed—170 lbs—would provide enough power to carry a useful load considerably greater than the minimum of 340 lbs. At one extreme, therefore, he could use an engine of the maximum weight and expect to carry six or seven hundred pounds of load with a correspondingly high fuel consumption, of the order of 17–18 m.p.g. in still air; at the other, he could fix the load at the minimum figure and be free to use a smaller engine such as the Bristol Cherub III, which would give about 35 m.p.g. In terms of ton-miles per gallon there was not a great deal to choose between these alternatives, since the extra load and the extra fuel consumption tended to offset one another, though the more powerful machine would have a higher speed and so be less affected by adverse winds. In theory any intermediate combination of power and load could be used, but in practice only one engine especially designed to 170 lbs maximum weight was available—the new Armstrong Siddeley five-cylinder Genet radial—and it turned out that the entries could be divided cleanly into two categories: the three machines with Genet engines and the remaining thirteen with smaller engines on the 1924 model and correspondingly small useful loads.

The 1926 competitions, in spite of the considerable prizes offered, attracted few new professionally built entries. The de Havilland Company, being unable to enter the Cirrus-Moth because of the limitation on engine weight, adapted one of these aircraft to take the Genet, and its smaller weight meant an increase of 50 lbs or so in the useful load which could be carried. A. V. Roe and Company also made use of the Genet in a totally

---

* The figure officially used at Lympne was 7·6 lb. Thus the little Wren of 1923, with its 87·5 miles per gallon carrying a 150-pound pilot, would have been assessed at 5·86 ton-miles per gallon or 1,727 lb-miles per lb.

new design called the Avian (Plate 18), a single-bay, equal-span biplane
of straightforward yet extremely light wooden construction, carefully
planned to be capable of cheap production for the flying clubs and the
private owner, and fitted for competition purposes only with a special set
of wings of larger area and span than standard. The Avis of 1924 was also

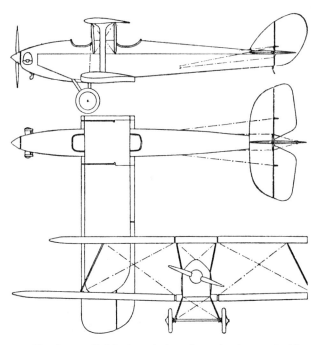

5. The Cranwell C.L.A.4, designed to take the new Pobjoy
radial engine and to compete in the 1926 Lympne trials

entered by its makers with its original Bristol Cherub engine replaced by
the three-cylinder Blackburne Thrush of 1,500 c.c. capacity. The third
Genet-engined type was the Blackburn Bluebird, which now reappeared
with some modification to its fuselage whereby the pilot's and passenger's
seats were slightly staggered in order to reduce the width to the 44 ins.
called for by the rules.

Apart from the graceful Missel Thrush or A.N.E.C. IV (Plate 20),
produced by the Air Navigation and Engineering Company to the design
of Mr J. Bewsher, the other new types were all the work of the amateur
clubs. The energetic Cranwell Club entered two similar C.L.A.4 biplanes
having the unusual arrangement (to British eyes at any rate) of an upper
wing of smaller span than the lower, with ailerons on the lower wing only
(Figure 5). It was intended that one of these aeroplanes should be fitted
with the first of a series of engines which also originated at Cranwell, for

Mr D. R. Pobjoy, at this time Education Officer of No. 4 Apprentices'
Wing there, had formed a small team unconnected with the Light Aeroplane Club to build to his design a 7-cylinder geared radial engine of
2·5 litres capacity, rated at 50 b.h.p. for the remarkably low weight of 100 lbs.
But the interesting combination never appeared, for the Pobjoy 'P', as the
engine was called, suffered a minor breakage during its type tests at Farnborough, after which the regulations governing type testing demanded a
completely fresh start. Due to the delay only one of the C.L.A.4 machines
—that fitted with a Cherub III engine—was ready in time to compete.

The Halton Aero Club, officially formed in December 1925 on the
same lines as the Cranwell and R.A.E. clubs with some 1,100 members
drawn from the staff and apprentices, entered their first production, whose
initial design had begun about a year previously. This was a wooden biplane with a Cherub III engine and folding wings braced by interplane
struts of a distinctive 'X' shape which avoided the necessity for fore-and-
aft wire bracing. The machine was called the H.A.C.1 or Mayfly, and was
designed by Mr C. H. Latimer-Needham, then also an education officer
with the R.A.F. He was later to become well-known for his work in the
glider and 'ultra-light' aeroplane fields in the 1930s. He based the propor-
tions of wings and control surfaces on a study of the 1924 Lympne two-
seaters, using average values with a bias towards the more successful
entries, and took unusual care to enclose control cables and similar items
within the fuselage. A very clean exterior was the result. The aeroplane
was built largely by the apprentices, partly as official training and partly in
their spare time, and great efforts were made to complete it for the meeting, but when this proved impossible work proceeded at a more leisurely
pace and the machine first flew in February of the following year. Later in
1927, in single-seater racing form with the front cockpit faired in, it won
a number of races and in this way contributed to the funds of the Club and
enabled its members to embark on further enterprises.

The R.A.E. Club's latest product was the Sirocco, a low-wing monoplane of straightforward wooden construction, but an enormous design
error resulted in the measured position of the centre of gravity being
twenty-nine inches aft of the estimated position, and work on the machine
was abandoned before it had flown. However, the Club had another aircraft to send to Lympne—Raynham's 1924 Cygnet, which had been presented to them by the Hawker Company several months previously and
which they had fitted with a Cherub III engine in place of the original
A.B.C. Scorpion. The other Cygnet (Plate 19), which had been flown by
Longton in 1924, was retained by its makers, strengthened to take a higher
all-up weight, and entered in their name also with a Cherub III. With
their new engines and extremely low structure weight the Cygnets were

capable of carrying a substantial load and their prospects of success in the competition were excellent.

The remaining entries were also familiar to those who had been at Lympne in 1924, although one—the Supermarine Sparrow—had been changed into a monoplane by attaching to the original fuselage a one-piece parasol wing intended for full-scale flight research on the American Clark 'Y' wing section. The all-steel Brownie reappeared with a Cherub III engine and a sprung telescopic undercarriage, the Pixie III was the machine flown by Sholto Douglas in 1924 in monoplane form, and the list was completed by the two entries of the Seven Aeroplane Club, the Satellite, which had been presented to them by Mr Oswald Short, and the Westland Wood Pigeon.

The absence of the Halton biplane, the Sirocco and the Pobjoy-engined Cranwell reduced the entries to thirteen, and the pretty Missel Thrush put itself out of the running on the Thursday, the day before the start of the eliminating trials. While landing at Lympne, piloted by Colonel G. L. P. Henderson, it had the misfortune to strike a slight bump in the grass; the rubber shock cord extended more than usual, allowing the end of an undercarriage leg to dig into the ground and the machine tipped over onto its back. The damage was too great for repair before the competition began, but the machine was airworthy again on the fourth day.

There were further eliminations which many competitors felt were due to an excessively strict interpretation of the rules by the stewards of the meeting, although in fairness it must be said that their task was far from being an easy one. It was laid down that all competing machines must be presented on the Friday morning in the precise form in which it was proposed to fly them during the following week, and that subsequent repairs were only to be of a minor nature, the definition of a minor repair being left largely to the stewards' discretion. No one who has tried to land a fully loaded small aeroplane over a 6-ft barrier and bring it to rest in 125 yds will be surprised to hear that more than one undercarriage was damaged during the pulling-up tests. The first casualty was the Bluebird, which Longton landed heavily, bending a lug which, it was ruled, could be bent straight but could not be replaced. The designer of the machine, Mr Thornton, asked permission to make a sounder alternative form of repair but this was also refused and he had no option but to withdraw the machine from the competition. The Cranwell met the same fate when Comper bent an undercarriage tube which was known to have a flaw in it, and the machine was eliminated even though an identical undercarriage had been brought to Lympne to meet this very eventuality. Less open to dispute perhaps was the refusal to allow a change of propeller on the Wood Pigeon. It had flown down to Lympne and been presented to the stewards with a

Fairey-Reed metal propeller which did not suit it instead of a wooden one which did, so the machine had to go forward to the competition with greatly reduced performance. This was unfortunate for the Seven Club since their other entry, the Satellite, had dismally failed to climb over the barrier in the getting-off test; from two aeroplanes they were reduced to something effectively rather less than one.

The nine aeroplanes which remained set off for Brighton in a stiff wind shortly after 8 o'clock on the Sunday morning, and by the end of the first day it was evident that the struggle lay between the Cygnets and Hinkler on the Avian, all of which were returning figures of merit well in advance of the rest of the field. The slow Sparrow could not maintain the required 50 m.p.h. against the wind, and Biard turned back, later to land on Beachy Head for the excellent reason that the pin holding one of his wing struts was nearly out of its socket. Once on the ground the machine promptly blew over, and after righting it and pegging it down the pilot spent an uncomfortable night in this exposed spot before flying back on the following day. The character of the competition differed from those of past years in that now, unless each day's task was completed before the close of flying on that day, there was no question of making up lost ground on a later day, so that the Sparrow was forced to retire, and the Avis quickly followed it by running into a ditch and damaging itself during a forced landing. The Wood Pigeon, last hope of the Seven Club, was also forced down on the Tuesday with a seized rocker; this was freed and the machine flew back to the aerodrome and set off on its last lap in gathering darkness, but try as he might Flight Lieutenant Ritchie could not quite urge his mount round the course fast enough to finish by the closing hour of 8 p.m. and he crossed the line 48 seconds late.

Hinkler's troubles began on the second day when the Avian's welded aluminium petrol tank began to leak, a fault which neither the overnight attentions of a local aluminium welder nor the liberal application of soap managed completely to cure, though it was possible to carry on with the tank only partly filled. It was not this, however, that robbed him of an almost certain second place, but an annoyingly small failure in his Genet engine—the breaking of the duralumin magneto shaft, which could not be replaced in time to finish the course. Had the shaft been of steel, at a cost of only a few ounces in weight, the result of the competition might have been very different. The same fault brought down Captain Broad on the Moth the next day, but his elimination was due not to this but to the fact that at the end of the day one of the 12-lb ballast weights which the Moth carried to simulate useful load was found to be missing, and it was believed that it had been removed by an inquisitive boy while the aircraft was on the ground after its forced landing.

The Moth was the last to go, and four remained to finish on the Friday. Although the weather was misty the two laps to Croydon and back presented little difficulty, and at 2.30 p.m. Courtney on the Pixie arrived back at Lympne to take fourth place, and shortly after three the winner, Bulman on the Hawker Cygnet, crossed the line to the accompaniment of hooting motor horns, closely followed by Uwins on the Brownie, winner of the third prize. The second prizewinner—the other Cygnet entered by the R.A.E. Aero Club—was slightly delayed by a landing at Biggin Hill with suspected low oil pressure, but this turned out to be only a faulty gauge so Chick and Ragg, who instead of taking turns were both in the machine for this final day's flying, took off again and reached Lympne safely.

The figures of merit achieved by the four machines that finished were:

1.	Hawker Cygnet	2,203 lb-miles per lb.
2.	R.A.E. Cygnet	1,808 ,, ,, ,,
3.	Brownie	1,687 ,, ,, ,,
4.	Pixie	1,541 ,, ,, ,,

From quite early in the meeting it had been apparent that Bulman was a certain winner if he could stay the course. His performance on the Cygnet was a remarkable one and is worthy of examination in more detail. The load carried, exclusive of fuel and oil, was equivalent to the weight of two people with a generous supply of luggage, and the machine had covered almost 2,000 miles at an average speed of 65 m.p.h. with a fuel consumption of 39.2 m.p.g., a feat which the two-seater motor-car of the day would scarcely have been able to equal even in the most favourable road conditions; in practice it would probably have done well to reach 30 m.p.g., or a figure of merit of 1,700, at only half the Cygnet's average speed. The minor fault which put the Avian out of the running should not be allowed to obscure the fact that at the time of its retirement it was returning a figure of merit of nearly 2,100, which if maintained would easily have brought Hinkler the second prize. The closeness of the figures indicates the small difference in efficiency (as measured by the chosen criterion) between the low-powered Cygnet with its 430 lbs. of useful load and the higher-powered Avian carrying almost double the amount (828 lbs) at some 7 m.p.h. higher average speed.

The Hawker triumph was shared by Mr Roy Fedden, designer of the Bristol Cherub III engines which had brought home all four of the machines which had stayed the course. The return to an economy formula had given all the engines an easier time than they had had in the high-speed tests of 1924, yet there had still been a number of failures and against the general background of reliability the Cherubs had performed out-standingly well. After the competition Bulman's engine was completely stripped down in public as a demonstration and was found to be in perfect order after its thirty-odd hours of almost continuous flying.

Thus ended the last of the three light aeroplane competitions at Lympne. In the thirteen years of peace that remained the aerodrome was the scene of many aviation meetings and the springboard for most of the famous flights across the world whose story will be told in later chapters, but never again was to be seen in England anything quite like the meetings of 1923, 1924 and 1926. In those years practically all the great aeronautical names of Britain—Blackburn, Hawker, Westland, Handasyde, Vickers, Avro, Gloster, Short, de Havilland, Supermarine and others—had made their contribution to the contests fought out from the turf of Lympne. Almost every designer of note, many of them today eminent men in an industry which has grown and changed out of all recognition, had pro-duced his own highly individual solution to the problem of the small economical aeroplane, had seen his ideas take shape in wood and metal, had blackened his hands preparing the finished product for the lists and as often as not had completed his task by taking it into the air himself; and alongside the established firms was ranged a band of knowledgeable and enthusiastic amateurs whose keenness to get their creations into the air overcame the many obstacles (including the financial) with which they were constantly faced.

Yet the results of the Lympne trials were curious in that the placing of the competing designs was almost exactly in inverse ratio to their future success. The Wren and A.N.E.C., Wee Bee and Cygnet won their prizes and had their hour of fame only to vanish quickly into obscurity, yet the Bluebird, Widgeon, Avian and Moth (and to a lesser extent the D.H.53), all of which were entirely unsuccessful in the competitions, later went for-ward to become popular club and private aeroplanes in the late 1920s and after. Perhaps the lesson to be learned is that a formal competition is not the best way to produce a satisfactory light aeroplane, or for that matter any other vehicle, since firstly the criteria which make for success or failure in engineering are often too subtle and complicated to be capable of defini-tion in a set of rules, and secondly, when the main object is to obtain marks, many competitors will be tempted to bend all their efforts to ingenious ways of defeating the rules rather than to producing the best machine according to their individual beliefs.

Nevertheless, the three competitions are of extraordinary interest in themselves. The search for aerodynamic efficiency allied to economy, unhampered by the requirement to accommodate commercial or military loads, resulted in a set of little machines which in many ways were considerably in advance of their time. In 1923, when the braced biplane reigned supreme in British aviation, three-quarters of the British types competing were monoplanes, many of them of cantilever type. The emphasis placed upon speed range in 1924 brought into prominence the landing flap, which was subsequently almost to disappear again until the rise of the efficient flapped cantilever monoplanes of the 1930s, when the light aeroplane was again to be in advance of its military and commercial contemporaries. On the structural side the Cygnet and Avian are memorable for their lightness of construction and weight-lifting ability, and the Satellite, though not especially successful as an aeroplane, must take an honoured place in any account of the development of the technique of stressed-skin construction.

For the aeronautical engineer who cares for the history of his art, the twenty-nine distinct and different aeroplanes which the three meetings brought into being form a rich field in which to browse with slide-rule in hand. There are many matters which must for ever remain pure speculation. How many miles could the Wren have flown on a gallon if conditions had been ideal? Would the altitude version of the Pixie have been able to go as high as the A.N.E.C.? How successful would the Pobjoy-engined Comper biplane have been in 1926 if it had been able to compete? These questions can still form the basis of an absorbing technical argument. But even the non-technical reader who cares for none of these things will be able to agree that Lympne occupies a unique place in the story of the light aeroplane and in the history of British aviation.

⤙ 6 ⤚

The Coming of the Moth

Captain Geoffrey de Havilland's decision not to participate in the Two-Seater Competitions at Lympne in 1924 was based upon his own clear idea of the form which a small, simple and practical aeroplane for the clubs and the private owner should take—an idea which could not be reconciled with those of the Air Ministry. Experience with the little D.H.53 had shown that in spite of its many excellent qualities its performance was not really adequate for serious air touring, due chiefly to its low cruising speed, which severely reduced its range and made it painfully slow when it was flying into the sort of stiff head-wind which is only too familiar to pilots in this country. What was now required, evidently, was a two-seater which would cruise at not less than 80 m.p.h., carry enough petrol for three hours' flying and a supply of luggage adequate for its occupants' needs when touring, and have a sufficient reserve of power to give a good take-off and rate of climb in the most adverse conditions which might be met in world-wide operation. All this, in Captain de Havilland's judgement and that of his chief engineer, Mr C. C. Walker, was a technical impossibility under the competition rules, which limited engine capacity to 1,100 c.c. and therefore held engine power down to something in the region of 35 h.p. A reasonable performance according to their specification could not, they believed, be looked for without an engine delivering at least 50 or 60 h.p., and no such engine suitable for use in aircraft existed in Great Britain at this time.

No progress seemed to be possible without the protracted and expensive process of development which must go on before a completely new design of engine can be placed in service, and the only way of circumventing the difficulty was to modify an already existing design in such a way that prolonged development work was unnecessary. Captain de Havilland therefore cast about him for an alternative solution on these lines, and the one that he found not only made it possible for him to launch upon the world the most successful light aeroplane of its time but also laid the foundation for the long series of Cirrus and Gipsy engines which were an essential element in the progress of the British light aeroplane movement as a whole.

The idea behind the original Cirrus engine, like so many good ideas, was a fundamentally simple one. The Aircraft Disposal Company of Croydon, formed in 1920 by a syndicate which included Mr Frederick Handley Page and Colonel M. O. Darby for the purpose of dealing with the vast stocks of aeroplanes, aero-engines and associated material left by the war, had from the first employed a considerable staff of skilled aircraft workers for reconditioning machines before sale. It was clear from the beginning that the 'disposals' business could not last for ever, and the firm therefore early turned its attention to the original design of both aeroplanes and engines. Under the supervision of Major F. B. Halford, who had had an outstanding record of engine design in the war years, an 8-cylinder air-cooled vee engine of 120 h.p. called the Airdisco was developed from the 80-h.p. Renault, and it occurred to Captain de Havilland that by using only one bank of cylinders from this unit a 4-cylinder in-line engine could be produced which would be of approximately the power required for a two-seater light aeroplane designed according to his ideas. Moreover, many of the existing Airdisco parts could be used in such an engine without modification, and these were available in large quantities from the Disposal Company's stocks, so that the problem of spares would not be a serious one.

Acting on this suggestion, Major Halford immediately set to work on the design of the smaller engine, and after only nine weeks the first Cirrus was running on the test bench. The only entirely new major component was the crankcase, to which was attached a large sump of motor-car type with an oil pump to lubricate the bearings under pressure. The cylinders and cylinder heads were identical with those of the Airdisco, and so was the five-bearing crankshaft, which with its bearings was carrying loads considerably smaller than those for which it had been designed and was therefore likely to be exceptionally reliable. The engines of the first batch were fitted with single ignition, though this was later duplicated to conform with normal aeronautical practice, and a mechanical device—later abandoned—was added at the rear of the engine to enable it to be started by the pilot without leaving the cockpit. The fact that some parts were more robust than was strictly necessary meant that the Cirrus was rather heavier in relation to its power than the average of contemporary designs, but events showed that this slight disadvantage did nothing to diminish its success.

In the meantime the design of the Moth was proceeding parallel with that of its engine, a rare and happy state of affairs compared with the much more usual case of a potentially successful aeroplane which comes to nothing for lack of a suitable power unit. It was a small biplane on perfectly orthodox de Havilland lines, with single-bay two-spar folding wings covered with fabric and a fuselage built as a plywood box on spruce longerons, closely resembling (except for its small size) its war-time predecessors the D.H.4 and D.H.9. Two more recent de Havilland designs may be considered to have led directly to the Moth, and for this reason require study in more detail: they were the D.H.37 private owner's machine which (as already noted) was built in 1921 to the special order of Mr A. S. Butler, and the lower-powered D.H.51 three-seater of 1923.

The D.H.37, with Rolls-Royce Falcon engine of 275 h.p., was by no means a light aeroplane, but it embodied a number of features which were continued into the Moth, notably the single-bay wings carrying differential ailerons on the lower planes only, the streamlined fuel tank in the centre-section, and the characteristic de Havilland fin and rudder. The empty weight of the machine was over two-and-a-half times that of the Moth, and with full load the wing loading was 8·55 lbs/sq. ft, a relatively high figure for the day. The D.H.51 which followed two years later was in effect an intermediate type of lower weight and wing loading, initially fitted with two-bay wings of the same span as the D.H.37 and with the 90-h.p. 8-cylinder R.A.F. engine, a batch of which had been bought as war-surplus at the very reasonable price of fourteen shillings and sixpence each. Owing to difficulties with certification of these engines with their single ignition, the 120-h.p. Airdisco was installed in the small number of D.H.51s built, and just before the first flight of the Moth the prototype of the larger machine was fitted with single-bay wings, in which form its resemblance to its smaller successor was remarkable, the principal distinguishing feature apart from size being the double bank of cylinders of the Airdisco and the large four-bladed propeller. The D.H.51 was still too large an aeroplane to find much favour as a private owner's machine and was soon overshadowed by the Moth with its engine of precisely half the size, but it is interesting to note that one of these machines was still in flying condition in Kenya in 1961, nearly forty years after leaving Stag Lane.

The Moth, then, was a miniature version of its two predecessors just described, carrying pilot and passenger in tandem cockpits with the latter seated immediately under the centre-section and very close to the centre of gravity of the machine, so that there was little change of trim due to the addition or removal of his weight. Access to the front cockpit was made easier by the absence of fore-and-aft wire bracing in the centre-section, the necessary rigidity being obtained by the use of a pair of inverted V-struts at the front. The wings were arranged to be easily folded back for storage in a shed or garage. The Cirrus engine was mounted high up on the top longerons with its four cylinders and exposed valve-gear protruding into the airstream, and was fed by gravity from the centre-section petrol tank. A characteristic feature of the Moth, which will be remembered by all who flew it, was the long exhaust pipe running down the side of the fuselage past the cockpits, and the excellent silencing of the engine, together with its low rotational speed, made the machine pleasantly quiet when in the air —a valuable feature for instruction or general conversation with a passenger through the speaking-tubes provided.

The small size of the Moth is best illustrated by a comparison of its leading particulars with those of the very much larger D.H.37 and the intermediate D.H.51:

	D.H.37	D.H.51	D.H.60 Moth
Empty weight, lbs	2,118	1,312	770
Loaded weight, lbs	3,318	2,240	1,240
			(Max. C. of
			A. weight:
			1,350 lbs)
Span, ft	37	37	30
Wing area, sq. ft	388	325	243
Wing loading, lbs/sq. ft	8·55	6·9	5·1

Thus the Moth was literally a 'halved' D.H.51 with just over half the empty and loaded weights, an engine derived by a direct process of bisection from the 8-cylinder Airdisco fitted to the earlier machine, yet a wing area some three-quarters as great to provide wing-loading low enough for safe operation from relatively small fields.

The de Havilland company, with their already long experience of aircraft design, launched their new type with every confidence of success, though few of those responsible can have imagined quite how astonishing this success would be or have dared to predict that the emergence of this small aeroplane would prove to be the turning-point of their company's fortunes. An advertisement published early in 1925, shortly before the Moth had flown for the first time, reflects this confidence and summarises the ideas underlying its design:

THE D.H. TWO-SEATER LIGHT AEROPLANE

The D.H. two-seater light aeroplane is being produced for the School, the Flying Club and the Private Owner.

Simplicity, robustness and ease of handling and maintenance are features which have been most carefully considered in its design.

The de Havilland Moth will not be a delicate and frail craft requiring highly skilled attention. It will be as sturdy and lasting as the modern Light Car.

The first cost of the D.H.60 will be low and its upkeep correspondingly cheap and simple.

On 22 February 1925, the prototype Moth was ready to fly and it was on that memorable Sunday afternoon that it first took the air at Stag Lane aerodrome in the hands of Captain Geoffrey de Havilland himself. After making a short flight to satisfy himself that everything was in order, he landed in order to pick up Captain Broad and took off again to check its behaviour with both seats occupied. The new machine was fully up to expectations; handling was found to be easy, and the performance was better than estimated, with a top speed of over 90 m.p.h. A few days later a demonstration was held for the benefit of the Press, and there were two aspects of this that were especially significant. First, the weather had been very wet, and the aerodrome was little better than a quagmire, but the power of the Cirrus engine was nevertheless ample to take the Moth into the air repeatedly on its demonstration flights with quite a short run, even when a passenger was carried. Second, throughout the demonstration the continued functioning and frequent re-starting of the engine was taken entirely as a matter of course—a totally different state of affairs from the troubles, the temperament and the continual forced landings of the Lympne meeting only a few months earlier. Looking back, it is clear to us today that Captain de Havilland and Major Halford had produced between them a new type of vehicle; not, to be sure, the aerial motor-cycle which had been dreamed of after Itford, but a robust 'motor-car of the air' on which the ordinary individual could learn to fly and thereafter, even if possessed of only average skill, conduct himself across counties or continents with a maximum of enjoyment and a minimum of risk to his own skin. Probably none of the journalists present at Stag Lane on this muddy Monday in February 1925 fully realised that they were witnessing the beginning of a revolution in flying, although the fact that the new machine had great potentialities must already have been evident, for *The Times*, reporting the demonstration under the heading 'An Aeroplane for Youth', presciently observed that the Moth was 'the most promising contribution yet made to the difficult problem of getting the youth of the nation into the air'.

Official reactions to the new type were somewhat mixed. The Moth's 4,500 c.c. engine put it well outside the category of light aeroplane as that term had hitherto been understood, and the Air Ministry, which had already refused to sanction the use of the well-tried Avro 504 by the State-subsidised flying clubs which were just coming into being, was at first reluctant to agree to its being ordered for the clubs. A considerable amount of public money had just been expended as prizes in a competition to find an economical two-seater aeroplane according to a formula limiting engine capacity to 1,100 c.c. and it was too much to expect an immediate welcome for an entirely new type of machine produced without official blessing and fitted with an engine four times as large. As time went on, however, it became clear that the Moth was admirably suited to the purposes of the

clubs and that the Lympne formula was most unlikely to produce a satisfactory competitor to it even if the various troubles arising out of the over-
loading of the small engines used could be overcome. It was officially
agreed, therefore, that the Moth should be used, on a temporary basis if
not a permanent one, and in April 1925 the Royal Aero Club, acting as
agent for the first five clubs (London, Lancashire, Midland, Yorkshire and
Newcastle) placed an order for a first batch of machines to be delivered in
June.

Towards the end of May the capabilities of the Moth for extended
travel were convincingly demonstrated in a flight by Mr Alan Cobham,
who had only recently returned from taking Sir Sefton Brancker, the
Director of Civil Aviation, to Rangoon and back in the Moth's very much
larger relative the D.H.50. Using the original Moth G-EBKT equipped
with extra petrol tanks in the front cockpit, he set out from Croydon just
before 5 a.m., crossed the Channel and set course for Switzerland across
the former battlefields of Northern France, landing at Zurich after a non-
stop flight of 500 miles in 6 hrs 6 mins. He remained at Zurich only long
enough to take on fuel and have a light lunch, and was in the air again at
11.45 on the return journey to England. Flying in this direction he was
meeting a stiff three-quarter head wind, and to minimise the effect of this
he flew much of the way in exceedingly bumpy air at a height of only a
hundred feet above the ground, but in spite of this the wind slowed the
Moth down and the return journey took 7 hrs 45 mins.

This showed once and for all that the new de Havilland machine was
perfectly suitable for flights of any length that its fuel capacity allowed, for
over the 1,000 miles covered at an average speed of over 70 m.p.h the
engine had run with perfect reliability, causing the pilot no anxiety of any
kind. The cost of fuel and oil used for the double journey, respectively
56 gallons and 14 pints, was only £4 12s., in comparison with which the
same journey by rail and sea would have cost £11 and occupied 37 hours.
The comparison in terms of cost was, of course, not a fair one, since the
aeroplane's fixed costs of insurance, maintenance and so on were not included, but it served to indicate that reliable personal air travel with all its
advantages of speed and simplicity had arrived at last at a price which was
within the reach of many. Had a passenger been carried in place of an
extra fuel tank, it would naturally have been possible to share even this
modest running cost with only the small added inconvenience of an intermediate landing to take on petrol.

Towards the end of the summer of 1925 the production Moths began
to appear. On 21 July Mr Cobham flew one of these machines to Woodford
aerodrome in Cheshire for the opening of the Lancashire Aero Club, and
although this was not strictly speaking a delivery flight it was not many

weeks before the new machines began to pass into the hands of the waiting clubs. The London Aeroplane Club began its operations in mid-August, and there followed two Moths each for the Newcastle and Midland clubs at Cramlington and Castle Bromwich and one for the Yorkshire Light Aeroplane Club, which, lacking its own aerodrome, had to receive its new acquisition in the open space known as the Soldier's Field at Leeds and subsequently fly it from Brough until the opening of Sherburn-in-Elmet aerodrome early in the following year. By the end of 1925 twenty-nine Moths had been completed, ten of which had been delivered to or were destined for the flying clubs at home, with a further six for Australian flying clubs, two for the Royal Australian Air Force, one for the Controller of Civil Aviation in Australia, five for the de Havilland School of Flying at Stag Lane, one for Chile, one for the Air Ministry and three for private owners.

Two days before Christmas one of the most active of British private pilots, Colonel the Master of Sempill, set off in a Moth for a demonstration tour of the Irish Free State, flying a Moth directly from Stag Lane to Dublin over the seventy miles of open water from Holyhead, the route over which Robert Loraine, the actor-pilot, had perilously flown for the first time in history in his Farman biplane in 1910. On his arrival Sempill was met by the Director of Civil Aviation, Sir Sefton Brancker, who had intended to be his passenger for the crossing but had been compelled to go ahead by sea when the departure of the Moth was delayed by bad weather. The tour was a most successful one, and at its end Sempill brought the machine back in foggy winter weather by the short sea route to Stranraer, landing on his way south on a sandbank off the Lancashire coast in order to fill up his tank from tins of petrol (which he carried with him) undisturbed by the crowds of onlookers who would otherwise have collected. In due course the Free State Government ordered four Moths, and these, smartly painted in green, white and orange, were flown across to Dublin in the following July, closing up into formation to pass over the city before landing.

The utility of the Moth for general transport purposes was shown soon after it had gone into service with the flying clubs, the occasion being the General Strike of May 1926. At 4.15 p.m. on the 2nd of May, the railways having ceased to function, one of the directors of the *Daily Mail* telephoned to the Royal Aero Club to inquire as to the possibility of flying to Manchester. By 5.30 he was in the air in a Moth of the London Aeroplane Club flown by Mr G. T. Witcombe, one of the club instructors, and two hours later he arrived at Woodford within a short car drive of his destination. The following day he returned by the same means carrying parcels of a specially printed leaflet, which were dropped from the machine on the

21.   Captain H. S. Broad after winning the 1926 King's Cup Race in a Moth
22.   Off for the week-end; a couple setting out in their Moth

23. The father of the flying-club movement: the Director of Civil Aviation, Sir Sefton Brancker (left) with Sir Philip Sassoon

24. Moths at the London Aeroplane Club, Stag Lane, in the late 1920s. G-EDCA is Sir Sefton Brancker's personal machine

return journey at Stoke-on-Trent, Macclesfield and Lichfield. In this way the proprietors of the *Daily Mail* (doubtless to their great gratification) received some return for the considerable sums which they had given away over the years for the furtherance of aeronautical progress. Later, eight Moths belonging to the clubs and to private owners were pressed into service for newspaper distribution, and between them flew a total of 15,455 miles on this duty, to which total one machine of the London Aeroplane Club alone contributed 3,384 miles.

Some Moths were fitted with the Armstrong Siddeley Genet radial engine, notably that flown in the third Lympne competition in September 1926, but subsequently the Genet Moth found little favour with civilian owners, and it is principally remembered for its aerobatic performances at the Hendon displays in the hands of pilots of the R.A.F. Central Flying School. At one display Flying Officers D. A. Boyle and R. L. R. Atcherley carried out inverted loops for the first time in these machines with the aid of special tanks attached to the undercarriage to supply petrol when upside down. The Cirrus Moth would not have been suitable for this purpose owing to its wet-sump engine, and a warning to this effect had to be issued to protect the more enthusiastic club members from the results of trying to emulate what they had seen at Hendon.

The annual race for the King's Cup, presented by King George V in 1922 and first competed for in that year, soon developed almost exclusively into an annual proving event for light aeroplanes. Nowadays it is of short duration and has little value except as a spectacle, but before 1939 it nearly always consisted of a complete circuit of Britain, of length up to 1,500 miles and sometimes occupying two whole days. Victory in the race therefore meant not only defeating the handicappers by subtle improvements to performance, but accurate navigation over every kind of terrain (and sometimes a sea crossing) and through all kinds of weather, with engines running at full throttle for many hours at a stretch. The advertisement value of such a win was consequently tremendous, and the de Havilland company were not slow to place their new product on the starting line. Two Moths started together as limit machines in the 1925 event, the prototype G-EBKT flown by Mr Alan Cobham and G-EBKU flown by Captain de Havilland himself. Unfortunately the race of this year was something of a fiasco, for by a freak of weather rare even in an English July dense sea-fog swept in across the course from the North Sea, and both Moths were forced down early in the race. Only four out of a total of fourteen starters completed the course on the first day, but in a consolation race for those that had fallen out the Moths took second and fourth place.

The following year, 1926, brought success when Captain Hubert Broad (Plate 21), flying the beautifully enamelled red-and-white G-EBMO, won the race by the narrow margin of only 22 seconds after flying for over sixteen hours at full throttle round two triangular circuits 1,464 miles in length, starting and finishing at Hendon. His speed of 90·4 m.p.h., an average figure indicating a higher maximum, had been achieved by a careful programme of 'cleaning-up' of the airframe which illustrates the large reduction in drag which can be achieved by attention to a number of minor excrescences. His engine, as the rules demanded, was a perfectly standard Cirrus, but the front cockpit was faired in and its windscreen removed, the rear cockpit aperture was reduced in size and fitted with a special long sloping windscreen, the exhaust pipes were taken off, plain bolts were substituted for the spring bolts used in wing folding and all joints between the fuselage, wing and tail were painstakingly filled in with fabric. Five Moths started in the race and two besides Broad's machine finished, but that flown by Captain de Havilland himself—the first to have the new Cirrus II engine—was forced out of the race at Chelmsford by a broken oil pipe, a minor defect which the testing conditions of air racing brought to light.

In the 1927 race a Moth won again, flown this time by Captain W. L. Hope of Air Taxis Limited and subjected to still more elaborate treatment in search of high speed. The handicapping formula of this year, which as it turned out grossly penalised the larger machines, was based on horsepower and wing-span, and Hope's Moth was therefore fitted with extended tips to the upper wings as well as a special pair of tiny wheels, the long windscreen which Broad had used in the previous year's race and a pressure-fed tank in the front cockpit in place of the bulky standard tank exposed to the airflow. In 1928 Hope won again, this time on a Moth with the new Gipsy engine, and this series of three victories, forming a curious and interesting parallel to the successes at Le Mans of another typical product of the age—the Bentley motor-car—added greatly to the reputation of the Moth at a time when it was beginning to venture upon a world-wide market.

The improved Cirrus II engine, offered as standard in the 1927 model Moth, provided an increase of power to 80 h.p. at 2,000 r.p.m. by virtue of its increased bore (110 mm. instead of 105), modified cylinder-heads, and other minor changes. With this engine the new machine—called the Moth X—was guaranteed to reach a top speed of 98 m.p.h., but not all this augmented performance was due to greater engine power, for the lines of the fuselage, as well as the pilot's view, had been greatly improved by lowering the engine to bring the cylinder-heads level with the top of the fuselage. There were other small alterations in the interests of comfort and convenience including a new type of windscreen and a luggage compartment accessible from the rear cockpit.

As production got under way and the success of the Moth became assured, it became possible to offer it more cheaply. As early as August 1926 the price of the original Cirrus I machine came down from £885 to £795, and very soon afterwards the faster Cirrus II Moth, originally £830, was on sale at £730 and was emerging from Stag Lane at the rate of three per fortnight. These reductions must in part have been stimulated by the competition of the Avro Avian, then available at £675 with the Cirrus II engine. At these prices the machine was in full flying order, but there were a few extra items: six guineas for Air Ministry fees in respect of certificates of registration and airworthiness, £17 10s. for a Hughes midget compass, £4 16s. for a set of telephones and helmets, £3 7s. for a Cirrus tool kit and £2 12s. 6d. for a set of engine, airscrew and cockpit covers. An important contribution to safety which soon became available on Moths was the Handley Page slot, demonstrated in an almost too convincing fashion by Captain de Havilland early in 1928 when, after a succession of fully stalled approaches and landings from 200 ft with the control column pulled hard back, a fuselage member gave way under the strain and the machine was wrecked. However, the fact that the pilot suffered no personal injury even after such an extreme demonstration must have persuaded many prospective owners to pay the extra £35 asked for this safety feature in addition to the basic price, which by now had fallen to £630.

The Mark III Cirrus engine appeared in 1928 and was fitted to the Moth of that year, offering a further rise in power to 94 b.h.p. at 2,100 r.p.m. through a higher compression ratio and the use of larger valves. The Cirrus III Moth also discarded the old-fashioned fixed-axle undercarriage in favour of the split-axle type with X-bracing, though the lower drag of the earlier kind often led to its retention for racing purposes when speed was of more consequence than pleasant landing qualities. In this same year of 1928 the de Havilland company began the manufacture of its own aero-engines—the famous Gipsy series—and equipped with these engines Moths went forward to even more spectacular successes; by 1929 they were coming off the production line at the rate of nearly three a day, and in the years that followed they made history over the long-distance routes of the world in the hands of such pilots as Chichester, Mollison, Scott and Amy Johnson.

The detailed story of the development of the Gipsy engine and of the numerous types of aircraft, including the Moth, to which it was fitted in its various versions will be told in a later chapter, and it is sufficient to say here that when the last Moth left the factory in 1934 some 1,800 of these aeroplanes had been sold all over the world—an extraordinary achievement for a period of nine years in which neither war nor the threat of war provided an artificial stimulus to the production of what was essentially an aeroplane for civil use. In fact, although some Moths found a military market and a few were used for light commercial work such as mail carrying, the vast bulk of the machines built went to private owners or to the flying clubs which (following the British example) came into being in every corner of the globe. In those days the flourishing light aeroplane movement at home absorbed a large proportion of the Moths which were made, and a good idea of the firm hold which the type had upon the home market may be gained from the following figures relating to the number and type of private aeroplanes on the British register:

	November 1927	March 1930	March 1935
Number of private aircraft	62	206	478
Number of Moths	27	135	147
Moths as percentage of total	43%	66%	31%

In each case the Moth was the most numerous type, and even as late as 1935, when the light monoplane was in the ascendant, it still accounted for nearly one in three of the total. If the figures for club aeroplanes were added to the above the balance would be shifted even further in the Moth's favour.

What was the secret of the Moth's success? Although it brought about an extraordinary revolution in flying and enabled thousands of ordinary individuals to take to the air with the subsidised flying clubs and in their own machines, there was nothing in any way revolutionary about the aeroplane itself. It was an ordinary biplane of most straightforward construction such as the de Havilland company had been building in various sizes and for various purposes for a number of years, and its performance (it has been pointed out) was not markedly superior to that of the Sopwith Tabloid which had caused such a sensation on its first appearance in 1913, though it offered a good deal more than the pre-war machine in reliability, economy and comfort. The fact was, however, that it had been planned from the beginning as a simple, robust, cheap and easily handled aircraft specifically intended for instruction and for the owner-pilot; it happened to be the right aeroplane at the right price, neither extravagantly large nor impractically small, and its sober and civilised qualities were placed before the public precisely at a time when the aeroplane's associations with warlike uses were beginning to be forgotten and when a new generation (as well as a good many of the old) was eager to rediscover the air and explore the world by way of a new element.

The qualities of the Moth, however, were not greatly different from those of its contemporaries such as the Avian and Bluebird, and its pronounced lead over these rivals must be attributed largely to the outlook of the de Havilland company and to the wide range of facilities which it offered to its customers. Throughout the twenty years between the wars, this firm more than any other believed in and supported civil aviation as an activity in its own right, and not merely as an offshoot of a more lucrative military business. Many of the leading figures in the company were practising pilots and used the aeroplanes which their firm built as if they had been motor-cars, not just as some kind of advertising trick but because flying was an ordinary and natural part of their lives. Captain de Havilland himself regularly flew his own products on business and pleasure—it was said that he never travelled a distance of more than ten miles otherwise than by air—and in this way he gained that unique knowledge of their defects and virtues which is only possible for the designer-pilot who has followed his creations over the whole of the long route from a crude sketch on the back of an old envelope to actual practical trial in the air. The purchaser of a Moth or one of its successors from Stag Lane or Hatfield could therefore be certain that all its features had been subjected to close scrutiny by men who were practical pilots as well as sound engineers.

The Moth began its career in the era when the idea of the 'service station' was beginning to take hold in the motoring world. Increasingly the motorist was coming to demand not only a reliable vehicle but widespread facilities for its maintenance and repair at standardised charges, and this idea was adapted by de Havilland to offer the same service to the owner of a light aeroplane as he would expect if he bought a high-quality car at a similar price. An example of this was the de Havilland Aero Garage, opened at Stag Lane aerodrome for the convenience of private owners of Moths shortly after the first appearance of these machines on the market. For the moderate sum of £4 a month, not greatly in excess of the cost of garaging a car in Central London, a private lock-up of suitable size to take a Moth with wings folded was available, complete with a small workbench at which minor repairs could be carried out. The charge included the services of wheeling the machine out on to the tarmac, unfolding its wings, starting the engine, attending to fuel and oil and wiping down after flying. All other work, ranging from inspections to complete overhauls, was available at fixed additional charges, so that the owner who lived and worked in London could keep his machine within easy reach by omnibus, Underground or private car, and a telephone call would ensure that it was waiting for him in perfect condition on his arrival, ready to carry him in entire freedom to any destination he chose. It is hard to realise today just what this freedom meant in an age when commercial air travel was still slow, infrequent and often inconvenient; the owner-pilot in the twenties had at his disposal, for only the cost of a medium-priced motor-car, a vehicle which was literally as fast as any then in existence (Plate 22).

The Moth owner who lived outside London was equally well catered for. He could keep his machine at the local aerodrome if one existed, or if this was not convenient he could make use of any suitable level field and the de Havilland company would supply all the extra equipment he needed to operate the machine away from professional assistance, such as special lightweight duralumin wheel chocks, screw pickets and a tail trolley (all portable and able to be carried in the aircraft), tail trestles, wheel jacks, and even a collapsible shed which could be erected to form a private hangar. Advice was also readily given by the company on all matters affecting the upkeep and operation of the Moth, and a rapid spares service ensured that the effects of a minor mishap could very quickly be made good, while for the foreign-going owner there were Moth agents and service stations in most European capitals and countries of the British Empire.

Skilful publicity, too, helped to keep the idea of 'the motor-car of the air' in the public eye. In January 1927 a Moth appeared in one of the Oxford Street windows of Selfridges, surrounded by figures in flying clothing and bearing the legend 'full particulars of garaging, oil consumption, mileage, landing facilities, etc. obtainable from the Motor Cycle Department, First Floor'. The motor department of William Whiteleys offered Moths for sale with easy terms spread over 12, 18 or 24 months, and advertisements showed the little aeroplanes skimming freely along above the crowded roads of which the public was already becoming painfully aware in the holiday season. The advertisement value of performances in the King's Cup Race has already been remarked upon, and these and other achievements such as long-distance flights in Moths were exploited to the full by the de Havilland publicity department. One original touch was a B.B.C. broadcast of a 'flying lesson' given by Mr Alan Cobham to Miss Heather Thatcher; this was not of course direct advertising for the Moth, but by helping to arouse interest in the flying clubs which were soon to receive their first Moths it provided useful publicity for the light aeroplane movement as a whole.

Thus the Moth represented the first serious attempt to make flying a practical everyday matter, to change the aeroplane from being a mysterious and dangerous apparatus for professionals into an ordinary mode of personal transport within the means and the understanding of the man in the street. As we have seen, there had been other attempts; the early beginnings of private flying had been frustrated by the 1914–18 war, and the Lympne competitions had failed in their primary object, although they left behind them some useful by-products. In the days of the Moth's greatest success, however, many really felt that the light aeroplane would follow the example of the motor-car which from its crude beginnings at the end of the nineteenth century had first become a rich man's toy and was by now, thanks to such men as Henry Ford and William Morris, accessible to a large and ever-increasing sector of the population and an accepted part of the life of all civilised countries. For a number of reasons it did not succeed in doing so; even with landing-grounds far more plentiful than they are in this country the aeroplane is not a substitute for a car, and its owner is therefore put to a double expense, while the excellence of communications in a small country such as England makes air transport relatively less useful than in countries the size of Australia. The poor climate and short winter daylight, too, must always subject the amateur pilot, unless he be very skilful and well-equipped, to some of the limitations which wind and weather impose upon the small-boat sailor. Nevertheless, in the great and golden age of the light aeroplane the Moth came nearer than any of its rivals to bringing personal aviation within reach of all. Perhaps the best measure of its success is the way in which, at the height of its fame, the word passed into the language, for to the great uninstructed public that paid its shillings to visit flying-club displays and the R.A.F. Pageants at Hendon, every little aeroplane was a Moth just as every big aeroplane in the Great War had been a Handley Page. The Moth revealed to the many thousands who learned to fly on it that special three-dimensional outlook on the world which only personal flying can offer, and it was the vehicle for the day-dreams of millions more who saw it passing across the sky and read in their newspapers of the exploits of a Lady Bailey or an Amy Johnson. To the many who still remember it with affection it remains not merely an aeroplane but an inseparable part of the legend of the 1920s, as much a part of that time as the Morris-Cowley or the Charleston or the novels of Michael Arlen.

7

The Flying Clubs

The formation of the State-subsidised light aeroplane clubs in Great Britain in 1925, which was soon followed by the rapid spread of the movement all over the British Empire and to a great many other countries, was largely due to the energy and vision of a single man, William Sefton Brancker (Plate 23), who in 1922 was appointed to the newly-created post of Director of Civil Aviation in the Air Ministry—a post which he held until his death. Brancker's immense enthusiasm drove forward many aeronautical enterprises during the eight years that he was in office, among them the cause of lighter-than-air commercial flying which led to his death, but it is the light aeroplane clubs above all else which remain as his most lasting memorial.

His interest in flying dated back to 1910, when the chief pilot of the Bristol company, M. Henri Jullerot, arrived in Calcutta with three of his firm's 'box-kite' aeroplanes, the first ever to be seen in India. After some wildly successful demonstrations on the Calcutta racecourse, Jullerot undertook a series of flights from Aurangabad in connection with certain military manoeuvres, and Brancker, then a young Army officer, was ordered to accompany him. After this experience, which included one of the mild crashes which were commonplace in those days, Brancker's career remained indissolubly wedded to aviation for the rest of his life. After returning to England he took his pilot's certificate at Brooklands in 1913, and the outbreak of war found him Deputy Director of Military Aeronautics. By 1917 he was in command of the Middle East Division of the Royal Flying Corps, and on the creation of the Royal Air Force in April 1918 he became Controller-General of Equipment and Master-General of Personnel, with the rank of major-general. His knighthood followed in the New Year's Honours of 1919. Immediately the war ended he turned to the new and promising field of commercial aviation by joining Aircraft Transport and Travel Limited, just formed by Mr George Holt Thomas, and then took office as Director of Civil Aviation in the Air Ministry in February 1922, only a few months before the announcement of the *Daily Mail* gliding prize which led to the meeting on Itford Hill.

It was no part of Sir Sefton Brancker's idea of his duties as a civil servant to try and run aviation at long range from behind a desk, and the figure of 'the General' with his glinting eyeglass was soon a familiar sight at flying events up and down the country. In particular he was present at the Motor Glider Competitions held at Lympne in October 1923, and the idea of popular flying in low-powered aeroplanes made an instant appeal to him. Through his influence, therefore, the official offer of £3,000 in prizes for the two-seater meeting of 1924 was made known not long after the end of the first set of trials, the stated intention of the offer being to bring about the design and construction of a large number of two-seater machines of economical type from which a selection could be made to equip a number of flying clubs throughout the country. Such clubs, offering cheap facilities for flying instruction and amateur aviation generally, would be set up specifically to encourage the ordinary man into the air, and would in this way help to spread 'airmindedness', stimulate a widespread and informed interest in aeronautical matters and create a reserve of pilots some of whom would be valuable to the country in times of national emergency. The movement was in no way intended, however, to have a military flavour, and the facilities which the clubs offered would be open to persons of either sex and of all ages, with no form of liability for service with the Reserve or any other body.

In June 1924 Brancker outlined to the Press the Air Ministry's intentions with regard to the clubs, and the official announcement which followed in August made the position quite clear. The proposal was to afford financial assistance for an initial period to ten clubs situated near the main centres of population, enabling them to purchase their own aircraft. The responsibility of arranging for aerodrome facilities, engaging ground engineers and flying instructors and dealing with all local matters of organisation would fall upon the clubs themselves, and the Air Ministry would undertake periodical inspections to see that their intentions were being correctly carried out. Certain other safeguards were insisted upon, such as the insurance of aeroplanes and equipment, and grants would be payable to the clubs in respect of each member who successfully learned to fly on its aircraft and obtained his licence.

The English have a propensity for forming clubs for every imaginable purpose, and it is not particularly surprising to learn, therefore, that the idea of associations of persons interested in the theory or practice of flying was by no means a new one at this time. Apart from the Royal Aeronautical Society and the Royal Aero Club themselves, the governing bodies respectively of scientific and sporting matters connected with the air, a number of smaller societies devoting their energies to model-building, discussions and the support of aviation generally had existed long before 1914. Among the oldest was the Coventry Aeroplane Building Society founded in 1905, which in its later form as the Coventry Aviation Discussion Group went in a body to the main Birmingham railway line in 1910 to see Louis Paulhan pass on his way to Manchester to win the *Daily Mail*'s £10,000. The Midland Aero Club, formed in 1909 with a hundred or so members, organised the British flying meeting of 1910 on the Dunstall Park racecourse at Wolverhampton, an event attended by Grahame-White, C. S. Rolls and other celebrated pilots of the day, and the Lancashire, Hampshire, Yorkshire and Brooklands Aero Clubs, which in revived form were to play a prominent part in the light aeroplane movement in later years, all enjoyed an independent existence in the years before the Great War.

Immediately after the war, as we have noted in passing in earlier chapters, there were a number of more or less abortive attempts to popularise flying by means of civilian clubs. Very much more successful were the Service associations of amateur constructors whose aeroplanes, designed and built by their members, competed with professionally-built types at Lympne. Such were the Cranwell and R.A.E. Aero Clubs, and these were later joined by the Halton club, which eventually became the largest organisation of its kind in the whole country in terms of membership. These pioneering Service associations carried out their work with no direct aid from the State, although naturally they were in a favourable position for obtaining tools, materials and labour, and their secretaries were often able to persuade their commanding officers to allow the building of machines to be carried on in working hours as part of the training of apprentices. The Lancashire Aero Club was also restored to life very early in the post-war years when Mr J. F. Leeming of Hale, Cheshire, began to build a glider (his fifth) in his garage in 1922. The difficulties were considerable, for the car had to be wheeled out and the fuselage lowered from its stowage place in the roof of the garage on each occasion before work could begin. In the end, however, the half-completed machine was moved into Mr Leeming's greenhouse, and it was here, in the course of its erection, that the first committee meeting was held of what was later to become one of the most active bodies in the light aeroplane movement. The L.P.W., or Leeming-Prince-Wood, as the glider was called after its three principal constructors, was subsequently flown (and crashed) at the Alexandra Park aerodrome in Manchester, and later Mr George Parnall, hearing of the Club's activities, presented it with the Douglas engine and propeller which had been used in his Pixie at Lympne. These were fitted to the L.P.W. to convert it into a powered aeroplane, and although in this form it was too under-powered to get into the air it was able to perform a series of prolonged bounds across the uneven surface of Woodford aerodrome, where the club had been offered a hangar for a nominal rent by A. V. Roe and Company.

The meetings at Itford and Lympne did much to stimulate amateur activity of this kind all over the country, and even at R.A.F. stations overseas—as witness the little single-seater on D.H.53 lines built by Flight Lieutenant Crawford at Hinaidi (Iraq) and later brought home to England. The hope that the 1924 trials would lead to cheap two-seater machines on which they could learn to fly attracted many members of the newly-formed clubs to Lympne in that year. The outcome of those competitions is already known to the reader; the trials, though exceedingly interesting from a technical point of view, did not result in the emergence of a single type of small aeroplane and engine which was fit to be placed in the hands of the waiting clubs. The Air Ministry was thus put in a very difficult position; its technical experts had carefully specified what was required, manufacturers all over the country had produced machines to meet their specification, and yet there was nothing to show for all this considerable expenditure of money and effort, whereas the new Cirrus-engined Moth which Captain de Havilland and Major Halford had jointly produced at Stag Lane by their own entirely independent efforts was showing every sign of being embarrassingly successful. Soon representative members of the various light aeroplane clubs which were already in being were invited to Stag Lane for a demonstration of the new type in flight, and after this the pressure on the Air Ministry to permit the clubs to use the Moth became irresistible. Sir Sefton Brancker's attitude in the matter, as expressed in conversation with one club member at this time, was characteristically direct. 'It's no good talking like a lot of old women,' he declared. 'What we've got to do is get on with the flying.' With such a highly untypical Civil Servant at the head of affairs past mistakes were quickly laid aside and the only possible course was taken: official permission was granted for the use of the Moth and orders were placed on behalf of the clubs with the de Havilland Aircraft Company.

Some time before this decision was made, however, the exact details of the proposed subsidy scheme had to be worked out with the Air Ministry, and for this purpose a committee was formed with representatives of the interested clubs. These were initially six in number, comprising the Royal Aero Club (represented by Commander Harold Perrin and Colonel M.O. Darby) the Lancashire Aero Club, the Midland Aero Club, the Newcastle-on-Tyne Aero Club, the Yorkshire Light Aeroplane Club and the Glasgow Light Aeroplane Club. The last-named of these eventually dropped out of the running, and the London area was served by the London Aeroplane Club, effectively the light aeroplane section of the Royal Aero Club and the successor to that body's earlier aircraft hire scheme but set up as an independent company in the summer of 1925. An initial conference held at the Air Ministry in November 1924 was followed by another at the Queen's Hotel, Leeds, in February 1925 to report progress. The Air Ministry's original proposal that the clubs should each receive a sum in cash for the purchase of their equipment was later modified to provide each club directly with two aeroplanes, a spare engine and incidental material up to a total value not exceeding £2,000, with an additional grant of £1,000 for the first year for general expenses, a payment of £10 for each pilot's licence obtained wholly by training on club aircraft and an undertaking to meet half the cost of replacement of a crashed machine. The agreement was to run for two years with a grant of unspecified size for expenses in the second year, and the position would be reviewed at the end of the period if the clubs were not by then self-supporting.

The prospect of trying to meet the needs of some two hundred eager members in each club with only two aeroplanes was a daunting one to club secretaries, and clearly long waiting-lists for flying lessons would be necessary; but the clubs realised that official generosity could hardly be stretched further and that they would have to augment their limited fleets later, either by subscription among their members or by talking persuasively to local benefactors. It was decided, therefore, to accept the offer. This was in March 1925, and soon afterwards the use of the Moth was officially approved and the clubs could look forward impatiently to the delivery of their machines. Sir Sefton himself lost no time in using the Moth, being flown to Cardington and Leicester in one by Mr Alan Cobham before it had even received the official blessing conferred by a Certificate of Airworthiness. Production began at Stag Lane, delivery dates were quoted, and there was keen rivalry to see which club would receive its Moth first.

The first headquarters of the London Aeroplane Club were in a wooden shed at Stag Lane (Plate 24), leased by the de Havilland company and adjacent to the factory from which Moths were soon to issue forth in such impressive numbers. Here on 19 August 1925, not quite six months from the day when the first Moth had left the ground from a spot only a few yards distant, a small crowd of members assembled with their two new, grey-painted aeroplanes drawn up alongside to hear the Under-Secretary of State for Air, Sir Philip Sassoon (Plate 23), perform the official opening ceremony. Sir Philip, congratulating the Club on having won for London, and rightly for London, the first light aeroplane club in the country, said:

> I am sure that it will be the precursor of many others all over the country, and that we shall soon see flying a popular and legitimate sport. As far as the Air Ministry is concerned, the clubs know they have their sympathy and

assistance within limits; the Air Ministry has never pretended, or hoped, to carry these clubs on its back, but it will do everything to help the clubs because the Air Ministry knows that the clubs can help aviation. They can help the State to build up that big reserve of pilots the nation needs, to popularise flying, and to create that 'air sense' which the Air Ministry looks forward to so much. The ideal is a nation of airmen and the light aeroplane clubs can help towards the realisation of that ideal. I want to congratulate the club very heartily on its work, and hope that their efforts, and those of the other clubs, will tend to wean the aeroplane from its warlike associations and develop it more as an agent for civilisation and peace.

When the cheers had died away, Sir Philip was installed in the front cockpit of one of the Moths and taken into the air for an inaugural flight by the Club's chief instructor, Captain G. F. M. Sparks (Plate 25), expressing himself on landing as delighted by its comfort and pleasantness. The aerial ice having in this way been broken, the rest of the day was devoted to the giving of instruction, and a ballot was held for the first twenty places on the list of those eligible to begin learning to fly. The winner of the first place, Mr David Kittel, later to be the first private owner of a Moth, gallantly gave it up to a woman member, Mrs Sophie Elliott-Lynn, who thus became the first person to receive flying instruction with the subsidised clubs. Later Mrs Elliott-Lynn, who by her second marriage became Lady Heath, turned out to be one of the best-known women pilots of the day and is particularly remembered for her solo flight from South Africa to England less than three years afterwards.

The sentiments which Sir Philip expressed at this little ceremony were unexceptionable, but there were those who disputed his facts, among them the ever-vigilant Mr C. G. Grey, who gleefully appended the caption 'What Lancashire Did Yesterday' to the photograph of the proceedings which he published in *The Aeroplane*, adding a note to the effect that 'entirely unsung, the Lancashire Club has been open for months'. The question of priority was in fact not quite so simple, and although the matter may not have been of cosmic importance the dispute which occurred in the Press at the time provided excellent advertisement for the flying club movement as a whole. The opening of the Lancashire Aero Club at Woodford had been planned for 21 July, nearly a month earlier, and the first Moth due for delivery, G-EBLR, was promised for this occasion. When the day came this machine was found to be suffering from engine trouble which prevented its leaving its makers' hands, and to avoid disappointing the large crowd gathered at Woodford Mr Alan Cobham flew another machine up for the ceremony and spent some time there giving joy-rides to members. The machine was wanted back at Stag Lane for demonstrations on the following day, and Mr Cobham had to leave in the morning, to the bafflement of certain club members not in the know who found that their new acquisition had suddenly vanished. The mysterious afflictions of G-EBLR continued for some weeks, in fact until just after the opening of the London Aeroplane Club, and certain Lancastrians voiced the suspicion that the delay had been deliberately engineered to ensure the maximum of publicity for the London Club, Stag Lane, the Moth and its manufacturers. Whatever the truth of the matter, the Lancashire Aero Club had at any rate the satisfaction of having been concerned with aircraft of their own design and construction for nearly two years by the time the Government subsidy scheme came into operation.

An intense enthusiasm for flying was the one common characteristic of all the members of the light aeroplane clubs in those early days. In spite of the subsidy, funds were generally low and such amenities as there were had to be provided by individual efforts, the social comforts which the clubs in later years offered for the attraction of new members being practically non-existent. Committees walked an uneasy edge between charging too little for flying and losing money on the one hand and charging too much and losing their members on the other, for by no means all their members were wealthy people. To begin with some clubs could not afford the luxury of engaging a full-time paid flying instructor, and in these cases the Air Ministry arranged for voluntary instructors with suitable experience to take a short course at the Central Flying School. When they returned, these instructors (like most members) had a living to earn, and flying operations were often restricted to week-ends and summer evenings. Mr Alan Goodfellow, an active member of the flying-club movement and a pilot in both wars, has recalled some of the early days of the Lancashire Aero Club, whose difficulties are typical of those of all the clubs in 1925:

> We had no clubhouse in those days. The hangar (which leaked badly) was our only shelter while waiting to fly and a temperamental stove our only means of keeping warm. When flying was over for the day we would adjourn to Mother Hooley's (the Davenport Arms) at the top of the aerodrome road and warm ourselves with Robinson's barley wine. The Committee met at the Nag's Head or Sawyer's Arms in Manchester, where hot-pot suppers constituted almost the sole social activities of the Club.
>
> The early days at Woodford are full of memories. Woodford aerodrome in those days more or less guaranteed that one's flying should be of an exciting nature. A spinney in the centre of the flying field, coupled with a cunningly concealed pond, were among the hazards. The usual take-off run was up a gradient so steep that there was no hope of becoming airborne before the crest, on reaching which it was not uncommon to meet another aircraft, previously hidden from view, which was taxying back after landing. Taking off to the south offered a choice of alternatives. There was an extremely short take-off run towards the aerodrome road, which involved

yanking the aircraft off the ground just before reaching the road, beyond
which the ground fell away and enabled the nose to be put down in order
to gain flying speed. The alternative was a longer run past the hangars, but
this involved a banked turn immediately after passing the hangar in order
to get through a gap in the trees. The prevailing winds called for an
approach over the high trees behind the hangars, and in order to land short
enough to make use of the uphill slope for braking purposes, it was customary to clear the tree tops by a matter of feet (or inches, according to the
skill of the pilot). This fact no doubt accounted for the high standard of
proficiency later shown in the Pemberton and Rodman forced-landing contests organised by the Club.

Take-offs were further complicated during the first winter (which was
a cold one) by the fact that the Cirrus engine in its early form was distinctly
temperamental in cold weather. It would run up perfectly on the ground,
but just as flying speed was reached the front cylinder (and sometimes the
front two cylinders) would cut out, necessitating a hurried descent into the
next field. It was this habit which led to the classic remark of Bartram, the
Club's first paid ground engineer: 'This 'ere flying wears yer boots out.'

The cost of flying on a strictly economic basis with machines of the
Moth type was about £2 15s. per flying hour, and with the help of the subsidy the average club was able to charge its members 30s. per hour for dual
instruction and £1 for solo flying. At these typical rates it was possible for
a reasonably apt pupil to obtain an 'A' licence for £20 or so, this amount
covering the club subscription, the eight hours or so of instruction
normally required, the statutory three hours of solo flying and the appro-
priate fees. The usual procedure was for the club member to pass the tests
for the Royal Aero Club certificate under the eye of an official observer
appointed at each club, and this certificate, with evidence of the necessary
solo flying, was then accepted by the Air Ministry for the issue of a licence.
Having acquired a licence, the member, still a very inexperienced pilot,
was delighted to learn that he was legally entitled to fly any type of aeroplane for any purpose he pleased, provided only that he received no payment for so doing. His ambitions in this respect, however, were sternly
held in check first by the benevolent despotism of his instructor, whose
concern was to preserve his club's aircraft intact, and second, by the difficulties put in his way by the British Aviation Insurance Group, whose
head, Captain Lamplugh—himself a keen pilot—was fully aware of the
risks involved by premature private ownership. So although the 'A' licence
was criticised even at this time as being an inadequate qualification the
system worked quite well in practice.

The light aeroplane clubs were fortunate in their early days in
receiving much support from interested and sympathetic benefactors. The
greatest of these was undoubtedly Sir Charles Cheers Wakefield, who in
the words of one club member 'gave away money like water'; his help to

the new movement and to the long-distance solo pilots of later years was proverbial, and he presented innumerable Moths to the clubs both at home and all over the British Empire. Several of the little Lympne machines, too, ended their days with the clubs, being sold or leased at reasonable rates by their manufacturers, and in this way members were enabled to broaden their experience on types very different in conception from the conventional club biplanes of the period. One of the curious Gnosspelius Gulls went up to the Newcastle Club at Cramlington, being later involved in an unusual and tragic accident in which the club's chief instructor, Major S. A. Packman, was thrown out and killed on landing. The Supermarine Sparrow went to Halton, one Brownie to the London Aeroplane Club, and another Brownie, together with one of the Parnall Pixies, later passed into the possession of the Bristol and Wessex Aero Club which began operations at Filton aerodrome in 1927. Those flying clubs which were in a close relationship to aircraft manufacturing firms could usually rely on a good deal of practical help; for instance, the Avro company presented the Lancashire Aero Club with one of their Gosport aeroplanes, a later version of the famous rotary-engined 504. It was in a similar machine fitted with an experimental Alpha radial engine that John Leeming and Bert Hinkler made their unique landing on the snow-covered top of Helvellyn, a feat vouched for by a professor of Greek who happened to be up there at the time and commemorated to this day by an inscribed stone near the summit cairn.

The great annual air show at Hendon, originally called the R.A.F. Pageant and later renamed the R.A.F. Display, used to attract crowds numbering a hundred thousand or more in the middle 1920s, and it was not surprising that the flying clubs should soon hit on the idea of staging smaller imitations of it on their own account as a means of arousing local interest in flying, gaining new members and improving the state of their finances. Nowadays few members of the general public would be greatly attracted by the prospect of watching a handful of light aeroplanes performing over their local aerodrome, but in 1926 the sight of an aeroplane at close quarters on the ground or in the air was still a considerable novelty to a great many people, and there were in the Midlands and North vast potential audiences who had neither the money nor the leisure to travel down to Hendon but who were only too ready for a Sunday outing a few miles from their own city.

The first of the club pageants was staged by the Lancashire Aero Club at Woodford on Sunday 18 April 1926, shortly after the club's fleet of aeroplanes had been doubled by the gift of a third Moth from Sir Charles Wakefield and of a fourth machine, the Avro Gosport already mentioned, from the managing director of A. V. Roe and Company, Sir William Letts.

25. A leather-clad instructor of the twenties: Captain G. F. M. Sparks
of the London Aeroplane Club

26. The unusual Parnall Imp of 1927, which required no wire bracing
of the wing structure

27. A popular type of private owner's aeroplane of the twenties: the
Westland Widgeon, shown with Genet and Cirrus engines

Participation by the R.A.F., which later became usual at these pageants, had not yet been arranged, and the whole show rested on the four club aircraft, but it was nonetheless immensely successful. Some 15,000 people visited the aerodrome, jamming the road for miles round with cars, bicycles and pedestrians, to watch a programme of events that included displays of aerobatics and inverted flying by Bert Hinkler and Captain Hubert Broad and a 'set-piece' (in imitation of Hendon) comprising an aerial attack with flour-bags on a wood-and-canvas fort garrisoned by Boy Scouts in Arab robes, terminating in a satisfactory fashion as the whole structure went up in flames to the accompaniment of loudly banging fireworks.

The Lancashire example was quickly taken up by the other clubs throughout the summer of 1926, their first full season of operation. The Southern Aero Club, which was not then included in the subsidy scheme, held its opening meeting at Shoreham in June, and this was soon followed by the Yorkshire Air Pageant at Sherburn-in-Elmet, when the first Moth to win the King's Cup was shown off by its pilot, Captain Broad. All these displays attracted large crowds. At one meeting, which had been widely advertised by posters and handbills placed in cinemas, cafés, shops, inns and filling stations, over 100,000 people saw the flying, and though only 25,000 of these paid for admission the pay office was soon swamped by the flood of spectators; the aerodrome was invaded from all sides, people swarmed across fields and over hedges, and one enterprising farmer opened an unauthorised way through his land at threepence a head.

This illustrates a difficulty which rapidly became apparent to the organisers of the early club pageants, namely that displays of 'crazy flying' or aerobatics could often be watched just as comfortably from outside the aerodrome as from inside, and as a result many thousands of 'hedge guests' (as they were called in Germany) lined the borders of neighbouring fields and roads for a free show. To counter this, novelty items were devised which could only be appreciated by those who were close at hand, and many of these 'turns' soon became traditional at every display. A typical one was the bombing of a supposed runaway couple from the air with flour bags until their decrepit car, usually an Austin Seven, was set on fire by concealed fireworks, causing the pair to abandon it and run for safety across the grass. Great alarm was caused to the uninitiated by another act in which a 'spectator', often faultlessly dressed in city clothes with bowler hat and umbrella, 'stole' an aeroplane and flew it round with a skilfully contrived display of incompetence which ended with some terrifying bounces as he attempted to land; a variation of this was to announce over the loud-speaker system that one of the onlookers had wagered that he could fly an aeroplane without any instruction, whereupon after a pretended show of reluctance an official would 'explain the controls' and send the 'novice' off alone and the same alarming exhibition would follow. Perhaps the most mystifying feat of all was that of the aerial sharpshooter who would climb into the passenger seat of a Moth or Avian armed with a revolver or an enormous blunderbuss, take the air and unerringly demolish one by one a row of bottles hung before a curtain. The mystery might never have been solved had not the curtain collapsed at a critical moment of one such display to reveal the mechanic concealed behind it with a heavy hammer.

Although the pageants and other activities raised money, the flying clubs had a struggle for existence in their first two years of life, and all were only kept going by the hard work, ingenuity, enthusiasm and sacrifice of their members. The original five subsidised clubs were joined in 1926 by the Hampshire Aeroplane Club, which began flying at Hamble with two Moths, G-EBOH and G-EBOI, in August, and in spite of all their difficulties the clubs were able to look back with satisfaction on the work they had done in their first two years of life. During this period they had trained without injury some 300 pilots, and by May 1927 almost 7,000 flying hours had been completed, made up as follows:

Club	Hours	Minutes
London	2,305	05
Newcastle	1,567	05
Lancashire	1,482	30
Midland	673	30
Yorkshire	477	40
Hampshire	392	55

By the end of the same year the London Aeroplane Club, which had had the distinction of training the first pupil (Mr G. N. Warwick) to 'A' licence standard under the subsidy scheme, was not far short of the 3,000-hour mark and numbered among its members twenty private owners. This was an excellent record, and other clubs were springing up all over the country. A great aerial rally at Mousehold aerodrome, Norwich, early in 1927 led to the formation of the Norfolk and Norwich Aero Club in July of that year, and almost simultaneously the Bristol and Wessex Aero Club began operations at Filton after an intensive publicity campaign in Bristol which included the exhibition of a Moth in a prominent position in the city and the holding of an air pageant in June to which the public were given free admission. The official opening of the Bristol club did not take place until October, but on this occasion the Secretary of State for Air, Sir Samuel Hoare, was able to announce a new three-year subsidy scheme which was to include more clubs and offer generous terms designed to encourage members to acquire their licences and to continue flying once qualified.

The grant to a club for each licence gained, formerly £10, was to be raised
to £50, with a further £10 for every member renewing his licence in the
current year, and to this would be added an allowance of 30s. per hour
flown by each member up to a maximum of twenty hours, the total grant
to each club being limited as before to £2,000 annually. These improved
subsidies helped considerably, and one leading club, which had lost
£1,350 in its first two years of operation, succeeded in wiping out its
deficit in the following three years, as well as greatly increasing its fleet
of aeroplanes and converting its hangar and club-house from their original
primitive state into comfortable quarters.

Other clubs soon came into being under the new scheme—the Suffolk
and Eastern Counties Aero Club, the Nottinghamshire Aero Club, the
Scottish Flying Club at Glasgow, the East Kent Flying Club at Lympne
(later renamed the Cinque Ports Flying Club in honour of its president,
Earl Beauchamp, who was Warden of the Cinque Ports), and the Liverpool and District Aero Club at Hooton Park. One of the few independent
clubs to survive without Government assistance was the Southern Aero
Club of Shoreham, founded in 1925 by Mr Cecil Pashley, who taught
himself to fly on a glider in 1908 and who is still actively flying as the club's
chief instructor at the time of writing, fifty-five years later. The Southern
club was unusual in that it operated rotary-engined Avros from its inception up till 1934, and its first pupil to obtain his licence was a young man
named F. G. Miles, later to become one of the best-known of light aircraft
designers.

As the clubs became more numerous it was soon necessary to form a
body through which affairs of common interest could be discussed and
representations made to the Government, and accordingly there came into
existence in 1927 the General Council of Light Aeroplane Clubs, with a
membership comprising six representatives of the Royal Aero Club and
one for each fifty members of the other clubs up to a maximum of two per
club. In return, this body was granted the right to nominate three members on the racing committee of the Royal Aero Club. It continued its
functions until the outbreak of war in 1939, by which time its membership,
originally fourteen clubs, had increased to seventy-one, and was eventually superseded by the Association of British Aero Clubs in 1946.

The second period of subsidy ran for three years—from 1927 to 1930—
and during these years the proliferation of flying clubs both at home and
in many other countries of the British Empire was nothing short of
astonishing. It stemmed almost entirely from the example of the five clubs
which had first received Government support in 1925 and of the small
handful of others which were already in existence independently at that
time, and by the end of 1928 there were no fewer than seventy-six

such clubs in Great Britain and British territories alone, made up as follows:

Great Britain	26
Canada	16
Australia	10
New Zealand	9
South Africa	8
India	4
East Africa	1
Singapore	1
Irish Free State	1

The Australians had been the quickest to follow the English example by instituting a subsidy scheme as early as December 1925. Indian interest in the light aeroplane movement was stimulated by the arrival of the Moths of Captain Neville Stack and Mr Bernard Leete at Karachi in early 1927 after a flight from England which at the time was the longest ever to be carried out in such small machines, and not many months after their appearance in India there came into being flying clubs on the English model at Karachi, Delhi, Calcutta and Bombay, followed in 1929 by others at Madras and Lahore. New Zealand witnessed a great wave of enthusiasm for flying clubs towards the end of 1928, and twenty-eight applied for Government recognition although not all were accepted. No subsidy was forthcoming from the South African authorities for the movement, but nevertheless it managed to take root in that country, whose climate and open spaces make it especially suitable for the light aeroplane. The Singapore flying club was unusual in that it operated exclusively with Moth seaplanes for many years in the absence of a suitable land aerodrome.

In the year 1928 alone, all these clubs flew between them a total of some 30,000 hours, and counted within their membership nearly 800 trained pilots. Over 12,000 of these hours were flown solely by the thirteen British clubs which were within the subsidy scheme, and by the following year the membership of these clubs, which had been only 780 at the end of 1925, had risen to over 5,000. As a direct result of their activity the number of private owners in the country had increased from twenty-four in August 1926 to 138 just over two years later and was still rising rapidly. Thanks to the phenomenal success of the Moth, by far the most popular type for club and private work, the fortunes of the de Havilland company had soared upwards over these years, and the flourishing light aeroplane business so created enabled this enterprising firm to survive through the years of depression which lay ahead. The cost to the taxpayer of the subsidies paid to the flying clubs from their beginnings in 1925 right up to the end of the financial year 1931–32 was £92,000, and for this sum the State had

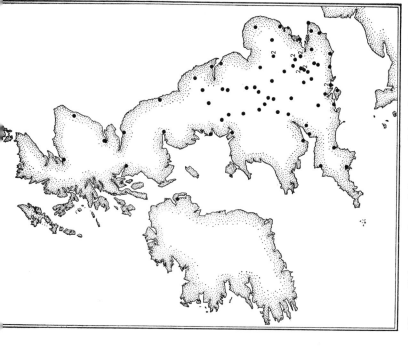

The 71 light aeroplane clubs comprising the General Council of Associated Light Aeroplane Clubs in September 1939. Of these, 64 were state-subsidised

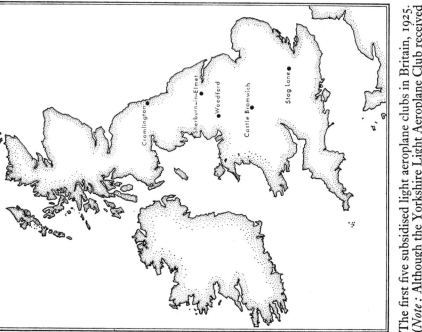

The first five subsidised light aeroplane clubs in Britain, 1925. (*Note*: Although the Yorkshire Light Aeroplane Club received its subsidy in this year, its aerodrome at Sherburn-in-Elmet did not come into use until early in 1926)

placed at its own disposal a considerable reserve of pilots, created a widespread interest in air matters which could hardly have come into being in any other way, and stimulated the growth of an important branch of the aircraft industry whose success helped in a modest way to alleviate the unemployment which was at that time so serious.

Over all this busy activity presided the genial and tireless figure of Sir Sefton Brancker, who gave broadcasts, attended dinners, delivered speeches urging city fathers to build airports, flew in Moths, Avians, Widgeons and Bluebirds, visited the clubs and toured the country from end to end to spread the gospel of civil aviation. He had once been called 'the best commercial traveller the aircraft trade has ever had' and without his stimulating presence, cutting through red tape and distorting or amiably ignoring official regulations to ensure that flying should proceed with the minimum of hindrance, it is doubtful whether the light aeroplane clubs could have succeeded as they did, and they might perhaps never have survived. Many of those now in high places in aviation whose flying careers began with the clubs at Stag Lane or Castle Bromwich, Cramlington, Woodford or Sherburn-in-Elmet, as well as the younger generation who are today becoming amateur pilots, owe to his memory a very considerable debt. Brancker was himself an extremely keen pilot, and soon had allotted to him for his personal use a Moth which, in consideration of his office as Director of Civil Aviation, bore the special registration G-EDCA. His flying ability was said to be somewhat erratic, and many jokes were made at his expense, but on one occasion at least he had his own back. When he was arriving by air as a passenger at a flying meeting, his pilot, trying to put his machine down within a few yards of the judges' table, landed very heavily indeed, and in the silence which ensued after the engine was switched off Sir Sefton was heard to remark loudly, 'I suppose they'll say I did that'.

The pioneering days of any movement tend to become invested with a special brilliance in the memories of those who in later years look back on them, but even when this natural effect of time is allowed for it seems that the early beginnings of the flying-club movement had a spirit and flavour that was all their own. These were great and growing times for aviation. They were the years when the momentous flights of Alan Cobham, Lindbergh, Kingsford Smith and others were astonishing the world, and when young men and women were setting out to emulate them in the small aeroplanes whose star was now fully in the ascendant. They were the years, too, when the beautiful and elegant seaplanes of the Schneider Trophy races were showing what mechanical sophistication and perfection of aerodynamic form would one day do for the commercial air liner and the interceptor fighter, and when the huge airships which would soon, it was confidently believed, bring unheard-of spaciousness, quietness and comfort to air travel were coming to birth in the lofty sheds at Howden and Cardington. There was much that was exciting and new. Aviation was the coming thing, and the light aeroplane movement in a very real sense formed a link between the man-in-the-street and the more rarefied and elaborate developments of the aeronautical art. Every amateur pilot felt himself to be an evangelist whose duty and pleasure it was to spread the gospel of flying among the sceptical and the unenlightened, and the influence on public opinion of thousands of such enthusiasts disseminated through every trade and walk of life must have been a profound one. The clubs, chronically short of money, continued nonetheless to thrive on the keenness and energy of their members, whose ranks had not yet been diluted, as they later became, by those whose interest in and devotion to the air were less single-minded. The amateur aviator enjoyed a wide freedom and his natural high spirits fitted well into the atmosphere of faint absurdity which then seemed to hang about all matters connected with flying—an atmosphere which, thank Heaven, is not yet entirely dissipated, in spite of the efforts of the public relations men to reduce the aeroplane to the mundane level of other forms of transport. In short, these were remarkable days; and although they can never return in quite the same carefree form, the modern descendants of the original light aeroplane clubs are with us still, offering to all who seek it the matchless experience of personal, individual human flight which will endure as long as the sky is open to its amateurs.

8

The Biplane Years

1926–29

The last years of the 1920s were indisputably the great age of the light biplane. The Moth and Avian, almost unchallenged, were then creating a world-wide reputation, to which they yearly added, by long solo flights across the immense distances and unfriendly terrain of Africa and Asia, as well as by more modest tours in the hands of private owners to the farthest corners of Europe and beyond. The Bluebird, less celebrated for its feats of long-distance flying, nevertheless achieved a certain popularity at home, as did the Widgeon monoplane, though for the essential but unspectacular work of club flying neither was able seriously to challenge the ubiquitous Moth, now emerging in great numbers from the de Havilland factory at Stag Lane. The story of that remarkable and archetypal light aeroplane has already been briefly told in a previous chapter as far as the year 1928, and it is now time to study the progress up to that year of its three contemporaries, all of which, as we have seen, appeared with somewhat limited success at one or other of the two-seater competitions at Lympne in 1924 and 1926.

The potentialities of the Avro Avian were hinted at in Chapter 5; it performed excellently in Bert Hinkler's hands at Lympne, and the minor breakage in its relatively untried Genet engine which caused it to withdraw from the competition in no way reflected upon the excellent conception of the machine as a whole. After the production of a relatively small batch of Avians in 1927, the extremely successful Avian III with Cirrus II engine appeared on the market towards the end of that year, moderately priced at £600. The mode of construction of this version, which was used for a number of the early long-distance flights, followed the lines which Mr Chadwick had originally laid down for easy assembly. The plywood sides of the fuselage were built up separately and finally joined, and the floor of the cockpits was also constructed as a single item carrying the complete set of dual control columns and rudder bars. A divided type of undercarriage was fitted in place of the original fixed axle, and many of the improvements which had been made to the prototype G-EBOV after Lympne were carried forward into production, among them the replacement of the rather crude squared-off wing-tips by a rounded contour and the abolition of the 504-type round rudder without fin in favour of a more conventional fin and rudder of triangular shape with a rounded top.

The original Bluebird came to an unfortunate end in the summer of 1927, not many weeks after Charles Lindbergh had startled the world by his solo crossing of the North Atlantic. While racing this machine round pylons at the Whitsun Meeting held on Bournemouth racecourse, Flight Lieutenant Longton, who had been the pilot of the winning Wren at Lympne in 1923, chanced to collide with a Widgeon flown by Major L. P. Openshaw of the Westland company and in the resulting crash both pilots were killed. A production version of the Bluebird subsequently appeared with the Genet II engine and certain modifications, some of which had been tried out in the original machine before its accident, and this was placed on the market in late 1927 as the Bluebird II. The new features included a wider-track undercarriage, lowered engine, and modifications to the cockpit to give more room and easier access. A number of these machines went to private owners and to the flying clubs, notably the Suffolk and Eastern Counties Aeroplane Club at Hadleigh aerodrome, near Ipswich.

The attractive little Widgeon monoplane, which had been blown into the ground by a down-gust at Lympne in 1924, was later rebuilt by its makers as a new version with a more powerful engine (the Genet) in place of the original Blackburne Thrush. After modification to make it more suitable for production it began to issue from the Yeovil works in 1927, the prototype Widgeon III being destroyed in the collision with Longton's Bluebird in that year. The modified version differed fairly considerably in appearance from the original Lympne machine, since for ease of manufacture the parasol wing had been altered to one of constant chord instead of the original double-lozenge shape in plan view, and was now arranged to fold about the fixed centre-section, which formed the fuel tank. The plywood fuselage contained two comfortable cockpits with a luggage compartment between them, and the front cockpit had a car-type door to enable the passenger to reach his seat without too much difficulty. Alternative engines could be fitted—the Genet II or Cirrus II initially, and later the more powerful Cirrus III—and to compensate for the lower weight of the Genet, provision was made for slightly increasing the angle of sweep-back of the wings by use of a modified centre-section, thus preserving the balance of the machine. The Widgeon was appreciably faster than the biplanes of the day with similar engines, and this combined with its other advantages of extreme robustness and excellent view made it popular with private owners, so that although production ceased at the end of the 1920s, the little monoplane—some thirty of which were built— remained in use for many years and at least two survived the Second World War (Plate 27).

In the years up to 1928, therefore, four light aeroplane types—Moth, Bluebird, Avian and Widgeon—met the demands of the clubs and the private owners, who were by then approaching a hundred in number in comparison with the half-dozen or so of the early part of the decade. There were also a few interesting but commercially unsuccessful machines built in these years which deserve mention before passing on to the great pro-liferation of new types which took place in 1929. First in chronological order was unquestionably the Short Mussel, which, apart from the Satellite and the little Cockle flying-boat, was the only light aeroplane to be built by a firm whose principal interest between the wars was the flying-boat of very much larger size. The Mussel was a braced low-wing monoplane which first flew in 1926, and was designed to take the A.D.C. Cirrus engine. Originally built and flown as a twin-float seaplane, it was later fitted with a wheeled undercarriage, and in this form it flew in the Gros-venor Cup race immediately after the 1926 Lympne meeting, though it did not take part in the competition itself. The fuselage, as might be expected, followed the Satellite's lead in being of duralumin stressed-skin type; the wings were of mixed construction with root spars of steel tube, outer spars of duralumin and spruce ribs throughout. On the Mussel's first flights the take-off and climb were found to be poor, but this was remedied by the addition of a fairing in the junction of wing and fuselage —a traditionally sensitive place for breakaway of flow in low-wing mono-planes, since the air there is being called upon to expand rapidly owing to the combined curvature of wing and fuselage.

Two years after its first flight came the Mussel's only noteworthy achievement, the establishment of an altitude record for light seaplanes, set up after the more powerful Cirrus II engine had been installed. Flown by Lady Heath and carrying a passenger and ballast, it lifted off the Med-way and climbed to 13,400 ft. Some time later it was broken up, and in 1929 Short Brothers built another—the Mussel II with Cirrus III engine —which was this time entirely of metal and was fitted with the patent Short amphibian undercarriage, comprising a central float to which was fitted a pair of retractable wheels which could be raised for water operation and lowered for land operation by means of a simple mechanical drive from the cockpit. This machine achieved no distinction other than the melan-choly one of being that in which Eustace Short, second of the three aero-nautical brothers, who had begun their career as official balloon-makers to

the Aero Club (not then Royal) at its inception in 1901, died at the age of
55 immediately after landing on the Medway.

The ingenuity shown in the design of the family of Parnall Pixies sug-
gests that further light aeroplanes designed by Mr Harold Bolas would be
of considerable interest, and this was indeed the case with his Imp biplane
of 1927 and the subsequent Elf of 1928, although neither went into production in quantity. The Imp (Plate 26), a two-seater built entirely of
wood, was most original in conception. The wings were completely covered
with a skin of spruce veneer which was tapered in thickness across the
span and designed to carry the loads imposed by bending. There were no
spars, but simply a number of light stringers and formers, the latter being
spaced along the wing at varying intervals in accordance with the stress
distribution. Discarding the conventional biplane system of freely hinging
upper and lower wings to the fuselage and centre-section and then bracing
them together with diagonal wires, Bolas made the lower wing a pure cantilever, hinged the swept-back upper wing to a central cabane of steel-tube
struts and joined it to the lower wing with a single broad interplane strut
on either side, so that in normal flight the lift loads on the upper wing were
carried by this strut in tension, no bracing wires being used. The wings
were not arranged to fold but the absence of wires made dismantling a
rapid operation, assisted by quick-release pins.

The Elf was a very much more conventional two-seater open cockpit
biplane with fabric-covered folding wings, closely resembling its contemporary the Parnall Peto which was a naval aircraft intended to be
carried by submarines. Its elegant lines were due to the cowled-in engine
—the new Cirrus-Hermes—and to the slightly swept-back wings, the
upper of which was of much larger span than the lower. Although he had
abandoned the Imp cantilever system, the designer again dispensed with
flying and landing wires by the use of a rather cumbersome arrangement
of steel-tube struts in the form of a Warren girder, which allowed wing-
folding without the need for a jury-strut at the cost (one would imagine)
of a considerable penalty in drag. Only one Elf was built in its original
form although two modified machines with Hermes II engine appeared in
the early 1930s.

In the summer of 1928 there appeared a serious rival to the three classic
biplanes of these early years. Mr O. E. Simmonds, a designer with the
Supermarine Aviation Works at Southampton, severed his connection
with that firm in order to form his own company and put into practice his
ideas for a light biplane of conventional form and normal wooden construction which would be especially cheap to build and repair. The result was
the Simmonds Spartan, in which the principle of interchangeability was
used for all aerofoil surfaces and some other parts in order to simplify

jigging during initial construction and to effect a drastic reduction in the number of spares needed for repair after accident. The four half-wings, with their ailerons, were identical and could therefore be fitted in any position, upright or inverted, since a symmetrical or uncambered aerofoil section was employed and attachment lugs were provided on both surfaces. Furthermore, the rudder was identical with each half-elevator and the fin with the outer portion of the tailplane, all bracing wires were interchangeable, and the two halves of the undercarriage, which was of split-axle type, could be fitted indifferently to the port or starboard side of the fuselage. Apart from these novel features, the machine was of the usual type with two open cockpits in tandem and a Cirrus III engine giving a cruising speed of 85 miles an hour.

The first Spartan was constructed in a bedroom of Mr Simmonds' house, and a certain amount of dismantling of the house was necessary in order to get the aeroplane into the outside world. After this, the machine was produced in considerable numbers in a factory at Weston, Southampton, forty-eight being built in 1928 and 1929, and although the type never achieved the world-wide success of its older rivals, it was a familiar sight on British aerodromes for many years. Some of the Spartans were built with a large front cockpit capable of carrying two passengers, which made the machine particularly suitable for joy-riding. The interchangeability which was the main feature of the type was made use of in unconventional fashion during the King's Cup Race of 1930, when Flight Lieutenant Gibbons had the misfortune to collide with another machine while waiting in his Spartan G-AAMG for the starter's flag to fall. Both his starboard ailerons were damaged, but instead of retiring from the race he calmly had the damaged surfaces removed and the upper port aileron placed in position on the lower starboard wing, leaving both upper wings without ailerons, and started thus in the race with somewhat reduced lateral control, which apparently caused him no embarrassment in the perfect summer weather which prevailed.

In 1927 Major Frank Halford, designer of the original Cirrus, broke his connection with the Aircraft Disposal Company in order to collaborate with Captain de Havilland in certain experimental engine work at Stag Lane. Difficulties with supply of the Cirrus engine at a satisfactory price had led de Havilland to the conclusion that it would be desirable to have the Moth and its engine manufactured under one roof and thus avoid the risk of deliveries being held up for lack of supplies from outside. The outcome of this was a batch of experimental engines of the same general appearance as the contemporary Cirrus II but developing 135 horsepower instead of the latter's 80, for a similar cylinder capacity. To test these highly developed engines in flight and obtain data on engine cooling, the de Havilland company built two small and fast single-seater monoplanes which were given the designation D.H.71 and the name of Tiger Moth—a name which, unfortunately for history, was later transferred to a biplane trainer whose widespread use in and after the Second World War has tended to confuse recollection of its earlier namesake.

The D.H.71, like the Moth, was built of wood, but the ply fuselage was of oval section in the interests of good streamlining instead of being flat-sided. The cockpit was tailored expressly to fit its pilot, Captain Hubert Broad, who had to squeeze himself into a fuselage only 17 ins. in width, and once in he was enclosed by a folding lid which formed part of a long fairing running the length of the machine, leaving only a small hole through which his head protruded. Thin wings of modified R.A.F.15 section were made in two halves set low on the fuselage, joined on the centre-line and braced above and below with streamlined wire. The upper bracing wires were carried to the top longerons of the fuselage, but the lower set were brought down to attachments at the centres of the undercarriage wheels which were internally sprung. The engine was very carefully faired into the lines of the fuselage and all the cylinders were totally enclosed.

Owing to difficulties which arose during type-testing the experimental engine could not be made ready for the 1927 King's Cup Race, so the second of the two Tiger Moths built, fitted with a Cirrus II, was entered and flown in the race by Captain Broad. He was compelled to retire at Spittlegate owing to difficulty with the controls in rough weather, but a month later, on a calm August evening which followed one of the soaking thunderstorms of a very wet summer, he took the machine with the 135-h.p. engine round a 100-kilometre course in just under twenty minutes, land-ing back at Stag Lane by the light of car headlamps after setting up a class record for aeroplanes of less than 350 kg empty weight by averaging 186·7 m.p.h., and a few days after this he reached a height of over 19,000 ft in the same machine, setting another class record.

The little Tiger Moth quickly disappeared from the active flying scene, but the experimental engine was de-rated by a reduction in the compres-sion ratio and the fitting of smaller valves to become the first of a line of engines which provided power for most of the British light aeroplanes (and not a few foreign ones) of the next decade and long after—the Gipsy I (Plate 28). In its design Halford had begun 'with a clean sheet of paper' and considered a variety of possible layouts before settling on the four-cylinder in-line air-cooled arrangement with which he was already very familiar. His choice was amply justified by events, for the line of Gipsy engines in a multiplicity of forms continues to this day. The Gipsy I, like the Cirrus, had cast-iron cylinders with detachable aluminium cylinder-heads carrying valves and sparking-plugs in bronze inserts, a five-bearing crankshaft, an oil sump of 'wet' type and exposed valve-gear operated in the usual way by push-rods. The bore was slightly greater than that of the Cirrus and the stroke slightly less, the result being a capacity of 5,230 c.c. in place of the 4,940 c.c. of the Cirrus II.

The new Gipsy engine began to be installed in Moths in 1928 and achieved publicity of a welcome kind when one of these machines won the King's Cup race and demonstrated that the 'hundred-mile-an-hour Moth' was now a reality. Throughout the rest of the year the Gipsy Moth was kept in the news with a series of exploits intended to show off its various good qualities. Almost immediately after the King's Cup race Captain de Havilland, accompanied by his wife, climbed to high altitude in his personal machine G-AAAA, the first to be registered under the new system of lettering (Plate 29). He reached an indicated 21,000 ft, which was later corrected to a true figure of slightly under 20,000 and officially recognised as a world record for light aeroplanes.* Later Mr A. S. Butler established another record in a Gipsy Moth by completing the 100-kilometre closed circuit at a speed of almost 120 m.p.h.

In view of the subsequent use of the Gipsy Moth for long-distance solo flying, however, Captain Broad's feat in one of these machines in August of the same year is perhaps the most significant of all. Taking off from Stag Lane with eighty gallons of petrol—the weight of which is equivalent to that of nearly four people—and well supplied with food and drink and a small library of novels, he set himself the task of keeping the Moth in the air for twenty-four hours. All that summer evening he cruised slowly about the south of England, and in spite of attacks of sickness brought on by the fumes of leaking oil he managed to carry on until 4 p.m. next day, when on his return to Stag Lane it was found that there were still twelve gallons left in the tanks. During the flight the engine had been well throttled back to conserve fuel, but even at the resultant low airspeed the Moth had covered almost 1,500 miles in its wanderings, and with its considerable initial overload it had left the ground without difficulty.

At the end of 1928 the Gipsy engine was subjected to a practical reliability test by its makers. A new unit taken at random from the production line was fitted into a Moth and all major components were carefully sealed together so that only routine maintenance work such as adjustment of valve clearances, changing of sparking plugs and cleaning of filters could be carried out. The aeroplane was then placed in service and flown by a number of different pilots for a total of 600 hours, at the end of which time, equivalent to a distance of 51,000 miles, the engine was removed

---

* In October 1928 Lady Heath attempted the same feat in a Cirrus III Moth, but fell short of Captain de Havilland's altitude by about a thousand feet. A few months before this she had established her seaplane record in the Short Mussel.

from the machine and subjected to a dynamometer test. This showed that its brake horsepower had fallen from its new value by only $2\frac{1}{2}\%$, and subsequent dismantling revealed that it was in good condition; the cost of necessary replacements was only £7 2s. 11d., or less than threepence for every hour flown. As a consequence of this test the de Havilland company were sufficiently confident in their new product to make a unique offer to the purchaser of a new machine, namely that subject to reasonable conditions as to maintenance they would indemnify him against any damage caused in a forced landing following the failure of a Gipsy engine.

The development of other engines was, of course, continuing parallel with that of the Gipsy. The Cirrus III of 1928, like the Gipsy, made its début in the King's Cup race of that year fitted to a Moth and an Avian, both of which completed the course. It was an improved version of identical capacity and completely interchangeable with earlier types, the main differences being modified cylinder heads, larger valves and a higher compression ratio, so that for the same weight its output was increased to a maximum of 95 b.h.p. In 1929 it was followed by an entirely new engine, the Cirrus-Hermes, which, although only five pounds heavier than earlier models and still fully interchangeable with them, developed the considerably increased maximum of 115 b.h.p. The smaller A.B.C. Hornet, a flat-four unit making use of many components of the earlier two-cylinder Scorpion, passed its Air Ministry type tests successfully in the furiously hot weather of July 1928, with temperatures in the test house rising to 100°F, and in the same year Mr D. R. Pobjoy's 'P' type seven-cylinder radial also passed its tests and was put into production by a company formed by its designer at Hooton Park, near Liverpool. The chief feature of this engine was that it provided a great deal of power for its weight (67·5 b.h.p. for 115 lbs) by running at high speed and driving a propeller through reduction gearing. Finally the five-cylinder Genet was succeeded in 1929 by the more powerful Genet Major, with larger bore and stroke giving an increase of power to a maximum figure of 110 h.p.

Although the open-cockpit biplane was to have many more years of useful life, its supremacy began to be challenged seriously for the first time in 1929, a year when the design of light aeroplanes in this country began to move forward along two new and distinct lines of development. The first of these was marked by the appearance of the high-wing monoplane with totally enclosed cabin for pilot and passengers, typified by the Desoutter (really an adaptation of a foreign design), the Civilian Coupé and the A.B.C. Robin; the second by the arrival on the scene of the low-wing cantilever monoplane, which had long been popular in Germany and which was soon to sweep all else before it with the efficient and successful designs of the 1930s.

Marcel Desoutter was a French pilot of pre-war days who had taken an active part in the meetings at Hendon. One day in 1913 he had crashed badly there on a Blériot and severely injured one leg, which had had to be amputated, and to avoid terminating his flying career he at once set to work with the help of his brother Charles to design a lighter and more efficient substitute. The result, an artificial leg built on engineering principles from aluminium alloy, was so successful that he was able to return to flying, and later went into business to place his invention on the market. The war gave rise to a large demand for artificial limbs and Desoutter was kept busy until 1929, when he decided to sell out his share in the business to his brother and form a company to manufacture the Dutch Koolhoven F.K.41 cabin monoplane. He had obtained the world rights in this machine from its designer, Frederick Koolhoven, and the new Desoutter Aircraft Company set up its works at Croydon with Mr G. H. Handasyde as works manager.

Though there was nothing completely new about the all-enclosed cabin, it was a distinct novelty for the club pilot of the day—who had been trained in an open cockpit and taught to judge the correctness of his turns by the absence of wind on one or other cheek—to find himself flying inside the equivalent of a saloon car. Even the professional air transport pilot had at this time only just begun to lay aside his leather helmet and goggles, though from the earliest days of regular air lines his passengers had been protected from the elements by a not always draught-proof cabin. The Desoutter and its contemporaries, which carried pilot and passengers in a single enclosed compartment, therefore represented the start of a new era in the history of the light aeroplane, when bulky flying clothing and Gosport speaking-tubes could be discarded and maps unfolded and handled in the air in comparative comfort.

The Desoutter company undertook considerable re-design of the original Koolhoven, a specimen of which was delivered to Croydon in April 1929, but the basic fuselage and wing structure were retained. The semi-cantilever wing arrangement was somewhat unusual; the ply-covered wing was constructed in one piece and the fuselage was suspended from it by three tubular steel struts on either side, leaving the centre-section above the cabin free to deflect vertically when the wing bent under load. The undercarriage was of especially wide track with a long vertical telescopic leg on each side extending up to the attachment point of the wing strut on the front spar. A door on the right-hand side gave access to the cabin, which contained a padded hammock seat for two passengers running across the full width at the rear and a single seat in front for the pilot. The Desoutter was manufactured in quantity and had a long and successful career as an air-taxi machine, for which it was ideally suited. In the

28. The first Gipsy engine, which after initial testing in the Tiger Moth monoplane of 1927 was adapted for Moths and other light aircraft and became one of the most successful and reliable small aero-engines ever built

29. The motor-car of the air: the Gipsy Moth. This machine, registered G-AAAA, was extensively used for personal transport by Captain de Havilland himself

30. The all-metal Blackburn Bluebird IV of 1929
31. Mr C. H. Latimer-Needham's H.A.C.1 'Mayfly', designed for the
Halton Aero Club and first flown early in 1927

long-distance flying role, however, it never seriously challenged the de Havilland Puss Moth, a superficially similar but structurally quite different high-wing cabin monoplane which first appeared in the same year.

There were two other less successful attempts to introduce the enclosed cabin to the light aeroplane pilot, the first a single-seater monoplane known as the Robin, intended as an economical form of transport and introduced by the engine firm of A.B.C. Motors of Walton-on-Thames. The engine chosen was the 40-h.p. A.B.C. Scorpion II. The larger of the current A.B.C. engines—the 4-cylinder 75/85-h.p. Hornet—was used in the Civilian Coupé, a side-by-side two-seater monoplane of the same general type, which in spite of its rather ugly appearance deserves credit as a brave early attempt to produce a simple enclosed two-seater for the private owner. The designer, Mr Harold Boultbee, had done his best to embody robustness and long life in the structure; the wings were completely covered with plywood and arranged to fold, and a feature rare in the light aeroplanes of the day was the use of push-pull rods in place of cables to operate all control surfaces. The cabin, which seated its two occupants side by side in slightly staggered seats to keep down the width of the fuselage, was entered by a door on either side, with a third door behind the cabin giving access to a luggage compartment, and a view to the rear— particularly lacking in the Desoutter—was provided through small windows at the back of the cabin below the trailing edge of the wing. In spite of its advanced features and moderate price of £650, which included dual control and wheel brakes, the Coupé did not find a ready market, and only five machines were built before the ultimate closing down of the Civilian Aircraft Company in 1933.

The first of the low-wing cantilever monoplanes to appear was the little single-seater Gadfly, built at Brooklands by Glenny and Henderson Limited in 1929 to the design of Captain K. N. Pearson. The empty weight of 455 lbs was rather more than the average of the 1923 Lympne single-seaters, but the A.B.C. Scorpion engine fitted provided more than twice the power of the 750 c.c. motor-cycle units of those days. Conventional ailerons were fitted at first, but these were later replaced by a curious form of lateral control invented by the aeroplane's designer—the Pearson rotary aileron, a form of oyster-shaped rotatable scoop projecting beyond each wing-tip and operated differentially to eliminate adverse yaw. Although the siting of these surfaces at the end of the main spar eliminated the twisting action on the wing associated with ordinary ailerons, they cannot have been very efficient aerodynamically and they were placed in a position which made them extremely vulnerable when the machine was on the ground. Some years later Captain Pearson embodied his special ailerons in another small monoplane called the Pickering-Pearson pusher, but there is no record of this having flown. The Gadfly at its price of £360 (or £370 with Pearson ailerons) was not a success, and its only claim to fame is an altitude record for single-seaters of less than 200 kg empty weight, set up by Colonel G. L. P. Henderson when he climbed to 3,021 metres in May 1929.

Later in the year a very similar single-seater flew for the first time at Shoreham in the hands of Captain E. W. Percival. The builders of the Hobo, as this small machine was called, were the Hendy Aircraft Company, formed by Mr Basil B. Henderson,* who had left his position with the Avro technical staff at Hamble to put into practice his own patented form of wing construction, the principle of which was to use the conventional arrangement of two spruce and plywood spars and to join them into a stiff torsion-resisting box by means of diagonal lattice strips applied to top and bottom. The Hobo embodied this idea, but was otherwise of straightforward wooden construction, with fully cantilever folding wings and a Scorpion engine. In later years the sole example built was fitted with a more powerful engine and extensively used for racing.

The advent of the more powerful Gipsy and Cirrus-Hermes engines infused new life into the classic biplanes of the day, and the successes of the Cirrus Moth were soon dimmed by the brighter star of the Gipsy Moth, which began to come into the hands of the clubs and private owners late in 1928. The luxury which the new Moth could offer was shown by the specimen delivered to the early private owner Mr Maurice Jackaman and named by him 'Peridot III'. This machine had the new coupé top which enclosed pilot and passenger from the slipstream, a cockpit heater operated from the engine exhaust, a chromium-plated exhaust pipe and manifold, and an extra fuel tank in the front cockpit, and the whole aeroplane was elegantly finished in a green and white colour scheme to the owner's choice. Moths, both standard and 'custom-built', were now beginning to emerge from the factory in hundreds, and their time of greatest achievement in long-distance flying still lay in the future.

An important technical development of 1929 was the introduction of metal versions of the famous quartet—Moth, Avian, Bluebird and Widgeon. The reason for this was an edict issued a few years earlier by the Air Ministry to the effect that no wooden construction would be acceptable for Service aircraft supplied after this date, the object being partly to prevent depletion of timber stocks (which had suffered badly due to aeroplane construction in 1914–18), and partly to obviate climatic troubles in aeroplanes which had necessarily to be capable of world-wide use. With an eye to possible applications of their light aeroplane designs as military trainers,

* Mr B. B. Henderson was not related to Colonel Henderson.

the major manufacturers with one accord set to work to plan the building of their well-tried designs entirely or partly in metal, and the new versions appeared almost simultaneously.

The most thorough-going of these was the Bluebird IV, wholly made of metal, with a fuselage built up into a beam of square cross-section using one size of steel tube throughout; light duralumin fairings were then sprung on to carry the fabric out into a good streamline form, and duralumin was also used for primary structure at the forward end in the form of transverse frames. Wing spars were formed of two lengths of thin rolled steel strip formed into a somewhat complex section to ensure rigidity, each strip forming one boom of the spar. There were many detailed differences from the earlier Bluebirds; the span was increased, a new undercarriage of divided type replaced the older fixed axle, and the rounded fin and rudder of the wooden version gave place to a rudder of trapezoidal shape without a fixed fin (Plate 30).

The D.H.60M or Metal Moth and the Avian IVM both retained their original wooden wing structure but had fuselages built up out of steel tube by bolting and welding. The former was made the basis for the military Moth Trainer and ultimately the D.H.82 Tiger Moth biplane; the latter became the Sports Avian with Cirrus-Hermes engine, the final development of the type with a top speed of 120 m.p.h. The steel Avian fuselage was also used for a braced low-wing monoplane version, which had been envisaged in Mr Chadwick's original design and which had a brief career in air racing in 1930. Finally the Widgeon IIIA* made use of square-section duralumin tubing for its fuselage, joined by riveting and stiffened with duralumin sheet in the region of the cockpits.

It remains to survey briefly some of the minor light aeroplanes of this exceedingly prolific period. One of the most original was the twin-engined Ibis, designed and built by Bert Hinkler after his solo flight to Australia in 1928. His long hours spent sitting behind a single engine while flying over inhospitable country had led him to the conclusion that a light twin-engined machine with side-by-side seating would be useful, and the considerable sum of money which his flight had brought him enabled him to return to England and put his idea into practice. The result was a very clean-looking monoplane with a cantilever wing of Henderson type designed for him by its inventor, carrying its pilot and passenger in a small cabin in front of the leading edge of the wing and equipped with a pair of

---

* It is perhaps not generally known that the fitting of a temporary or 'mock-up' cabin to a Widgeon III, creating a version known as the IV, led to the initial design of a cabin Widgeon V which was extraordinarily like the Puss Moth, though the Westland Company were quite unaware that the de Havilland Company were working along the same lines. It was not developed, however, and the Widgeon ceased production owing to pressure of work on the military Wapiti contract.

40-h.p. Salmson A.D.9 engines mounted in tandem in a nacelle which was carried above the wing on struts. The whole aircraft somewhat resembled in general outline the Saunders-Roe flying-boats of the time such as the Cutty Sark, and although it was in fact a land machine its designer hoped to be able later to offer an amphibian version. Unfortunately, however, the project came to nothing.

Parts of the Avro Baby, which Hinkler first made famous, reappeared in a new guise at Shoreham in 1929. The firm of Southern Aircraft Limited, whose managing director was Mr F. G. Miles, produced a small single-seater biplane with wings taken from the Baby but with a new fuselage and tail unit, a steel-sprung undercarriage replacing the old-fashioned arrangement of rubber cord, and an A.B.C. Hornet engine in place of the venerable Green. The result, intended for aerobatics and sporting flying, was named the Martlet; five machines were built, and a later version known as the Metal Martlet with steel fuselage, folding wings and Cirrus-Hermes engine, appeared in 1931. Two relatively undistinguished wooden biplanes of the same year were the D.W.2,* designed for Mr Dudley Watt by Captain K. N. Pearson, and the A.L.1, built by Surrey Flying Services at Croydon to the design of Mr J. Bewsher. Only one of each was made, and neither seems to have offered any particularly desirable feature that was not already available in other designs. The first was based on the notion that a low landing speed was more important to some owners than a high top speed, and was therefore provided with large wings 350 sq. ft in area instead of the 250 which was average for the two-seater light biplanes of the day, with the result that the cruising speed with Cirrus III engine was only 75 m.p.h. The A.L.1 had side-by-side seating in an upholstered cockpit beneath the centre-section and a roomy luggage locker behind the seats which could be adapted to form a third seat for a child. The Salmson A.C.7 radial engine of 95 h.p. provided a maximum speed of 110 m.p.h.

The Halton Aero Club's Mayfly or H.A.C.1 biplane (Plate 31), which had just failed to get to Lympne in 1926, had a successful racing season in the next year, and the Club then set about a drastic re-design. Since the original competition requirement for a two-seater no longer applied (the Mayfly had in fact done all its racing in single-seater form) it occurred to Mr Latimer-Needham that by permanently eliminating the weight of the passenger it would be possible also to dispense with the small lower wing and the X-shaped interplane struts, converting the original biplane into a parasol monoplane like Comper's C.L.A.3 by the addition of a pair of long parallel lift struts on either side. This work, together with a certain amount of detail re-design, was carried out at Halton during the winter of 1927–28

---

* The D.W.1, also built for Mr Dudley Watt, had been a converted war-time S.E.5.

with the result that the H.A.C.2 or Minus was ready in time for the events of the following summer. The change in wing arrangement raised the maximum speed to 95 miles an hour, and the Minus was very successful at racing, winning the Wakefield Cup at Hamble in 1928 in addition to a number of other events. As its predecessor the Mayfly had done in 1927, the Minus flew in the King's Cup Race in 1928 and 1929, and in the first of these years it had the distinction of taking part in the fly-past of new air-craft types at the Hendon Display, being almost certainly the only aero-plane built by a club which ever did so.

The discarded wings and X-struts of the Mayfly were taken over by Flying Officer J. Clarke of the Royal Air Force, who had built himself a parasol monoplane named the Cheetah out of D.H.53 parts, and were used to convert this machine into a biplane, with quickly-detachable fittings which enabled it to be flown in either form.

The influence of Captain G. T. R. Hill's tailless aircraft with Cherub engine, first flown in 1923 and subsequently developed into the Westland-Hill Pterodactyl, may be traced in two amateur-built light aeroplanes of the late 1920s. The Experimental Light Plane Club of Nottingham, formed by the brothers R. and J. Granger, had been building gliders since 1921, and after an unsuccessful attempt at a powered biplane they began on the ambitious project of a tailless design. Mr. Latimer-Needham, who had come into contact with the Grangers in the winter of 1926–27, carried out a stress analysis of the machine and recommended certain modifications, the most fundamental being the substitution of a normal fuselage with fin and rudder (but no tailplane) for the two wing-tip rudders originally pro-posed after the manner of the Hill design. Several advantages were claimed for this arrangement: the rudder was given greater effectiveness by being placed in the propeller slipstream; a tail-skid could be fitted for better control when taking-off or landing; and the design of the wing spars was much simplified by the removal of rudder loads from their tips. Longi-tudinal stability was provided by the usual device of sweeping back the wings, and control in roll and pitch by the use of controllers at the wing tips which fulfilled the functions of both elevators and ailerons, being operated by a pilot's handwheel which could be rotated for lateral control and slid forwards and backwards for longitudinal control. This machine, named the Archaeopteryx by way of analogy with the Pterodactyl, was extremely successful; it was flown for some years without registration marks, as was then permissible for experimental aircraft flown within three miles of an aerodrome, but was later registered and thus enabled to carry out flights across country to aviation meetings.

Experience with the Archaeopteryx led Mr Latimer-Needham to em-bark on a tailless design of his own in conjunction with the Halton Aero

Club, and the result was the H.A.C.3 or Halton Meteor, a racing mono-plane with two Bristol Cherub engines arranged in 'push-pull' fashion at either end of a central nacelle (Figure 6). It was intended that the Meteor should be as nearly as possible a flying wing, but owing to its small size this ideal could not be completely realised and it was necessary to provide a small nacelle for the accommodation of the pilot. A particularly good

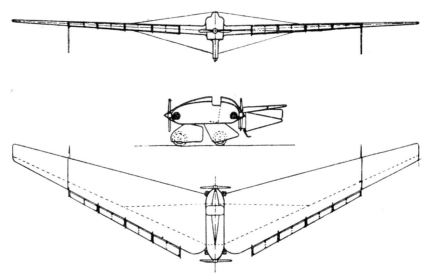

6. A novel tailless racing machine of 1928, which unfortunately never flew: the Halton Aero Club's H.A.C.3 Meteor

speed range was aimed at by the provision of 'pilot planes' similar in their action to Handley Page slots along the greater part of the leading edge of each wing, and with these in operation it was calculated that the stalling speed would be only 25 m.p.h., little more than one-fifth of the estimated maximum of 120 m.p.h. Had this interesting machine flown it might have imparted a futuristic touch to the air races of later years, but although practically completed it was not allowed to take the air because of official misgivings over so unconventional an arrangement. The design activities of the enterprising Halton club ended with its successor the H.A.C.4, which was to have been a six-seater high-wing monoplane with three Cherub engines but which did not proceed beyond the stage of preliminary drawings.

⊸⊷ 9 ⊷⊶

Widening Horizons
1926–29

It requires a certain effort of the imagination, in these days of journeys into space, to appreciate quite what a revolution in travel was brought about by the light aeroplane when it first began to appear in the middle 1920s. Commercial air transport had been in existence for only six years, and although the crudities of the very early days had been improved upon, the air liner of the time still left a good deal to be desired in terms of speed, regularity, comfort and quietness. When the first Moth took the air at Stag Lane in February 1925, Imperial Airways Limited had been in existence less than eleven months, and its fleet of machines—taken over from its predecessors, Instone Air Lines, Daimler Airways and Handley Page Transport Limited —consisted principally of the single-engined D.H.34 and the twin-engined Handley Page W.8b, both of which were biplanes carrying nine and twelve passengers respectively in wicker chairs within a cramped cabin. The safety provided by the two engines of the Handley Page machine was illusory, for it would not maintain height on one engine, and it was not until the following year that the three-engined Armstrong Whitworth Argosy and de Havilland Hercules came into use. All these machines still carried their leather-coated pilots in open cockpits, and their cruising speed was only in the region of 90 m.p.h., so that the journey from Croydon to Le Bourget could easily take three hours if there was a stiff head-wind or a spectacular ninety minutes with the wind behind. Imperial Airways flew three services between Croydon and Paris in each direction every weekday and one on Sunday, the return fare being £11 5s., or well over £30 in present-day terms. Their other services, to Zurich, Cologne and Amsterdam with connections by foreign lines to Berlin and Malmö, operated only once a day, and this (with a weekly flight between Southampton and Guernsey) represented the sum total of British services at the time. It is hardly necessary to add that commercial air transport to Australia or South Africa, let alone across the Atlantic, was entirely non-existent. Wireless, though in use for communications and for fairly cumbrous position-finding by means of bearings from ground stations, contributed nothing to the problem of accurately locating the terminal aerodrome in bad weather, and for this much depended on the pilot's local knowledge and skill. Really bad visibility or a strong and gusty wind meant cancellation and delay, and those in a hurry would then make a quick dash for the Channel ports to board the slower but more reliable steamer, justifying the old saying of the cynical: 'time to spare, go by air'.

It is against this background of rather primitive commercial flying that we must view the advent of the Moth, Avian, Bluebird and Widgeon, all available on the market at reasonable prices and offering the independence and flexibility of the motor-car combined with speed, safety and reliability; any convenient field could be used as a landing ground, and maintenance of the machine and its engine had been brought within the capabilities of the ordinary mechanically minded motorist. The prospective owner who was not yet a pilot could quickly learn to fly with one of the new State-subsidised clubs for a sum which was a negligible fraction of the cost of his aircraft, and once he had obtained an 'A' licence and a small amount of additional flying experience the world was at his feet. This was a new kind of freedom, and the great upsurge of private ownership and personal flying brought about by the Moth and its contemporaries reflected the keen desire of those who could afford the luxury of a light aeroplane to take full advantage of the benefits it had to offer. Flying, only a few years previously an affair for the young and daring, had suddenly come within the grasp of the comfortably-off middle-aged professional man who might perhaps be a keen motorist but who did not see himself as endowed with any unusual qualities of fitness, courage or skill.

The cost of owning a private aeroplane, though not yet so low as the 'motor-glider' enthusiasts had once hoped that it might be, was not much greater than that of running a large car, and it was easy to imagine that as private flying became more and more widespread it would also become cheaper. The possession of a machine of essentially war-time design had often involved its owner in an alarming number of unlooked-for expenses, but this situation was greatly changed by the coming of the Moth with its simplified maintenance at standardised charges, and with the experience of many others to draw upon it soon became possible for the prospective purchaser to estimate quite accurately what his flying would cost him. One such estimate, made for the Cirrus Moth, suggested that an annual total of 250 hours could be flown for about 23s. an hour exclusive of depreciation, equivalent to some 20,000 miles of personal air travel at threepence-halfpenny a mile. The initial cost of a new light aeroplane of Moth type in 1926 was in the region of £800, but as has been shown elsewhere this figure was soon reduced by increased production and competition. There soon developed a flourishing second-hand market in light aeroplanes, with the standard biplane type selling for £400–£600 according to age, and occasionally one or two of the surviving machines used in the Lympne trials would be offered for £100 or less; in 1930 one of the Westland Wood Pigeons was advertised in the technical press for only £35 including a complete spare Anzani engine. It must of course be remembered when making comparisons that the purchasing power of the pound was at this time at least three times as great as it is today (1963).

By early 1926 the Moth was beginning to pass into the hands of private owners and its possibilities for touring at home and abroad were soon being thoroughly explored. Colonel Sempill carried out a tour with his wife at Whitsun 1926 which admirably demonstrated how the light aeroplane could be used quite independently of aerodromes and thus made to live up to the claim that it was an 'aerial motor-car'. Leaving Stag Lane he set off for Aberystwyth, making one stop in a field in Wales to fill up the tank from a roadside petrol pump, and since there was no aerodrome at his destination he landed the machine on the sands at Borth. From Aberystwyth he flew directly across the Bristol Channel to Instow in Devon, a journey of little over an hour's duration which would have taken all day by road, and later continued to Cheltenham (landing on Cleeve Common) and to Broadway. When it eventually returned to Stag Lane the Moth had covered a total of 800 miles in 12 hours' flying time and during the whole tour had not been near an aerodrome, but had spent its nights either picketed in the open or with wings folded in some convenient outbuilding. Later Colonel Sempill gave a further demonstration of the convenience and speed of the Moth by flying the red-and-white G-EBMO, which had recently won the King's Cup in the hands of Captain Broad, from Land's End to John o' Groats in a flying time of eight hours and fourteen minutes.

Folding wings were provided on all the light aeroplanes of the time chiefly in order to facilitate 'garaging', and although much use was made for publicity purposes of the fact that a Moth could be towed behind a car with its wings folded this must have been a somewhat unwieldy procedure even on the relatively quiet roads of the 1920s. There is, however, at least one case on record of this facility having been put to practical use. Mr A. G. Wilson, a motor agent from Leeds who was a member of the Yorkshire Aeroplane Club, flew down from Sherburn-in-Elmet to Oxford with a companion to collect a new Morris car on the understanding that the aeroplane would be returned to the club for the week-end's flying. They landed in Port Meadow and took over the car, but finding that the weather had turned too bad for flying they folded the Moth's wings and set off northwards by road with it in tow. By the time they reached Banbury the weather had improved, so after manhandling the aeroplane through a gate into a convenient field and spreading the wings, Mr Wilson's companion took off for Yorkshire leaving his friend to follow behind by car.

Although the Moth was by far the most popular type of light aeroplane in these early days, its contemporaries were not neglected. Colonel Sempill made much use of a Bluebird seaplane flown from the Welsh Harp as a London base, and travelled in it to Aberdeen and to the Berlin Aero Show, taking advantage of the seaplane's greater safety on a long sea crossing to fly directly from Amsterdam to Felixstowe on his return. The Westland Widgeon, too, had its small band of devoted owners, who were attracted by its robustness and good cruising speed, which was rather higher than that of the biplanes. One of these owners, Squadron Leader Harold Probyn, had the original idea of using his machine G-EBRQ for camping holidays, and took it round the country loaded with a tent, a collapsible rubber boat (used either as a bed or a bath), bedding, stove and cooking utensils, in addition of course to pilot and passenger. In the carefree days of the 1920s when almost any field could be used as a landing ground and camp site, there can hardly have been a pleasanter way of spending a holiday. Later Squadron Leader Probyn and his wife set out on a more ambitious tour to North Africa and back in the same machine, covering over 4,000 miles with a load of 800 lbs which included a spare propeller, a spare magneto, five suitcases and an inflatable raft in case of a forced descent into the Mediterranean.

All this sudden enthusiasm for light aeroplanes gave rise to some curious suggestions, many of which did not come near being carried into practice, but the very fact that they could be seriously put forward is an indication of how bright the prospects of private flying seemed in 1926. In the *Tatler* for 3 November of that year there appeared the following paragraph:

> An interesting glimpse of the possibilities of the future is provided by the scheme which was explained by Lord Apsley last week for the provision of an aerodrome for light aeroplanes and a taxiplane rank in Hyde Park. . . . A machine like the Moth only requires, under ordinary conditions, about 100 yards in which to take off, [so that] an aerodrome in Hyde Park in the shape of an L, each arm being 200 yards or more long, with a breadth of 50 yards, would provide for the landing of these machines whatever wind was blowing.

Alas for progress! Thirty-seven years later the whistle of the gas turbine pervades the air of the West End by day and night, but the very appearance of a Moth over Hyde Park would call down the most ferocious penalties upon the head of its pilot and he would be unable to find a welcome at any landing place less than twelve miles from Marble Arch

Perhaps by the standards of today the light aeroplane of 1925 seems a somewhat crude vehicle for long-distance touring, with its two open cockpits exposing their occupants to all the rigours of wind and weather, but again it is essential to consider it against the background of other modes of transport. Most travellers in those days expected to have to wrap up warmly, for this was still the spartan era of the dickey seat and the open-topped General omnibus. Cars were for the most part of the tourer variety with hood and sidescreens provided purely to keep out the rain (though not the draughts), and the saloon body, as yet something of a rarity, was entirely unheated and frequently let in the wind after its woodwork had settled a little in use. Motoring coats, gloves and rugs were therefore normal accessories for a journey of any length outside a few weeks of high summer, and so dressing up to go flying was equally a natural, and indeed rather pleasant, part of the aeronautical *mystique*. All professional pilots were clad in leather, and there can hardly have been a single amateur in the early days of the flying clubs who on first buying his helmet with its Gosport tubes and goggles did not try them on at once before a mirror to see if he looked like Alan Cobham. But apart from these accessories, essential for taking instruction, the clothing required was only that worn in the motor-cars of the day, and when one flying club advertised that 'Moths are as warm as open cars' it was if anything understating the case, for the pilot, sunk in his cockpit up to his ears, was probably more comfortable in the air at moderate altitudes than huddled behind the windscreen of his tourer in an icy sidewind. Women pilots found the close-fitting felt hat which was then fashionable a convenient substitute for a leather helmet when flying solo, and as private flying grew in popularity 'modes for airwomen' soon made their appearance in the London shops. Some of these embodied trousers which, though practical, were not particularly suitable for arriving by aeroplane at a garden party or similar elegant gathering. Ingenuity was brought to bear on this difficulty, however, and one result was the 'Itylus' ladies' quick-change flying-suit, designed by Mrs Patrick Ommanney and smartly cut in dark blue cord. A contemporary description of this remarkable garment ran:

> The lady flies in trousers, changes in a very few seconds in the cockpit of the 'plane while in the air and alights at her journey's end wearing a Skirt and Hat, properly dressed to take part in any social function, Luncheon Party, etc.

The exact mechanism of this transformation must be left to the imagination of the reader, but it is worth noting that the invention of the zip-fastener was contemporary with the D.H. Moth.

It was not long, naturally, before the private owner began to use his aeroplane to explore the Continent by air just as the more enterprising motorist was beginning to explore it by road; a new form of holiday described by one light aeroplane owner as 'sight-seeing for those who are not content to count the telegraph poles from the window of a train'. A typical Continental tour was that carried out in September 1927 by Mr David Kittel, the first private owner of a Moth, who had by this time accumulated some 400 hours of flying. It was most comprehensive, taking in Cologne, Berlin, Breslau, Prague, Vienna, Budapest, Venice, Rome, Naples, Pisa, Milan, Zurich and Paris, and was carried out without trouble except for a single alarming incident when the engine failed from fuel blockage at 150 ft just after taking off from the Lido at Venice; fortunately however the blockage cleared itself and an awkward forced landing was avoided. One striking feature of the journey was that the last stage from Paris to London was flown in company with an Imperial Airways machine, forcibly illustrating the point that the light aeroplane could at this time offer personal transport which was as fast as that provided by the regular air lines. All the air tourists of the day were struck by the contrast between the freedom offered by the personal aeroplane on the one hand and the old international suspicions and jealousies on the other, exemplified by the military precautions of each state against its neighbour and the difficulty of obtaining even weather information across a national boundary.

There were indeed occasions when the light aeroplane displayed even greater advantages than usual over other means of travel. At the time of the Carnera-Stribling fight in Paris early in December 1929, a furious gale in the Channel stopped all boats and air-liners and made it impossible for many English boxing enthusiasts to travel over to France for the occasion. Mr A. S. Butler, chairman of the de Havilland company, accompanied by Mr Nigel Norman, boldly set forth in a Moth and crossed the water at an astonishing 160 m.p.h. with the wind behind. Ground staff at the St Inglevert aerodrome had been warned of their coming and were ready to seize the Moth's wing-tips as soon as it touched the ground to prevent it from blowing over. With this help they landed successfully and the machine was safely manhandled into shelter, where it remained while its pilots took the train for Paris. This kind of flying was not for the inexperienced, but it was a good demonstration of the light aeroplane's possibilities in skilful hands and provided excellent material for the de Havilland publicity department.

Foreign touring, by air as by road, involved a number of preparations including the provision of up-to-date maps and information on aerodromes, weather forecasts, Customs carnets and similar documents, and as private aeroplanes grew in popularity it was soon evident that a central organisation for dealing with these matters would be most useful. The Automobile Association, with its experience of meeting the requirements of travellers by road which dated from the earliest days of the motor-car, was the obvious body to take over similar duties for tourists by air, and in 1928 its Aviation Department came into being under Mr Ivor McClure and Mr O. J. Tapper. The services it offered, developed in the next few years and continued up to 1939, were most comprehensive. Strip maps covering air journeys to any part of the world could be supplied on hire, thus saving pilots the very considerable cost of buying them, and up-to-date aerodrome and weather information was collated and made available to those contemplating flights to any destination in the world. Almost as soon as the new aerodrome at Heston was opened in 1929 the A.A. installed a wireless station there and began a system of regular weather broadcasts at fixed times which could be picked up by an ordinary domestic receiver or by wireless apparatus carried in aircraft. All these services were extensively used, and many long-distance flights of the period were planned by the A.A. and carried out with the aid of maps supplied on hire. An ingenious form of liaison with the network of road patrols was arranged by issuing weighted message bags to members, who could drop them near any A.A. box with a distinctive streamer attached if they wished to pass a message ahead to their destination or communicate with the ground in any other way. Later came the A.A. Register of Landing Grounds, intended to increase the usefulness of the light aeroplane for travel in Britain by providing details of fields all over the country whose owners were agreeable to their being used for landing in return for a small fee. Since it was unreasonable to expect farmers to notify the A.A. when a particular field was ploughed up or rendered useless for landing by some obstruction, the Register was kept up to date by the reports of road patrols, who were provided with special forms for this purpose. Finally, a number of patrols with experience of aircraft in the R.A.F. were selected for special training in picketing down machines, folding wings, starting engines and putting on cockpit and engine covers, and these men in the familiar yellow uniform were soon to be seen in action at every air pageant and meeting, at each of which hundreds of private aeroplanes were by now arriving.

Although many pilots were quite content to tour England and the Continent in their machines, there were those—amateur and professional —to whom the wider possibilities of cheap personal flying offered an irresistible challenge. In this way began the brief era, little more than a decade, of famous long-distance solo flights for which the rapid growth of the light aeroplane movement was largely responsible. This was the adolescent period of aviation, when the aeroplane had travelled far enough along the road of technical development to allow outstanding feats to be attempted in reasonable safety, yet not so far that the element of individual enterprise and courage had been entirely eliminated, so that the figure of the pilot who set out alone for the ends of the earth still retained some of the attraction and romance of the pioneering days. No attempt has been made in this book to deal with the important flights made by the larger commercial and military aeroplanes of this period, and their contribution must not be forgotten: but it was the light aeroplane above all, offering as it did a performance little inferior to that of larger machines at a small fraction of the cost, which was used for the great majority of the solo flights of these years and which showed the way which the commercial aeroplane was later to follow. In his book *First Flights*, Major Oliver Stewart has written of these fascinating years:

> During the period of the solo flyers, aviation was at its most attractive. It did not show its warlike qualities in excess and it did not seem to dote on commercial achievement. There was flying for the sake of flying: and there came into existence this great body of men and women who flew because they loved flying. We must for ever regret the passing of that period. It was historically less significant than the time when the first powered flights were made, but it was a better period in that it placed the emphasis upon the creative and the peacefully entertaining sides of aviation. It showed aviation as a means of touring the country and of visiting friends. It showed it partly as an entertainment and partly as a technical enterprise. It combined the merits of these two things.

There were two routes across the world which held an especial interest for British pilots and the British public. The first was that joining England and Australia, first traversed by air by the Australian brothers Ross and Keith Smith in a Vickers Vimy biplane in 1919, and it was perhaps this route, running almost half-way round the earth, which caught the popular imagination above all others. The shortest, or great-circle, track from London to Darwin, as anyone can verify with a piece of string and a geographical globe, passes approximately through Moscow, across the north of Tibet into Indo-China and thence over the South China Sea and North Borneo, and therefore was (and is) highly impractical for both political and geographical reasons, much of the way being barred by the highest mountains in the world and very sparsely provided with aerodromes. The practical alternative, used by the brothers Smith and almost all who followed them, possessed the great advantage for English-speaking pilots that it traversed a large part of the British Empire; a variety of routes ran through Europe, and possibly North Africa, to the Middle East and from there led to Karachi and across India to Calcutta. After Calcutta came the extraordinary chain of coastline and islands, 4,000 miles in length, that stretches from the Sunderbunds at the mouth of the Ganges to the island of Timor, and the journey was completed by a long flight over water—the crossing of the Timor Sea, usually associated in the Press with the hackneyed but only too accurate adjective 'shark-infested'. The town of Darwin marked the goal for most record flights from England to Australia, but to reach the populous areas in the south-east of that continent the weary long-distance pilot was faced with a further two thousand miles across some of the most desolate and waterless country on the face of the earth.

The second of the great routes, much shorter but with its own peculiar hazards, was that joining England to the Cape of Good Hope. Here the great-circle track lay down the west side of Africa, and involved a direct crossing of the Sahara, so that the eastern route by way of Cairo, Khartoum and East Africa, pioneered by van Ryneveld in 1920, was generally chosen by pilots of light aeroplanes in the early days although it presented problems (unfamiliar to the pilot trained in England) of take-off and landing at aerodromes where the air was thin by reason of high altitude and great heat. In later years, as the range and reliability of machines increased, the emphasis shifted to the considerably shorter western route by way of Oran, Gao, Duala and Mossamedes to Cape Town, and it was this route which was used from 1933 onwards for a series of fast journeys to the Cape.

It was not perhaps surprising that the first pilots to attempt a long-distance flight by light aeroplane should choose to set out part way along the Australia route, since at the time this route was in the forefront of everyone's mind. On 1 October 1926, Mr Alan Cobham completed his historic return flight from England to Australia by landing his D.H.50 seaplane on the Thames at Westminster to receive a well-earned knighthood and the acclamation of a crowd estimated at one million people. Six weeks later, on 15 November, two Moths flying in company set off from Stag Lane on a journey eastwards towards India. Each carried an extra petrol tank of 37 gallons capacity in the front cockpit; but suggestions in the Press that a 'non-stop record' was to be attempted were strenuously denied by both pilots, who described the venture as a 'holiday jaunt and not a Cook's Tour'. The pilots thus aspiring to be 'junior Cobhams' were Captain T. Neville Stack, instructor of the Lancashire Aero Club at Woodford, and Mr B.M.T.S. Leete a member of the club, the former flying the King's Cup winner G-EBMO and the latter a similar machine G-EBKO. Both aircraft were fitted with the new and improved Cirrus II engine which had made its public début in the same race. Since each aircraft had to carry spares and other items for the journey, luggage space was restricted and each pilot limited himself to a single small suitcase. Captain Stack, however, was a notable performer on the ukelele (he had, in fact, been persuaded to leave a lucrative job with a dance band in a London night club to become the Lancashire Aero Club's first paid instructor) and he therefore managed to find a small corner in which to stow his instrument, subsequently bringing it out at the various landing places along the route for the entertainment of the local inhabitants.

The start from Stag Lane was made in cold and blustery November weather, and a gale held up the travellers for three days at Lympne before they could even cross the Channel. Eventually, however, they got away, overtaking a Farman Goliath passenger machine of the French air-line near Abbeville, and landing at Paris where they were held up for two more days. Violent thunderstorms accompanied them down the flooded Rhone valley and at Lyons they were faced with a landing in the dark since the storms had put all the aerodrome lighting out of action. At Pisa the aerodrome was under water and they had to land their Moths on the only dry portion, a strip about ten yards wide and a hundred yards long. The weather improved as they flew south, though on the long sea crossing from Naples to Malta the visibility was very poor, but they managed to find the island successfully and remained there seven days for engine overhaul and the enjoyment of social pleasures before setting out again for the North African coast. The stage from Homs to Benghazi passed over territory occupied by hostile tribes, and rain and low cloud forced the two machines to cover this stretch at a height of only 200 ft, fortunately without incident.

On 16 December the Moths reached Baghdad, where the two pilots had an enthusiastic reception from their old squadrons and arrangements were made for the cutting of a new sprocket-wheel for one of the magnetos of Leete's machine, which had been out of action during the desert crossing. After spending a cheerful Christmas with their old friends, during which no doubt the ukelele was extensively brought into service, the pair continued to Bushire and here they were overtaken by the three-engined D.H. Hercules of Imperial Airways which was carrying the Air Minister, Sir Samuel Hoare, and Lady Maud Hoare on the inaugural flight of the desert air route from Cairo to Karachi. Stack's engine was by now giving trouble with a cracked cylinder-head, but they managed to patch it up well enough to complete the journey to India and in the afternoon of 8 January the two little machines appeared over the Drigh Road aerodrome near Karachi after a flight totalling 5,500 miles. Certainly it was the longest that had ever been carried out by a light aeroplane at the time, and one that was considered sufficiently meritorious for the award of the Air Force Cross to both pilots, who were flying officers in the R.A.F. Reserve. The arrival of Stack and Leete at Karachi aroused great interest in India. Special trains were run for the crowds that came to watch the exhibition flights which they subsequently gave, and one direct result of their tour was the formation of Indian flying clubs, first at Karachi and later at other cities.

In the spring of 1927 there appeared on the scene one of the most remarkable airwomen of the period, who turned to the light aeroplane as a new means of travel at an age when most of humanity has its mind fixed on retirement. This was the Duchess of Bedford, whose varied interests included radiography (at which she was fully qualified), skating and ornithology. In the more prosperous days before 1914 she had been able to satisfy a restless desire for travel by bird-watching expeditions round northern waters in the ducal yacht, *Sapphire*, but this vessel having long since been disposed of she was compelled to seek another outlet which did not involve her in the boredom of long train journeys. In 1926 she made her first aeroplane flight, from Croydon to her home at Woburn, and this immediately became her new interest, helped by the fact that flying appeared to benefit the severe deafness from which she suffered. Almost at once she engaged Captain C. D. Barnard as her personal pilot, hired a Moth and set off to tour Europe and North Africa in it. Leaving Woburn on 21 April 1927, she and Barnard completed a tour which involved 55 hours' flying in three weeks, travelling through France and Spain to Tangier and crossing the Pyrenees, the Guadarramas and the Sierra Nevada. At Seville, one of their stopping-places, Captain Barnard demonstrated the Moth before the King of Spain and the Prince of Wales.

The Duchess was so fascinated by the freedom which personal air travel offered that later in the summer she set forth again with her pilot, this time to Venice, Pisa and Rome, covering 3,500 miles in an eventful week which included flying over Vesuvius and crossing the Alps at 14,000 ft, a considerable achievement for a woman of sixty-one travelling as a passenger in an open cockpit. She was not content to remain a passenger for very long, however, and the following year she began to take flying lessons from Captain Barnard on her own Gipsy Moth. She flew solo for the first time in April 1930, immediately before her flight to the Cape and back with Barnard in the Fokker monoplane 'Spider' which they had used for a journey to India and back in less than eight days in the previous August. During her flying career the Duchess owned five light aeroplanes in succession, all of them Moths, and kept them at her private aerodrome at Woburn Park, and it was in the last of the series, a Moth Major, that she eventually vanished in mysterious circumstances over the North Sea while flying solo at the age of seventy-one.

The unsuccessful pioneer is rarely remembered, however great may be the tribulations which beset him before he is finally forced to admit defeat. Such was the unfortunate Mr Dennis Rooke, an Australian who bought a Moth in England early in 1927 with the intention of flying it home. He had served in the Royal Air Force but had not flown for seven years and therefore took a course with the de Havilland School at Stag Lane before setting off alone from Croydon on 24 May. Following the route of Stack and Leete by way of Malta he reached North Africa successfully at Homs on the 31st, but after this his troubles began with a forced landing in the desert, where he spent three days with almost no food or water trying to repair his engine. Eventually he was able to get off and continue to Aboukir for a more permanent repair, in the course of which it was found that the bearings had been damaged by sand. A subsequent delay in Persia caused him to arrive at Karachi very late in the evening of 20 June, and mistaking a cricket ground for the aerodrome in the bad light he landed and damaged his machine, although he himself was unhurt. Repairs occupied about a month and Rooke set off again for Jodhpur, Cawnpore and Allahabad, at the last of which places he was further delayed by engine trouble and illness. Finally he got away again for Calcutta, but when taking off after an intermediate landing the Moth crashed into a tree and was wrecked, putting its unlucky pilot into hospital. Rooke was therefore compelled to abandon his flight, and with it the distinction of being the first man to fly solo from England to Australia.

The first member of the London Aeroplane Club to receive instruction was, as we have already noted, Mrs Sophie Elliott-Lynn, a young woman of twenty-two who was destined to play an important part in the light aeroplane movement. Born in Limerick, she had studied agriculture in Dublin with the intention of taking up farming overseas, but like many another she found a satisfaction in aviation that made her adopt it as a career, and after first flying solo at Stag Lane on 18 October 1925 she quickly obtained her certificate and 'A' licence and went on to become a professional pilot in the spring of the following year. Her aeronautical experience also included a voluntary parachute descent which she performed successfully after a first attempt had been frustrated by the engine failure of the Avro from which she was to jump, so that she had the alarming and possibly unique experience of undergoing a forced landing as a passenger while standing on the wing and clinging to the side of the machine. During her flying career she owned a number of different aeroplanes, and it was in her Avian G-EBRS that she performed a remarkable and unusual flight which, overshadowed perhaps by her later activities, seems to have been little remembered. Setting off alone before dawn on 19 July 1927 from Woodford Aerodrome, where she had slept in the hangar, she carried out a complete tour of all the aerodromes and landing grounds in England south of Manchester and then flew up to Newcastle, covering a total distance of 1,300 miles and making 79 landings, the last being at 9.27 p.m. The distance in itself would have been astonishing in a machine such as the Avian if carried out in a single flight, but the interruption of repeated landings, each at a different place with its own special difficulties, made her achievement a particularly striking one.

Most of the little machines which had competed at Lympne later vanished into obscurity or ended their days with various private owners or flying clubs, though there were some whose careers were more distinguished, such as Mr W. S. Shackleton's A.N.E.C. two-seater, which enjoyed some racing success in the hands of Mr N. H. Jones, and his Wee Bee of the same year which had a long flying life in Australia. In the summer of 1927 there was a brave attempt to carry out a long-distance flight in one of the Hawker Cygnets which had done so well in the *Daily Mail* trials the previous year. Flight Lieutenant R. L. Ragg of the R.A.E. Aero Club planned to fly it non-stop from England to Bucharest, and to this end the fuel capacity was increased to 38 gallons with tanks in the passenger seat, bringing the total loaded weight up to 1,000 lbs—a fairly considerable overload relative to the figure of 850 lbs used in the trials. With this fuel the Cherub should have run for some seventeen hours, sufficient to carry the machine over the journey of 1,250 miles given favourable winds. Ragg taxied out at Lympne in the early hours of August 23rd with his heavy load of petrol and began his take-off towards a road which was lined with telephone wires and which had behind it a thick belt of trees, after which the land fell away to the marshes. Unfortunately its fully-loaded condition, coupled perhaps with a down-draught at a critical moment, made it impossible for the Cygnet to be coaxed over the wires, and it hit them head-on, becoming a total wreck; Flight Lieutenant Ragg, however, was unhurt. It is satisfactory to record that the other of these two historic aeroplanes survived the 1939-45 war, was rebuilt and made airworthy and is today still in the care of its makers.

The route to the Cape, so far traversed only by Colonel Pierre van Ryneveld in 1920 and by Alan Cobham's far-ranging D.H.50 six years later, had not yet been attempted by the light aeroplane, but this deficiency was soon made good. Lieutenant R. R. Bentley, an Englishman who had joined the South African Air Force after war service with the R.F.C., managed to obtain some financial assistance from the Johannesburg *Star* towards the purchase of a new Moth with which he hoped to cover the distance from Stag Lane to Cape Town in fourteen days.* When the Moth was ready for its flight it was christened *Dorys* in honour of Bentley's fiancée, Miss Dorys Oldfield, who was awaiting him in Pretoria, and the bottle of South African wine that was smashed against the propeller boss was wielded by Lady Bailey, president of the Suffolk and Eastern Counties Flying Club, who herself was soon to follow Bentley down the same route. Leaving Lympne on 1 September 1927, Bentley reached Paris to find that his Customs triptyque had been left behind, and had to wait until it caught

* Cobham had made the journey in the opposite direction in fifteen days on returning from his survey flight, leaving at the same time as the *Windsor Castle* and just beating her on her voyage from Cape Town to Southampton.

him up by the regular service of Imperial Airways. After this the pilot kept to a regular routine of flying four to six hours each day and aimed to reach his daily destination by 3 p.m. to allow a comfortable period for checking over his machine and engine. On arriving at Kosti he made a halt of two days to investigate an unusual noise in his engine—attributed to a distorted cylinder—and at Kisumu, still not satisfied with its condition, he stopped to give it further attention. Apart from this, however, he encountered no difficulties, and although his intended time of fourteen days proved rather optimistic he was at Johannesburg on the twenty-fifth day and his arrival at Cape Town on 28 September caused a sensation, since the journey was by far the fastest ever made in this direction. Moreover, Bentley had thought it unnecessary to lay down spares along the route, relying entirely on the small quantity which he carried in the machine, so that much credit for the success was due to the reliability of the Moth and its Cirrus engine. *The Times* commented:

> Perhaps the greatest compliment that can be paid Lieutenant Bentley as an airman and to his Moth as a machine is to say that the flight was almost entirely without incident.

For this flight Bentley, like Stack and Leete, received the Air Force Cross.

By the end of 1927 Australia had yet to be reached from England by a light aeroplane, although one was proceeding there by slow stages. This machine, the first of the Mark III Avians with Cirrus III engine, was flown by Captain W. N. Lancaster and named (for fairly obvious reasons) *Red Rose*. It carried as passenger the wife of an Australian journalist, Mrs Keith Miller, and the flight, like Bentley's, received the support of newspapers, in this case the Melbourne *Herald* and the Sydney *Sun*. The original intention was that another Avian flown by Flying Officer Galpin should accompany Captain Lancaster's, but this plan came to nothing and *Red Rose* set out alone from Croydon on 14 October 1927. There were numerous delays along the route, and the coming of the New Year saw them only at Rangoon. Shortly after taking off from there for Tavoy on 2 January they had the unnerving experience of finding a live snake on board and Mrs Miller, displaying great resource, managed to kill it by hitting it with the spare control column, which was usually detached and stowed in the front cockpit when a passenger was being carried.

Meanwhile Bert Hinkler was making preparations for his third attempt at the journey. He had not been allowed to try for the Commonwealth Government's £10,000 prize in a Sopwith Dove in 1919 because his machine's range was thought insufficient, and in spite of his fine non-stop journey from Croydon to Turin in the Avro Baby the following year the authorities had withheld permission for him to cross the Syrian Desert.

He now chose an Avian, in fact the identical aeroplane which he had flown in the 1926 Lympne trials but with a Cirrus II engine fitted in place of the Genet, and set about embodying several ideas of his own to make the task of maintenance easier on the journey. One ingenious modification was to attach the undercarriage to the wings in such a way that when the wings were folded the wheels moved backwards and upwards in relation to the fuselage; in this way the nose was lowered to facilitate work on the high-set upright engine and at the same time the load on the tail-skid was reduced, making the machine easier to handle on the ground. He also constructed a simple form of lightweight vice which could be attached to a strut during maintenance operations and a special hand-pump for refuelling the aeroplane from tins placed on the ground.

From the financial point of view Hinkler's flight was decidedly a gamble. He had given up his job of test pilot to A. V. Roe and Company in order to undertake it, his funds were extremely limited and his wife was to remain behind in England, so that an accident somewhere along the route would have left him in a serious position. He was an exceptional pilot and mechanic, with qualities once described as 'gentleness, kindliness, magnificent endurance and stubborn determination', but it was not in his nature to thrust himself forward and therefore the monetary support which a more forceful individual might have gained did not come his way, although the ever-helpful Sir Charles Wakefield put up some of the £730 which the Avian cost him.

His preparations were simple but thorough. He took with him an alarm-clock to ensure an early start after each night's halt and a rubber boat for extra safety in case of a descent into the sea. A complete set of proper maps would have been a great expense to buy and he therefore cut up an atlas and stuck the pieces on to card, the best of the maps thus made having a scale of 30 miles to the inch, and left the deficiencies to be made up by his own skill at navigation. By way of a preliminary test of his machine's range and fuel consumption, he carried out a non-stop flight of 1,200 miles from Croydon to Riga in September 1927, at the time when Bentley was on his way to the Cape. After this test he did not set out at once, being occupied with an attempt to reach India non-stop with Captain R. H. McIntosh in the same Fokker monoplane which later carried the Duchess of Bedford on some of her long journeys, but the attempt ended unsuccessfully and by the beginning of February he was again making preparations for his projected solo flight. The early hours of 7 February saw him installed in his Avian at Croydon, and at 6.48 a.m. he was in the air bound for the far side of the earth.

The whole of that cold winter day he sat in his open cockpit flying on across France and over the Alps until the short daylight failed as he carried on down the length of Italy. The last three hours to Rome were flown in darkness, and when he arrived over the city no aerodrome lights were visible and he was forced to put the Avian down as best he could. It was not until after he had landed that a well-meaning aerodrome official fired off a rocket which almost set the machine on fire and ended the enterprise before it had fairly begun. This first stage of 1,100 miles non-stop in fourteen hours was a magnificent start, but his task was not over when he switched off at the end of the day's flying, for like all the early solo pilots he was his own mechanic and had always to refuse the rest and hospitality offered him until the essential schedule of work on his engine had been completed.

The next day's run was shorter, only 450 miles to Malta, and then, unable to complete the long stage to Tobruk because of a head wind, he landed the Avian in the desert and spent the night in his rubber boat under its wings, clearing clumps of thorn in the morning to make a take-off path. His next difficulty was that he could not land in Egypt, having failed to give the necessary two weeks' notice, so he tried to fly directly on to the R.A.F. station of Ramleh in Palestine but was again forced to land in the desert seventy miles short of his destination. Having reached Ramleh he spent a whole day using the facilities of the R.A.F. for a careful inspection and overhaul of his machine, making up the time lost by flying right through to Shaibah, near Basra, the next day. Thereafter he carried on steadily, covering six or seven hundred miles each day, and on the thirteenth day out from England he was at Singapore. Here he overtook the unlucky Captain Lancaster and Mrs Keith Miller, who had met with further delays on their way down the Malay peninsula. Two more days of flying took him to Bima, on the island of Sumbawa, and then, unlike most of those who later followed this route, he decided to omit a landing on the island of Timor itself and instead to fly the thousand miles to Darwin in a single stage. To ensure an early start he slept on the aerodrome rather than go into the town of Bima 15 miles away, and a night made restless by mosquitoes was ended by the clatter of the alarm-clock at 4 a.m. The Avian was quickly in the air, cruising at 2,000 ft above the lonely Timor Sea, and the islands were soon left behind; at about 4 p.m., after interminable hours spent between blue sky and blue water, the desolate northern shores of Hinkler's own country at last came into view on the horizon.

Hundreds of people had waited at the Darwin aerodrome all the afternoon scanning the western sky, but had dispersed again after a wireless message from the cruiser *Melbourne* had announced that nothing had been seen of the Avian. It was almost six o'clock in the evening when the tiny machine at last came into sight over Fanny Bay and began its glide in to land, bringing its pilot home to find a permanent place in aviation

history. Hinkler, worn out and sleepy, was welcomed by the Government
resident and hustled into the town of Darwin, where at a reception in the
Victoria Hotel a bag containing 476 telegrams was thrust into his hand.
One, from the Royal Aero Club in London, consisted of the single word
'Bravo'. At the end of a short stay at Darwin, Hinkler was away again
bound for his native Bundaberg, over 1,600 miles further on, and he
promptly vanished in the vast spaces of the Northern Territory. After an
anxious wait for news the public learned with relief that he had found the
combination of fatigue and the furious heat of a North Australian February
too much for him, had landed for a drink between Brunette Downs and
Alexandria and had easily been persuaded to stay the night. His reception
at Bundaberg was tremendous; the whole population turned out to greet
him and he was escorted through the town by an immense procession
which included the local fire-engine and four brass bands. All his financial
worries for the future had now entirely vanished, for his flight, which had
cost him in direct expenses only £50, brought him a flood of commercial
offers in addition to a gift of £500 from the Queensland Government, one
of £2,000 from the Commonwealth Government, the rank of honorary
squadron leader in the Royal Australian Air Force and the award of the
Air Force Cross.

What was the significance of Hinkler's flight? He had covered the
distance between England and India in seven days and that between
England and Australia in fifteen days, both journeys being by a considerable margin the fastest ever made in the world's history, and over the
whole 11,000 miles, the longest light aeroplane flight ever made, he had
flown and maintained his little Avian entirely single-handed. Though himself no amateur, he had established that a light aeroplane costing only a
few hundred pounds could be used to travel quickly, cheaply and un-
eventfully over a distance almost equal to half the circumference of the
globe, and had been the first to show the way along a route which was
shortly to be followed by many less experienced pilots in similar machines.
This flight had none of the desperate quality which later crept into record-
breaking, driving pilots dangerously near the limits of human endurance,
but was instead a competent demonstration of what aviation had to offer,
given at a time when there were many who had still to be convinced. It was
a splendid achievement (Map p. 249).

Meanwhile, Captain Lancaster and Mrs Keith Miller followed on in
Hinkler's track, their performance now much overshadowed by his own.
At the aerodrome of Muntok, situated on a small island off the north coast
of Sumatra, the Avian crashed, injuring them both slightly and damaging
itself severely. There were no facilities for it to be repaired locally and it
had to be shipped back to Singapore, whence eventually it set out again.

This time there were no difficulties; the last two thousand miles were covered in good time and the travellers arrived at Darwin on 9 March, nearly five months after leaving Croydon.*

After Hinkler's flight the rest of 1928 saw attention largely focused on the Cape route again, with women pilots playing a leading part. In the previous October Mrs Elliott-Lynn, who was a widow, had married Sir James Heath, and shortly afterwards the couple departed by sea for South Africa taking with them a new Mark III Avian G-EBUG. During her stay of several months in the Union, Lady Heath did much to stimulate the growing interest which was being shown in the light aeroplane movement in that country, and the passenger flights which she gave raised the sum of £1,200 in support of the clubs. Then, early in 1928, she made plans to fly her machine home alone by the eastern route, and set off from Pretoria on 17 February, her aeroplane heavily loaded with 112 lbs of luggage and equipment which included engine spares, medical supplies, day dresses, an evening dress, tennis rackets, a Bible and a shotgun and cartridges in preparation for every possibility of success or failure. (The tennis rackets and some other inessential items were thrown overboard to lighten the machine when the high altitudes of East Africa were reached.) She was accompanied as far as Warmbaths, about a hundred miles north of Johannesburg, by the pioneer African airman Sir Pierre van Ryneveld, but from here onwards she struck out on her own. Approaching Bulawayo over the Matopo country she had the terrifying experience of being overcome by sunstroke while in the air. She was flying without a helmet and was suddenly afflicted with severe pains in the head and the back of the neck, accompanied by a sensation of approaching unconsciousness. She at once throttled back her engine at 6,000 ft and headed the Avian towards grassland, but of what happened after this she could later remember nothing; somehow the machine landed without damage and she awoke to find herself under some thorn bushes with milk being dabbed on her head by three native girls. In due course she was put to bed in a nearby farm and her aeroplane was flown to Bulawayo, whence she resumed her journey after she had fully recovered.

As a woman flying alone she was forbidden to cross the troubled areas of the Sudan, but fortunately an escort was easily arranged; Lieutenant Bentley, now just married, had installed his bride in the front cockpit of his Moth (which had been presented to him by the Johannesburg *Star* in recognition of his flight) and was proceeding northwards through Africa on a leisurely honeymoon journey back to England. He readily consented

---

* Five years later Captain Lancaster disappeared in the Sahara while trying to fly solo to the Cape. It was not until 1962 that his body and the wreckage of his Avian were discovered in the sand.

to act as escort as far as Khartoum, and from there Lady Heath was able to carry on alone to complete the first solo flight ever made between the Cape and Cairo, 5,132 miles in seventy-two flying hours. The final stage to Cairo from Wadi Halfa was the longest (700 miles), and as the Avian pursued its slow way down the interminable length of the Nile its pilot read a novel and ate chocolates to alleviate her boredom, until with her destination in sight she felt impelled to prepare for the reception which awaited her by donning a pair of silk stockings in the air before landing and finally celebrated her arrival at Heliopolis with a series of loops over the aerodrome. At Cairo she was again recommended to arrange for an escort along the North African coast and across the Mediterranean, and she obtained the services of an Italian military seaplane by the simple expedient of sending a telegram addressed 'Mussolini, Italy'. Unfortunately, the seaplane itself was forced down in the water with engine trouble and the crew had to be rescued. The stony aerodrome at Sollum caused the whole rear part of the Avian's fuselage to break off on landing, and there was some delay while it was repaired. On 6 May she made the crossing from Tunis to Naples, escorted once again by the Bentleys in their Moth, and wearing round her waist a couple of motor-cycle inner tubes in case of a descent into the sea. These safeguards did not last long, for over-inflation at ground level caused them to burst after a climb to 7,000 ft. Her long and leisurely journey came to an end when she landed at Croydon on 17 May, emerging from her cockpit wearing a fashionable dress and a black straw hat to face the crowds which had gathered to welcome her (Plate 32).

After Lieutenant Bentley's return to England he took the post of instructor to the Liverpool and District Aero Club at Hooton Park for the summer, and when autumn came he and his wife set out for Africa again in the same Moth, which had been brought up to date by the fitting of the more powerful Cirrus III engine. When they reached Malakal it was thought safer for Mrs Bentley to travel the next stage to Mongalla across the troubled areas in a large three-engined Fokker which was being flown out to East Africa on a big-game hunting tour by Lieutenant-Commander Glen Kidston. As it turned out, however, she would have fared better in the Moth, for the Fokker was forced down in wild country and the five occupants had to be rescued by motor-boat, whereas Bentley, flying solo, completed the journey without incident. The couple travelled on to Pretoria, and not long afterwards Bentley made yet another flight up the length of Africa in the same veteran Moth, this time taking a business man as passenger from Johannesburg to Frankfurt in Germany.

While Lady Heath was flying northward towards Cairo, another equally indefatigable airwoman, who had also learned to fly at the London

Aeroplane Club at Stag Lane, set out in a Cirrus Moth in the opposite direction. This was Lady Bailey, wife of the South African millionaire Sir Abe Bailey, who had launched Lieutenant Bentley's Moth on its success-ful journey to the Cape in the previous September. She was no bright and irresponsible young thing, but a woman approaching middle age and the mother of a large family, and like Lady Heath she did not intend in any sense to break records. Instead, as she modestly explained on her return to England, she 'wished simply to reach the Cape to see her husband, did not at first know if she could do it, but found everything all right and thought how interesting it would be to go on'. She left Croydon on 9 March, reached Khartoum on 5 April and was escorted thence to Malakal by the obliging Lieutenant Bentley, who had just performed the same service for Lady Heath in the opposite direction. Having reached Kisumu she found herself without a map for the next stage to Tabora in Tan-ganyika, but cheerfully set off none the less to follow the shore of Lake Victoria and the railway. Being unable to find Tabora, she landed at Shinyanga to enquire the way and then flew on to her destination only to damage her Moth severely in a crash on landing owing to the unfamiliar condition of increased landing speed at the high altitude.

This setback might have led many people to abandon the whole enter-prise, but Lady Bailey was not deterred; she merely telegraphed to her husband, who arranged for a new Moth to be flown up to her from the Cape by an officer of the South African Air Force, and after a delay of only twelve days at Tabora she was in the air again—a remarkable demonstra-tion of the world-wide nature of the de Havilland sales and service organi-sation in these early days. The last stage of her flight was an especially uncomfortable one, with mist and cloud driven by a strong and bumpy wind over the hills, but eventually she managed to find a way through to Cape Town and her greeting to her husband after she had taxied the Moth in at the Wynberg aerodrome was a casual one: 'Hello, Abe, how are you? I am a bit late, but I got muddled up in the mountains'.

Lady Bailey was not content, however, to complete the journey in one direction only and to be the first woman ever to have done so. After a stay of some months in the Union she decided that owing to the political diffi-culties of traversing the Sudan she would return to England by the more westerly route through the Belgian Congo and French West Africa, but since no one had flown over this route from South Africa before she was forced to set out with very little idea of what was available in the way of petrol supplies and landing facilities. Her maps were also of the sketchiest, and for the section from Salisbury to Elizabethville she had to rely on an extremely small-scale map in booklet form issued by the Union Castle steamship line. Quite undeterred by these deficiencies she set out from

Broken Hill in September 1928 and was pleasantly surprised to find an adequate chain of aerodromes all the way through Belgian and French territory as far as Dakar, after which she was able to follow the Aéropostale route along the desolate West African coast, finally reaching Croydon in January 1929 after having covered 18,000 miles alone by air since leaving England. On the return journey she met with no real setbacks, although there were the usual minor adventures. Landing on one occasion near a remote village to ask the way, she bent the axle of the Moth and had to borrow a horse from the local chief to go in search of a mechanic, and her subsequent presentation of some dress material to him in recognition of his kindness was at once countered by the embarrassing gift of six eggs and two live chickens. These had to be stowed away in the luggage locker of the Moth and the chickens arrived at the next aerodrome perfectly contented after their unusual experience.

These African flights of Lady Heath and Lady Bailey were exceptionally fine ones by any standards, and it must be remembered that they were undertaken in an age when women's emancipation was still a comparatively recent issue, hardly yet accepted by many of the older generation. They traversed vast areas where an aeroplane was still a complete novelty. Engine failure over large segments of the route would have been fatal, or unpleasant in the extreme, and the maintenance of the aircraft was in both cases largely carried out by their pilots without assistance. Lady Bailey in particular was a relatively inexperienced pilot who confessed that she had little knowledge of technical matters, so that she looked after her aeroplane purely by following the routine which she had been taught. Her flight, aptly described by the Air Minister, Lord Thomson, as 'just pottering round Africa', was therefore a striking example of the capabilities of the light aeroplane used as simply and naturally as a motor-car in the hands of the ordinary non-professional owner-pilot (Map p. 207).

There were other African flights in 1928, a year when the Moth and the Avian were beginning to carry their owners far and wide across the globe in rapidly-increasing numbers. Lieutenant Patrick Murdoch, a brother officer of Bentley, made an attempt to fly to the Cape and back in 24 days (Plate 33), but though he accomplished the outward trip in thirteen and a half days various misfortunes delayed his return and finally the Avian hit a tree, crashed and caught fire while flying low over forest country in the Congo. Fortunately he escaped uninjured. While he was waiting at the Cape to begin his return journey, a fellow-countryman, Captain S. S. Halse, who had been a pilot in the R.F.C., set out from England with his wife in a brand-new Gipsy Moth to fly back to his South African farm. On their way they encountered the Bentleys, who were bound in the same direction after their summer in England. Such meetings on remote aerodromes between aerial travellers were becoming increasingly common; another occurred on Boxing Day 1928 when Captain R. L. Rattray, flying alone from England to the Gold Coast in his Cirrus Moth, arrived at Mogador in Morocco to find the returning Lady Bailey there in a similar machine.

The coming of the Gipsy Moth inspired many air tourists to long journeys and among the most ambitious of these was the flight through Europe, North Africa, Asia and America undertaken by the Vicomte and Vicomtesse de Sibour in 1928 and 1929. They fitted their new silver and cobalt Gipsy Moth *Safari* with extra fuel tanks and departed from Stag Lane on 14 September 1928. The first part of their journey took them south through France and Spain to Gibraltar and then by easy stages along the North African coast to Cairo. Here they too overtook the Bentleys on their way home to South Africa, and were greeted by a telephone message from Heliopolis stating that Captain Halse, now some hundreds of miles south of Cairo, had broken his propeller and urgently needed a spare. The Sibours, who were carrying a spare propeller themselves, immediately transferred it to the Bentleys' machine and watched it vanish to the southward to the aid of their fellow airman. Luckily their own propeller remained intact for the rest of their journey.

There was a long delay at Baghdad with engine trouble, and eventually the aeroplane was taken on by sea to Karachi. Here the old engine was exchanged for a new one through the kindness of the new Karachi flying club, and when they had seen the club officially opened at Drigh Road aerodrome the travellers continued on their way across India. Later, while trying to reach Bangkok, they were forced down on the restricted space of Moulmein racecourse, to be informed gloomily by a local resident that their Moth was the third aeroplane to visit Moulmein and that the other two had crashed. On leaving they came near to continuing this unfortunate tradition, for the engine cowling, which had not been properly fastened, flew open just after taking off and they only just succeeded in getting through a gap in the trees and making a circuit and landing to put it right. The rest of the journey to Indo-China was relatively uneventful and in due course the Moth was loaded on to a steamer for the crossing to the United States. After flying it across that country and visiting the Vicomtesse's native city of Chicago, the couple crossed to Havre by sea and had the machine erected again for the final stage to England, which they reached in the middle of July 1929 after a journey of 33,000 miles carried out in the space of ten months.

Lieutenant-Commander H. C. MacDonald took his 'A' licence at Stag Lane just before Easter of 1928 and only a fortnight later set off for India in his own Gipsy Moth. This flight had the usual share of adventures, including a forced landing in North Africa which resulted in the pilot's capture by hostile Arabs and subsequent rescue by Italian armoured cars, but after his return to England MacDonald was tempted by the experience he had gained to try the far more hazardous feat of an Atlantic crossing in his little machine. Inspired perhaps by Captain Broad's demonstration of flying a Moth non-stop for 24 hours in August, he equipped his aircraft with tankage for 100 gallons of fuel, which in favourable conditions should have carried him from Newfoundland to Britain, and set out from St John's on 17 October, very late in the year for an attempt on a stretch of water notorious for its unpredictable weather conditions. MacDonald's tiny bi-plane was sighted by a ship when 600 miles out from land and then, like more than a few others in the past year, it vanished for ever. Since Lindbergh's success in the previous year the Atlantic had been much in the news and there had been a number of attempts to fly across it in either direction, many of them disastrous. The Moth had many virtues as a long-distance aeroplane for the amateur, but to attempt such a long flight out of sight of land in so slow a machine with few aids to navigation was too much of a gamble.

The Blackburn Bluebird in its wooden form achieved little in the way of long-distance flying, but the all-metal version—the Bluebird IV—had more success, although it was never so widely used as the Moth and Avian. The prototype of the all-metal version, G-AABV, fitted with a Gipsy engine, was bought not very long after its first flight by Squadron Leader L. H. Slatter and flown by him to his home in South Africa on leave. He left Croydon in March 1929 in company with the India-bound Moth of Captain Donald Drew and Mrs Hylton-Cleaver, and after an overhaul at Aboukir and the fitting of a new petrol tank the Bluebird reached Durban safely in rather more than a month, while the Moth went its separate way to Karachi and in due course returned to England.

By 1929 that which had only a few years earlier been a matter for wonder had become commonplace, and many a Moth or Avian, Bluebird or Widgeon was carrying its owners on their journeys about the world entirely unremarked. Five years before, after the two-seater competitions at Lympne, it had been possible for the Press to comment with surprise on the fact that Hinkler had flown a light aeroplane from Lympne back to Hamble, a journey of a hundred miles across English fields, 'entirely without incident'. Now far greater journeys failed to reach the headlines, for the light aeroplane had already come to be accepted as just another means of transport, and in order for a flight to be worthy of more than the briefest mention in the Press it was necessary for the time taken to constitute a record or for the pilot to be especially noteworthy as to age, sex or other qualities.

Particularly remarkable, too, is the safety of the light biplane of that day in relatively inexperienced hands. Minor mishaps of the kind which provide harmless amusement to all but the unlucky pilot were plentiful enough, and the forlorn sight of a Moth or Avian on its nose or upside down after a landing in soft ground or an unskilful attempt to take off was not too uncommon either on home fields and aerodromes or down the long routes of the Empire. On the whole, however, these aeroplanes suffered fools gladly, and their low landing speed and light but sturdy wing structure, capable of absorbing much of the shock in an accident, meant that little harm resulted to their occupants even after the most spectacular of crashes. In these early years, when so many comparative novices had begun to venture in light aeroplanes over jungle and desert, sea and mountain, with engines which were considerably less reliable than those of today, the number of fatalities and serious injuries was negligibly small. All forms of transport have their special risks, and if a comparable fleet of small boats manned by single-handed sailors, some of whom had done little more than a fortnight's cruising round the Solent, had been sent out to find their way independently with watch, chart and compass to Australia and the Cape, it is hard to believe that they would have met with fewer disasters than the pioneering pilots whose adventures have just been described. The successful completion of each flight in safety made its small contribution to the future of aviation as a whole, and little by little the achievements of the light aeroplane prepared the way for today's world-wide acceptance of flying as an everyday means of transport.

Towards the Monoplane
1930–34

Throughout the 1920s the majority of small aircraft built in this country were fitted with air-cooled four-cylinder in-line engines of upright type such as the Cirrus and the Gipsy, most of the remainder having small radial engines such as the Genet and Pobjoy and a small minority the horizontally-opposed A.B.C. Scorpion or Hornet or the Bristol Cherub, but the year 1930 witnessed an important engine development which was to alter the appearance of the British light aeroplane for several decades to follow. Major Halford's Gipsy I of 100 h.p. was followed early in 1930 by the Gipsy II, a more refined version with enclosed valve-gear and a longer stroke offering an increased power output of 120 h.p., and at about the same time an inverted form of this engine made its appearance as the Gipsy III.

Arranging for an engine to run inverted, that is to say with the cylinders below the crankshaft, brings with it certain problems of which the most obvious is that of adequately lubricating the bores without oil draining down into the cylinder heads, but this difficulty was overcome by using suitable baffles and by incorporating a dry-sump oil system with separate tank in place of the car-type sump below the crankcase which had been employed on the upright types. The advantages of the inverted arrangement were numerous, so much so that the upright engine quickly became obsolete for aircraft use. In the first Cirrus Moths the pilot had been confronted with a forest of exposed valve gear on top of a line of high-set cylinders, and although on later models the engine had been lowered the improvement of forward view so obtained was not nearly so striking as that offered by the smooth cowling line covering the crankcase of a Gipsy III. Further, the raising of the thrust-line produced by inversion enabled a lower undercarriage to be used without detriment to the ground clearance of the propeller, and at the same time the vital parts of the engine were brought within comfortable reach of a man standing on the ground, so that maintenance was made far easier.

The Gipsy III was used as the basis for an important new type of cabin monoplane in direct line of descent from the Moth, intended as a luxurious and fast tourer for the private owner or air-taxi operator. This machine was for a short time called the Moth Three after its new engine, but soon received the name of Puss Moth by which it was quickly to become famous for its performances at long-distance flying (Plate 34). The prototype, which flew at Stag Lane in September 1929, was a two-seater built entirely of wood, but in production the fuselage structure was radically changed to follow the technique of metal construction which had been used in the larger Hawk Moth a year or two earlier, being built up entirely of welded steel tube in three portions which were then bolted together. Square-section tube was used for the front two portions and round tube for the lighter rear part, and when the steel framework was complete, light wooden stringers were clipped on to the outside to support the fabric covering. The original cabin doors were both on the starboard side, but this was replaced by a far more convenient arrangement of motor-car type with a door on each side. The wooden wings differed from those of the Desoutter in that instead of being in one piece they were separately hinged to fittings on the top longerons and braced by V-struts, allowing a transparent panel to be provided above the occupants' heads to give them the upward view often lacking in high-wing monoplanes and to provide a means of emergency exit after a forced descent into water. Other features included in the price of £1,000 were dual controls, wheel brakes, a fitted map board for the pilot, provision for an occasional third seat beside the passenger, and standard tankage for over five hours' flying.

Compared with its biplane antecedents the Puss Moth was a very clean machine, capable of cruising at over 100 m.p.h. and 20 m.p.g., so that one of its characteristics was a very flat gliding angle (1 in 11) and a tendency to 'float' which made getting into small spaces difficult.* To steepen the glide for landing it was therefore arranged that the streamlined casings of the main undercarriage compression legs could be rotated through 90° by means of a lever in the cockpit, thus offering a braking surface to the air-flow and increasing the angle of descent to 1 in 7, a figure comparable with that of the average biplane. These air-brakes had the great advantage that their centre of resistance was so placed as to cause no change of trim when they were opened, and moreover—unlike the wing-flaps which were soon to come into general use—they could be opened and closed at will, without danger of the machine suddenly sinking owing to loss of lift.

The inverted Gipsy III was also used in place of the Cirrus-Hermes

---

* One well-known pilot, accustomed to biplanes, made a number of attempts to land one of the early Puss Moths at Brooklands and finally gave it up, returning to his starting place and saying that 'there wasn't enough room'.

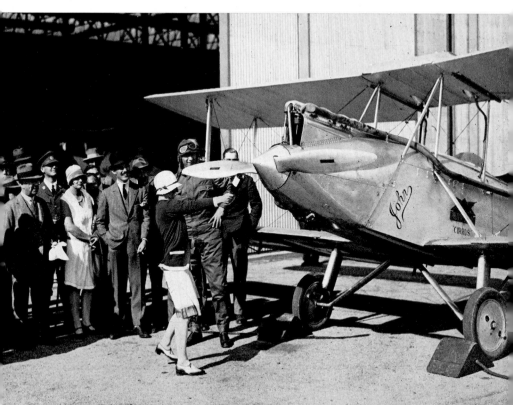

32. Lady Heath in front of her Avian after completing her flight from the Cape to Croydon in May 1928

33. The 'launching' of Lieutenant Patrick Murdoch's Avian before his flight to the Cape in July 1928

34. The de Havilland Puss Moth used by Mr J. A. Mollison
35. A rival to the Moth, Bluebird and Avian: the Robinson Redwing
of 1930

in the Desoutter II of 1930, and the manufacturers were able to take advantage of the better ground clearance offered by the higher thrust-line to fit a shorter undercarriage. At the same time they introduced many other improvements including re-designed windows for better vision, pilot's seat adjustment, individual passenger seats with fitted suitcases beneath them, a re-designed tail unit with trimming tailplane and a larger fuel tank giving a range of 500 miles. In this form the Desoutter had a long career at air-taxi work and one example was still surviving in Australia as late as 1959.

In 1930 the Gipsy Moth was flowing from Stag Lane in such numbers that a further substantial price reduction was possible. The standard all-wood Gipsy I Moth, finished in a uniform colour scheme of silver surfaces and azure blue fuselage with black registration letters, could now be obtained brand new for £595, and this price included standard instruments, parachute seats, a luggage compartment with lock, speaking tubes, a tool kit, log books and covers for engine, airscrew and cockpits.

By paying a little more the purchaser could specify a steel fuselage, the Gipsy II engine, or the seaplane version of any model, and the very wide range of accessories available included a coupé top, cockpit heater, slots, aerobatic harness, streamlined headrest, pneumatic cushions, rubber floor mats, various extra instruments, a specially finished exhaust pipe and silencer and a large variety of extra fuel tanks for increased range. The makers were thus in a position to meet the requirements of practically any customer, and it was not surprising that Moths sold quickly at home and abroad. To save flying clubs the expense of buying their own machines, the de Havilland company in its usual enterprising way instituted a hire scheme under which new wooden Moths could be supplied fully equipped and insured for a monthly payment of £60, reducing to £50 for periods exceeding six months.

A pretty biplane which achieved a more limited success as a club aeroplane in the early 1930s was the Robinson Redwing (Plate 35), designed by Mr John Kenworthy and therefore a descendant of the Austin Whippet of 1919. It was conventionally built of wood with folding wings and a wide cockpit situated immediately below the centre-section and seating two side by side; behind the cockpit was a large compartment for luggage. The control system was noteworthy in that it used cables only in straight lengths without pulleys or fairleads, extensive use being made of push-rods to achieve this end, and with the instructional uses of his design well in mind Mr Kenworthy had provided a split type oleo undercarriage of wide track with the compression legs carried up to the top fuselage longerons. The Redwing was placed on the market at £575 with Genet IIA engine and full equipment and saw service with a number of flying clubs, notably the London Omnibus Company's club at Broxbourne in Essex, the Eastern Counties Flying Club at Colchester (whither the manufacturers later transferred themselves from their original works at Croydon) and the Wiltshire School of Flying at High Post near Amesbury. A feature of the Redwing was its generous wing area to ensure a low landing speed, but this naturally resulted in a somewhat modest cruising speed, and a version with drastically reduced area—the Redwing III—was offered in 1933, but found little favour.

The novel interchangeability feature of the Simmonds Spartan had dictated the use of a wing of symmetrical section so that a given half-wing could be fitted either way up, but it was found in practice that the stalling qualities of the section used caused some concern, and in 1930 the manufacturers of the machine, now called Spartan Aircraft Limited, produced a replacement type with cambered Clark Y-section which was called the Spartan Arrow. Considerable ingenuity was brought to bear on the problem of retaining interchangeability; the rear portion of each wing was made removable from the cambered front portion, and a system of detachable tips with provision for fitting an aileron at either end enabled a single half-wing still to be adapted for fitting in any of the four possible positions on the machine. Apart from this change and a new shape for the fin and rudder, however, the two-seater Arrow and a three-seater version which was built for joy-riding were structurally closely similar to the original Simmonds Spartan of 1928.

After his activities in the years of the Lympne trials it was not surprising that on leaving the Royal Air Force in 1929 Nicholas Comper should have gathered a few friends together to finance the setting up of the Comper Aircraft Company at Hooton Park aerodrome near Liverpool, with himself as chief designer and managing director. The first of the new company's products was the little single-seater Comper Swift or C.L.A.7, which was a natural development of the C.L.A.3 racer of a few years earlier. In the Swift, however, Comper had greatly improved on the aerodynamic cleanness of his original parasol design by placing the wing directly on top of the fuselage and the pilot was accommodated in an open cockpit situated immediately behind the wing in a cutout in the trailing edge. The Swift was made entirely of wood with a girder-type fuselage built up in three sections and wings of conventional two-spar type braced with V-struts and capable of being folded to a width of only 7 ft 6 ins. The undercarriage arrangement was especially neat with its rubber-cord suspension totally enclosed in the fuselage, and the total loaded weight of only 600 lbs ensured a lively performance for the first machine even on the limited power of its A.B.C. Scorpion II engine.

In its original form the Swift was placed on the market at £400 as a cheap aeroplane which would enable pilots who had already obtained their 'A' licences to keep flying at a moderate cost. Its suitability as a racing machine was evident, however, and some Swifts were soon equipped with more powerful engines in order to exploit the high-speed potentialities of the compact airframe. The association of Comper and Pobjoy which had

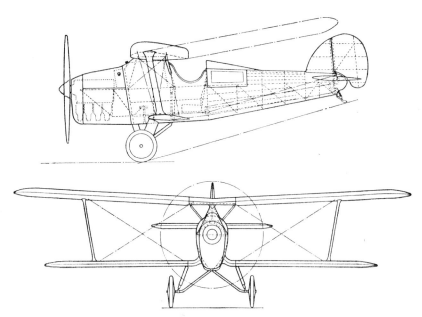

7. The Arrow Active, a single-seat sporting biplane of 1931 built entirely of metal

met with bad luck on the occasion of the 1926 Lympne trials was revived when the latter came to Hooton to begin manufacture of his light geared radial engine, and when a development of the original 'P' engine, the 75-h.p. Pobjoy R, made its appearance in 1931 it was quickly fitted to the Swift. It is perhaps the Pobjoy-Swift which has gained the most secure place in aviation history with its racing successes and long-distance flights, and one or two machines of this type still remain in flying order today, competing in air races as they began to do over thirty years ago; but it is worth remarking that the few Swifts which were fitted with the 130-h.p. Gipsy Major engine later in the 1930s (Plate 42) were capable, after the aerodynamic cleaning-up which is customary for racing purposes, of a top speed little short of 170 m.p.h. None of Comper's later designs, original though they all were, came near to achieving the wide appeal and the versatility of the Swift, and it is by this single type above all others that his name is remembered today.

    Somewhat similar in intention to the Swift was the Arrow Active, a small single-seater biplane which was almost a miniature replica of the fighter aeroplane of its day (Figure 7); it was produced in 1931 by Messrs Thornton and Oddy of the Arrow Aircraft Company of Leeds. Mr A. C. Thornton had previously been with the Blackburn company and had been closely concerned with the metal Bluebird, so that he was able to put his experience to good use in the new design, which was also made entirely of metal. The fuselage of the Active consisted of three separately built sections, a forward one carrying the engine, a central one of almost monocoque type with a duralumin skin riveted to steel longitudinals and duralumin box frames, and a rear portion of triangular section with three tubular longerons, the whole being constructed without the use of welding. The wing spars were of rolled figure-eight section in high-tensile steel strip and carried built-up duralumin ribs with fabric covering. In spite of its considerable technical interest the little Active did not go into production, but the second machine of the two built—the Active II with Gipsy III engine —has of recent years been completely restored to flying order by the Tiger Club of Redhill.

For the private owner who is able to afford the greater cost of purchase and upkeep, the extra safety provided by a light twin-engined machine is an important point in its favour, and it was this consideration that led Hinkler to build his Ibis. An interesting twin-engined aeroplane whose advanced appearance was such that it would excite little comment if it were seen at an aerodrome today was the Segrave Meteor, a cabin four-seater with two inverted Gipsy III engines mounted upon a wing of full cantilever construction. The design was due to the well-known racing motorist Sir Henry Segrave, and was the embodiment of his ideas for a fast private or light commercial touring machine. The prototype was built on the Isle of Wight by Saunders-Roe Limited, but after Sir Henry's death in his racing boat 'Miss England' production was taken over by the Blackburn company, who radically altered the form of construction by converting the fuselage (originally of wood) into a metal stressed-skin structure. The three machines built in this form became known as Blackburn Segraves and they and the prototype saw some service with private owners and on charter duties. One of the Blackburn machines was later used for an interesting structural experiment when it was fitted with the Duncanson wing, whose single tubular duralumin spar effected a considerable weight saving and enabled the performance to be markedly improved.

Another form of single-spar wing formed the basis of what was perhaps the best-known and most successful of the light twin-engined aeroplanes of the 1930s, the Monospar. The wing was the invention of a Swiss engineer named H. J. Stieger, formerly of the Beardmore company, and was built upon a single fabricated duralumin spar of I-section whose resistance to torsion was immensely increased with little penalty in weight by the addition of a series of pyramidal tie-rods, forming in effect a double-helical coil round the spar. After several trial wings had been constructed in 1929 and 1930, a complete experimental aeroplane named the ST-3 was designed and built by the Gloster Aircraft Company in 1931, and this formed the basis of all future developments of the type. It was a low-wing cantilever monoplane with a cabin for three persons and two 50-h.p. British Salmson A.D.9 engines, which were at this time being manu-factured in England under licence from the French Salmson company, so that the advantages of twin engines were offered for a total power output less than that of a single Gipsy II. After extensive trials had been carried out with this machine a company known as General Aircraft Limited was established at Croydon and a four-seater version, the ST-4 with Pobjoy R engines, was put into production in 1932 and soon appeared in consider-able numbers. It was followed in 1933 by the ST-6, which had the unusual feature for its day of a retractable undercarriage which could be manually wound up into the engine nacelles to provide a useful improvement in speed. After the General Aircraft Company moved its works from Croy-don to Hanworth in 1934, an improved Monospar with more powerful Pobjoy engines known as the ST-10 was built, and it was in this prototype that Flight Lieutenant H. M. Schofield won the King's Cup of the same year (Plate 43). The development of this useful type of small aeroplane continued until 1939, and throughout the 1930s private and club-owned Monospars were a common sight at aeronautical gatherings and on aerodromes generally in this country and abroad.

An unsuccessful contemporary of the ST-3 was the twin-engined four-seater Henderson Falcon Four, a low-wing monoplane employing the Henderson type of wing construction and designed by the Southern Air-craft Company at Shoreham. Its most outstanding feature was the arrange-ment of the twin Cirrus-Hermes engines on stilts above the wing driving pusher propellers. It was unfortunate that this comparatively advanced design, which embodied such unusual features for its day as electric engine starters and differential wheel brakes, had to be abandoned before it reached the stage of flight testing.

The Henderson wing was also used in the Hendy 302, a cabin mono-plane of especially clean design which succeeded the Hobo and was designed as a fast machine for Captain Percival to fly in the 1930 King's Cup race. The construction was entrusted to the firm of George Parnall and Company, and the complete process of design, building and flight testing took only four months. The choice of the 105-h.p. Cirrus-Hermes engine allowed the nose to be neatly cowled, and the good lines of the machine were continued aft into a well faired and completely enclosed cabin seating two people in tandem. Two fuel tanks, each of 16 gallons capacity, installed in the wings and a nine-gallon gravity tank provided a cruising range of 750 miles, and although no slots or flaps were fitted the 302 had an excellent speed range, being able to land at only 44 m.p.h. with a top speed of 132 m.p.h. Captain Percival flew the machine as intended in the King's Cup and was reasonably successful although he was not placed, and he showed its capabilities further by subsequently flying it non-stop from England to Cannes in $5\frac{1}{2}$ hours and back in 6 hours (Plate 39).

A military development of the Moth appeared in 1931 in the shape of the Moth Trainer, with Gipsy II engine and metal fuselage, in which an increase of all-up weight and a new wing section allowed the carriage of the necessary equipment for a wide variety of training duties including air fighting, bombing, wireless and photography. The front cockpit of the ordinary civil Moth, situated under the top centre-section and normally occupied by the instructor or passenger, was not well adapted for the military need of a quick exit by parachute in emergency, and the Trainer was therefore modified by the provision of deeper doors to the front cockpit, a larger cutout in the wing trailing edge and a change in the wing-bracing arrangement so that the attachment point of the rear lift wires was carried forward to leave the lower wing-root free from obstruction. A more satisfactory solution was clearly to carry all the centre-section struts forward of the cockpits and to give stagger and sweep to the mainplanes to retain correct longitudinal balance, and it was not long before a new version of the Moth Trainer on these lines made its appearance fitted with the inverted Gipsy III. The changes made were sufficient to justify a new type number, so the D.H.60T was thus transmuted into the D.H.82 and was shortly afterwards given the name of Tiger Moth. Soon after this Major Halford increased the capacity of the Gipsy III to slightly over six litres to produce the 130-h.p. Gipsy IIIA or Major, and this engine was standardised for the Tiger Moth, a combination of aeroplane and engine which is still familiar thirty years later. Most of the Tiger Moths manufactured went to the Royal Air Force, to foreign air forces and to the Elementary and Reserve flying training schools, and it was not until 1937 that they began to replace the standard Moths of the ordinary civilian clubs. The Tiger Moth in the 1930s was thus largely a military training aeroplane, and its counterpart for the private owner was first the Gipsy III Moth and later (in 1934) the Gipsy Major Moth or Moth Major, the last of a long line.

The weight-carrying abilities of the light biplane, illustrated by Captain Broad's 24-hour flight, were further exploited in 1932 when the de Havilland company adapted standard Tiger Moth wings and tail unit to fit a specially designed plywood fuselage with a Gipsy III (later a Gipsy

Major) engine, wheel brakes, a tailwheel and a small cabin for four passengers in place of the single front cockpit of the military trainer. The pilot flew the machine from a cockpit aft of the cabin and could communicate with his passengers by means of telephones and a small shuttered window. The aeroplane which resulted, called the Fox Moth, was capable of lifting a disposable load almost equal to its own empty weight of 1,050 lbs and could therefore carry four passengers for short joy-rides, while with three passengers the fuel allowance was enough for a range of 350 miles. At its price of under £1,000 the Fox Moth was essentially intended as an economical commercial machine, and few were privately owned; the majority saw service for the transport of passengers and goods of all kinds, especially in the remoter regions of the world such as New Guinea, and even after the Second World War the Fox Moth was still being built in Canada to meet the requirements of 'bush' operators in that country.

Another—though less important—case of adaptation of old wings to new fuselages took place in the same year when the Spartan company built a cabin monoplane called the Clipper, with two seats side by side in a plywood fuselage, and outer wing panels identical with those used on the twin-engined Monospar ST-4. A Pobjoy radial engine was fitted at the extremity of a slender nose and the general appearance of the machine was pleasing, but only one Clipper was made, and after an uneventful life whose most important moment was its participation in the King's Cup Race of 1933, its days were ended by a German bomb on the Isle of Wight nine years later.

After the outstanding Avian, originally produced for the Lympne trials, A. V. Roe and Company continued the theme of the small two-seater biplane with a series of types which had something of the size and and solidity of the Service trainer in comparison with the lighter machines such as the Redwing or the Spartan. The Type 621 or Tutor, a military trainer intended as a replacement for the ageing 504, appeared in 1930 and was followed by the Type 626 advanced trainer, later put into R.A.F. service as the Prefect. These aeroplanes were of all-metal construction with fabric covering and were fitted with engines of relatively high power such as the Armstrong Siddeley Mongoose or Lynx. In 1931 appeared the Cadet, in effect the same design but of reduced size with wooden wings and a Genet Major engine, and in the following year the series ended with the Type 638 or Club Cadet. In the Tutor and Cadet the wings had been heavily staggered to provide for a satisfactory exit from the front cockpit in emergency, but since parachutes were not in common use with private owners and club pilots this feature was not carried into the Club Cadet and the wings were arranged without stagger to facilitate folding; in fact the procedure which had led from Moth to Tiger Moth was here put into reverse. The type underwent various modifications, including the fitting of in-line engines in place of the more usual Genet Major radial, and in addition to building a joy-riding version with a front cockpit seating two passengers the Avro company modified one Club Cadet as a cabin machine. This was not developed, but instead a larger single-engined cabin biplane intended as a luxury private-owner type on the lines of the American Waco and Beechcraft was later built at Woodford and named the Commodore. It carried four or five occupants in a roomy cabin at a cruising speed of 110 m.p.h. and enjoyed a limited popularity; five were sold in Britain and a sixth went overseas for the personal use of an Indian maharajah.

The all-metal Blackburn Bluebird IV was in due course fitted with the Gipsy III engine and a further development of the type made its first public appearance in the summer of 1932 using the same engine. This machine, called the B.2, was essentially a Bluebird in outward form but was strengthened to meet the needs of military training and had a fuselage which was completely covered in Alclad sheet in place of fabric. The B.2 in its production form with Cirrus-Hermes IVA engine was used almost exclusively by the Reserve schools and those built did not find their way into the hands of the flying clubs or private owners; when war broke out they continued in use as instructional machines, notably at their makers' aerodrome at Brough, but today only one—G-AEBJ—remains in existence, preserved in flying condition by its manufacturers.

After the great success of the Cygnets at Lympne the Hawker company almost entirely abandoned the light aeroplane in favour of larger military types, but one Service trainer of their manufacture found a limited use for private flying: the Hawker Tomtit, built to the standard pattern of the military trainer of its day with an all-metal structure covered with fabric, tandem open cockpits and an Armstrong Siddeley Mongoose radial engine. It appeared in civil form in small numbers from 1930 onwards and competed in the King's Cup race of that year and in other sporting events where its excellent aerobatic capabilities could be shown off to advantage. It was not until 1935, however, that the release of a number of these machines as obsolete by the R.A.F. caused them to pass into the hands of the clubs (in particular the Leicestershire Aero Club) and of such private owners as were more interested in pleasant handling qualities than in the cabin comfort which was by then readily available in light aircraft designed more specifically for civilian uses.

The R.A.E. Aero Club of Farnborough embarked on a further enterprise in aircraft building in 1930 and 1931 to the design of Mr P. G. N. Peters and Mr C. R. Brewer, and the result, named the P. B. Scarab after its designers' initials, first flew early in 1932 and rather resembled the Widgeon in its general layout, though it was considerably smaller and was a single-seater. The specification was similar to that laid down for the Motor Glider Competitions of 1923, which was hardly surprising since the machine was in fact simply an ingenious remodelling of the little D.H.53, the original low wing having been raised to the parasol position and arranged to fold and a split-axle type of undercarriage fitted. Equipped with the Bristol Cherub III engine of 1,228 c.c. (which would of course have excluded it from Lympne) and having a loaded weight of 650 lbs, the Scarab had a reasonable top speed of 78 m.p.h. and a rate of climb of some 600 ft/min.

When Captain Edgar Percival set up his own aircraft company he made use of the experience gained with the 302 to produce an entirely new design of cantilever low-wing type, which he named the Gull. The first machine (Plate 38), which appeared in 1932, was a three-seater with the occupants seated in clover-leaf layout, staggered laterally to provide leg-room and enclosed by a glazed lid hinged along one side of the fuselage. It embodied the Henderson type of wing torsion bracing, the patent rights in which were half owned by Captain Percival; for production, however, a lighter and less complicated form of wing bracing was devised by Percival and used.

The exceptional aerodynamic cleanness of the Gull* led to the usual problem of a flat glide on approaching to land, and therefore a small flap type of air brake was fitted under the fuselage in line with the leading edge of the wing. With the inverted Cirrus-Hermes IV engine of 130 h.p. the machine had the remarkable top speed of 147 m.p.h. and would cruise at 125 m.p.h. with three occupants and luggage and sufficient fuel for 700 miles. The 160-h.p. Napier Javelin engine later fitted to the prototype improved the maximum speed still further to 165 m.p.h. In these years the long-standing prejudice against the monoplane on the part of the designers of military and commercial aircraft was still strong, and as a result the standard fighter of the Royal Air Force, the Bristol Bulldog biplane with 450-h.p. Jupiter engine, was capable of flying only three miles an hour faster than the clean Javelin Gull.

The good qualities of the Gull quickly made it popular, and production in quantity began in 1933, the first batch of machines being built for Percival by the Parnall company at Yate, near Bristol. They were identical with the first aircraft in all important particulars, although small improvements were made to the wind-screen and cabin top. As an alternative to the two engines already mentioned, some Gulls were fitted with the Gipsy Major. In 1934 the Percival Aircraft Company began to construct its

---

* On applying the Everling formula for overall aerodynamic efficiency in its technical appraisal of the Gull, the journal *Flight* remarked that the efficiency figure so obtained was the highest ever recorded up to that time.

own aeroplanes in its new works at Gravesend, and when the de Havilland company announced its new six-cylinder engine, the 200-h.p. Gipsy Six, this was quickly used in the clean Gull airframe to produce the Gull Six, which in its various forms has a good claim to have been the most widely used of all light aeroplanes used for long distance flying in the years immediately before the war.

The motor-glider of Lympne days, offering cheap flying at very low speed, had been in eclipse in the late 1920s, when the more powerful biplanes typified by the Moth were in the ascendant. In 1932, however, when pure gliding had begun to flourish once again as a sport, there appeared a small economical single-seater of true motor-glider type. In November of that year Mr C. H. Lowe Wylde, who was at this time managing director and designer of a small glider-building concern named the British Aircraft Company of Maidstone, introduced a version of his B.A.C. VII glider on which had been mounted a Douglas motor-cycle engine of only 600 c.c., a capacity well within the 1923 rules at Lympne. The Planette, as the Lowe Wylde 'baby' was first called, attracted much attention on its first appearance, since it was economical in fuel and had the low landing speed of a glider and extremely safe flying characteristics. At the first demonstration of the type at Hanworth early in the New Year of 1933, the pioneer pilot Mr Claude Grahame-White took himself into the air in one with his cap back to front in the manner of the old days, though he had not flown since 1921.

Unfortunately, however, the Planette's designer was killed in one of his machines in the following summer, an accident apparently due to no fault in the aircraft but to his fainting in the air, and the Austrian gliding expert Herr Robert Kronfeld then took over the firm and began production of a modified version at Hanworth, fitting a Douglas Sprite engine and giving it the name of Drone. Under this more familiar name the type continued in various developed forms throughout the 1930s and offered a relatively cheap way into the air for many people (Plate 36).

Not long after the appearance of the Lowe Wylde single-seaters a monoplane employing the same pusher layout made its first flight at Sherburn-in-Elmet. It was in part due to Mr W. S. Shackleton, designer of the A.N.E.C. and Wee Bee, who after a period in Australia had returned to England to set up in business as a consultant at 175 Piccadilly, London. His partner in this enterprise was an Australian pilot, Mr Lee Murray, who had travelled to England by way of the United States and Canada. While there he had been struck by the virtues of the pusher type of light aeroplane as exemplified by the Curtiss Junior, so that when in 1932 the two partners began the design of a small two-seater according to their own ideas, it was this arrangement that they decided to adopt.

The Shackleton-Murray or S.M.1 (Plate 37) was designed at the Piccadilly offices and built by the Airspeed company at York, and its first trials were carried out early in 1933. The construction was of plywood and spruce and the wing was carried some way above the fuselage on steel struts. The engine chosen was the 70-h.p. four-cylinder Hirth, a German 3½-litre unit which had no exact counterpart in Britain at this time, and which was mounted in the centre-section driving a pusher propeller behind the wing. The attractiveness of the pusher arrangement, which eliminated much of the noise and all of the battering from propeller slipstream experienced in conventional tractor aeroplanes with open cockpits, was very favourably commented upon at the time, but no more aircraft of the type were built since Mr Shackleton, after giving consideration to the idea of building another pusher type in collaboration with M. Desoutter, abandoned design work to build up the aircraft sales business which still bears his name, and his partner joined the de Havilland company. The single S.M.1 nevertheless had a long life as a private aeroplane under the ownership of Lord Apsley, who used to fly it from his home at Badminton until petrol shortage one day brought him down in the sea off the Isle of Wight, and then the soaking in salt water which it received put an end to its career.

When production of the de Havilland Puss Moth ceased in 1933, it was replaced by the Leopard Moth, an aeroplane of generally similar appearance except for its tapered wings of smaller area and the shorter undercarriage legs, whose fairings still performed the function of air brakes. A fundamental though less superficially apparent difference was the abandonment of welded steel tube in favour of the traditional spruce and plywood for the fuselage, a change made on grounds of cost and weight saving. Thanks to its lighter structure weight, the Leopard Moth was a full three-seater carrying two passengers side by side behind the pilot, and with the Gipsy Major engine giving it a cruising speed of 120 m.p.h. it was an ideal private owner's machine. The new type was well launched when Captain de Havilland won the King's Cup Race of 1933 in the prototype and another Leopard Moth came into third place flown by Mr A. J. Styran.

After the Southern Martlet of 1929 Mr F. G. Miles applied the experience thus gained to the design of a single-seater biplane with Pobjoy R engine intended for aerobatics and named the Satyr. This machine attracted the attention of the director of a motor business at Reading, Mr Charles Powis, and in this way began the association of Miles with the firm of Phillips and Powis, by whom all pre-war aircraft to his design were built and sold. In 1933 the first Miles aeroplane to the low-wing cantilever formula was constructed in the workshops of the Reading firm, and first flew in the hands of its designer on an evening towards the end of March.

The purchase of a batch of Cirrus IIIA engines at a low price from a firm which had gone into liquidation made it possible for the Miles Hawk, as the new machine was called, to be offered at the low price of £395, and with its ply-covered folding cantilever wings, two seats, luggage locker and top speed of 115 m.p.h. it was an immediate success (Figure 8).

The Hawk appeared in great numbers and in a variety of forms, some with three seats, some with cabin tops and other modifications, and the

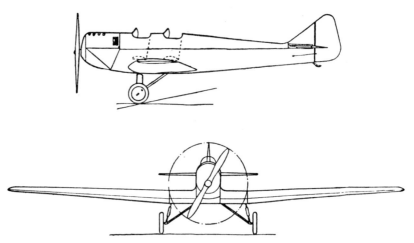

8. The first of the low-wing cantilever designs of Mr F. G. Miles:
the Hawk of 1933 with Cirrus IIIA engine

original Cirrus of 95 h.p. was in some instances replaced by engines of higher power such as the Gipsy III and Hermes IV. Its successor of 1934 was the Hawk Major with Gipsy III engine and an undercarriage enclosed in faired 'trousers', an improvement in appearance and aerodynamic cleanness over the bare struts of the original Hawk. The prototype gained second place in the King's Cup in its first year, and in the same race there took part, though unsuccessfully, a special version with Gipsy Six engine and a single cockpit. Split flaps, also to become a standard Miles feature, were added to the Hawk Major design towards the end of 1934 as an aid to reducing landing speed and steepening the very flat glide. One Hawk Major took part in the 'MacRobertson' race from Mildenhall to Melbourne in October 1934 and with it over the same course flew the prototype of the first of the cabin Miles designs, the three-seater Falcon, forerunner of a series of graceful monoplanes which allied the docile handling qualities of the original Hawk to an unusually good performance with comparatively low power.

The development of the low-wing cantilever monoplane in Germany had been several years in advance of that in England, and as early as 1929 a popular German machine of this type—the Klemm L25—had begun to be imported in considerable numbers. Its success encouraged the holder of the British selling rights, Major E. F. Stephen, to promote its construction at Hanworth, and the British Klemm Aeroplane Company was formed in 1933 under the chairmanship of Lord Willoughby de Broke, himself a Klemm owner, with Mr G. H. Handasyde as works manager and Mr Harold Boultbee as chief designer. The new company immediately set to work to produce a British version of the Klemm which was substantially the same as the original except for such modifications as were necessary to meet British airworthiness requirements, and the first British-built machine, which was named the Swallow, was demonstrated in December 1933. It quickly developed the reputation of being one of the safest aeroplanes in the world by reason of its totally innocuous stalling characteristics and inability to spin, and it could be landed so slowly that no flaps or air brakes were necessary even though the clean design had resulted in the extremely flat gliding angle of 1 in 12. The first machine was fitted with the Salmson A.D.9 engine and the Pobjoy R was offered as an alternative; early in 1934 however a new range of Pobjoy engines was announced and later production Swallows could be equipped with the Cataract, which delivered 80 h.p. at 3,200 r.p.m. (Plate 51).

Closely following the Swallow came the British Klemm Eagle of 1934, this time a three-seater cabin monoplane of similar wooden cantilever construction whose extremely clean lines could be further improved after take-off by winding up its mechanically retractable undercarriage to lie flush with the underside of the wing. This feature was one which conveniently accompanied the cantilever wing, since the relatively great wing thickness imposed by structural considerations made it easy to house a pair of wheels, and it enabled the Eagle to fly at almost 150 m.p.h. on the power of its Gipsy Major engine. The Eagle offered a great degree of technical refinement for its day and was suitable for the more well-to-do private owner at its price of £1,375.

Cantilever monoplanes were now appearing in wide variety, and three were produced in quick succession by Comper between the middle of 1933 and the end of 1934. The Comper Mouse, originally called the Aircar, was designed at Hooton Park very shortly after the Swift and was an attempt by Comper to meet the many requests which he had received for a multi-seat version of that machine. With the better facilities available to him after his company had transferred to Heston, Comper was able to set to work to construct the prototype Mouse, and this first flew on 10 September 1933. It was a clean three-seater with a Gipsy Major engine, seating two people side by side in front on adjustable seats with full dual control and a third on a full-width seat at the rear. A sliding hood, which could be opened in flight, provided easy access after climbing on to the low-placed fully cantilever wing. For convenience as a touring machine the Mouse was provided with fitted suitcases and it had a mechanically retractable undercarriage which folded backwards, leaving a portion of each wheel protruding to minimise damage if a landing was made with wheels up (Comper did in fact land the machine in this way at Heston on Christmas Eve 1933, and the principle was vindicated, for there was no damage apart from a broken propeller).

The Streak, Comper's next product, was designed to compete in the Coupe Deutsch de la Meurthe race in France in 1934. It was a high-speed single-seater with a modified Swift fuselage and scaled-down Mouse wing, but its unsupercharged Gipsy Major engine, though of special high-compression type, was scarcely a match for the supercharged 8-litre engines allowed by the rules, and when he had completed part of the race with his undercarriage jammed down Comper was forced to retire.

The last of his three designs of this period was the Kite, a two-seater version of the Streak of elegant design with a remarkable performance which included a top speed of over 150 m.p.h. on the 90 h.p. of its Pobjoy Niagara, but like the Mouse it was not a commercial success. Comper's undoubted gifts as a designer were not matched by business ability. In 1934 his small company went out of existence and apart from a high-wing pusher monoplane named the Scamp, built to Comper's design at Brooklands, his work was not seen again. The Scamp was overtaken by the war, and although an attempt was made to develop it into a military observation machine it had little success, while Comper himself did not live to see it, for he died at the early age of 42 as a result of becoming involved in a street fight in Hythe in June 1939.

The Snark monoplane, designed for his own personal use by Dr N. A. de Bruyne and built at Duxford, was intended as a machine which would carry four people on the power of a single Gipsy Major engine, with a low wing loading and a good ratio of loaded to empty weight, and was built entirely of wood with a stressed plywood skin for the fuselage, tail surfaces and fully cantilever wing. The occupants sat in two pairs in the cabin, which was generously provided with window area, and a jointed swing-over control column allowed either of the front pair to fly the machine. The wing contained a luggage compartment and fuel tanks holding a total of 32 gallons, which with a maximum permissible weight of 2,200 lbs allowed four people to be carried over a range of 500 miles. Although the first flight was carried out by the designer in December 1934, the first conception of the machine dated back some years and Dr de Bruyne's stress analysis of what was at the time a somewhat novel type of construction led him into difficulties with the airworthiness authorities which took some time to be fully resolved. When the machine eventually received its certificate it was used by its designer for a European tour and eventually passed into the hands of the R.A.E. at Farnborough for research purposes.

A word must be said here about the autogiro, a form of light aircraft which enjoyed a few brief years of popularity before the Second World War eclipsed it* in favour of its immensely more costly and complicated relative the helicopter. The principle of the autogiro, invented by the Spaniard Don Juan de la Cierva, is that a rotor consisting of freely spinning blades of aerofoil section, maintained in motion by the speed of flight, produces lift in a manner which is largely independent of the forward speed of the machine as a whole. Unlike the fixed-wing aeroplane, therefore, which has a definite stalling speed below which it cannot sustain level flight, the autogiro can be brought in to land at low forward speeds of the order of 10 m.p.h. and can be landed with almost no ground run. Since the blades are not driven by the engine as in the helicopter, true hovering is not possible, but in a light wind the machine can be brought to rest relative to the ground without difficulty while in full flight. The use of conventional aerodynamic controls on the early autogiros led to difficulty at very low forward speeds since these controls were then almost totally ineffective, but in 1934 there appeared the first direct-control autogiro, the C.30, built by A. V. Roe and Company. In this machine the rotor could be spun up to its flying speed by a drive from the engine and then declutched for flight, and in the air a hanging-stick control operated directly on the rotor head to tilt it forward and aft for pitch control and laterally for turns, which were automatically given the correct angle of bank.

Unlike the helicopter, the autogiro was quite easy to fly, and an ordinary 'A' licence pilot trained on conventional machines could fly it solo after only an hour or so of dual instruction. It was also relatively cheap to buy—the C.30 cost £1,250, or about the same as a medium-priced light aeroplane—and a number were sold to private owners and flying clubs and schools, among the latter being the Airwork School at Heston, the Lancashire Aero Club, the Bristol and Wessex Flying Club and the Hanworth Flying School.

Since it offered, as a private vehicle, almost all the advantages of the present-day helicopter at only a fraction of the cost, it may be wondered why it was not more successful. There were several reasons. The intensive development of the fixed-wing light aeroplane had overtaken the autogiro, for by the time the C.30 appeared as a practical vehicle its two open cockpits were beginning to appear old-fashioned in the face of such new types

---

* It has recently been revived in England in the form of the Beagle-Wallis single-seater, originally based on an American design.

as the Leopard Moth and the Percival Gull, and further, its performance was markedly inferior to that of comparable fixed-wing types, as a comparison with one of its contemporaries will show:

	C.30 *Autogiro* (*Genet Major*)	British Klemm *Swallow* (*Salmson A.D.*9)
Max. horse-power	140	75
Useful load, lbs	580	540
Range, miles	285	420
Max. speed, m.p.h.	110	104

The Swallow would provide a very similar performance on about half the power and fuel consumption, and although it could not equal the autogiro in landing performance its low wing loading enabled it to use comparatively small fields. Then, Cierva's death in December 1936, ironically enough in one of the fixed-wing aircraft whose hazards he had done so much to eliminate in his invention, was a blow to the progress of the type, and it turned out that the full potentialities of the autogiro as a personal vehicle were not really exploited in the few years of peace which remained.

One of the most technically advanced light aeroplanes of 1934 was the Hendy Heck, built to the design of Mr B. B. Henderson to meet the requirements of the racing motorist and pilot Mr Whitney Straight. The object was to produce a fast machine with Gipsy Six engine while still preserving a low landing speed, and to achieve this the designer seated the two occupants in tandem in a cabin of the minimum frontal area and used a small cantilever wing faired into the deep fuselage by a large expanding fillet. The wing loading was necessarily high—nearly 25 lbs/sq.ft—so that plain flaps and leading-edge slots were provided for landing, with aileron droop of 15° to augment the effect of full flap travel of 40°, and furthermore the undercarriage was made retractable by means of a mechanical hand-winding gear which folded the legs outwards and upwards into the wing surface. The outcome of these many refinements was an aeroplane with a top speed of 170 m.p.h. which could still be landed as slowly as a Moth—an excellent illustration of the possibilities of clean design coupled with the use of high-lift devices.

Shortly after the appearance of the Heck the Hendy Aircraft Company was absorbed into Parnall Aircraft Limited, but subsequent efforts to sell the machine in three-seater form with fixed undercarriage were unsuccessful, and the only claim to fame of the type other than as a technical *tour de force* was the record flight of the prototype from the Cape to England in 1935, piloted by Mr David Llewellyn. A two-seater open cockpit version with all the aerodynamic refinements of the original was later offered as a Service trainer, but it did not secure a contract and only one was built.

36. An economical 'motor-glider': the B.A.C. Drone, originally called
the Lowe Wylde Planette

37. An unusual design of 1933: the Shackleton-Murray S.M.1 pusher
monoplane

38. The Percival Gull in its original form with strut-braced
under-carriage and air-brake (in lowered position)

39. The Hendy 302 monoplane, flown in the 1930 King's Cup Race by
its owner and co-designer Captain E. W. Percival (in front seat)

To take an engine and a pilot and encase them in the minimum aerodynamic form to produce a high-speed racing single-seater is an absorbing
intellectual exercise which must have stirred the minds of most people
with an interest in the art of aircraft design. Having created in the Gull a
vehicle capable of 160 m.p.h. on the power of a Napier Javelin, it was not
difficult for Captain Percival to imagine the racing potentialities of a
smaller Gull in which everything was sacrificed to high speed, and in the
spring of 1934 he put these ideas into practice in the first Mew Gull,
designed and built at Gravesend and demonstrated there in a blustery
March wind before being entered for the King's Cup Race of that summer.
First flights were made with a Javelin engine but this was replaced by a
Gipsy Six for racing purposes; the original braced Gull-type undercarriage gave place to a pair of streamlined single struts and split flaps
were added to hold down the landing speed, which with a wing loading of
some 21 lbs/sq.ft at maximum weight was fairly high for the day. In the
race the Mew was competing against a field which included such new types
as the Klemm Eagle, Comper Streak and Hendy Heck, and in spite of his
average speed of 191 m.p.h., Percival was unable to prevail against the
handicappers. The Mew Gull was then broken up and in preparation for
the following season an entirely new version was built, a description of
which will be found in a later chapter.

In the same race was the T.K.1, first of an interesting series of small
aircraft which were designed and built entirely by the staff and students
of the de Havilland Technical School. The letters T.K. were an indication
of the international flavour of that institution, having their origin in the
phrase 'Tekniese Kollege' inscribed upon the drawings by a Dutch student
there. The design was under the control of Mr Marcus Langley, at that
time lecturer in aircraft design at the College, and was a conventional
wooden biplane with two open cockpits in tandem and a Gipsy III engine.
It was at Mr Langley's request that permission was granted for the
students to build the machine—a novel idea in England at the time—and
when it was completed Captain de Havilland's eldest son Geoffrey asked
if he might fly it in the King's Cup. The aeroplane was hurriedly put
through its tests at Martlesham Heath in a single day just before the race,
and after certain last-minute changes everything was made ready just in
time and the machine successfully reached the finals although it was un-
placed. This minor triumph encouraged the continuation of the series and
thus a family of aircraft was developed along lines which were not necessarily those of the parent firm. Since commercial success was not a requirement many original ideas could be tried out in complete freedom, to the
great benefit of students and company alike.

By the end of 1934 the British light aeroplane had undergone a great transformation. Apart from the de Havilland Hornet Moth—a new design which harmoniously combined the cabin comfort of the Leopard Moth with the original Moth biplane wing arrangement—the age of the light biplane was quickly passing. The many Moths, Spartans, Redwings, Blue-birds and Avians which still made up much of the background were begin-ning to look old-fashioned against the new monoplanes that were taking the front of the stage—the Gull and Mew Gull, the Hawk and Falcon, the Swallow, Eagle and Heck, all with the new and clean outline and some with the flaps and retractable undercarriage which were its natural con-comitants. These important advances had taken place in a period when the Royal Air Force was entirely equipped with biplanes, and when (except for the Armstrong Whitworth Atalanta) the same was true of Imperial Airways. Just as the long-distance pilots of light aeroplanes showed the way for the commercial machine to follow, so also in the technical field the smaller private and sporting types pointed the road to the future.

Hanworth, Heston and
the King's Cup

Looking back today, few people would claim that State expenditure on the
light aeroplane clubs in the 1920s was in any way excessive. The cost to the
taxpayer of the subsidies paid to the flying clubs from their beginnings in
1925 right up to the end of the financial year 1931–32 was some £92,000,
and for this the State had placed at its own disposal a reserve of pilots comparable in number with those then on the strength of the Royal Air Force,
created a widespread interest in air matters which could hardly have come
into being in any other way, and stimulated the growth of an important
branch of the aircraft industry whose success cannot have been without
influence on the outcome of the Second World War. During the second
period of subsidy from 1927 to 1930, however, there were those who were
critical of the use of public money for something which did not seem to
provide any direct and tangible return, and at the end of 1928 a scheme
was proposed which was intended not only to place on a centrally organised
basis the running of such clubs as were willing to join it, but also pro-
gressively to reduce the taxpayer's share of the burden until eventually the
movement would be independent of the Treasury and self-supporting.
The originator of this scheme, for the promotion of which a company
named National Flying Services Limited was later formed, was Captain
F. E. Guest, a former Air Minister who was at this time commanding
officer of No. 600 (City of London) Squadron of the Auxiliary Air Force.

The Guest scheme was a most ambitious one. The country was to be
covered by a network of 22 main aerodromes, each of which would be
equipped with four aeroplanes, two flying instructors and the necessary
ground staff and would act as a flying school, club and air centre for its
locality. In addition there would be 100 landing grounds, without facilities
for flying instruction but with the necessary minimum of petrol, oil and a
telephone to meet the needs of the air tourist. The complete system of
aerodromes and landing grounds would be distributed over the country in
a uniform fashion so that each was within a quarter-of-an-hour's flying

time of its immediate neighbours, thus offering landing facilities within easy reach of every area. The main centre for London would be at Hanworth Park, Middlesex, and here would be the headquarters of the controlling company with extensive facilities for flying instruction, air hire, air taxi services and the maintenance, overhaul and storage of privately owned aircraft. Any machine of the company which was damaged in an accident at one of the outlying aerodromes would immediately be replaced by another flown over from Hanworth, where a central pool of aircraft and spare parts would be maintained for this purpose. The Air Ministry's liability for the entire project would be limited to a maximum subsidy of £15,000 a year for the first three years on the basis of an annual £10 for each qualified pilot who was a member of N.F.S., falling to £7,500 a year and £5 per pilot over the ensuing seven years and then ceasing entirely. Thus in no case could the Government be required to lay out a greater sum than £97,500 and this amount would be spread over ten years until National Flying Services was in a position to operate wholly on a commercial basis without outside help.

⸴ The scheme was on the face of it most attractive. It offered the possibility of economies brought about by centralisation, and the proposed chain of landing grounds, if completed, would immensely increase the usefulness of the aeroplane as a means of rapid communication within the country, as Sir Alan Cobham had been energetically preaching to local authorities in his Aerodromes Campaign. The existing flying clubs, however, were bitterly opposed to it, and their reasons were easy to understand. It was they who had been solely responsible for starting the light aeroplane movement and for keeping it alive in its critical early years. They were, their supporters claimed, essentially non-profit-making enterprises. Each club had grown up as a local organisation with its own particular character, its own special difficulties to overcome, and often its own local benefactors who had frequently been persuaded to contribute towards the cost of a new aeroplane or a new clubhouse. All this, so carefully built up at the cost of many generosities and sacrifices and much hard work, would now be exposed to the risk of forcible absorption into a large centralised organisation which was to be run on a purely commercial basis and which would inevitably lack the essential spirit of enthusiasm which had borne the clubs along since their earliest days.

The Government, however, irresistibly attracted by the prospect of reducing expenditure, decided to adopt the Guest scheme, and the terms of the agreement were set out in a White Paper* published in January 1929. They contained one important proviso: the Government wisely stipulated that payment of the subsidy was to depend upon the company's

* Cmd. 3264.

fulfilling its agreement to provide and equip at least 20 new aerodromes and 80 new landing grounds in its first three years of operation. The clubs were not to be forcibly included in National Flying Services but were given the cold comfort of being allowed to continue as independent units if they wished to do so provided that they were prepared to operate on the very much reduced subsidy offered to the new organisation. The future looked bleak, and one or two clubs found themselves compelled to merge with the N.F.S. scheme; others decided to struggle on.

The scheme went ahead. At Hanworth Park, which had been used as an aerodrome in the 1914–18 war, the work began of clearing the ground to make it fit for operations to start later in the year. Captain T. Neville Stack was appointed chief pilot to the company, and various types of light aeroplanes were tested to find which were most suitable for the purposes of the new organisation, those finally chosen being the Spartan, the all-metal Bluebird IV and the Desoutter. A booklet entitled *The World on Wings* was produced in which were set out the many facilities which N.F.S. was to offer to the public, and a standard colour scheme of orange and black was adopted for the company's aircraft and for the high-collared uniforms which were specially designed for the pilots. These uniforms came in for much criticism, being unfavourably compared by some to those worn by bandmasters and members of the Boys' Brigade, while irascible ex-members of the R.F.C. wrote to the press complaining that they had been flagrantly copied from the 'maternity jackets' of their former Corps.

The opening of National Flying Services took place on the first of September 1929, and the ceremony was performed by the Duchess of Bedford. The weather was kind and the green lawns of Hanworth House and the wide expanse of what was now to be called the London Air Park were bathed in warm sunshine. Captain Guest, speaking at the inaugural luncheon, sketched the history of Hanworth House, which had been a seat of Henry VIII, and outlined the company's plans for the future. They hoped, he said, to have most of the 71 landing grounds which had so far been planned in operation within a year, and of these thirteen or fourteen would be air parks like Hanworth itself. Two subsidiary aerodromes, Reading and Hull, were about to begin work and negotiations were in progress for eight more.

Hanworth House was pleasantly situated in the middle of its park, all of which was used for landing, the north side being reserved for commercial operations and the south for private flying. For the latter purpose twenty lock-ups were provided as well as a large communal hangar, and on the commercial side the new cabin Desoutters soon began to appear in their role as air-taxis. An office was opened in Trafalgar Square and the air-taxis could be booked here at the rate of a shilling a mile for a single passenger or 1s. 6d. for two, with a car provided to take passengers to the aerodrome.

There was some antagonism between the new company and the old-established flying community and most of the members attracted to Hanworth were new to aviation; nevertheless, in its first six weeks of operation Hanworth gained 534 members, and throughout the following spring and summer the figures of membership continued to increase. In spite of this activity, however, the picture presented to the shareholders at the first annual general meeting was a gloomy one: instead of the net profit of £32,000 which the prospectus had confidently predicted for the first year, a trading loss of nearly £40,000 was reported and the flying carried out by the company's fleet of 46 aircraft had only succeeded in earning £740 out of the available £15,000 of Government subsidy. Various reasons were advanced for the failure, but the underlying one was the onset of the world-wide depression which was now spreading to England, following the collapse of the American stock market only a few weeks after the opening of Hanworth. Less money was available for private flying, and National Flying Services, which had lavishly equipped itself throughout 1929 with everything from aeroplanes down to special cutlery and crockery, had been caught by worsening trade conditions just at the very moment when those in control were expecting to see a good return on their investment.

After the first annual general meeting the Board was reorganised and some economies were effected, but in spite of this the second year's working showed no improvement and at the annual general meeting of March 1932 a loss of £68,000 was announced. There was now no possibility of the company's meeting its obligation to provide twenty aerodromes and eighty landing grounds; instead it could only show seven and in July the Government had no option but to cut off its subsidy. In the three years a mere £4,160 had been earned out of a possible £45,000, and when even this trickle of State assistance was cut off the ultimate outcome was no longer in doubt. The company managed to struggle on for a while, but the end came in 1934, and in June of that year a receiver was appointed.

The failure would not have been so serious had it not also depressed the fortunes of those clubs which had elected to remain independent. Once it became clear that the N.F.S. agreement could not be fulfilled, however, the Government was quickly forced to make amends for its parsimony, and after representations by the General Council a new five-year agreement was drawn up to take effect from April 1932. This new subsidy plan was not quite so generous as that which had been put forward in 1927, but it was still a great encouragement to the clubs after the dark days through which they had been passing. It offered once again the sum of £25 for each 'A' licence gained and £10 for each renewal, with a maximum annual grant of £1,500. The spring of 1932 was thus something of a turning-point in the history of the British flying-club movement and from this time onward, with the international situation steadily worsening, the clubs had little reason to complain of insufficient support.

In contrast with National Flying Services, one of the most successful aviation projects of the day was the opening in 1929 of a new aerodrome to the west of London which was intended specifically as a centre for private flying. This was Heston in Middlesex (Plate 41), constructed for the firm of Airwork Limited, whose directors, Mr Nigel Norman and Mr F. A. I. Muntz, were themselves both practising private pilots. As the years went on Heston gradually came to replace Stag Lane as the principal London aerodrome for private flying. Stag Lane itself finally closed down in 1934 after the departure of the de Havilland company to their new home at Hatfield and in due course suffered the irreversible fate of unwanted aerodromes by disappearing under bricks and mortar. Work having begun on the Heston site in 1928 it was opened to air traffic in July of the following year, some two months before the opening of Hanworth, its inauguration being arranged to coincide with the 1929 King's Cup Race which was to begin and end there.

From the beginning it was the intention of Airwork Limited to provide at Heston every amenity which the amateur pilot could desire, and these included a set of private lock-up garages for aeroplanes in addition to a large general hangar, three exhibition shops let out for the sale of aircraft and their accessories and a central building forming a 'social focus' and including within it the control tower. There soon followed a wireless station from which the aeronautical weather broadcasts of the A. A. were periodically transmitted, a clock with large horizontal face legible from 2,000 ft for the information of pilots in the air, overnight accommodation, a restaurant and full Customs facilities. It was not long before Heston was fully established as a busy and fashionable rendezvous for those interested in amateur flying, and the annual garden party of the Household Brigade Flying Club, which had moved from Brooklands into one section of the central building at Heston as soon as it was opened, became an important social event of the summer with something of the character of an aeronautical Ascot.

The Airwork School of Flying under one of the best-known instructors of the day, Captain V. H. Baker (formerly of the Lancashire Aero Club), soon acquired an exceedingly high reputation for the quality of its instruction both in the air and on the ground, although its charges of £4 4s. per flying hour were considerably higher than those of the average subsidised light aeroplane club. Many distinguished people from all walks of life learned to fly there, and the fact that it succeeded so well in spite of the economic situation must be attributed partly to the comparative wealth of many of its supporters. In 1936 the Airwork School gained some publicity on a national scale when Mr Filson Young of the B.B.C. described in a series of broadcasts his experiences at becoming a pilot under Captain Baker's care. Subsequently these talks were gathered into book form, and they not only make an interesting study of the first-hand reactions of an ordinary middle-aged man to the novel sensations of flight but also present an excellent picture of the thriving days of a place which, like so many of the small aerodromes easily accessible to London before the war, today lies derelict and silent under the thrall of its giant neighbour at nearby Heathrow.

In a somewhat similar way the flying ground in the centre of Brook-lands motor-racing track in Surrey, which had witnessed so many of the early efforts of the pioneers of aviation in the years before 1914, was developed in the 1930s into a popular centre for private flying (Plate 40). In the latter part of the 1920s Colonel G. L. P. Henderson had based his school of flying there, and on his death in 1930 his second-in-command, the experienced war-time instructor Captain H. D. Davis, took over con-trol and formed the Brooklands School of Flying. To provide social facilities in addition to flying instruction the Brooklands Aero Club was opened in the same year, and after a new clubhouse in modern style had been built beside the war-time hangars the historic aerodrome took on a new and vigorous life. In due course the Brooklands group absorbed with-in itself the Northamptonshire Aero Club at Sywell, the Southern Aero Club at Shoreham and the Cinque Ports Flying Club at Lympne, so that membership of any one carried with it the right to use the facilities of the other three, and the Moths of the group in their smart colour scheme of red, black and silver were soon carrying as diverse a range of pupils of all professions, nationalities and races as Captain Baker's Club Cadets on the other side of the Thames.

The coming of the light aeroplane, simple and safe to fly, had opened up the freedom of the air to many who might otherwise have felt that flying was altogether too difficult and exacting an art to be learned by those no longer in their youth. There was little official obstruction placed in the way of either the old or the very young who wished to learn to fly. In the 1920s and 1930s the pilot under instruction required neither licence nor medical examination in order to fly solo provided that his flying was restricted within a three-mile radius of an aerodrome, and as a result of this freedom quite a number of boys and girls from the age of fourteen upwards were able to gain experience on their own in the air until they became eligible for 'A' licences at seventeen. This practice was eventually prohibited by the Air Ministry in 1934 and thereafter young pilots had to postpone their first solo flights until their seventeenth birthday.

At the upper end of the age scale there was (as today) no limit as far as the private pilot was concerned, and it would be possible to quote a long list of those who took up flying as a sport well into their sixties and seventies. The Duchess of Bedford has already been mentioned; Mr J. A. McMullen, aged 71, took up autogiro flying at Hanworth with no previous flying experience of any kind and later owned his own autogiro, and Colonel A. J. Richardson, of the Norfolk and Norwich Aero Club, used regularly to fly his Klemm across the North Sea to Holland in his late sixties. Another who came to flying late in life was Mr Douglas Fawcett, brother of the explorer who disappeared mysteriously on the Amazon. Although interested in aviation from an early age, he was careful to keep a promise made to his wife that he would not fly in her lifetime, and it was not until 1933, when he was a widower of 67, that he took his first flight as a passenger. He was so attracted that he at once consulted Captain Baker at Heston and took a trial lesson, and a flying course followed in the summer of 1934, after which he returned to his home in Switzerland to use his new skill for studying from the air the mountains which he had climbed on foot in his younger days. Later, at the age of 71, he was back at Heston again for a refresher course and to qualify himself at aerobatics.

Although the subsidies paid to the clubs brought the cost of an 'A' licence down to £20 or so, well within reach of the professional classes, there was still a vast untapped market for personal flying. In an age when cigarettes were ten for sixpence the cost of learning to fly was an insuperable obstacle to thousands who wished to do so, and for the many who had just come within reach of a Morris Cowley or an Austin Seven the ownership of an aeroplane was an impossible dream. The elusive ideal of the 'aerial motor-cycle' costing £150 or less which had first been seriously discussed at the time of the first Lympne trials in 1923 had largely been lost sight of in the early years of the Moth, and during those years the power output and fuel consumption of small aero-engines had climbed steadily upward. This was acceptable when flying was confined to the relatively well-to-do, but in the depression years of the early 1930s this trend began to be reversed to some extent, and the minds of flying enthusiasts turned once more to study the problem of getting into the air at the lowest possible cost.

Those who sought ways of learning to fly cheaply on standard machines came up against the fundamental difficulty that a light aeroplane such as the Moth could not be operated for much less than £2 10s. per flying hour, and even with their subsidies the clubs could rarely afford to offer flying instruction at less than 30s. an hour. The only way round the difficulty was a form of collective effort in which the small subscriptions of a large number of interested people could be used to provide flying at acceptably low rates for a few of their number selected by ballot. The pioneers of this type of poor man's flying club were the 'flying busmen'. In 1930 the sports association of the London General Omnibus Company, which had already started its own gliding club, set out to explore the possibilities of light aeroplane flying at low cost and with 1,500 members, each of whom contributed sixpence a week, they managed to buy the prototype Redwing biplane and to persuade its manufacturers' test pilot, Flight Lieutenant N. M. S. Russell, to act as unpaid instructor at their aerodrome at Broxbourne in Essex. Instruction was offered to those chosen for the privilege at the very low rate of 5s. an hour, and although the financial structure of the club meant that progress was necessarily slow, twenty-five of its members took their 'A' licences in the ensuing six years. This extremely successful club is at the time of writing still in operation as the London Transport (C.R.S.) Sports Association Flying Club.

The enterprising busmen soon had a number of imitators. In 1931 their example was followed by the employees of United Dairies, whose club was formed with 400 members and operated on the same principle of sixpence-a-week subscriptions. The United Banks Flying Club, offering bank staff an 'A' licence for £12, was formed in the same year, and later the Midland Bank began a flying club on its own. The Civil Air Service Corps, operating from Cambridge, offered cheap flying at weekends to young men of limited means, and its members used to perform various duties in uniform at flying displays and meetings. In December 1931, through the efforts of Mr Geoffrey Dorman, formerly of *The Aeroplane*, a flying club was formed for the messenger boys of the Commercial Cable Company, and well-known persons in the world of aviation and motoring were invited to lecture to them and to give flights. A summer camp was arranged at Hanworth and the club managed to obtain flying scholarships from various organisations so that one boy was selected to learn to fly on fixed-wing aeroplanes, one on autogiros and one on gliders. The messenger who won the autogiro scholarship offered by the Cierva company—F. J. Cable, aged 17—handsomely repaid the investment by becoming chief test pilot to the company and later, after a distinguished war record, one of the first three helicopter pilots in Britain.

For the benefit of the ordinary citizen who was not fortunate enough to belong to an organisation with its own cheap flying scheme and who was unable to meet the cost of an 'A' licence obtained in the ordinary way, there were numerous flying scholarship schemes run by newspapers and weekly magazines, for the great public interest in aviation in these years ensured that the publicity so gained would have a satisfactory effect on circulation. One of the first newspapers in this field was the *Newcastle Evening World*, which in 1929 offered ten free courses of flying lessons to selected applicants of either sex between the ages of 17 and 35. Two years later the society magazine *Tatler* launched its own scheme, according to which the first fifty applicants to go to each of certain specified flying clubs would receive free trial lessons. The six who were considered to show most promise would then be encouraged to take an hour's dual instruction and the best of these would be awarded a free course up to the standard of the 'A' licence. The *Daily Express* ran a similar scheme in conjunction with National Flying Services, and in 1935 the Air League of the British Empire set up a Young Pilots' Fund from which half the cost of flying instruction was met for approved applicants between 17 and 26 years of age. It is therefore fair to say that in the early 1930s quite a considerable number of people who would not normally have been able to afford the cost of learning to fly were in various ways enabled to do so.

Those who could not, or did not wish to, participate actively in flying had ample opportunities of watching it. Although the purely commercial uses of the light aeroplane do not strictly fall within the scope of this chapter, it is impossible not to refer briefly to a phenomenon of the 1930s which will be remembered by almost everyone old enough to recall those days—namely the travelling air displays which toured up and down the country every summer, operating from suitable fields near large towns. The organisers of these shows normally tried to include in their fleet as wide a range of aircraft as they could lay their hands on, and much of the work of joy-riding and aerobatics rested upon the Moths, Avians, Bluebirds, Spartans and other light types which have already been described. Probably the most famous of the displays was Sir Alan Cobham's National Aviation Day, which from 1931 onwards visited almost every town of importance in the British Isles, performing before audiences which in the aggregate ran into millions and giving practical flying experience to tens of thousands. The display was taken over in 1935 by Mr C. W. A. Scott, joint winner of the Mildenhall to Melbourne race, and it continued its itinerant operations under his control until shortly before the outbreak of war. Another well-known 'air circus' was the British Hospitals Air Pageant, with which was associated the experienced joy-riding pilot Miss Pauline Gower, who, assisted by her friend Miss Dorothy Spicer as ground engineer, gave flights to more than 10,000 passengers in her three-seater Spartan biplane.

Apart from the commercial displays, innumerable private flying events filled every summer and often attracted large numbers of spectators. There were race meetings, club displays, aerial garden parties, Continental tours, *week-ends aériens*, and other activities in which the keen club pilot, even if he did not own an aeroplane, was freely encouraged to take part. The success of these events depended greatly upon the ability and good sense of their officials, who had the delicate task of ensuring a necessary minimum of discipline for safety's sake without detracting from the general atmosphere of high spirits. Much responsibility rested upon the secretary of the Royal Aero Club, Commander Harold Perrin, and mention must also be made of the 'triumvirate' which officiated at nearly every one of the larger meetings—Major Alan Goodfellow as clerk of the course, Captain Lamplugh as chief marshal, and the popular and much respected 'Jimmy' Jeffs* as aerodrome and air traffic control officer. The great sporting event of each summer was the King's Cup Race, which in the years of which we are speaking generally consisted of a long circuit embracing most of the country and often taking two days to complete. The race provided an exciting test for the keen private owner or amateur club pilot, but at the same time it had the more serious purpose of serving as a proving ground for new types of aeroplane and engine; the publicity value of winning or putting up a good performance was much prized and manufacturers were always anxious to prepare their latest products to be shown off on the King's Cup circuit. Such a blend of pure sport and new technical interest made the race attractive to competitors, spectators and the aviation world as a whole, and it had then a character which has been largely lacking in post-war years owing to present-day restrictions and the depressed state of the British light aircraft industry. Seventeen King's Cup Races were flown between 1922 and 1938, that of 1939 having to be cancelled because it was arranged for the week-end of Hitler's attack on Poland. Their story would fill a book in itself, but we will here confine ourselves to a description of the race of 1930, when the effects of the gathering economic storm had hardly yet been felt in aviation and private and sporting flying were flourishing as they had never done before.

The King's Cup of that year attracted the largest entry list ever, consisting of 101 aeroplanes of 22 distinct types. These included no fewer than thirty-nine of the Moths which were now at the height of their career, as well as fourteen Bluebirds, eight Avians, nine of the new cabin Puss Moths, two Comper Swifts and a considerable number of individual machines such as Captain Percival's Hendy 302 monoplane, the Parnall Elf, the Redwing and the twin-engined Segrave Meteor. The circuit chosen on this occasion started and finished at Hanworth and its 750 miles were to be flown in a single day. The first turning-point was situated on the south coast at Hamble, and from there competitors would fly to a compulsory

---

* Later, as Group Captain G. J. H. Jeffs, c.v.o., o.b.e., to become Commandant of London Airport.

halt of forty minutes' duration at Bristol (Whitchurch), taking off again to travel by way of the Midlands to a second stop at the Manchester airport of Barton, then crossing the Pennines to Newcastle (Cramlington) and finally setting off southward to Hull (Hedon) and back to Hanworth after rounding a last turn at Desford.

The morning of the race, Saturday 5 July, dawned fine and still with a promise of great heat, and Captain Entwhistle, the 'gust guesser' of the Air Ministry's meteorological department, unable to find anything more sinister on his charts than the usual industrial haze over the Midlands, recommended pilots to fly low as far as Hamble and then climb to 3,000 ft to catch a southerly wind for the long run up to Newcastle. With the first competitor due to leave at 7 a.m., Hanworth was a bustle of activity from a very early hour. There were a dozen or so non-starters, including both Comper Swifts and a handful of Moths and Bluebirds, but this still left Colonel Lindsay Lloyd and Mr A. G. Reynolds, who were respectively starter and time-keeper, with the formidable task of despatching eighty-eight aeroplanes over a period of nearly four hours.

Promptly at seven o'clock the first machine was away—G-EBOT, an aged Cirrus I Moth flown by Mr W. H. Sutcliffe which was rumoured to be something of a dark horse since its entrant, Mr. D. M. K. Marendaz of motor-racing fame, was known to be a skilful hand at the tuning of engines. Sixth away was G-EBOI, one of the original Moths of the Hampshire Aeroplane Club, now entered and flown by a future gliding expert, Mr Philip Wills, and some way after him came a long line of the new metal Bluebirds numbering among their pilots Captain Norman Blackburn, Colonel Sempill, Flight Lieutenant 'Tommy' Rose and two famous names of the Schneider Trophy—Waghorn and Orlebar. In the midst of them was a popular woman pilot of several years' experience, the international hockey player Miss Winifred Brown, flying a Cirrus III Avian with her fiancé Mr V. H. Addams travelling in the front cockpit as navigator, and soon after her came Lieutenant-Colonel Strange, managing director of the Spartan company flying one of their biplanes with its interchangeable wings. As the twentieth machine, one of the last of the line of Bluebirds, was climbing away for Hamble, Sutcliffe's Moth was already gliding in for his first stop at the Bristol control at Whitchurch, and the news was at once passed back to Hanworth to be displayed on the big boards from which the public could learn of the progress of the race.

Two hours after the departure of the first aeroplane, Mr F. G. Miles was taking off in the Southern Martlet with Lady Bailey close behind him, and then one of Sir Philip Sassoon's entries, the large three-engined Avro Five, stopped a propeller as the flag fell and wasted some seconds as it was hurriedly restarted. A Gipsy II Moth in the hands of Captain de Havilland's eldest son Geoffrey was followed by a pair of Avians, and then came another Moth, carefully streamlined, flown by the de Havilland chairman Mr A. S. Butler and entered by Mrs Butler, who was already waiting to pursue her husband round the course in a Puss Moth. Captain Percival was next to leave in the Hendy 302, and after him came the two royal entries, Prince George's Hawk Moth flown by Flight Lieutenant Fielden and the Hawker Tomtit carrying Squadron Leader Don and entered by the Prince of Wales; then the eight Puss Moths were away in quick succession, that of Captain Barnard carrying Mrs Barnard and Bert Hinkler in the passenger seats and the last of them being flown by Captain de Havilland himself. In among the Puss Moths was the Martlet of Miss Winifred Spooner, one of the most competent of professional women pilots of the time, and after them came the two unusual-looking Avian monoplanes and the twin-engined Segrave Meteor with two more well-known pilots of the Schneider races—Atcherley and Stainforth—followed at last by the scratch machine, the big 1,000-h.p. Vickers Vellore freight-carrier, which thundered heavily into the air in strange contrast to the dozens of light aeroplanes which had preceded it. It was 10.41, and as the officials were at last free to relax into deck-chairs on Hanworth's shady lawns the leading Moth, almost 240 miles in front of the Vellore, was pursuing its slow way over Staffordshire towards the turn at Hooton Park. An immense string of aeroplanes, numbering among their pilots two Members of Parliament, a large proportion of the de Havilland board of directors and their dependents and a host of others distinguished in the flying world, was spread out across the wide map of the sunlit English countryside, and at last peace reigned at Hanworth.

At the Manchester aerodrome of Barton 20,000 visitors were waiting to see the first arrivals, and twice as many more lined the hedges and filled the neighbouring fields. Some had arrived by air, most by road and train, and there were even a few who had come by boat along the Ship Canal. Mr John Leeming, in charge of proceedings, had been visited briefly by the Director of Civil Aviation, who after inspecting the arrangements had instructed him to hold up the race at Barton if, as reported, the weather turned out to be bad over the northern hills. 'Use your own judgement', Sir Sefton had said in his brisk way before climbing into his Desoutter to fly on to Newcastle, and Mr Leeming, understandably disturbed by the responsibility of arresting the progress of nearly ninety aeroplanes on his own initiative, had hurriedly prepared a paper for all pilots to sign stating that they were aware of the reported conditions and would proceed at their own risk. Just after half-past eleven the limit man, Sutcliffe in his Moth, appeared from the direction of the Hooton turn, and soon after him other

machines began to swarm in. Miss Brown, a local girl who had learned to
fly with the Lancashire Aero Club, was loudly acclaimed when she arrived at
Barton in third place, having started fourteenth; she had made a quick run
to Manchester, but there was still nearly 450 miles to go and she had many
much faster aeroplanes in hot pursuit of her little Avian. There had been a
few retirements by this time: Atcherley and Stainforth in the twin-engined
Meteor had soon had to turn back to Hanworth with engine trouble, and
the two Sports Avians flown by Mr J. C. Cantrill and Flight Lieutenant
John Oliver had suffered the unusual fate of having almost simultaneous
forced landings at Slimbridge in Gloucestershire, one of them being put
on its back by hitting a rough patch of ground.

As must occur in every well-arranged handicap race, the field was
beginning to bunch together as the miles went by, and the running of the
controls, staffed by voluntary officials drawn from the local flying clubs,
consequently became more and more difficult. Somewhere in the haze
above the West Riding of Yorkshire Miss Brown moved ahead into the
lead, and at eight minutes past two she was gliding in at the Cramlington
aerodrome at Newcastle, followed by Waghorn's Bluebird and the Moth
of Philip Wills. Twenty minutes later the aerodrome was a whirling chaos
of machines arriving in bunches of three, four and five, landing in groups
and taxying in fierce competition to be first at the petrol pumps; the organisation broke down completely as harassed officials tried desperately to keep
pace with the arrivals and to despatch each exactly forty minutes after it
had landed, and at one instant a state of panic prevailed as a starting sheet
was found to be missing with seventeen aeroplanes due to leave in the next
five minutes.

Promptly at 2.48 Miss Brown and her fiancé departed, skilfully thread-
ing their way through the press of machines like a London taxi-driver
through a traffic block, but for over an hour the confusion at Cramlington
continued, and not until the last of 71 arrivals had been dealt with and
despatched could the weary staff collapse upon the grass. In spite of the
chaos there were only two minor accidents at this control, and Flying
Officer Summers' big Vellore, hopelessly out-handicapped, followed the
race fulfilling the useful function of collecting stranded pilots within its
capacious cabin. A similar confusion prevailed at Hedon, the aerodrome
of Hull, from which sixty-five machines had to be despatched, the field
still led by Miss Brown with Waghorn behind her and the Hermes Spartan
of Flying Officer McKenna in third place.

Since the departure of the last machine at 10.41, Hanworth itself had
been comparatively peaceful, with only the constantly changing marker
boards to indicate the state of the prolonged struggle in the distant north.
The winner could hardly be expected before six, and to amuse the crowds

through the long hot afternoon a flying display was staged with a fly-past of different types, demonstrations of aerobatics and of the curious properties of the autogiro, and a parachute descent by Mr John Tranum. Soon afterwards there was a stir of interest as the Avro Five appeared, followed by a Redwing and a Puss Moth, but it was learned that all these had retired from the race for various reasons. By six o'clock all eyes were turned to the north, the direction of the last turn at Desford from which the winner must eventually come. The issue was still doubtful, for although it was known that Miss Brown had left Hull in the lead, faster machines were quickly closing the gap behind her, among them Mr A. S. Butler's very fast Moth and Captain Barnard's Puss Moth, both of which were overhauling the Avian by almost half-a-mile in every minute.

Just after ten past six a speck appeared, grew larger, was seen to be a biplane and was at last identified as an Avian, and at 6.16 Miss Brown swept across the line after more than seven hours' flying at full throttle to become the first woman pilot ever to win the King's Cup Race. Her old Avian had covered the course at 102.7 m.p.h., an excellent average speed which indicated that engine, pilot and navigator had all performed faultlessly. Ten minutes later Mr Butler came into second place with the fastest time of the race, an astonishing 129.7 m.p.h. from an ordinary Gipsy II Moth biplane on which every unnecessary crevice and excrescence which could produce unwanted drag had been painstakingly eliminated. Mrs Butler was not far behind her husband, following Flight Lieutenant Waghorn's Bluebird in to take fourth place at 129.6 m.p.h., and Captain Percival on the Hendy 302 had reached Manchester with a speed of 129 m.p.h. which would certainly have assured him second place if he had only been able to maintain it to the finish. Third place had been within the grasp of Flying Officer McKenna when his Spartan had run out of petrol within sight of Hanworth; in the nonchalant fashion of the time he landed, filled up at a nearby garage and took off again but was too late to stay in front of Waghorn. The regularity of speed of the Puss Moths in their first King's Cup was particularly striking, as a few examples will show:

Captain Broad	128·3 m.p.h.
Lieutenant-Commander Kidston	127·7 m.p.h.
Captain Barnard	127·6 m.p.h.

but the unfortunate Vellore, which had been held back by the handicappers for more than half an hour after the last Puss Moth had departed and yet had only averaged 126·8 m.p.h., did not come droning over the scene with its load of passengers until the moment when Sir Philip Sassoon was handing the Cup and the Siddeley Trophy to a smiling Miss Brown and Mr Addams. The crowd then began to disperse in search of refreshment and

40. Brooklands from the air, 1931

41. A meeting of the Household Brigade Flying Club at Heston in 1932

42. This version of the Comper Swift with Gipsy Major engine was entered for the King's Cup Race of 1932 by the Prince of Wales

43. The Monospar light twin, popular as a private owner's type. This example, an ST-10, won the 1934 King's Cup

transport, and the biggest—if not the greatest—of King's Cup Races, flown in rare and perfect summer weather, was at its end.

It is interesting to contrast this race with the Jubilee King's Cup of five years later. In 1930 three-quarters of the aeroplanes entered had been biplanes, but by 1935 the picture had changed utterly: out of thirty-six entries thirty were low-wing monoplanes, and the solitary Genet Avian of Mr A. H. Tweddle was the only biplane to reach the starting-line, the new D.H.90 Dragonfly having failed to appear in time. The race in this year was a two-day event starting at Hatfield, with an eliminating circuit of 953 miles to be flown on a Friday and a final the following day consisting of seven laps of a 50-mile course. The eliminating circuit, after running up the east coast to Edinburgh then across to Glasgow, for the first time swung over the Irish Sea to Belfast and then led back to Hatfield by way of Dalbeattie, Blackpool, Woodford and Cardiff. During the sea crossing Mr Alex Henshaw had the misfortune to fracture the crankshaft of his Miles Hawk Major so that his propeller flew off. As he was prudently flying at 2,000 ft, however, he was able to glide back and alight beside a mail steamer and was picked up safely while other competitors circled overhead.

The final, flown in excellent weather, resulted in an overwhelming victory for the Miles team, thirteen of whose machines had been entered with seven going forward to fly on the Saturday. 'Tommy' Rose, the test pilot for Miles, swept into the lead in his Falcon Six and won at 176·28 m.p.h., followed by two Hawk Trainers which were barely 20 m.p.h. slower, and all were cheered wildly by 200 employees of Phillips and Powis who had come by motor-coach to watch their products perform. Captain Broad concluded his long career as test pilot to the de Havilland company by flying the Technical School's graceful T.K.2. into fourth place, and the elegant white Mew Gull with Gipsy Six engine, flown by Captain Percival and entered by the Duke of Kent, overtook most of the other machines at almost 210 m.p.h. to finish sixth. Five years earlier Percival's Hendy 302 had been the sole representative of the clean low-wing type of light aeroplane which now, technically in advance of most of the larger commercial and military types of the day, had swept the field.

Record–Breaking

1930–34

In terms of achievement and sheer activity over the long-distance routes to Australia, to the Cape and across the North and South Atlantic, the period with which we shall now deal was probably the most remarkable that the light aeroplane has ever known. It began with a fine flight by an amateur, Mr Francis Chichester (Plate 44), a young Englishman who was in partnership in an aircraft business in New Zealand, and who left that country in April 1929 to travel to England with the idea of flying himself back single-handed. He was not yet a pilot, and a delay of two months in California with illness meant that he did not reach England until the summer was well advanced. Once arrived he wasted no time but immediately began flying lessons at Brooklands, made his first solo flight in August and bought a Gipsy Moth in September, not without some financial difficulty, since his business in New Zealand was starting to feel the effect of the depression. The autumn was spent in getting the machine ready, applying for the necessary permits to cross the various territories along the route and making a trial run round Europe. By December all was ready, and at 2.30 a.m. one morning *Elijah*, as the Moth had been named, took off from the frozen grass of the Airport of London and climbed away in the darkness with its pilot holding as accurate a course as his inexperience and lack of blind-flying instruments would allow.

The first day was a long one and ended with a night landing at Pisa. Leaving there soon after midnight Chichester reached Catania in Sicily at 9.45 a.m. and snatched a few minutes' sleep before getting back into his machine for the sea crossing of 285 miles to Tripoli. He arrived over the African coast in pitch darkness and was at first unable to find the aerodrome, although he circled a bonfire which (it later turned out) had been lit to guide him. Eventually he found what appeared to be his destination, but landed by mistake in a flooded salt pan which adjoined it, as a result of which *Elijah* tipped on to her nose and broke the propeller and a front interplane strut.

This was an unfortunate end to a very fast first stage of nearly 2,000 miles, and Chichester had no alternative but to remain at Tripoli over the New Year until the Italian mechanics had put right the damage. He was away again on 9 January and successfully reached the R.A.F. station of Abu Sueir in Egypt two days later after a long non-stop flight of 854 miles from Benghazi. The regulations in Egypt dictated that he should fly back sixty-five miles to Heliopolis in order to clear Customs, but once in the air again Chichester managed to forget this inconvenient instruction and turned eastward for the Imperial Airways aerodrome at Gaza and the route across the desert to Baghdad. From Abu Sueir his engine began to give trouble with a defective exhaust valve, and a mechanic of Imperial Airways attended to this at the desert halt of Rutbah Wells, enabling him to carry on for a more detailed overhaul in the hands of the de Havilland agency in Karachi.

The rest of the flight followed the usual route across India and down the long Malay Peninsula, with heavy rainstorms and sodden aerodromes in the East Indian islands, one of the wettest regions in the world. Chichester's last stopping-place before the crossing to Darwin was Atamboea on the island of Timor, and after leaving here he flew along the length of the eastern half of the island before turning southward into the blue for the 320-mile stage over water to Australia. His Moth reached Darwin at 1.20 p.m. local time on 25 January, completing the second solo flight ever to be made from England. Since the mishap at Tripoli the journey had been reasonably free of trouble, but after leaving Darwin for the flight to Sydney, Chichester had another adventure. When approaching Camooweal from Brunette Downs he found himself running short of fuel, and being unable to see any sign of his destination in that lonely area, he decided to land near a deserted pumping-engine shed and water-hole. After waiting here in vain for help he concluded that the only thing to do was to make use of his remaining three gallons of fuel for a short and carefully timed flight of fifteen minutes out and back again. As chance would have it, a cattle station appeared below exactly at the fifteenth minute, and he was able to land and establish that Camooweal lay only four miles to the southward. After this all went well, and *Elijah* was met by a formation of aircraft over Sydney Harbour Bridge and escorted in to a landing and an enthusiastic reception. The flight from Tripoli had taken 22 days and his average daily run had been 575 miles in comparison with the 760 covered by the much more experienced pilot Hinkler.

Late in 1929 the Aga Khan offered a prize of £500 for the first solo flight to be carried out in 1930 between England and India by an Indian pilot, the direction of the flight being immaterial. The growth of the flying-club movement in India had enabled a large number of Indians to obtain licences, so that this prize offer stimulated a good response. The first pilot to attempt the journey was a student at Bristol University, Man Mohan Singh, who left Croydon on 11 January, but the weather was extremely unfavourable, and after being forced down a number of times he returned for a fresh start on the 25th, shortly afterwards to crash in the extreme south of Italy. In March Mr R. N. Chawla, who had learned to fly with the Nottingham Aero Club, left Karachi in a Moth and reached England in seventeen days, but although this was the first flight to be made over the route by an Indian pilot (and indeed the first to be made in a light aeroplane by a pilot of any nationality) it did not qualify for the prize since a passenger was carried. However, Mr Chawla's achievement was recognised by an award of 7,500 rupees. By April three pilots were in the running, one of whom, a seventeen-year-old Parsee named Aspy Merwan Engineer, had been Mr Chawla's passenger. After reaching England, young Mr. Engineer—whose unusual last name had been adopted by reason of his passion for things mechanical—set off alone in the same aeroplane and won the prize by arriving at Karachi on 11 May, just one day before his compatriot Mr J. R. D. Tata reached Croydon after a flight in the opposite direction lasting only nine days. Man Mohan Singh completed the eastward journey on his fourth attempt, overtaking Engineer on the way, but he failed to comply with a condition that the journey must not occupy more than a month and was therefore disqualified.

The flight of Flying Officers H. L. Piper and C. E. Kay from Croydon to Darwin early in 1930 established no records but is worth mention as being almost the only long-distance flight carried out in the Desoutter cabin monoplane. The Desoutter passed its tests at Martlesham Heath in November 1929 and deliveries then began, principally to National Flying Services but also to other users. The machine flown by Piper and Kay, who were New Zealanders returning to their own country on leave, was registered G-AATI and named by them *Oarangi*, and in it they set out on 9 February 1930 for an entirely uneventful journey to Sydney lasting six weeks. The aeroplane was subsequently taken on to New Zealand by sea, and it had a long and useful life in that country carrying tourists until it was irreparably damaged in an accident in 1950. Less than a year after this flight, Miss Winifred Spooner and Flying Officer E. C. T. Edwards used a Desoutter in an attempt to fly to the Cape and back in ten days, but the attempt failed when they crashed into the sea off Italy and were rescued after clinging to their floating machine for many hours.

One flight of 1930 stands out above all the rest as having caught the imagination of the public of Britain and the world, less for its exceptional speed than for its element of persistence in the face of difficulties. This was Miss Amy Johnson's flight from England to Australia in May. Miss

Johnson, whose conveniently short Christian name was often to be in the headlines over the next decade, began her career with none of the financial advantages possessed by the women pilots such as Lady Bailey and Lady Heath who had gone before her. Her father was in the trawl-fishing business in Hull, and her introduction to flying was a five-shilling joy-ride on the annual visit of Surrey Flying Services to her local aerodrome. After obtaining a B.A. in economics at Sheffield University, she began an office career in Hull at a salary of £1 a week, moved to London and after a short period as a saleswoman found a post in a solicitor's office. One day, while taking a Sunday bus ride, she passed Stag Lane aerodrome and finally persuaded herself to call in at the London Aeroplane Club to inquire the cost of flying lessons. She was placed on the waiting list and remained there a year through the summer of 1927. Eventually her turn came to take instruction, and then began a period of many sacrifices in order to continue her lessons through the winter. She did not fly solo until 9 June 1929. By the end of the month she had passed the tests for her 'A' licence and she at once set to work to study for her ground engineer's licences—'C' for rigging and 'A' for engines—which involved her in practical work in the hangars from 6.30 a.m. to 8 a.m. and in the evenings after finishing her office work, in addition to which she was studying navigation and the theory of flight. As a result of this strenuous existence she lost her job and had to ask her father to help her with the £150 she needed towards the cost of the pilot's 'B' licence.

She was now determined to fly to Australia, and cast round for a suitable aeroplane and for financial backing in order to buy it. Finally she wrote to Sir Sefton Brancker, who arranged for her to have an interview with Lord Wakefield, formerly Sir Charles Wakefield, and his well-known generosity to aviation did not fail her. He agreed to put up £300 as half the cost of the second-hand machine which she had decided upon, and once again her father came to the rescue with the balance of the money although, like the rest of her friends and relatives, he had little confidence in her projected flight. She named the green and silver Gipsy Moth *Jason* (Plate 46), after her father's trade-mark, and spent some of her remaining money on maps of the route and on a parachute, a rare item of equipment outside the Service but one which she felt to be desirable for such a long and uncertain undertaking.

By 4 May all was ready and Miss Johnson flew *Jason* over from Stag Lane to Croydon where she had booked a room at the Aerodrome Hotel to be sure of an early start the next morning. For the short trip over to Croydon fellow members of the London Aeroplane Club provided an escort of five Moths as a send-off. One or two friends and her father were there to see her start, and just before 8 a.m. she was installed in the cockpit with all her equipment on board, including a spare propeller lashed to the centre-section struts. Her first attempt at taking off was unsuccessful and she taxied back to try again; then she got away and the little biplane headed away to the south-east and was lost to sight. Few among those watching imagined that it would get very far.

Miss Johnson had carefully considered the various possible routes to the Middle East and had chosen that by way of Vienna and Constantinople, avoiding the crossing of the Mediterranean. She had never before been out of England and her longest cross-country flight had been from Stag Lane to Hull, but she found her way safely across Europe and landed at Vienna after nearly ten hours in the air, and the next evening she was at Constantinople, having covered 1,600 miles in two days. Two years earlier Hinkler had only reached Malta on the second evening, a distance of 1,500 miles, and it now began to appear that he had a serious challenger in the unknown office girl. The next day, after an alarming experience flying up a cloud-covered ravine in the Taurus mountains, she reached Aleppo, and took off for Baghdad on the fourth morning. When she was almost within sight of the city, however, a violent sandstorm reduced visibility to nothing and the Moth was forced down in the desert. To prevent it being blown over in the violent wind, she was compelled to unload luggage and pile it against the wheels, hanging on to the machine for two hours until conditions improved sufficiently for her to take off again and reach Baghdad.

She had now flown nearly as far in four days as Hinkler had done in five, and although it was not her original intention to break records it was impossible to resist the temptation to improve on his time. She therefore passed by Basra, where Hinkler had spent his sixth night, and flew 830 miles to Bandar Abbas, whence she took off again having had only two hours' sleep after working on her machine until the early morning, and reached Karachi in a further nine hours.

This was the fastest journey to India that had ever been made. Miss Johnson was two days ahead of Hinkler and it seemed that she was within reach of a new record from England to Australia, but on the way to Allahabad she ran short of fuel and had to land on a military parade ground at Jhansi. She hit a notice board in doing so but without serious damage; repairs were carried out by the regimental carpenter. Two days later, after a frightening passage across the Arakan Yoma in rain and wind, she failed to find Rangoon in very bad visibility, landed on a football field at Insein and could not prevent the Moth from rolling into a ditch, breaking her propeller and damaging the undercarriage and starboard wing. Her two-day lead dwindled to nothing while her machine was repaired by the Government Technical Institute, a task which included the letting in of a new three-foot section into the wing, and not until the morning of the 16th was it ready. Since the football field was too small for taking off, arrangements were made to tow her aeroplane to Rangoon racecourse by road, and she was in the air by 9.30 in the morning, faced with a long struggle to cross the mountains into Siam in appalling weather. She landed at the Don Muang aerodrome, Bangkok, at 6.30 p.m. local time on her twelfth day out from England; Hinkler, following the west coast of the peninsula, had at the corresponding time been at Victoria Point, almost three hundred miles further south.

More rain and wind in southern Siam finally spoiled her chances of beating Hinkler, and it was a further two days before *Jason* appeared over Singapore Island to be escorted in by Moth seaplanes of the local flying club. At Singapore a new starboard lower wing was fitted in place of the damaged one, and the next day she was off for Sourabaya. Shortage of fuel drove her down in a sugar plantation at Tjoemal where her aeroplane's wing was again damaged by some sticks and local help had to be called upon for repairs. After flying on to Sourabaya next day in company with a Dutch mailplane she set off down the long chain of islands for Atamboea on Timor and vanished into a long and worrying silence, which caused the Dutch authorities to make preparations for a search. Finally it turned out that she had been overtaken by darkness crossing the sea to the island of Timor and had consequently decided to put the Moth down in a clearing at Halilulik, twelve miles short of her destination and a long way from a telephone.

Next day came the wide emptiness of the Timor Sea. The Shell oil tanker *Phorus* was ordered to keep a lookout for her, and when the little Moth skimmed low across the ship hundreds of miles from land a wireless message was sent out to Darwin, now only hours away. She was sighted off the coast at 3.30 p.m. and it was not long before *Jason* was landing to the cheers of the crowd which had gathered to welcome her. When she arrived in the sunshine of an Australian winter afternoon, Londoners were still asleep in a summer dawn, but within an hour or two the posters were out in the capital with the simple but adequate words 'She's There'. She had fulfilled her ambition, but the strain of almost twenty days had begun to tell on her, and on the way to Sydney a few days later she crashed the battered Moth into a boundary fence and finished her journey in a commercial aeroplane of Australian National Airways, flown by a young Scotsman called James Mollison.

After a wonderful reception in Sydney Miss Johnson set out for home by sea, travelling the last stages by Imperial Airways air liner to Vienna and London. Strong headwinds delayed the machine, and it was not until 9 p.m. on 4 August, a showery Bank Holiday Monday, that it appeared

The flights of Hinkler, Chichester and Amy Johnson from England to Australia. Hinkler's route is shown by the solid line. This was substantially the route followed by Chichester, and any differences are noted in the text. Amy Johnson took a different route across Europe, as shown by the dotted line, joined Hinkler's route at Baghdad and thereafter followed it with only minor variations to Darwin. All three pilots continued on to Sydney, but for simplicity only the actual England–Australia section is shown here

ROUTES

HINKLER

Croydon, Rome, Malta, Tobruk, Ramleh, Basra, Jask, Karachi, Cawnpore, Calcutta, Rangoon, Victoria Point, Singapore, Bandoeng, Bima, Darwin

CHICHESTER

Croydon, Lyons, Pisa, Catania, Tripoli (crashed), Benghazi, Abu Sueir, Gaza, Rutba Wells, Baghdad, Bushire, Jask, Charbar, Karachi, Nazirabad, Jhansi, Allahabad, Calcutta, Akyab, Rangoon, Victoria Point, Singapore, Batavia, Pemalang, Sourabaya, Bima, Atamboea, Darwin

AMY JOHNSON

Croydon, Vienna, Constantinople, Aleppo, Baghdad, Bandar Abbas, Karachi, Jhansi, Allahabad, Calcutta, Insein (damaged wing), Rangoon, Bangkok, Singora, Singapore, Tjoemal (Java), Sourabaya, Bima, Atamboea, Darwin

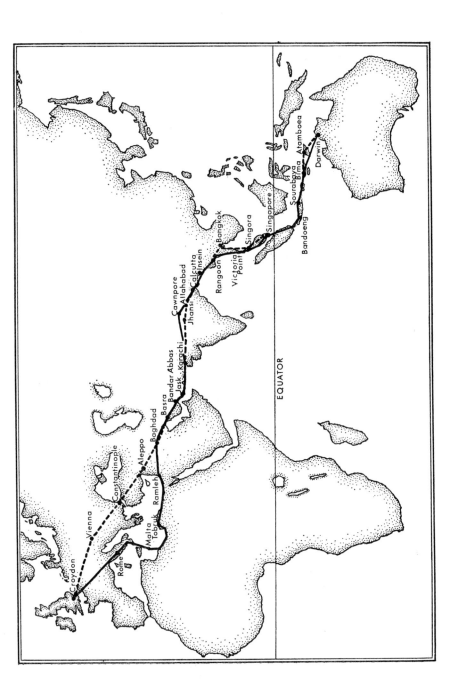

over Croydon in the dusk. 'She's stalling', explained the B.B.C. announcer helpfully, causing the hearts of several thousand flying-club members to miss a beat; but this slur on Captain Youell's ability proved to be unfounded and the Argosy landed smoothly on the turf from which *Jason*—now repaired, shipped home and standing by the reception dais—had climbed away three months earlier. The welcome which awaited its pilot was overwhelming; the public, touched by her struggle against odds both before and during her flight, took her to its heart. What she had done seemed to many to be a new statement of woman's freedom, for starting with no advantages of wealth or influence she had planned and completed an adventure to stir the imagination of all. Instead of the doubting few who had watched her departure, there were now 200,000 people impatiently waiting, as well as an official reception committee which included the Air Minister (Lord Thomson), Lord Wakefield, Miss Margaret Bondfield (the first woman Minister to hold office), the Mayor and Sheriff of Hull and Amy's parents. Sir Sefton Brancker was also there, to see his attempt to bring flying to the ordinary man and woman bear fruit in the triumph of an unknown Yorkshire girl. The route from Croydon to her hotel in Park Lane was lined four or five deep with cheering crowds, and the cheque for £10,000 presented to her by Mr Esmond Harmsworth at the *Daily Mail* luncheon at the Savoy next day was only the beginning of a shower of gifts and honours, which included the C.B.E., an M.G. sports car from Sir William Morris, a gold cup bearing an inscription from the youth of Great Britain, a silver globe from the people of Hull, honorary membership of the Guild of Air Pilots and Air Navigators, a brand-new Gipsy Moth subscribed for by readers of the *Daily Sketch* and *Sunday Graphic* and presented by Sir Sefton Brancker in Hyde Park before a crowd of 100,000, and an equally new Puss Moth presented by the de Havilland Aircraft Company. It was not perhaps surprising that she subsequently became ill and had to terminate the aerial tour of the seaside towns which had been arranged by the *Daily Mail* in order to retire into a nursing home.

After Amy Johnson's flight a stream of pilots set off for Australia with the idea of bettering Hinkler's still unbroken record of 15 days. One of the rare tragedies of long-distance flying at this time occurred in July, when two Australians bound southward through Burma in a Moth—E. L. Hook and J. Matthews—crashed in a remote area between Akyab and Rangoon and Hook died while his companion went for help. In September a namesake, Captain F. R. Matthews, formerly chief instructor at the London Aeroplane Club, left Croydon flying alone in one of the new Puss Moths with special tankage for 100 gallons of petrol. He crossed India and Burma successfully but a crash some distance north of Bangkok caused some delay. In spite of this he later continued and managed to reach

Darwin thirty-two days after leaving England. This was the beginning of a long series of distinguished flights by the Puss Moth. Its capabilities had been effectively shown at the end of July when Captain C. D. Barnard had flown one 1,400 miles from England to Malta in thirteen hours, returning next day and flying both long stages in his shirt-sleeves as an illustration that the age of cabin comfort for the light aeroplane pilot had at last arrived. Shortly afterwards he capped this performance with a similar pair of non-stop flights from Lympne to Tangier and back.

By October 1930, when the bad flying conditions in India and Burma had improved with the easing of the south-west monsoon, departures along the Australia route were an almost daily occurrence. On 5 October, the fatal Sunday when R.101 crashed into a wood near Beauvais killing Lord Thomson, Sir Sefton Brancker and forty-six others, the Gipsy Moth of Flight Lieutenant C. W. Hill passed over the skeleton of the great airship only a few hours after the disaster on the first stage of his flight to Darwin. The day after he was followed from Croydon by a Puss Moth flown by Flying Officer C. J. Chabot and Major C. E. M. Pickthorne, and three days later, at 5.35 a.m. on 9 October, a special Avro Avian departed from Heston carrying an Australian pilot, Charles Kingsford Smith (Plate 45). An unofficial race to Australia and a concerted attack upon Hinkler's record was under way. Kingsford Smith was already well-known for his flights in the historic three-engined Fokker monoplane *Southern Cross*, which had carried him and his crew across the Pacific in 1928, across the Tasman Sea in both directions a few months later, from Australia to England in June and July 1929, and finally across the Atlantic from east to west in June 1930 and back to California to complete the circuit of the earth.

As might have been expected from Kingsford Smith's great experience of long-distance flying, his Avian, which he named *Southern Cross Junior*, was most comprehensively equipped, carrying a two-gallon drinking-water tank, an extra oil tank, a supply of emergency rations, a revolver and ammunition, a spare propeller enclosed within the fuselage decking, a Pioneer turn-and-bank indicator, two compasses and instrument lighting operated by flash-lamp batteries. With all this equipment and a full load of fuel, the take-off run was 360 yards, or about three times the distance for an ordinary club machine.

Kingsford Smith's first day's journey was to Rome, as Hinkler's had been, and here an attempt to make an early start was frustrated by the absence of the official who was to sign his papers, but he was finally off at 10 a.m., reached Athens that night and Aleppo the night following. While crossing the desert to Baghdad he met severe sand-storms, and these seriously reduced visibility for some hours, but he got through successfully and continued to Bushire and Jask. At Jask he encountered the stranded Mrs Victor Bruce, who had left Heston in her Bluebird on a world flight about a fortnight before him. Arriving at Karachi, which he reached in one day less than Amy Johnson, he found Pickthorne and Chabot awaiting him, with the news that they had decided to give up their attempt because of various delays and that Matthews had also fallen out after his accident in Siam. Only Hill remained, therefore, flying on to-wards Australia some unknown distance ahead. After a fine day's run of 1,111 miles in under twelve hours from Allahabad to Rangoon, Kingsford Smith continued down the Tenasserim coast and, arriving very tired at Seletar aerodrome on Singapore Island, landed down-wind in error and broke the Avian's undercarriage. With full R.A.F. facilities available, how-ever, this was not too serious; it was repaired overnight and he was away across the Equator before sunrise, hard on the tail of his only remaining competitor. He was told on reaching Sourabaya that Hill had spent the previous night there, and the next day arrived at Atamboea to find his rival's Moth damaged after a crash on take-off. The two pilots spent an interesting evening together in the rest-house exchanging stories* and Kingsford Smith was full of plans for taking Hill with him in the Avian, but this proved impossible for reasons of space and weight, and finally Hill lent him his rubber boat for the crossing of the Timor. In the morning, there-fore, the Avian took off with a disappointed Hill waving goodbye, and Kingsford Smith landed safely at Darwin at 1.50 p.m. local time on 19 October, after a fine flight from Heston in under ten days.

There is a great deal of difference between the breaking of a record by a pilot of great experience and a flight round a large part of the globe by an optimistic novice, and to those who believe in the light aeroplane as a vehicle for the ordinary man and woman the latter performance is in many ways more satisfying. Thus the flight of Mr Oscar Garden from Croydon to Australia in eighteen days in his Gipsy Moth, *Kia Ora*, though over-shadowed by that of Kingsford Smith which just preceded it, was a most meritorious one in view of his very small flying experience. Even more remarkable was the flight of the Hon. Mrs Victor Bruce (Plate 47), an experienced sporting motorist who (according to her own modest account) was shopping in London one day when the sight of a Blackburn Bluebird in a showroom window with a ticket 'Ready to Go Anywhere' inspired her with the idea of flying round the world and visiting her mother's birth-place in America. She at once began to make the necessary preparations quite regardless of the fact that she had not yet learned to fly, and had soon purchased the Bluebird—a metal Mark IV type with Gipsy II engine—

---

* Hill had much to contribute, for it was he who played a leading part in the extraordinary story of bogus spiritualism in a Turkish prison camp which is described in Lieut. E. H. Jones' book, *The Road to Endor*.

and arranged for the installation of extra tankage and a specially-designed automatic wireless transmitter which would enable the sending of selected messages of reassurance or distress without the need for a knowledge of the Morse Code. When the weight of the machine and its fuel and equipment was reckoned up, Mrs Bruce found that she would have to choose between taking a parachute and installing a dictaphone to record her impressions in the air, and she promptly chose the latter.

In the intervals of buying maps and making other arrangements for the flight she was taking flying lessons, and when the time came for her departure she had held an 'A' licence for only eight weeks and had done no more than forty hours of solo flying. In consequence there were many who thought little of her chances of completing the flight successfully, among them the ground engineer who when asked by an inquisitive bystander the meaning of the registration letters G-ABDS painted on the Bluebird, wearily replied 'a bloody daft stunt'. In spite of her inexperience, however, Mrs Bruce was firmly determined to carry on, and in the early dawn of a September morning in 1930 she climbed into her machine at Heston and waved goodbye to her husband, her small son and the party of friends that had come to see her off.

Her adventures were many and various. A strong headwind forced her to come down short of petrol in the Syrian desert, and she had to ride to a nearby village on the back of an Arab's horse (an incident later transformed by the popular Press into 'abduction by a sheikh') and there buy a small tinful at an exorbitant price. Later, when crossing the hundred miles of sea across the Strait of Hormuz, at the mouth of the Persian Gulf, rapidly failing oil pressure forced her to land on the first available piece of dry land, which turned out to be quicksand and tipped the machine on to its nose, breaking the propeller. With the help of some tribesmen, she righted the aeroplane, fitted the spare propeller with unsuitable tools at the cost of severely lacerated hands, and then found that it was impossible to take off from the soft sand, so that it was several days before she could be rescued by a search party sent out from Jask. In the meantime, a party of brigands, fortunately of fairly amiable type, had descended on the Bluebird and relieved her of more money, and some of the friendly tribesmen had eaten one of her dictaphone records in the mistaken belief that it was made of chocolate. When she reached Jask, she was overtaken by Oscar Garden in his Moth and they flew in company to Karachi and again from Calcutta to Rangoon. Thereafter their ways parted and he continued to Australia while Mrs Bruce turned eastwards for Siam, Indo-China and Japan.

She reached Bangkok without difficulty, but while attempting the crossing of the mountains to Hanoi in bad weather she set out and flew eastward over unbroken cloud for four hours, her first experience of this type of flying. At the end of this time, uncertain whether the mountains still lay below, she took her courage in both hands, breathed a tense last message into the dictaphone, closed the throttle and sank into the clouds. With the extraordinary luck of so many amateur pilots in these years, she emerged from the clouds directly over a railway which in a few minutes led her to Hanoi, and thence to Japan.

After an enthusiastic reception in Tokyo, the little Bluebird was loaded on board the *Empress of Japan* for the Pacific crossing and re-assembled in Vancouver for a flight across America, in the course of which Mrs Bruce fulfilled her original intention of dropping a flag by her mother's old house. Before reaching New York she had two crashes, and during repairs the old fabric was carefully replaced to preserve the thousands of signatures collected during the tour, including that of the notorious Al Capone, who had inscribed his name on the tail at Chicago. The Atlantic was crossed by sea, and the final stage from Havre to Croydon was followed by a great gathering of Bluebirds at Heston. The much-travelled G-ABDS was exhibited in Charing Cross Underground station after a journey of nearly 20,000 miles through twenty-three countries in less than five months. The stunt had not, after all, turned out to be such a daft one.

On the other side of the world Francis Chichester was preparing for a comparatively short but exceedingly difficult flight. After his arrival in Australia in January 1930, Chichester took his Moth on to New Zealand by ship, but thereafter the idea of flying it solo across the Tasman Sea, and so completing his link with England, continued to exercise his mind. But the distance across that stormy stretch of water from Wellington to Sydney is 1,450 miles and by no artifice could the range of *Elijah* be sufficiently extended to make the journey possible. Browsing over a globe one day, however, Chichester noticed two specks in the ocean, Norfolk Island and Lord Howe Island, which could serve as stepping stones across the Tasman and reduce the journey to one of three stages, the longest of which would be only 560 miles. Since the islands offered nothing in the way of aerodromes, the crossing could only be made by a seaplane, and Chichester therefore cast around for a pair of floats for the Moth, eventually managing to borrow a discarded pair from the Auckland Air Base. At the cost of a considerable drop in performance, therefore, *Elijah* was converted into a seaplane, though a tiny and fragile enough machine for operation over the open ocean, and in the meantime her pilot had taken a course of sea-plane training with the Territorial Air Force.

The most difficult problem, however, was navigation. Ordinary light aeroplane flying was (and for the most part still is) carried out by dead reckoning—the steering of a calculated course for a calculated time, any errors from the intended track being corrected by the pilot from time to time by observation of landmarks on the surface. This method is perfectly satisfactory for flying over populous country and can be made to serve for crossings of sea or desert provided that the distant objective is broad enough to absorb the accumulated errors; but Chichester's project involved striking islands only a few miles across after flying over five hundred miles or more of featureless ocean—islands, moreover, which were themselves so remote from the nearest land that no alternative lay within the range of his Moth. The only reliable solution lay in the use of celestial methods, but to use a sextant and carry out the subsequent calculations in spherical trigonometry while flying solo in an open cockpit, battered by the slipstream and having the continuous responsibility of keeping the machine on course and on a level keel, would appear to most pilots a quite impossible task. Nevertheless, this was what Chichester planned to do, in the face of all advice to the contrary, and he settled down to studying astro-navigation and practising the use of a sextant from an open car driven at high speed.

In January 1931 his hopes of being the first man to fly solo across the Tasman were dashed, for the Australian Guy Menzies, flying the Avian with which Kingsford Smith had set up his England-to-Australia record, took advantage of that machine's exceptional range to cross from Sydney to South Island. Nevertheless, Chichester continued with his plans, and although some of his trial shots with a sextant led to dangerously large errors which would be serious on the actual crossing, he continued cheerfully to assume that everything would be 'all right on the night'. *Elijah* was loaded up with equipment including sextant, chronometer watch, barometer, navigation tables and charts, position-line slide-rule, protractors, rulers, camera, rubber boat and transmitting wireless set, and early on the autumn morning of 28 March 1931 Chichester took off from Auckland on the long journey to Norfolk Island—an island he had never seen and which was a mere speck in the ocean subtending only half a degree at the extreme northern tip of New Zealand.

The risks were immense. Refuelling at Parengarenga Harbour held up his departure until 11.50, which meant that even in still air his estimated time of arrival had gone back to ten minutes after sunset, so that a headwind would mean an arrival in darkness, and not only was the island unlighted but he had no astronomical tables for use after dark. Apart from the normal and ever-present possibility of engine failure over a most unfrequented stretch of ocean, there were the chances that heavy cloud would obscure the sun and make observations impossible, that a single error in calculation would lead him wildly astray, and that the island would be buried in cloud and invisible even at the small distance to which accurate navigation ought to bring him. To avoid the dilemma of not knowing which way to turn if his objective failed to appear at the calculated time, he planned to fly to a point to one side of the island and then run down an astronomical position line passing through it. After hours of flying over the open ocean, the time to make the turn finally came and, overcoming with difficulty the powerful psychological resistance against such a sharp alteration of course in the empty mid-ocean, he swung the Moth round and ran on down the line until the calculated instant came. There was no sign of land, and an agonising ten minutes passed, with false islands end-lessly looming and then dissolving into cloud, before his real destination appeared at last.

The difficulties of alighting in open sea, refuelling, repairing a fault in the engine and finally taking off from a narrow strip of sheltered water three days later (Plate 48), were formidable enough, but there was worse to come. After another interminable flight over 561 miles of water to Lord Howe Island, once more with hours of nerve-racking uncertainty until it too eventually loomed up out of the cloud, Chichester moored the Moth on the lagoon only to return the next morning after a squally night and find it sunk, upside down, with only the tail and the after-ends of the floats above the water. This should by any ordinary reckoning have ended the adventure, but *Elijah*'s indefatigable pilot, helped by the islanders, sal-vaged the machine and its engine, stripped them down to the last nut and bolt, cleaned and painted everything and rebuilt it from top to bottom using new fabric, dope and spare parts forwarded by sea from Australia. Nine weeks of this labour, interspersed with fishing and enjoying the leisurely life of the sub-tropical island, sufficed for Chichester to have his aeroplane ready for flight again, and after carrying out a series of test flights and giving joy-rides to his willing helpers he set off again for Sydney which he reached successfully. The rebuilt machine flew perfectly, and ironically enough his chief anxiety on this stage was rough running of the engine due to intermittent defects in both magnetos—the only com-ponents which had been sent to the mainland for professional overhaul.

Few of the cheers, acclamations and gifts which greeted Amy Johnson came to Chichester for this flight, but it remains one of the most remark-able in aviation history, and in recognition of it he was awarded the Johns-ton Memorial Navigation Trophy, subscribed for in memory of the navi-gator of R.101.

Having flown from England to Australia and completed the crossing of the Tasman, Chichester planned to finish his circuit of the world back to England by way of New Guinea, Japan, Alaska, Canada, Greenland and Iceland, and he set off again from Sydney only a few weeks after arriving in Australia, still in his little seaplane. The project came to a sudden end,

47. Mrs Victor Bruce after her world tour
by Bluebird

46. Miss Amy Johnson and *Jason*

44. Mr Francis Chichester
45. Sir Charles Kingsford Smith

48. Mr Francis Chichester's Moth seaplane in Emily Bay, Norfolk Island, during his flight across the Tasman Sea in 1931

49. Two record-breakers: Mr J. A. Mollison (left) and Mr C. W. A. Scott

however, when *Elijah* hit a telegraph wire in Japan while taking off for Tokyo and was completely wrecked. Chichester was injured but his passion for adventurous travel continued; he flew a Puss Moth from Australia to England several years later and in more recent times came into

Mr F. C. Chichester's seaplane flight across the Tasman Sea

prominence at the age of 59 by winning a single-handed race across the North Atlantic in his yacht, significantly named 'Gipsy Moth III'.

While Chichester was on Norfolk Island in the middle of the Tasman, another pilot was just setting out from Lympne in an attempt to reach Australia in a shorter time than Kingsford Smith. This was Mr C. W. A. Scott, who after the expiry of his short-service commission with the Royal Air Force had gone to Australia to join the Queensland and Northern Territory Air Service. Scott had taken part in the search for Hinkler near

Camooweal in 1928 and he had also been present at Darwin on the day in 1930 when Amy Johnson, dressed in an oily shirt and shorts, had climbed out of her Moth after flying alone from England. Having determined to try long-distance flying for himself, Scott had found someone in Brisbane who was prepared to buy his machine from him at the end of his flight, so he gave up his job and set out for England by sea to collect a Moth from Stag Lane and fly it back. His start was delayed until 1 April 1931, but on that day he was able to get away to a fine first stage from Lympne to Belgrade non-stop. Progress for the next two days was slower, but he left Baghdad on the fourth morning with the intention of reaching Karachi, 1,700 miles on, by nightfall. After a hopeless race with daylight he was compelled to spend the night at Gwadar on the deserted coast of Oman— a stopping-place which, curiously enough, he found himself using on his two subsequent Moth flights along the same route. By the end of the seventh day, when Kingsford Smith had been at Rangoon, Scott was ahead of him at Victoria Point, and another losing battle with daylight brought him to a landing in pitch darkness at Bima, where the aerodrome was under six inches of water. He was able to make no check on machine or engine owing to the darkness, and set off at dawn for the crossing of the Timor. Water in the petrol caused the engine to cut out twice while he was flying along the island of Flores, but in spite of this ominous beginning the Moth carried him safely across to Darwin to touch down on Australian soil, having improved on Kingsford Smith's time by seventeen hours.

Although he was feeling somewhat unfit after this flight, Scott allowed himself to be persuaded to attempt the return journey in a similar aeroplane and took off from Wyndham for England again less than two months after his arrival. His flight was not without setbacks—an oil leak over the Timor Sea and sunstroke in India—but with a last stage of thirteen and a half hours non-stop from Brindisi he landed at Lympne in the evening of 5 June to complete the first light aeroplane flight ever made from Australia to England and to break by two days the absolute record for the journey set up by the *Southern Cross* almost exactly two years earlier.

Scott's achievement was quickly capped by James Mollison, another short-service officer who had known Scott during his time in the R.A.F. and who, like him, had gone to Australia when his term of service had expired. After a leisurely journey out by way of Tahiti, spending his gratuity on enjoying himself in the sunshine, Mollison had ended up as a bathing-beach attendant at Bondi Beach, and it was only the sight of one of the aeroplanes of the local flying club passing over his beach that recalled him to the air. After a short time as a club flying instructor he became an air line pilot with Australian National Airways, and it was while performing this duty that he flew Amy Johnson to Sydney. Mollison heard of Scott's preparations for a flight to England and, although completely unknown, audaciously persuaded Lord Wakefield through his Australian agent to provide a Moth and the necessary financial backing for a similar attempt. He set off from Darwin before Scott but flew no further than the length of that rather small aerodrome before crashing the heavily loaded machine into some telegraph wires and completely wrecking it. This neither deterred nor seriously injured him, and he at once despatched a cable to Lord Wakefield asking for a new Moth—a bold request to which that generous peer long-sufferingly acceded. For his next attempt Mollison followed Scott's example and chose the larger aerodrome of Wyndham, and from here he successfully took off just after midnight on 30 July. The journey was relatively uneventful except for one unsuccessful attempt to cross the Arakan Yoma due to the heavy monsoon clouds, which he overcame next day by flying high. In conditions of low cloud and poor visibility he reached the English coast at Pevensey having flown some 11,000 miles from Australia in 8 days, 19 hours and 25 minutes, but the weather and his extreme fatigue made it impossible for him to carry on to Croydon, so he put the machine down on the beach while he had a few hours' rest in a bungalow before completing his journey. He had left Australia entirely unknown, without a job and with only £5 in his pocket, but this flight, which in all earned him some £7,000, set him firmly on the road to becoming one of the most celebrated long-distance pilots of the 1930s (Plate 49).

Only a few weeks after Mollison's arrival at Pevensey, Kingsford Smith set out once more from Melbourne bound for England in a specially-built Avian similar to that which he had used for his outward flight. The torrential rainstorms which Mollison had encountered gave him a good deal of trouble along the west coast of the Malay peninsula, and he had to make a forced landing on the beach eighty miles south of Victoria Point. From then on continuing bad luck and illness made it impossible for him to reach England in time to beat Mollison. However, the flights of Scott and Mollison and the unsuccessful attempt by Kingsford Smith did not complete the story of the Australia route in this busy year of 1931, for they were soon followed by a surprising achievement by Nicholas Comper's tiny single-seat monoplane, the Swift, a machine which hardly appears a suitable vehicle for long-distance record-breaking. A few months previously Lieutenant C. Byas, R.N., had flown a Pobjoy-engined Swift from England to the Cape in a matter of ten days, and a similar machine was chosen by Mr C. A. Butler for his attempt on Scott's record. Mr Butler, an Englishman who had spent some years in Australia, had in the previous year designed, built and flown an all-metal monoplane on very similar lines to the Swift, and this no doubt much influenced his choice. His machine, G-ABRE, was modified to carry extra tankage holding 42 gallons of fuel, equivalent to the weight of two passengers, and a cruising range of 1,075 miles was thereby obtained. Naturally the pilot's luggage could not be very extensive, and Mr Butler was able to restrict his belongings to a total of one-and-a-half pounds, excepting only the pair of carpet slippers which he wore for the whole journey. Leaving Lympne on 31 October and reaching Naples in a single flight, he arrived at Darwin without incident in a fraction over nine days.

Another unusual feat to the Swift's credit was the double crossing of the Andes by Comper's representative in the Argentine, Mr C. Taylor. Leaving Buenos Ayres early in the morning of Sunday, 6 March 1932, Mr Taylor flew a Swift up to Las Jamarindas (Mendoza) on the Argentine side of the range, and after spending a few days there to get his papers in order, took off for Chile on the Wednesday morning. He had been offered oxygen equipment for the crossing by Pan-American Grace Airways but was unable to fit it into his aeroplane, so he climbed to 18,000 ft without it and cleared the Puerto del Inca (14,500 ft) with no distress from the high altitude other than a slight pain in the temples. After a two-hour flight he was forced down unintentionally by thick fog at Nogales, Chile, where the police detained him for six hours to check on his unconventional mode of entry. A fortnight later he flew back again, this time taking only an hour and forty minutes. There is something particularly impressive about this traverse of so high a range of mountains by so small an aeroplane, and it seems unlikely that the feat has ever been repeated by a machine of comparable size.*

The achievements of Chichester, Amy Johnson and Kingsford Smith on the Australia route had somewhat diverted attention from flights down Africa in 1930. The solo record still rested with Murdoch, though it had been unsuccessfully attacked by Mr Roy Tuckett, who in November 1929 had set out from Croydon in a Gipsy Moth. Six months after starting, Mr Tuckett, surely the most unfortunate of long-distance pilots, was seen by the residents of Touws River, a small village in Cape Province, wearily pushing his aeroplane down the main street in search of a petrol pump. His forced landing with dry tanks on the Touws golf course was the last of a long series of misfortunes, including an accident at Alexandria when the engine was started with no pilot on board, a somersault in Uganda after losing a wheel and a forced landing in a forest clearing near Abercorn.

In October 1930, however, both the solo record and the absolute record for the outward journey to the Cape fell simultaneously to a former pilot of the South African Air Force, Lieutenant R. F. Caspareuthus, who

* The Andes have, however, been crossed in more recent years by a de Havilland Chipmunk.

was delivering a new Puss Moth from Stag Lane to South Africa. Caspareuthus left England on the same day as Flight Lieutenant Hill—5 October —and like him passed over the scene of the disaster at Beauvais in which Sir Sefton Brancker had met his death; he was in fact carrying on board his machine letters from Sir Sefton to South African officials. He completed the journey in eight days, the Puss Moth effortlessly covering the 8,000 miles in just under 77 hours' flying time. Later its pilot joined Imperial Airways and had the distinction of flying the D. H. Hercules machine *City of Karachi* on the first air mail flight from the Cape to London in January 1932.

In February 1931 a very experienced war-time pilot with over 8,000 hours' flying—Flight Lieutenant 'Tommy' Rose—unsuccessfully attempted the Cape record in both directions in a Sports Avian and then Commander Glen Kidston and Mr O. Cathcart Jones completed the outward journey in six-and-a-half days in an American Lockheed Vega. This was a fast cabin monoplane with extremely clean lines, capable of 180 m.p.h. and extensively used for long-distance flying by American pilots at this time. It was therefore a formidable rival to the little Puss Moth, a light aeroplane of roughly one-quarter the power and one-sixth the price, yet only a few months passed before a Puss Moth was again attempting the Cape record. Its owner was a nineteen-year-old débutante, Miss Peggy Salaman, who had been given it as a birthday present by her mother and had flown in it as a passenger in the King's Cup Race. Miss Salaman had herself learned to fly with N.F.S. at Hanworth, but at the time at which she planned to start for the Cape she had a mere ten hours' solo flying to her credit, and a South African instructor at the London Aeroplane Club, Mr Gordon Store, was therefore engaged to go with her. They departed from Lympne on 30 October 1931 and made a fast flight to Athens (1,563 miles) by the evening, reaching Wadi Halfa at sundown the next day. Between Abercorn and Broken Hill gathering darkness forced them down and they had to spend the night in a clearing in the bush, taking off early next day for Bulawayo and continuing to Kimberley, where two small lion cubs that Miss Salaman had bought in Juba were deposited with the Mayor to be forwarded to Cape Town by train, having proved something of an embarrassment in the Puss Moth's small cabin. Their aeroplane landed at the new Windermere aerodrome at Cape Town early in the morning of 5 November having flown from England in 5 days 6 hours and 40 minutes. Although Miss Salaman received the larger share of attention from the Press, it was obvious to those with a knowledge of flying that much of the credit was due to her very much more experienced companion.

So far no light aeroplane had made a successful crossing of the Atlantic

Ocean. Lieutenant-Commander MacDonald had been lost in his Gipsy Moth between Newfoundland and Ireland in 1928 and two years later Squadron Leader C. S. Wynne-Eyton had crashed at St John's in one of the early Puss Moths while taking off to attempt the same flight, escaping with his life, although his aeroplane was very heavily loaded with petrol and caught fire after the accident. Bert Hinkler, who after his flight to Australia in 1928 had vainly tried to make a commercial success of his Ibis, had later given it up and moved to Canada. He took with him a Puss Moth with which he hoped to make a living in the air transport business, but this too was unsuccessful, and with no prospects and few assets except his aeroplane, he resolved to attempt another long-distance flight, this time across the South Atlantic. His first stage, begun on 27 October 1931, took him non-stop from the North Beach airport, New York, to Kingston, Jamaica, a distance of 1,850 miles, and since the Puss Moth had no navigation lights and therefore did not comply with United States regulations he was forced to fly well out over the sea during the hours of darkness. His machine also lacked any form of instrument lighting, and he used the moon and a luminous compass, estimating drift over the water as best he could. On 9 November he crossed another 700 miles of water to Maracaibo, and by the 24th, he was at Port Natal. Next day he took off for the long flight to Africa.

The weather was clear when he left, and to minimise the effect of a north-easterly wind he held the aeroplane down to a height of only a few feet above the sea. By nightfall heavy clouds were gathering and he climbed to 10,000 ft, flying through violent storms for over four hours with the instrument panel lit up by the continuous lightning. The crossing took 22 hours through these varied and unfavourable conditions, yet he made landfall on the Bissagos Islands south of Bathurst within ten miles of his intended position. This remarkable flight was not only the first crossing of the Atlantic Ocean by light aeroplane but also the first solo flight across the South Atlantic and the first crossing from west to east by any type of machine, and on his return to England Hinkler was awarded the Gold Medal of the Royal Aero Club and became the second holder of the Johnston Trophy.

After this long flight he began to fit out his machine *Karohi* for another attempt at the Australia record, equipping it in his usual ingenious and painstaking way with a special flowmeter to check fuel consumption in the air, a fresh-oil replenisher and a hooded instrument panel with flash-lamp lighting. By the end of 1932 he was ready, and on 7 January 1933 he took off in the small hours from the Fairey aerodrome at Feltham. After this he vanished utterly, and searches revealed nothing, although an aeroplane believed to be his was reported to have been seen crossing the Alps. It was

not until 28 April that his body and the wreckage of *Karohi* were discovered by some charcoal-burners in a remote spot in the Pratagnano
mountains north-west of Arezzo. The reason for the crash was never
established, although it was known that conditions at the time were likely
to cause ice formation. Bert Hinkler, with his modest personality and
exceptional skill as pilot and engineer, had contributed much to the aeronautical scene, and in particular to the development of the light aeroplane.
His death at the age of forty-one was a severe loss.

In the meantime Mollison, after a tour of Scotland during which he
gave broadcast flying lessons from the air on behalf of the *Daily Mail*, was
making preparations for a fast solo flight to the Cape. He left England in
November (on Friday the 13th), and some way up the Nile he found that
the pump which forced petrol up to the gravity-tank was not working
properly. He therefore decided to land by moonlight in a large open field
at El Minya, two hundred miles from Cairo, but unfortunately it happened
that the field was under a crop of maize five feet high, and the flight ended
abruptly as the aeroplane went over on to its back.

For his next attempt Mollison decided to use a Puss Moth and to take
the direct western route across the Sahara, saving a matter of 800 miles and
accepting the risk of the long desert crossing. The date fixed for his
departure was 21 March, which would enable the necessary night flying
to be carried out in the light of the full moon, but as it turned out the
weather was unfavourable on that day and the two succeeding days; so
that Scott, who was waiting with him at Lympne to attempt the Australia
record, decided to postpone his start for another month. Mollison, however, was set upon going in the early morning of the 24th at latest, regardless of the conditions, and at 1.05 a.m. he boarded his machine and took
off for the Cape. With daylight fading at the end of 1,450 miles of flying he
decided to land a little short of his objective at Colomb-Bechar. Here the
French authorities, though helpful, refused to waive the regulations for-
bidding night flying over the Sahara and insisted on Mollison carrying a
supply of food and water, so that he was unable to get away until 2.30 in
the morning. After a halt of an hour at Reggan just after daybreak, during
which he quietly jettisoned his supplies in the interests of saving weight,
he took off from this last outpost following the tracks of the Trans-Sahara
car service southward as far as they went; when these at last petered out he
had to set on his compass a course for the Niger, over five hundred miles
away across an ocean of sand.

As he flew on, Mollison noticed from the blowing sand that a head-
wind had arisen, one of such force that he would be unable to reach the
great river before nightfall, and he was aware that there would be two
hours of complete darkness before the moon rose. He therefore made the

risky decision to land in the desert and have a short rest so that his arrival would be delayed until moonrise. This time he made no mistakes in his choice of a landing-place, and after spending three-quarters of an hour on the ground drowsily smoking cigarettes he swung the propeller, climbed in again and carried on. Near sunset the sight of occasional patches of grass and shrubs suggested that he was approaching watered country, and just as the moon appeared, the gleam of the river showed in front. He turned the Puss Moth down past Gao towards his destination but was unable to pick out the town or the aerodrome and a sudden fall in the oil pressure drove him down to a hurried landing on a mud-flat, which fortunately proved to be hard. Here he spent the rest of the night fending off curious natives and flew on to Niamey at daybreak.

Long delays with refuelling kept him on the ground most of the day, and he was forced to telegraph to Duala, his next stop, saying that he could not reach there that evening as he had planned. He was in the air by late afternoon and flew through the night, landing at Duala early on the Sunday morning. The lonely desert stage of the flight was behind, and there remained rather less than 3,000 miles of coastline to the Cape, but he had had little rest since the previous Wednesday afternoon and in the oppressive heat fatigue was beginning to tell upon him. With a heavy load of fuel the Puss Moth struggled into the air again and its weary pilot flew on all day through low cloud and rain to arrive at Loanda shortly before sunset, refilled the tanks and carried on through the night to his last halt at Walvis Bay.

It was almost eight o'clock on Monday evening when Mollison's little machine came in sight of Cape Town, and in the extremity of his fatigue he was suffering from double vision. The glare of the aerodrome lights was too much for his tired eyes, and after circling once or twice he turned away to try and land on an unlighted strip of beach. The machine touched down on the sand but the slope of the beach swung it round into the sea, where the drag of the water tipped it gently on to its back. Mollison splashed his way ashore and finished the journey to the aerodrome in a taxi, to be greeted by a large crowd, after a flight which had been an astonishing feat of endurance: he had flown solo from England in 4 days, 17 hours and 19 minutes and of this time 64 hours had been spent in the air. Among those who greeted him was Amy Johnson, who was recuperating in South Africa after an operation for appendicitis.

Scott set off on 19 April 1932 and made a fast and uneventful journey to Australia by way of Brindisi, Aleppo and Bushire, to follow the usual route across India and reach Darwin some six hours ahead of Butler, thus regaining the record. This flight may be regarded as the last occasion on which the classic light biplane with open cockpit was used for serious record-breaking over really long distances. Its day had begun with Stack and Leete only six years before, and now it was done, although it had still a long and useful life ahead of it for less spectacular purposes. The cabin Puss Moth and the clean low-wing cantilever monoplanes such as the Percival Gull, with their greater comfort and better performance, quickly improved on the times set up by the Moths and Avians. It is doubtful, however, whether in terms of human achievement the Australian flights of Scott, Mollison and Kingsford Smith in the older type of aeroplane have ever been excelled. To cover 11,000 miles in a machine cruising at less than 100 miles an hour, flying and navigating for periods of up to eighteen hours at a stretch in the continuous battering of the propeller slipstream, and to keep this up continuously for nearly nine days, is a feat coming very near the limits of human endurance. A machine of Moth type flying continuously was capable of traversing the distance between England and Australia after spending something like five days in the air; the balance of the time was imposed simply by the natural limitations of the human frame.

James Mollison and Amy Johnson were married in London on 29 July 1932, and thereafter the flying exploits of 'Jim and Amy', sometimes as rivals and sometimes as collaborators, not to speak of their personal affairs and eventual matrimonial difficulties, provided material in profusion for Fleet Street. At the time of his marriage, Mollison was already planning the first solo crossing of the North Atlantic Ocean from east to west. For this attempt he had once more selected the Puss Moth, and a new machine of this type was already receiving special attention on his behalf at Stag Lane, so after a very brief honeymoon in Scotland the couple travelled south again to make final preparations. The North Atlantic had still at this time not been flown by a light aeroplane. The crossing from east to west is always more difficult than in the reverse direction because of the prevailing westerly winds, and this difficulty is much increased for aeroplanes with a low cruising speed since the effect of wind upon range is proportionately greater than for faster machines.

Mollison's Puss Moth was named *Heart's Content* (Plate 34) after one of a group of small villages in Newfoundland lying near the track along which he intended to fly. It was specially strengthened to carry an overload of 700 lbs, and to save weight a number of items were discarded. The standard tankage was supplemented by two large tanks in the cabin, one behind and one in front of the pilot, whose position had been shifted aft to what was normally the passenger seat. With a total of 162 gallons of petrol, enough for 33 hours' flying, the machine was greatly overloaded, and this would inevitably mean a very long take-off run and a poor initial rate of climb. No aerodrome was adequate to provide a safe margin of length for Mollison's departure, and he therefore decided to follow the example of Kingsford Smith's *Southern Cross* two years earlier and use the long stretch of level beach at Portmarnock Strand, north of Dublin. He flew *Heart's Content* over with a light load of fuel, had the tanks filled on the beach, and after waiting for a satisfactory weather report drove out from Dublin for the start on Thursday, 18 August 1932. Five thousand people had assembled to see him go, among them the Lord Mayor of Dublin, who gave him a letter for Mayor Walker of New York. It was Mollison's intention to complete the double crossing and be back in Ireland on the Sunday.

At about 11.30 a.m. the engine was started and the little machine moved out to begin its run. It rolled heavily along the beach for 28 seconds and at last climbed away with its enormous load of fuel, whose weight was equivalent to that of seven people and rather greater than the empty weight of the aeroplane itself. Flying low across Ireland, it cleared the west coast of Galway at a quarter past one, and its pilot soon saw the Irish mountains fading below the horizon.

To simplify navigation, Mollison was flying the whole way to Newfoundland on a constant magnetic track, which with the changing magnetic variation across the ocean would conveniently take him along a line situated between the great-circle, or shortest, track and the rhumb-line, or track of constant true bearing. Allowance for drift was made by estimating the wind direction and strength from observation of the water surface and the movement of cloud shadows, and for the first four or five hours, flying at only fifty feet or so, he kept the machine heading three or four degrees to starboard to counteract the effect of light northerly winds.

Five hundred and fifty miles out, the Puss Moth passed low over the Cunard steamship *Ascania*, and shortly afterwards it encountered another ship, the *Beaverbrae*. The sight of these ships was encouraging since the position of both was marked on Mollison's shipping chart, and thus provided a check on his own position. After this no more ships were seen, and as the sun set in front and the clouds thickened Mollison judged it wise to climb for the hours of darkness. Through the night it remained cloudy, although there were fitful glimpses of the moon, and before daybreak, with fatigue beginning to tell, he encountered the eastern edge of the notorious summer fog which covers the Newfoundland coast. After some hours of instrument flying the fog cleared momentarily, and the moonlight shining through a break in the clouds revealed a coastline which Mollison identified as Grates Point, only some twenty miles north of his intended track and close to the village after which the Puss Moth had been named. He had made a fast crossing of the ocean from

Galway—1,972 miles in just over nineteen hours, or well over a hundred miles an hour.

After this satisfying revelation the fog closed in again, but cleared a second time to reveal the town of Halifax. After checking the amount of petrol that remained, Mollison decided to carry on for New York, but the fog then returned in full force and after many hours of uncertainty he decided that it would be wise to take advantage of a brief clearance to land in a convenient field. More than thirty-one hours after leaving Dublin the Puss Moth, first light aeroplane to cross the North Atlantic, came to rest on Canadian soil near the small town of Pennfield Ridge, New Brunswick, and the first of the local inhabitants who reached the machine was incredulous at its pilot's claim to have flown from Ireland. He was soon convinced, however, by the flood of telegrams which poured in as soon as the position of Mollison's landing-place became known to the outside world. After a night's rest he took off again for New York, where he was accorded a tumultuous welcome; the American Press quickly seized on the notion that an economical crossing of the ocean had been made by a Scotsman, and made much of the fact that the cost of fuel and oil was only sixty-five dollars, or approximately half the minimum first-class fare by sea.

The strain of the flight had been considerable, and Mollison did not feel equal to a quick return. It was important, however, to make use of the moon before it had waned too much, and it was with some impatience that he received a series of unfavourable weather reports. Two attempts at the crossing from west to east in the week following Mollison's arrival were unsuccessful, one machine being lost at sea and the other forced down by fog and wrecked in Newfoundland. Eventually, ten days after leaving Dublin, Mollison set off again for Harbour Grace, but fog and storms forced him down at Sydney, Nova Scotia, and a doctor in whose house he stayed cabled to England expressing his anxiety as to his fitness for the flight. The result was a series of telegrams from Mrs Mollison, Lord Wakefield and others urging him to abandon the attempt, and in due course he was persuaded to do so and made arrangements to return with his machine by sea.

It was at about this time that Mr John Grierson was touring the remote regions of the Soviet Union in his Gipsy Moth *Rouge et Noir*. This machine, named from its curious colour scheme—it was painted red on one side and black on the other—had been bought third-hand from Glen Kidston in 1930, and in it its owner, then a pilot officer in the R.A.F., had flown to India in October of that year. After a year's service on the North-West Frontier he became dissatisfied with life in India and attempted to resign, but was not allowed to do so; he therefore set off without official permission to fly his aeroplane back to England, and arrived at Lympne in May 1931 completing the journey in a record four-and-a-half days. For this he was not court-martialled but simply released from the Service and in the following year, wanting to obtain a first-hand view of Russia, he set out for Estonia in *Rouge et Noir* with a passenger before Russian visas had been obtained. The visas did not come through and he was compelled to take his passenger back to England. When they did arrive Grierson started again, alone this time with an extra fuel tank in the passenger seat. He reached Moscow successfully but could not get permission to continue to Samarkand, so he telegraphed to Sir Malcolm Campbell who asked Mr George Bernard Shaw to use his influence with the Russian Government. By this roundabout method he eventually obtained the necessary permit and set out by way of Astrakhan, using a small-scale borrowed map of the pre-Revolution era which showed no aerodromes; he was recommended on arrival at each town to 'fly round it and look for the aerodrome'. With these somewhat vague directions he successfully reached the Caspian and continued to Tashkent, to which remote place his Moth had already been preceded by that of the pioneering air tourist Mrs Edwin Montagu and her pilot Mr Rupert Belville in 1931. After reaching Samarkand and exploring that legendary city, he eventually returned to Moscow, 'losing' his map on the way in order to avoid a tiresome diversion between Uralinsk and Stalingrad, and reached England again after a flight of 9,300 miles in which the only mechanical trouble had been a broken valve spring.

In November 1932 Amy Mollison successfully attacked her husband's record to the Cape and beat it by 10½ hours, using her own Puss Moth *Desert Cloud* which had a Gipsy Major engine in place of the standard Gipsy III. She flew over the desert by night, and in spite of irritating delays managed to reach Cape Town by the afternoon of the fifth day. She returned by the same route three weeks later, meeting appalling weather up the African coast which at times compelled her to fly a hundred miles offshore in order to get enough height, and landed at Croydon on 18 December after a flight taking 7 days, 7 hours and 5 minutes—a considerable improvement on the time of the Duchess of Bedford's 'Spider' almost three years earlier. Soon afterwards a nineteen-year-old South African, Mr Victor Smith, made three attempts on her newly-established outward record in a Comper Swift and would undoubtedly have beaten it if he had not been unlucky enough to run out of petrol hardly an hour's flying from Cape Town.

In February Mollison was off again in *Heart's Content*, this time with the intention of making the South Atlantic crossing from West Africa to Brazil. This route had already been flown many times since the first crossing of Admiral Coutinho and Commander Saccadura Cabral in a Fairey

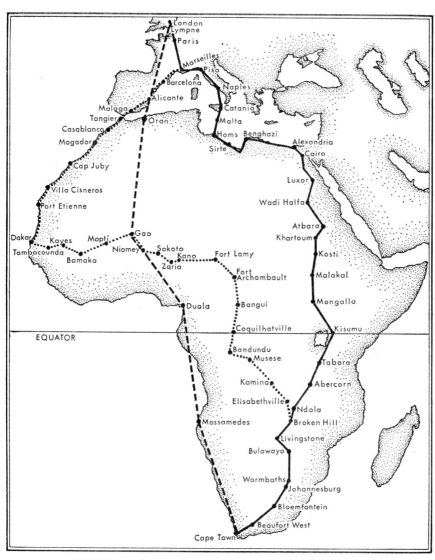

The African flights of Lady Bailey, 1928–29 (solid and dotted lines), and Mrs Amy
Mollison's flight to the Cape in November 1932 (broken line). The eastern route
followed by Lady Bailey on the outward journey was substantially the same as that of
Lieut. Bentley in 1927 and of Lady Heath (in the homeward direction) in 1928.
On her return journey she took the western route as shown to Dakar and then followed
the French Aéropostale route to Paris

seaplane in 1922, and a regular French mail service was about to be in-augurated between St Louis and Port Natal, but Hinkler's feat of flying across this ocean solo from west to east had not as yet been paralleled in the opposite direction. Mollison left the aerodrome of Thies, near Dakar, at 12.50 a.m. on 9 February, and sat all day in the Puss Moth's little cabin, flying on through the equatorial heat and removing his clothing piece by piece until he wore nothing but a solar topee. When he was within a few hundred miles of South America the sunshine gave way to pouring rain, and after donning his clothes again Mollison managed to find his way to the aerodrome at Port Natal and land after a crossing which had taken seventeen hours and forty minutes. He continued to a reception at Rio, and after three weeks the little *Heart's Content*, which had crossed both North and South Atlantic Oceans, was swung aboard a steamer for the return journey to England. Its achievements had earned it a place in a museum alongside *Jason*, but this was not to be, for a year later the York-shire pilot Mr H. L. Brook, while attempting the Australia record in it, was driven down by ice in the Cevennes and wrecked it completely in a crash though he himself managed to escape with bruises. Mollison, who now had the distinction of having crossed both oceans single-handed, followed Chichester and Hinkler in becoming the holder of the Johnston Navigation Trophy for the year 1933.

A significant event of October 1933 was the appearance of the new Percival Gull for the purpose of long-distance record-breaking. The machine used—G-ACJV or *Miss Southern Cross*—enabled Sir Charles Kingsford Smith (as he now was) to better Scott's time from England to Australia, in spite of a recurrence of the nervous sickness and inability to eat which had troubled him on his unsuccessful flight in the other direction. He landed at Wyndham on 11 October after a journey taking just over seven days, having covered the stage of 1,600 miles from Brindisi to Baghdad non-stop. This record, viewed as an absolute one, lasted only a week, for on 19 October Kingsford Smith's old co-pilot Mr C. T. P. Ulm, with three companions, beat it in a three-engined Avro Ten monoplane; considered as a solo record, however, it remained unbroken until it was bettered by Mr H. F. Broadbent in a Gipsy Six Gull two years later.

The 24-year-old New Zealand airwoman Miss Jean Batten first enters this story in 1933. Her career had been in many ways parallel to that of Amy Johnson. Visiting England in 1929, she had taken her 'A' licence at Stag Lane, but her subsequent ambition to fly to Australia met with family opposition and it was not until a second visit to England in June 1931 that she managed to proceed to the 'B' licence, finding the money for the necessary hundred hours at 30s. an hour out of her small allowance.

She then persuaded a fellow-member of the London Aeroplane Club to put up a half-share in a second-hand Moth, took off in it in April 1933 and reached India, but here a serious mechanical failure left her stranded almost penniless. Lord Wakefield arranged for her journey back to England, and a year later, flying a fifth-hand Gipsy I Moth that had cost her £260, she set off once more, this time to arrive over Rome in pitch darkness and driving rain and carry out an emergency landing short of fuel in a tiny field surrounded by wireless masts and high-tension cables. The subsequent removal of her aeroplane from this awkward place took time, and she therefore decided to return to England for a third attempt. This time the weather along her route gave her great difficulty, especially in Burma and Malaya; furious squally tropical rain after leaving Rangoon made the stage to Victoria Point an anxious one, and at times the rain was so heavy that the wing-tips were invisible and she could only catch glimpses of the heavy rollers and jungle-covered shore of the coast below Mergui. When she approached Victoria Point she was nine hours out of Rangoon with a diminishing fuel supply, but the weather forced her to fly up and down the coast for some time waiting for the rain to clear, and when it did she had to land on a flooded aerodrome. The next morning's take-off was alarming even with a light fuel load, and at the next stop—Alor Star—the Moth became bogged and had to be lifted to dry ground. Later, at Batavia, Miss Batten was faced with dense morning fog, and after the Dutch fuel agent had endeavoured to disperse it by driving up and down the aerodrome in his car she took off blindly into it on his assurance that there would be sunshine immediately above, which fortunately proved to be correct. She eventually reached Darwin in slightly less than 15 days, more than four days faster than Amy Johnson, and thus gained the women's record although she had of course taken considerably longer than the existing holder of the solo record, Kingsford Smith.

Mr John Grierson's flight across the Atlantic has many points in common with Chichester's crossing of the Tasman Sea. Both pilots used seaplanes and adopted techniques of navigation which were decidedly original for single-handed use in light aircraft, and both began with the intention of flying round the world; although neither succeeded in this aim, an enterprising and unusual flight resulted in each case. After his flight to Russia in 1932, Mr Grierson equipped *Rouge et Noir* with floats and with a Marconi-Robinson direction-finding wireless receiver with which it was possible to 'home' on an ordinary transmitting station, and then he planned to use this technique to fly to Canada by way of the Orkneys, the Faroes, Iceland and Greenland. No record-breaking was involved, the whole enterprise being a serious attempt to pioneer the use of wireless navigation over a little-known route.

After obtaining advice about conditions from various authorities Grierson carried out a test flight to Kiel and then took off from the Humber on his long journey on 4 August 1933. The wireless failed as he was passing Berwick, but he reached Scapa Flow without difficulty and carried on to the Faroes, whence he homed successfully over the long open-sea passage to Reykjavik. On this stage the engine began missing badly while flying over unpleasantly rough water, a trouble later traced to sticking exhaust valves due to the accumulation of salt on their stems, which were exposed on the Gipsy I engine. Curiously enough the extra engine vibration entirely cured the unserviceability of the wireless! All was now going well, and on taxying out for the stage to Greenland Grierson could already clearly hear the transmission from Angmagssalik, 500 miles distant across the Denmark Strait, towards which he hoped to fly; but he never left the water, for a heavy swell put the little Moth on its back, and the remains had to be loaded on board ship for the return to England.

Grierson was not discouraged and was quickly making plans for another attempt in the following year. By January he was touring Europe in his machine, demonstrating the homing apparatus to various governments, and while on honeymoon in Rome in April he made a personal approach to Marconi asking for assistance with his project. Although his wireless apparatus was lent by the Marconi company, little other help was forthcoming and he was compelled to provide most of the necessary finances himself, as well as combining the functions of organiser, pilot, navigator, wireless operator and mechanic, photographer, fitter, rigger, mooring assistant and newspaper correspondent. He ordered a new Fox Moth from the de Havilland company, choosing this type for its good weight-lifting ability, and equipped it with floats, tankage for 1,400 miles, the homing receiver, a small 5-watt short-wave transmitter, and a directional gyro to simplify course-keeping in high latitudes.

On 20 July he left Rochester for Londonderry, whence he intended to fly directly to Iceland. His attempt to take off next day was a failure owing to water in the floats, but on the 23rd he was away and made a successful 10-hour flight to Reykjavik during which his little transmitter was heard at a distance of 500 miles. By an extraordinary coincidence, however, he crashed again while taking off from Reykjavik by hitting a moored rowing-boat. His damaged float was hastily rushed south, repaired and loaded on a trawler at Hull together with a new wing, and Grierson was quickly back at Reykjavik and ready to try again. This time he was successful in getting off and the Fox Moth set out across the water for Greenland. Failure of the wireless, however, prevented him from finding Angmagssalik, and after fruitlessly searching the lonely coast he had to alight in an ice-free fjord from which he was rescued by a Danish pastor and a party of Eskimos

50. The de Havilland Hornet Moth neatly combined the Moth type of biplane wing
structure with the cabin comfort of the Puss and Leopard Moths

51. One of the safest aeroplanes ever built: the Pobjoy-engined B.A.
Swallow of 1935

52. A British-built Pou du Ciel—a revolutionary French design, a craze
for which swept the country in 1935–36
53. Flying Officer David Llewellyn in his Aeronca for the Cape in 1936

after several days. Having established his position he was able to fly to Angmagssalik and from here he successfully crossed the lonely ice cap to Godthaab, passed over the Davis Strait to Baffin Island and eventually reached Ottawa on 30 August to complete a fine flight over some of the remotest and most unfriendly regions ever traversed by a light aeroplane.

Early in 1934 the Australian millionaire chocolate manufacturer Sir MacPherson Robertson offered a cup and prizes totalling £15,000 for an air race from London to Melbourne on the occasion of the centenary of the latter city and of the state of Victoria. This race took place in October of the same year and was won by one of the specially built de Havilland Comet racing aeroplanes flown by Mr C. W. A. Scott and Mr T. Campbell Black, which covered the distance from the start at Mildenhall in Suffolk to the finish at Melbourne in the astonishing time of 71 hours. The Comet, with its two high-compression Gipsy Six R engines of 230 h.p. each and its loaded weight of 5,320 lbs, hardly falls within the same category as the light aeroplanes which are the chief subject of this book, and even less so do the Douglas and Boeing air liners which took second and third place and whose advanced design left their British counterparts looking decidedly old-fashioned. Nevertheless, the smaller type of machine was well represented among the twenty starters, since the race was arranged to have both a speed and a handicap section with a proportion of the prize-money allotted to each. Several months before the start Mr Bernard Rubin and Mr K. H. F. Waller, entrant and pilot respectively of one of the Comets, flew out to Australia to survey the route in one of the new Leopard Moths, and in this machine they broke Mollison's old record for the return journey with a time of 8 days and 12 hours. Soon afterwards another pilot who was travelling to England for the race, the Australian Mr C. J. Melrose, unofficially bettered their time by some three hours in his Puss Moth, flying solo.

In the race itself Melrose, this time with a companion, gained third place in the handicap section with the same machine by reaching Melbourne in a little over five days. He actually won the second handicap prize of £1,000, since the Dutch pilots Parmentier and Moll who occupied the second place had already taken a prize in the speed section and were not eligible for both. A Desoutter flown by two Danish pilots, Hansen and Jensen, completed the course successfully in the stipulated time of 16 days but did not win any prizes. The light cantilever low-wing monoplane, now coming to the fore, was represented by the Miles Hawk Major flown by Captain Malcolm MacGregor and Mr H. Walker, which easily beat the existing record to Darwin, and by the prototype Miles Falcon of Mr H. L. Brook and the British Klemm Eagle of Flight Lieutenant G. Shaw. Unfortunately, these last two achieved little; the Falcon suffered various misfortunes which prevented it from reaching Australia in less than a month and the Eagle had to retire after its retractable undercarriage had suffered damage in a landing at Bushire.

The 'MacRobertson' race marks something of a turning-point in aviation history. From 1926 up to 1934 many, indeed most, of the outstanding long-distance flights stood to the credit of the light aeroplane, and in these years it performed feats which could as yet scarcely be matched by the larger commercial machine. When the red Comet of Scott and Black landed at Melbourne the pattern was beginning to change, for the high speed and great range of that remarkable aeroplane were soon to place permanently out of reach of the small private-owner type many of the long-distance records which it had formerly held. The age of record-breaking was by no means over, and fast solo flights in small aircraft were to continue for another five years, but for the most part the light aeroplane had completed its pioneering work. Looking back today, we can see that its achievements in the hands of Hinkler, Mollison, Chichester, Scott and their contemporaries played an important part in the development of commercial flying, for where these pilots led in their small machines, not without risk, the larger transport aeroplane would in due course follow in greater safety, and their feats served continually to keep aviation before a public which was still far from being fully converted to a belief in its possibilities. To regard their flights purely in this light, however, is to take too utilitarian a view, for apart from its usefulness each was in itself an extraordinary achievement by an individual, an outstanding example of human persistence in the face of fatigue, boredom, occasional danger and the vagaries of an element as unpredictable as the sea. Except perhaps in the fields of mountaineering and single-handed sailing, the particular flavour of the performances of the long-distance solo pilots has almost entirely been lost today, and it has certainly long since vanished from aviation. The first travellers into space need qualities of a different kind, for they stand at the summit of a fantastically complex pyramid of expensive communal effort which can leave little room for personal idiosyncrasy. Whatever their achievements, it will never be possible to regard them in quite the same light as the men and women who climbed into their own small aeroplanes in the dark of the morning to fly to the ends of the earth.

⤖ 13 ⤖

Flying for All?

The private pilot in the 1920s, as we have seen, enjoyed an exceptional degree of personal freedom; regulations affecting him were very few, and under the benevolent rule of Sir Sefton Brancker even those which did exist were not always too severely applied. Aerodromes in those days were open to aircraft of every type, and landing a Moth at Croydon among the air liners of Imperial Airways caused no more concern than the sending of one of those same air liners to give joy-rides at a pageant at some provincial aerodrome—indeed both were quite frequently done. With the rapid growth of commercial air traffic in the early 1930s, however, rules for its control near busy airports in bad weather were gradually introduced and in such conditions the absolute freedom of the amateur pilot to fly where he pleased began to be somewhat restricted in the interests of safety, though to a vastly lesser extent than is the case today. The first of the new 'control zones' appeared round Croydon in 1933, and within this zone, extending for a radius of some ten miles from the aerodrome, aircraft without wireless were not permitted to fly when the visibility and cloud-base fell below certain limits. A similar zone was introduced in 1935 for Heston, which by then had acquired a considerable volume of commercial traffic with the appearance of such internal air lines as Jersey Airways. The fact that weather conditions were such as to cause these zones to come into operation was conveyed to the knowledgeable by the mysterious letters QBI, an arbitrary combination from the international wireless Q-code which was freely interpreted by the less serious-minded to mean that the weather was 'quite bloody impossible'. When the zone system was first introduced there was naturally some consternation among amateur pilots, who saw themselves being steadily driven out of the air, and one of them submitted a plaintive article to the journal *Flight* entitled 'Private Owners, Are We the Last of our Race?'. In practice, however, the new arrangements did not turn out to be unduly restrictive to the average amateur, who was then fortunately unable to foresee the formidable maze of air traffic regulations which were to confront his successors in the years after 1945.

If the private pilot was thus having his freedom slightly curtailed in one sphere in the 1930s, in another it was soon to be greatly enlarged. The control of all matters concerning civil aviation by the Air Ministry, an essentially military body on to which had been grafted a civilian Directorate, was a legacy of the 1914–18 war which was held by many to be unduly hampering to aircraft constructors and to civil flying generally. Increasing restrictions, such as the Air Navigation Directions of 1932 which abolished the freedom formerly granted to experimental aircraft to be flown without official permission within three miles of an aerodrome, led to a widespread demand for the system of administration to be radically altered, and in 1933 a committee under the chairmanship of Lord Gorell was appointed to look into the matter. Its members included the aviation pioneers Mr E. C. Gordon England, Lieutenant-Colonel J. T. C. Moore-Brabazon and Mr Frederick Handley Page and the active private pilot Mr W. Lindsay Everard.

The report of the Gorell committee, issued in 1934, contained a number of important conclusions from which sprang far-reaching recommendations for changes to the existing system. After examining the evidence the members of the committee decided that a relaxation of the existing system of Government control would be beneficial to civil aviation and could have no harmful effect upon the community. A careful analysis of accident statistics since 1926 revealed that the majority of accidents had been attributable to human error rather than to faults in aircraft, and on the basis of this it was concluded that the existing close control of aircraft manufacture through the medium of detailed structural requirements was unnecessary. Further, the committee felt that subject to third-party insurance being carried a certificate of airworthiness could be made optional for private aircraft and that with the same proviso any builder of experimental types should be free to fly them without special permission being granted if such flying was not carried out over large numbers of people. The most sweeping recommendation, however, concerned the administration of civil aviation, which it was proposed should be transferred in due course to an entirely civil body, with the responsibility for all matters concerning airworthiness relegated to an independent organisation for which the name of Air Registration Board was suggested. Air Ministry control of civil flying in fact continued until the outbreak of war, and it was not until 1945 that the Ministry of Transport and Civil Aviation came into being; the Air Registration Board, however, was duly established in 1937 and the severity of official control over the activities of amateur constructors and the world of private flying was appreciably relaxed, to the general satisfaction. One important change was the introduction of Permits to Fly for amateur-built machines, for which lower standards than those of the full

Certificate of Airworthiness were permitted subject to certain restrictions in the operation of such aircraft.

The easing of restrictions which was set in motion by the Gorell committee's report encouraged a return to the Lympne formula of motor-cycle engines and low wing-loadings as a means of reducing the cost of learning to fly and of keeping in practice after obtaining a licence. This trend really began before the report was issued with the Lowe Wylde 'Baby' of 1933, developed as the B.A.C. (later Kronfeld) Drone. Since this was a single-seater there was no possibility of the ordinary kind of dual instruction, but it was so easy to fly that the technique of solo training which had been employed in the earliest days of flying proved quite satisfactory. Mrs S. M. Green, a director of British Aircraft Limited, taught herself on one of the original Lowe Wylde machines by the time-honoured method of 'rolling', or taxying, followed by short 'straights' which ultimately led to turns and a circuit and landing. Later in the year the Drone was made available for hire at 19s. an hour, and some years later it was extensively used for flying training, notably by the County Flying Club of Leicester and the Ely Aero Club. Mr Lindsay Everard, who was M.P. for Leicester and the owner of the aerodrome at Ratcliffe, purchased for the County Flying Club the prototype Kronfeld Ground Trainer, a wingless contrivance built on the same lines as the Drone which was incapable of flight but which had large control surfaces with which it could be manoeuvred while taxying at speeds up to 50 m.p.h. After three hours of dashing across the aerodrome on this apparatus at 10s. an hour, pupils were up-graded to the flying trainer, which was capable of short straight flights, and two to three hours on this enabled them to be put in the Drone itself and allowed to fly. After two hours on the Drone they were usually capable of carrying out flights of up to half-an-hour's duration at heights up to a thousand feet, and this stage was reached for a total expenditure of only £4 5s. Such a course led to a restricted 'A' licence, which could be converted to a full licence after the pilot had gained more experience.

Perhaps the most astonishing phenomenon of the 1930s in the field of cheap flying was the affair of the Pou du Ciel. Its designer, M Henri Mignet, has received brief mention in an earlier chapter, when in the year of the Motor Glider Competitions at Lympne he was already experimenting in France with a low-powered monoplane. All through the rest of the '20s he continued a tireless search for a small aeroplane of really simple design which could easily be built and flown by the true aviation amateur, the enthusiast with little time, money or skill who longed to seek mild adventure in the air in the spirit of the mountaineer or the dinghy sailor. Such a machine, he was firmly convinced, would have to be of radically different conception from the current light aeroplanes of 100 h.p. and he laid down as his objective the single-seater aeroplane of less than 100 kg empty weight.* After many experiments and much careful thought he arrived at his ultimate design, which he named the Pou du Ciel, variously anglicised as Sky Louse or Flying Flea and once described by its designer as 'a small insect which has made people in France scratch their heads'.

The Pou was indeed a radical design (Plate 52). Mignet had reasoned that the standard biplane of the day was a complicated structure consisting of ten, twelve or fourteen fixed and moving aerodynamic surfaces: in the case of the monoplane these could be reduced to eight, but this was still complex enough to make aircraft construction by the amateur costly in time and money. The Pou, by contrast, consisted simply of a wooden box fuselage built up like a packing-case, to which were attached only three surfaces—a movable front wing braced to the fuselage by cables, a fixed rear wing and a large rudder. Control in pitch was obtained by pivoting the front wing about its central pylon support, and turns were made on rudder alone; there were no ailerons, and bank was applied merely by the action of sideslip on the wings, whose generous dihedral angle and short span ensured a quick response. The rudder was operated not by the conventional rudder-bar but by lateral movement of the control column, and with this simplified two-control system the pilot could, as Mignet put it, 'stamp his feet to keep them warm' as he did not need them for flying. Three advantages were claimed for the wing arrangement: first a beneficial slot effect from the relative situation of the front wing and rear wings, second a direct control of lift, and third a pull on the hand which enabled the pilot to feel the lift and alleviate the effect of up-gusts in rough weather by allowing the wing to reduce its incidence. To make the last arrangement satisfactory an approximately stationary centre of pressure was called for, so Mignet employed a wing section with reflex curvature at the trailing edge.

Using the simplest of materials—commercial grade wood for the structure and mild steel for the fittings—Mignet assembled the first real Pou in the late summer of 1933 and began its tests precisely one month after the start of construction. After painstaking trials and endless repairs and modifications he succeeded in flying it, and by the middle of winter he had spent ten hours in the air. He thereupon wrote his book *Le Sport de l'Air*, which was partly an exposition of his philosophy of life and aviation, partly an account of his trials and experiments and partly a guide to how to build the Pou. It sold rapidly, and soon Poux were being assembled by his followers all over France. By the time of the 'MacRobertson' race to Melbourne, October 1934, Mignet's fame had spread to England, and his book, translated into English as *The Flying Flea* by the Air League of the British

---

* The English Electric Wren of 1923 weighed 232 lbs, or 105 kg.

Empire, was published here in the following year. The first edition of 6,000 copies was sold out within a month, and throughout the summer of 1935 the craze for the Pou spread all over the British Isles. The dream of the Lympne pioneers had come again and in sheds and garages, basements, attics and living-rooms, amateurs were gluing and nailing their way towards their objective of cheap and simple flying for all.

The cost was small. Many firms offered raw materials—plywood, spruce, fabric, sheet steel, tubing, cable, glue, dope, wheels and tyres—and a complete set of these could be bought for the sum of £25 or so. The remaining expenditure was £30 to £60 for the engine, which could be of a wide variety of types in the range from 20 to 30 h.p., including converted water-cooled car units such as the Carden-Ford and the Austin Seven, modified motor-cycle engines like the Douglas Sprite or Scott Flying Squirrel or aero-engines of the Lympne era such as the A.B.C. Scorpion, the Anzani or the Bristol Cherub. Thus the Pou could be built for the moderate sum of £50-£90, and for those who did not wish to do all the work themselves there were plenty of enterprising firms who offered ready-built units, or a complete professionally-built machine could be purchased ready to fly at prices in the range £150-£200 according to engine. The motor-cycle of the air had arrived at last.

On 14 July 1935 the first British Pou left the ground at Heston. This was Mr S. V. Appleby's machine with Carden-Ford engine, and although a few days later it ended on its back in a field of cabbages it subsequently turned out to be one of the most successful of the British machines built. After its first flights it was modified somewhat from the original Mignet specification by the sailplane designer Mr L. E. Baynes, who also produced the Abbott-Baynes Cantilever Pou in which, among other alterations, the bracing and control cables for the main wing were replaced by rigid struts. The Cantilever Pou was offered for sale at £198, and sixty were ordered, though as it turned out only three were built.

M. Mignet himself, who had by now completed 145 hours' flying in his tiny machine, crossed the Channel by Pou on 13 August and appeared with his wife at Shoreham to begin a demonstration tour of Britain. He was enthusiastically received and was able to report that 500 of his machines were under construction in France and that fifty had flown. British constructors were thus stimulated to greater efforts, Pou clubs proliferated from Devonshire to the north of Scotland and all through the winter the fever of manufacture, engine running, testing, crashing and repairing continued its course. By April 1936 there were some eighty Poux flying or nearly ready to fly, and a great rally was held at Southend on Easter Monday. Although seven Poux put in an appearance, one being flown all the way from Heston by Mr Appleby, only two were actually demonstrated in the air to an impatient Bank Holiday crowd of 5,000 people. Throughout the summer Poux continued to appear at every aviation event, sometimes as unintentional comic relief, and on August Bank Holiday there took place at Ramsgate the first international Flying Flea Trophy Race, at which Mignet himself appeared with his smart new 100-m.p.h. cabin version, the H.M.18.

Meanwhile there had appeared the first shadow of the hidden defect which eventually ended this extraordinary attempt to bring flying to the man-in-the-street. A fatal accident at Renfrew on 20 April had been followed by another on 5 May which had caused the death of the Air League's test pilot, Flight Lieutenant A. M. Cowell. Five similar fatal accidents had been reported from France and in all the cases the circumstances were the same: the aircraft would be reported as flying normally, would then enter a shallow dive as though to descend for landing and would finally dive straight for the ground with increasing steepness, often going over the vertical before striking it. A third British crash in May at last began to arouse concern, and Captain Lamplugh of the British Aviation Insurance Group, upon whose shoulders rested most of the financial risks of British private flying, wrote to the Press calling for an investigation. After some initial reluctance the Air Ministry agreed to carry out wind-tunnel tests of the Pou at Farnborough, while in France preparations were made for a similar study at the aerodynamic research centre at Chalais-Meudon.

The French tests were completed on 20 August. They showed that with the specified maximum positive setting of the front wing with the control column hard back, the Pou would still trim into a dive if a certain negative angle of incidence were reached. The R.A.E. tests confirmed this, and the mechanism of the eleven fatal accidents which had occurred was now clear. In normal flight at positive incidence the Pou was both stable and controllable, and could be flown satisfactorily for months or years until one day, due to a down-gust or a rapid push on the control column to initiate a dive, the critical incidence was attained. Thereafter no amount of pulling back would produce a recovery, and the little machine would carry its unfortunate pilot into the ever-steepening dive which had so often been reported by eye-witnesses. This dangerous characteristic, an aerodynamic interference effect between the front and rear wings, could not have been predicted by any method other than wind-tunnel tests on the full-scale machine or on a model.

The results brought the great Pou fervour to an abrupt end in England. British Permits to Fly were withdrawn and most of the aircraft built met an obscure fate, though one or two survive to this day collecting dust as somewhat pathetic curiosities. Henri Mignet himself never suffered serious injury in any of his own machines; he continued with his experimenting in France up to the outbreak of war and is actively concerned with modern developments of the Pou to this day. Perhaps the secret of his personal success has been that, unlike some of his followers, he has brought to his beloved aviation something of the painstaking and single-minded devotion that was characteristic of the Wright brothers. He is the archetype of the true aviation amateur, describing himself justly as one 'qui aime l'Aviation comme il aime ses enfants, comme il aime sa femme, de tout son cœur'.

Much of the cheap flying instruction offered by certain clubs between 1936 and 1939 was carried out in small aeroplanes of foreign origin which were then beginning to be imported, and in some cases manufactured, in this country. The chief of these were the Aeronca, the Taylor Cub and its later developments the Piper Cub and Taylorcraft—all American—and the Hillson Praga from Czechoslovakia. The main British aircraft firms were by now engaged on work connected with military expansion and had little time or inclination to produce economical two-seaters or the engines of 40 or 50 h.p. with which they were fitted. The Aeronca was an original little high-wing cabin monoplane whose wing was braced with a multitude of wires to the fuselage and to a cabane, or pylon, above the centre-section. A solitary example of the earlier single-seater version had been imported into England as early as 1930, and in the autumn of 1935 the first of the two-seaters was demonstrated at Hanworth by Light Aircraft Limited, a firm which had been formed to sell a British-built version. The fuselage and tail were constructed of welded steel tubing, with a spruce wing and ailerons of pressed duralumin, and with the Aeronca engine of only 38 b.h.p. the machine would carry two people and a modest amount of luggage at a cruising speed of 87 m.p.h. and a fuel consumption in still air of 28 miles to the gallon. Considerable interest was aroused, for here was a two-seater machine offered at a price (£395) comparable with that being asked for existing British single-seaters, and in early 1936 construction of Aeroncas began at Peterborough, the engines being built by the motor-cycle engine manufacturers J.A. Prestwich as the Aeronca-J.A.P. In addition a batch of sixteen American-built machines was imported, and with these the Hanworth Aeronca school was opened in November 1935. It offered an 'A' licence for the low price of £14 with deferred terms, and Aeronca flying was available to qualified pilots at £1 an hour (Plate 53).

Flying instruction at cheap rates was also obtainable on the Hillson Praga* from 1937 onwards. The Northern School of Aviation at Barton operated a number of Pragas on instructional work and they were also used by Mr Whitney Straight for his chain of flying clubs at Ramsgate, Ipswich, Exeter, Plymouth and Weston-super-Mare. When the original Praga

* See Chapter 14 for details of this type of aircraft.

engines were replaced by British Aeronca-J.A.P.s the type qualified for a subsidy and the Straight Corporation was then able to offer courses leading to the 'A' licence for £12 10s., or about half the average cost on larger aircraft of the Moth type.

The Aeronca was quickly followed to Britain by the Taylor Cub, a small braced high-wing monoplane with a 40-h.p. Continental engine and a welded steel-tube fuselage seating its occupants in tandem in a small cabin under the wing. It was an extremely simple, cheap and slow little aeroplane which had enjoyed enormous successes in the United States, and had no direct equivalent in England. In 1937 the American manufacturer of the Cub, originally the Taylor Aircraft Company, became the Piper Aircraft Corporation, and Mr C. G. Taylor, president of the original concern, set himself up in business independently. The original Taylor Cub thus became the Piper Cub, and the new Taylor-Young Airplane Company began to develop a machine which followed the same structural lines as its forerunner but seated its two occupants side by side. The Taylorcraft Model A, also with a 40-h.p. Continental engine, soon appeared on the American market and was imported into England. Manufacture was begun under licence by Taylorcraft Aeroplanes (England) Limited at Thurmaston, Leicester, in late 1938, and after the British prototype had flown in April 1939 a production run of these aircraft, fitted with the 55-h.p. Lycoming engine and known as the Taylorcraft Plus, began to issue to the clubs and private owners. Its further developments were significant. With war impending, the use of such a machine for Service purposes was fairly clear, and in June 1939 a Taylorcraft fitted with the new Cirrus Minor engine of 90 h.p. was submitted to the Air Ministry for trials under the name of Taylorcraft Auster. In this way began the long line of Auster light aeroplanes—all of essentially similar design to the original Taylorcraft—which formed the mainstay of the much diminished British light aeroplane industry in the years following 1945.

Although cheap aircraft were abundantly available in the late 1930s, the rise in the number of privately-owned machines did not continue at the spectacular rate at which it had begun after the coming of the Moth. The hope that the light aeroplane would become a 'motor-car of the air' did not come to pass in the way that many had imagined in the '20s; instead, it had taken on more of the character of a small aerial yacht than of a really popular vehicle, and fewer than 700 private aircraft were in use in Britain by 1937. This was in part due to their cost of ownership, but also because the aeroplane's real utility lay in long-distance travel and not in the short journeys of a few miles which make up by far the greater part of the annual task of the average motor-car. Those private owners who had the will, the enthusiasm and the means to fly themselves about Britain and Europe found that their light aeroplanes amply fulfilled their needs; but they remained comparatively few. Had England been a larger country with a better climate, had the authorities possessed the foresight to lay down a small permanent landing-strip near every town of importance, had the habit of European travel not at this time been confined to a fairly limited few, then a widespread demand might have made it possible for the cost of personal aircraft to be drastically reduced by large-scale production.

The increase in the club flying movement, however, was more spectacular. The new subsidy agreement of 1932 and the improvement of economic conditions which was beginning to make itself felt at that time gave the movement a new lease of life. The fifteen clubs which entered the new scheme were joined in 1933 by the Northamptonshire, Brooklands, Cardiff and Scarborough clubs, and in each of the following two years a further twelve were added. By the end of 1935 there were forty-two State-assisted clubs in action, as well as twenty-eight run on an independent basis; the movement now numbered 11,000 members and the facilities which it offered were easily accessible (geographically at any rate) to most of the inhabitants of the country. The progressive extension of State-assisted light aeroplane flying was reflected in the annual Air Estimates, for the £16,000 set aside for subsidies in 1934 rose in the following year to £25,000 and had reached £35,000 by 1937. These were the years of the expansion of the Royal Air Force, and with the international situation becoming ever more troubled the Government was coming to recognise that a flourishing popular flying movement and the large reserve of pilots which it created could have a direct military value.

At the end of the five-year period of subsidy in 1937 a further agreement was concluded for a similar period, with the maximum annual payment to any one club raised once more to £2,000 and made payable in the form of a new pilot's grant of £25, a sum of £10 for each renewal of licence and a flying grant of 10s. an hour up to a maximum of twenty hours per member. In ordinary circumstances the new scheme would have run until 1942, but the steadily worsening outlook for world peace led to a radical extension of it which brought flying within reach of almost all pockets. This was the Civil Air Guard, first announced in July 1938, which opened the floodgates to let thousands of aspiring pilots into the clubs. Unlike the old subsidy arrangement, which had imposed no obligations upon its beneficiaries, the Civil Air Guard carried a direct military liability; all joining it were obliged to sign an undertaking to offer their services in a 'national emergency' and were warned that such services would not necessarily involve flying duties. Those joining had to be British subjects of either sex between the ages of eighteen and fifty who were without Reserve commitments. The Government was prepared to pay a grant of £50 for every 'A' licence gained on standard types of light aeroplane, or £30 if on 'ultra-light' types, with additional payments for practice flying up to ten hours a year after qualifying. This enabled clubs to offer flying training on standard aircraft for 10s. an hour at week-ends and 5s. at other times, or half these amounts for the smaller machines below 1,200 lbs all-up weight. Any club was eligible to operate the scheme whether or not it had been receiving a subsidy before, provided that it agreed to set up a C.A.G. section of at least twelve members, and was entitled to make a small annual charge for membership. Ordinary club flying with the existing subsidy would continue side by side with C.A.G. training.

Here was flying for everyone at last, even though it had a National Service string firmly attached. The response was tremendous as thousands seized their chance to get into the air, so that within a week 16,000 applications had been received by the Air Ministry, and they continued to pour in throughout the rest of the summer. In order to deal with these and to control the scheme generally it was thought desirable to set up an administrative body of persons with experience of flying and of the club movement, and this took the form of a sub-committee of the General Council of Light Aeroplane Clubs, with Lord Londonderry as Chief Commissioner, Air Commodore Chamier as honorary secretary and Mrs F. G. Miles, Sir Lindsay Everard, Major Alan Goodfellow and Mr Robert Murray as Commissioners for their respective areas. In addition to the formidable amount of routine work which the scheme presented to them the Commissioners were faced with several new problems, including that of arranging a comprehensive plan for personal accident insurance on behalf of the many thousands of members.

The scheme was welcomed by the clubs, which had been suffering severely from the competition of the recently-formed R.A.F. Volunteer Reserve and had been forced to pay higher salaries to instructors and ground staff to prevent their absorption by the Reserve schools. Among many of the older members and the private flying movement generally, however, its reception was in some cases less enthusiastic. Some of the reason for this may have been mere snobbery, but those who over the years had become fairly experienced pilots at considerable expense to themselves had a genuine grievance in that the C.A.G. did not cater for them in any way; indeed the influx of new pupils would often make it impossible for the established members upon whose support the clubs had relied in harder times to obtain a machine at all for week-end flying.

Operations began on 1 September 1938, and about thirty per cent of the total number of clubs were involved. A simple uniform was soon issued for C.A.G. members consisting of a one-piece boiler suit in R.A.F. blue with a wings badge for those who had obtained 'A' licences, and the semi-military nature of the new organisation was thus made apparent; a very different situation from the old days of club flying when in spite of State aid there had been more than a semblance of self-sufficiency. There was a considerable variation in the attitude adopted at C.A.G. clubs throughout the country, however, for according to the particular whims of chief instructors some tended to an excessively military outlook while others tried to retain something of the old spirit of individuality. Certain clubs, too, gained an unpleasant reputation for giving their C.A.G. pupils as little as they possibly could for the subsidy, and to combat this and to ensure uniformity of training methods standard syllabuses were drawn up and an inspector was appointed to tour the clubs testing pupils and instructors.

By October 30,000 applications had been received and the clubs were forced to call a temporary halt in recruiting, although applications were still accepted by the Commissioners. Training proceeded through the autumn and by January 1939 a total subsidy payment of £40,823—almost as much as had been paid to the original clubs in the first four years of their existence from 1925 onwards—had produced 1,380 'A' licences out of a total of 5,550 members enrolled, and the Royal Aero Club was kept busy issuing aviator's certificates at the rate of over 200 a month, or more than four times the usual rate. By this time some sixty clubs were participating. There was some criticism of the scheme at about this time because women and older men, who it was thought would be less useful in war than younger men, received exactly the same training and privileges, and although this view turned out to be mistaken a modification was announced at the end of January to meet these objections. Those enrolled were henceforth to be divided into three categories, the first a supplementary pilots' reserve for men from 18 to 30 years of age, or older if with special experience, the second including men up to forty who might be eligible for secondary flying duties and the third comprising all those who did not come into the first two classes, including all women. Different training syllabuses were prepared for these categories and the first two were allocated an extra ten hours' flying each year.

In this way thousands took to the air against the troubled background of the spring and summer of 1939. Some talked optimistically of a great growth in private flying to be stimulated by the C.A.G. scheme, with the development of cheap popular aeroplanes and five or ten thousand private owners by 1941 or so if there should be no war; but this was not to be, for the happy days of *le sport de l'air*, like so much that was good and bad in the 1930s, were near their end, and the aeroplane was shortly to be turned once more to less civilised uses.

The New Look

1935–39

Although the de Havilland Company's Hornet Moth cabin biplane was flown by Captain de Havilland in the 1934 King's Cup Race, it was at that time regarded by the firm as a purely experimental type and a prolonged programme of flight testing followed before production began in August 1935. The design was a logical sequel to the Puss Moth and Leopard Moth, combining the cabin comfort of these machines with the biplane wing structure used in the original open-cockpit Moth (Plate 52). It is apt to be forgotten that the arrangement of side-by-side seating used was something of a novelty at the time, for the earlier de Havilland types just referred to, as well as such aeroplanes as the original Miles Falcon, Percival Gull and B.A. Eagle, had carried their pilot on a centrally-mounted single seat ahead of his passengers. There were those who believed that placing a passenger beside the pilot would result in his attention being diverted from his task of flying the machine, but this notion was quickly proved to be erroneous, and another important stride from the austerity of the early years towards the motor-car type of comfort and convenience had soon been taken.

The Hornet Moth followed the practice of the Leopard Moth in being built entirely of wood, and the engine was the 130-h.p. Gipsy Major. The wings of the first Hornet Moths were sharply tapered in plan view in accordance with current de Havilland ideas as embodied in the racing Comet, the Dragon Rapide and the D.H.86 Express Air Liner, but the tendency of such wings to tip stalling was thought undesirable for a private owner's machine, and in 1936 new wings with square tips were introduced in manufacture and for fitting on an exchange basis to aircraft already sold. According to their usual policy the de Havilland Company spared no detail that could contribute to the comfort and convenience of the owner, and the price of £875 asked for the Hornet Moth included leather upholstery of motor-car type, carpets, a pilot's map-board, a walnut instrument panel, a sun blind, and even a bottle of polish for cleaning the windscreen and windows. With its refined aerodynamic form in which the centre-section gap of the Moth Major and Tiger Moth was eliminated, the machine was appreciably faster for its power than these earlier biplanes and could be cruised comfortably at speeds up to 110 m.p.h., and a large fuel tank at the rear of the cabin provided a range of up to 700 miles, so that with its ample baggage space the Hornet Moth offered excellent touring facilities for two people. Dual control was ingeniously arranged by means of a single control of 'Y' shape placed in between the occupants and fitted with two hand-grips, and those who flew Hornet Moths in R.A.F. service during the Second World War will recall that any tendency to fly one wing low could be corrected by the convenient though unorthodox method of hanging a forage-cap on one side or the other!

The de Havilland Technical School's T.K.1 biplane was followed the next year by a more advanced type, the T.K.2 low-wing cantilever monoplane fitted with a special high-compression Gipsy Major engine for racing purposes. Once again the work of design was carried out under the supervision of Mr Marcus Langley, and after a number of schemes had been presented for Captain de Havilland's judgement an extremely clean and compact aeroplane embodying the best features of each eventually appeared on paper and was built by the students (Plate 55). The construction of T.K.2 was entirely of wood; a shallow box fuselage was given streamline form with a light deck fairing aft of the enclosed cockpit, and a one-piece cantilever wing carrying a pair of single telescopic undercarriage legs fitted into a cut-out underneath it. In its original form (it was much modified later) the T.K.2 had the remarkable maximum speed of 174 m.p.h. and with its disposable load of nearly 500 lbs it would have been the fastest two-seater light aeroplane in the country; since it was used mostly for racing, however, it rarely flew in two-seater form, and for the King's Cup Race of 1935, which involved a long leg from Hatfield to Renfrew, a special tank was fitted in the passenger space to supplement the normal wing tankage. After its début in this race it enjoyed a number of other racing successes before being finally broken up in 1947.

After the prototype Miles Falcon had taken part without success in the 'MacRobertson' race the type went into production early in 1935 with various modifications of a minor nature, the chief of which were a wider fuselage capable of taking four persons, an 'undercut' windscreen arrangement and the aerodynamically balanced split flaps which had earlier been used on the Hawk Major. The first Falcons to be built were for the most part fitted with the Gipsy Major engine, but a more powerful version had been envisaged in the original design of the airframe and very shortly the Falcon Six appeared on the scene. It was in this type of machine that 'Tommy' Rose won the King's Cup of 1935 and subsequently set up a record time for the flight between England and the Cape (Plates 54, 60).

The success of the Falcon led to several adaptations of it being produced in the same year, all with the 200-h.p. Gipsy Six engine. The first was the Merlin, a five-seater intended as a high-speed air taxi for Birkett Air Service Limited and claimed to be the first British aeroplane (other than purely racing types) to be fitted with a controllable-pitch propeller. The Nighthawk of the same period was specifically intended as a trainer for instrument flying and was fitted with a special blind-flying hood; the type later formed the basis for the three-seat Mentor communications aeroplane which was supplied to the Royal Air Force. The single Hawcon, as its name suggested, was in effect an amalgam of the Falcon and the Hawk and was constructed specially to Air Ministry order to enable research to be carried out into the properties of thick wing sections.

The Miles Hawk Major, introduced in 1934 as the successor to the original Hawk of the previous year, appeared in a new guise in 1935 as the Hawk Trainer, differing from its predecessor by having a slightly increased wing-span and wing area and being fitted with split flaps and comprehensive blind-flying equipment for the use of the Elementary and Reserve flying training schools. Like the Tiger Moth, the Hawk Trainer had only a limited use for civil flying, its primary role being that of a military training aeroplane, and by 1937, when the expansion of the Royal Air Force was fully under way and that Service was at last coming to abandon the biplane for first-line duties, it took its final form as the Miles M.14 or Magister which went into production in quantity to introduce future military pilots to the novel handling techniques of the monoplane. An intended replacement for the Magister, the M.18, was constructed immediately before the war, and although it did not fulfil this function it is interesting to note that one of the four examples built has had a long post-war racing career in the hands of Squadron Leader H. B. Iles, who finally succeeded in winning the King's Cup in it in 1961.

A development of the Hawk specially constructed for racing purposes in 1935 was the Sparrowhawk, designed by Mrs F. G. Miles and built as a single-seater out of standard Hawk components for Mr F. G. Miles to fly in the King's Cup of that year. A reduction in wing-span, achieved by attaching the wing panels directly to the fuselage sides instead of to the normal centre-section, combined with the fairing-in of the front cockpit and a modification of the fuselage lines in the interests of lower drag, raised the machine's top speed to 180 m.p.h. with a special high-compression Gipsy Major engine and in this form it was placed on the market for the sporting owner-pilot at a price of £825.

The high-wing cantilever monoplane, in spite of its aerodynamic

54. The Miles Falcon, first of a line of fast cabin touring aeroplanes to the design of Mr F. G. Miles

55. The extremely clean T.K.2, built by the de Havilland Technical School in 1935 under the direction of Mr Marcus Langley

56. The three-seat Miles Monarch of 1937
57. The Chilton single-seater of 1937, in which careful streamlining gave
a good performance with a low-powered engine

virtues, has never found much favour with British light aeroplane designers, largely perhaps because of the inherent difficulty of providing an
adequate upward and backward view for the pilot. In the summer of 1935,
however, the demonstration of a foreign machine of this kind, the Czechoslovakian Praga E.114 or Air Baby, aroused sufficient interest to stimulate
its production under licence in England by the woodworking firm of F.
Hills and Sons at Trafford Park, Manchester. The Hillson Praga, as the
British version was called, did indeed suffer from the defect that the rear-
ward view from the cabin was poor, but the designer had secured an
upward view for the two occupants by placing them side by side under the
leading edge of the wing with a hinged and glazed lid forming the cabin
top and the front of the centre-section. The structure was generally of
wood and the wings were not arranged to fold, but they could be very
quickly removed by two people after four bolts had been undone. With
the Praga B flat-twin engine of 40 h.p., also built under licence in England,
the performance was naturally modest. In spite of its price of £385,
extremely low for a two-seater, the Hillson Praga did not particularly
appeal to the private owner in this country and the majority of the
machines built went to flying clubs.

At quite the other end of the price range, in fact costing some five times
as much as the little Praga, was the luxurious five-seat Heston Phoenix,
which was intended for the more prosperous private owner or for light
commercial purposes such as air-taxi work. The Heston Aircraft Company
took over the assets of the Comper firm when it fell into financial difficulties in 1935, and Mr George Cornwall assumed the duties of chief
designer to the company after Comper himself and his fellow directors had
resigned their positions. The Phoenix was the first product of the new concern and was a wooden high-wing monoplane of unusual though pleasing
layout, fitted with a Gipsy Six engine. The fuselage, seating the occupants
in two pairs with a fifth at the extreme rear, consisted structurally of a
braced rectangular truss in the region of the cabin, becoming a semi-
monocoque of elliptical section at the rear. The wings were of orthodox
construction with plywood leading edge and fabric covering and were
braced with N-struts of comparatively shallow angle, terminating at their
lower ends upon a small stub wing which served as a passenger step for
access to the cabin doors and also as a support and housing for the retractable undercarriage, which was arranged to fold inwards by hydraulic
means leaving a flush underside to the wing-stub and the fuselage. The
cabin was roomy, effectively soundproofed and generously upholstered,
and dual control was provided for the pilot and front passenger by means
of a swing-over wheel. At £1,980 the Phoenix was one of the more
expensive private aeroplanes, but the fortunate owner was offered a

reasonable cruising speed with five persons and 120 lbs weight of luggage
over a range of 500 miles. No flaps were fitted, and the landing speed of
55 m.p.h. was rather higher than that of similar types.

The British Klemm Company was reorganised in 1935 under the new
and all-embracing title of the British Aircraft Manufacturing Company,
and it then offered the Swallow and Eagle in a new form which made production easier. The B.A. Swallow 2, in spite of a more angular outline to
wing-tips and rudder than its predecessor, retained a graceful appearance
(Plate 51) and exceptionally safe handling qualities, and was offered in
standard form with wings arranged for single-handed folding, a cable-
operated hand starter in the cockpit and a Pobjoy Cataract engine for the
price of £725. A later refinement which further improved the Swallow's
performance was the installation of an inverted in-line engine, the new
Cirrus Minor of 90 h.p. and 3,605 c.c. capacity which had recently been
introduced. The B.A. Eagle 2 went into comparatively large-scale production, thirty-seven machines being constructed, and several of these were
taken into service by the R.A.F. on the outbreak of war although none
appear to have survived to return to civil life. In addition to the larger
twin-engined six-seater Double Eagle, the same company built in 1935
one example of a two-seater cabin aeroplane with side-by-side seating and
a Gipsy Major engine named the B.A. Cupid, but after a brief career,
which included flying in the King's Cup Race, this machine was sold in
South Africa.

The Percival Gull Six was followed early in 1936 by a four-seater
development known as the Vega Gull, with a longer and wider fuselage
than its predecessors coupled with increases in wing span and wing area.
At its price of £1,650 the Vega offered refinement for travel at cruising
speeds up to 163 m.p.h., including as optional extras an electric engine
starter, sun blinds, cabin heating and a constant-speed airscrew, and for
solo long-distance flying with the Series II Gipsy Six engine the tankage
could be increased to 140 gallons and the cruising range to a matter of
2,000 miles. Next year the Percival company brought out their first twin-
engined design, the six-seater Q.6 with a pair of Gipsy Six engines. In
its day this aircraft, considerably larger and more powerful than the
original Monospar 'light twin', would hardly have been considered a light
aeroplane, and a number of them were in fact used for scheduled airline
work in various parts of the world; such has been the increase in size and
complexity of commercial transport aircraft over two decades, however,
that today the Q.6 would be classified as a relatively low-powered business
or 'executive' machine.

The original Mew Gull racing aeroplane was broken up after its failure
to gain a place in the 1934 King's Cup, and in the next year it reappeared

as an entirely new and much refined design, with a different shaped fuselage and an increased maximum loaded weight, which associated with the unaltered wing area of only 88 sq. ft gave it a stalling speed, flaps down, of 64 m.p.h. and the very high maximum of 228 m.p.h. In the two years which followed four more Mew Gulls were built, one of which, the Cape record-holder G-AEXF, is still in active use at the time of writing. Throughout their lives these aeroplanes had great success at racing and record-breaking, notably in the hands of Mr Charles Gardner and Mr Alex Henshaw, and the imperturbably trilby-hatted figure of Captain Percival himself, swiftly overhauling the field in his Mew Gull at nearly four miles a minute, was a familiar sight at the King's Cup and other races in the years immediately before 1939. For those who are able to find aesthetic pleasure in aeroplanes—whose design is indeed a form of three-dimensional sculpture subject to the stringent rules imposed by function yet allowing wide scope for individual expression—the slender little Mew Gull of the late 1930s, seen in its natural element against a blue summer sky, must rank high in any list of beautiful man-made objects (Frontispiece).

The light aeroplane built entirely out of metal was at this time rare, for the traditional spruce and plywood had much to offer in cheapness and lightness, but when stressed-skin light-alloy construction was coming into use for the larger military and commercial aircraft some attempts were made to extend it to smaller types. One such attempt by the C.L.W. Aviation Company of Gravesend resulted in an extremely clean-looking low-wing monoplane prototype, the Curlew. In this design the C.L.W. patent wing, entirely of metal except for the covering of the main panels, was neatly allied to a shapely semi-monocoque fuselage of Alclad, not unlike that of the Short Satellite and carrying the two occupants in tandem open cockpits above the wing. The neat appearance was enhanced by the careful cowling of the 90-h.p. Pobjoy Niagara III radial engine and by the extremely simple cantilever undercarriage.

Despite its technical promise the Curlew was not a commercial success but a more successful essay in all-metal construction took place in the same year in the form of the C.W. Cygnet, designed by Messrs. C. R. Chronander and J. I. Waddington. The wing of this machine was built up on two main spars with booms of R.R.56 light alloy, stiffened light alloy ribs and sheet duralumin covering. The cabin section of the fuselage, wide enough for two seats abreast, was built up as a skinned box with structures of welded steel tubes fore and aft to carry the Cirrus Minor engine and the stressed-skin rear fuselage. Even the control surfaces were metal covered, and in these great lightness was achieved, for the one-piece elevator weighed only $3\frac{1}{2}$ lbs and the rudder $4\frac{1}{2}$ lbs. After a number of modifications the design passed into the hands of General Aircraft Limited and in due course appeared with a tricycle undercarriage, twin fins and rudders and the new Cirrus Major engine of 150 h.p. In this new form it was a most advanced and entirely viceless aeroplane, capable of a top speed of 135 m.p.h. with two occupants, luggage and fuel for 445 miles. Although relatively expensive at £1,250 it was expected to sell in considerable numbers, but the coming of war dashed these hopes and only nine were built. A development named the Owlet, retaining the same layout except for the substitution of tandem open cockpits in place of the cabin, was built as a Service trainer in 1940, but was unsuccessful.

The Australian designer Mr G. N. Wikner, cousin of Captain E. W. Percival, came to England in 1934 and joined Mr V. Foster with the aim of producing a really cheap two-seater monoplane using a converted motor-car engine. The result was the Wicko, a neat-looking machine with a braced high wing, a well-faired undercarriage with wheels enclosed in streamlined 'spats' and a cabin with side-by-side seating. It was first flown by Mr. Wikner himself in the autumn of 1936, but the Ford V8 engine, which drove the propeller through reduction gearing, proved very heavy for aircraft use and had the disadvantage of being water-cooled. The original plan of offering the aeroplane at the low price of £450 had therefore to be abandoned and the prototype was modified to carry the more expensive but very considerably lighter Cirrus Minor. With this engine it was put into production in 1937 at Southampton, certain modifications having been made which included the substitution of plywood for the original fabric wing covering and the separate jigging of the four sides of the rectangular fuselage, these being finally joined together using split longerons. Subsequently the Gipsy Major engine replaced the Cirrus and nine Wickos with this engine were built, the extra power giving a top speed in the neighbourhood of 140 m.p.h.

The single-seater Drone, originally conceived by Lowe Wylde and developed after his death by Robert Kronfeld, appeared in various forms, notably as the Super Drone with Douglas Sprite engine and the heavier and more powerful Drone de Luxe with the 30-h.p. water-cooled Carden-Ford. The Drone was indeed a 'motor-glider', but in 1935 there appeared another type to which the name could be even more aptly applied since it was intended to lift its pilot into the air with even less power than had been available in the English Electric Wren of 1923. This was the Carden-Baynes Auxiliary, designed by Mr L. E. Baynes and built at the Abbott Motor Works at Wrecclesham, Surrey. The airframe was essentially that of a Scud III sailplane with the pilot seated in an open cockpit in front of a wing of high aspect ratio. Aft of the wing there was fitted (at the suggestion of the engine designer Sir John Carden) a single-cylinder Villiers two-stroke motor-cycle engine of only 249 c.c. capacity, modified to run

inverted and to drive a small pusher propeller. By operating a crank in the
cockpit the pilot was able to wind the engine down into the fuselage while
flying, and a spring lid would then close over the opening leaving a smooth
outline for flight as a pure glider. The output of the little engine, about
nine h.p., was adequate for level flight or slow climb and a fuel supply
sufficient for about half an hour's running could be carried. An interesting
refinement was the fitting of a duplicate engine throttle at one wing-tip so
that the pilot could taxi the machine single-handed. The designer's intention was that the machine should be used as a glider in the ordinary
way with the engine held in reserve for occasions when exterior sources of
lift had failed, rather after the manner of an auxiliary sailing boat; unfortunately, however, the idea had no great appeal for glider pilots, who,
apart from their natural distrust of machinery, would have been disqualified by the use of mechanical assistance from such merit as their
flights might have earned them. Nevertheless the Auxiliary remains a most
interesting technical achievement, and it seems likely that it was (as its
designer claimed) the lowest-powered aeroplane ever to lift its pilot off the
ground without external assistance.

The short-lived Pou du Ciel was followed by quite a number of small
single-seaters, some of which copied Mignet's tandem-wing principle and
others which (more successfully) were designed on more orthodox lines.
Certain designers attempted to correct the shortcomings of the Pou by
adopting a normal control system, and a typical small machine in this
category was the Perman Parasol, built by E. G. Perman and Company of
Gray's Inn Road, who were one of the main suppliers of Pou components.
The Parasol, with its 30-h.p. Perman-Ford engine, was little more than a
Pou with fixed front wing, ailerons and a conventional tail unit, and it was
intended that it should be sold for substantially less than £200, but these
plans came to nothing once the Pou itself had come to an end in England.
A development of the Parasol, similar in general outline, was the Brough-
ton-Blayney Brawney, built at Hanworth; this had a particularly unfortunate record, since out of the three aircraft built two were involved in
fatal accidents.

It was at about this time that a remarkable and somewhat eccentric
figure of the early days of British aviation came forward with a proposal
for a light aeroplane capable of being manufactured and sold for £100.
Mr Noel Pemberton-Billing, founder of the Supermarine Aviation Works,
is also remembered for having with extraordinary foresight prepared an
aerodrome in Essex complete with all accommodation some considerable
time before there existed any aeroplanes in England to make use of it.
Later—in 1913—he won a wager of £500 by the surprising feat of learning
to fly and taking his pilot's certificate between dawn and breakfast-time

on the first day in which he had ever sat in a practical aeroplane. The light aeroplane which he now proposed, to be called the Skylark, was to be made entirely of welded bicycle tubing and covered with aluminium sheet, in spite of which the weight of the structure was optimistically expected to be only 140 lbs. This idea, though nothing if not original, was not translated into practice and the £100 aeroplane remained a dream except for those energetic persons who were ready to face the labour of doing their own constructional work.

Mr C. H. Latimer-Needham, designer of the Halton biplane of 1926 and other light aeroplanes and gliders, left the R.A.F. in 1935 to become managing director and chief designer of a new small company, Luton Aircraft Limited. His first powered design was the Buzzard, a wooden single-seat pusher with 35-h.p. Anzani twin-cylinder engine which made its maiden flight in the autumn of 1935. The construction of this machine owed much to sailplane practice, with removable outer wing panels of very high aspect ratio and a narrow boom fuselage carrying a tail with all-moving control surfaces. A concession to powered practice, however, was the fitting of split flaps which could be set in six or seven different positions to regulate the steepness of the approach. After a crash in the winter of 1936 the original Buzzard was rebuilt as the Mark II Coupé with wings of lower aspect ratio, a fixed tailplane and a neatly enclosed cockpit which enabled the engine, immediately behind the pilot, to be carefully cowled in. These modifications raised the top speed from 80 to 90 m.p.h. Two experimental types followed the Buzzard, one having tandem wings, and then came the single-seater L.A.4 or Luton Minor. This was a direct successor to the Halton Minus, and was designed specifically for the amateur builder who would be expected to have little expert knowledge and few facilities at his disposal. The parasol wing of the Minus was retained and the structure generally was arranged to provide duplicate stress routes as an insurance against inexpert workmanship. With the Anzani engine and a loaded weight of 600 lbs it was capable of a cruising speed of 75 m.p.h. By the time of the outbreak of war a considerable number of Luton Minors were under construction by amateurs all over the world.

The L.A.5, or Luton Major, which appeared in 1939, was a two-seater high-wing braced monoplane with Walter Mikron engine, having several of its components in common with the Minor and being equally designed on robust and simple lines for amateur building. To make it suitable for training the machine was fitted with dual control as standard, and the wings were arranged to fold for storage by releasing two pins. The flight trials of the Major, carried out at Denham aerodrome in March 1939, showed it to perform satisfactorily and indicated a top speed close to

105 m.p.h. A further version, to be known as the Sports Major and using the Gipsy Minor engine, was under development but all work had to be discontinued on the outbreak of war; in more recent years, however, the earlier Luton series of designs have been revived and brought up to date. In 1937 Mr Latimer-Needham was also responsible for the design of a light single-seater to special order—the Martin monoplane, which used a number of components from the D.H.53 of fourteen years earlier.

The designer of the interesting Snark, Dr N. A. de Bruyne, later produced a small single-seater monoplane called the Ladybird, whose construction was begun by Dr de Bruyne's company Aero Research Limited and completed by a young Dutch student named J. N. Maas. Its first flight took place at the Cambridge aerodrome (Marshall's) shortly after Christmas 1937. The layout was unusual, with a shoulder-wing arrangement and a tricycle undercarriage employing Dunlop pneumatic-tyred wheelbarrow wheels for the main units; these were carried below the wing in streamlined fairings, the trailing edges of which could be splayed out as airbrakes. The long-nosed wooden monocoque fuselage accommodated the pilot beneath a transparent canopy immediately behind the single wing spar, and the 25-h.p. Scott Squirrel engine (later changed for a Bristol Cherub) was mounted in the extreme nose with the castoring nosewheel immediately below it.

On more traditional lines was the Currie Wot biplane built to the design of the ground engineer at Lympne, Mr J. R. Currie, in the same year and fitted with an Aeronca-J.A.P. flat-twin engine. The Wot had the appearance of a diminutive Moth or Avian, the span of its unstaggered wings being only 22 ft. The two machines built before the outbreak of war had a relatively undistinguished career and were both destroyed by enemy action at Lympne in 1940, but eighteen years later a third was built to the original drawings at Eastleigh and was experimentally fitted with a small Rover gas-turbine engine.

Contemporary with the Luton series were the single-seaters produced by the glider-building firm of Zander and Weyl at Dunstable, later renamed Dart Aircraft Limited. The Dunstable Dart, which upon its makers' change of name became the Dart Pup, was a parasol pusher type of the same general class as the Shackleton-Murray but on a smaller scale, fitted with an Ava engine of 27 h.p., later replaced by a Bristol Cherub III. The Ava engine was also used initially in the Dart Kitten, a low-wing cantilever monoplane of which three were built; two of them, developed versions with Aeronca-J.A.P. engines, are still in existence. Finally there was the Flittermouse, built to private order in 1936 and fitted with a Scott Squirrel engine of 25 h.p., the tail unit of this machine being carried on an open arrangement of booms which provided room for the small pusher propeller. Like most 'ultra-lights' of their day, the Dart series were of a certain technical interest but extremely limited popular appeal, and were built in ones and twos rather than in dozens or hundreds.

Perhaps the most elegant, and at the same time practical, small single-seater aeroplane of the period was the Chilton (Plate 57), designed by two ex-students of the de Havilland Technical School—the Hon A. W. H. Dalrymple and Mr A. R. Ward—who had been concerned with the T.K.2. Their object was to build an economical small machine on modern lines capable of a good performance on an engine of low power, and the result was a cantilever low-wing monoplane of exceptional cleanness, built of wood with fuselage and wings completely ply-covered. The plan-form of the wing approximated to the elliptical, theoretically the most efficient shape from the point of view of induced drag, but was made up out of a judicious combination of straight lines to simplify manufacture. The whole machine had something of the appearance of a miniature Miles Sparrow-hawk, with its carefully fitted 'trouser' type fairings over the wheels, three-position split flaps and fin and rudder of low aspect ratio, and the designers' careful attention to detail repaid them with a maximum speed which was surprisingly high: with its neatly cowled water-cooled Carden-Ford engine the Chilton was capable of 112 m.p.h. Later substitution of a lighter and more powerful French air-cooled engine, the 44-h.p. Train, further improved the performance and raised the top speed to 125 m.p.h. At its price of £315 it offered excellent value as a delightful little sporting aeroplane, which unlike some of its small single-seater contemporaries was fully capable of acting as a fast and practical means of transport across country.

Two interesting and somewhat similar single-seat racing types made their appearance at the time of the 1937 King's Cup Race. After their successful T.K.2 the de Havilland Technical School constructed a tiny low-wing monoplane which was at the time reputed to be the smallest aeroplane ever to have been built in Great Britain, and was numbered T.K.4, the intermediate T.K.3 never having proceeded beyond the initial design stage. The span of T.K.4 was under 20 ft and it embodied every possible aerodynamic refinement including a retractable undercarriage and flaps operated by hydraulic handpump, fixed slots and a special nose cowling with circular intake. Structurally it was also noteworthy, for the wooden fuselage was of semi-monocoque type and the wing was built up on four spars with spruce laminations as top covering and plywood below. Balsa wood was used for wing-tips and leading edges and (in sandwich form) for all control surfaces—a structural technique pioneered by de Havilland in their four-engined Albatross transport aeroplane of 1936 and later used to good effect in the war-time Mosquito. The wing loading of the little T.K.4 was naturally high, giving a landing speed of 62 m.p.h., and some indication of its top speed is given by the fact that it completed the 1937 King's Cup course at 230·5 m.p.h. Unfortunately its life was very brief for it crashed while practising for a record attempt in October of the same year, killing de Havillands' chief test pilot R. J. Waight. No other aeroplane of the T.K. series flew, for the T.K.5 research machine of 1939, which employed the unusual canard or 'tail-first' layout, failed to leave the ground in its first trials and its development was abandoned on the outbreak of war.

The other single-seat racer was the Miles Hobby or M.13 whose active career was also short. Like the T.K.4 it was fitted with the Gipsy Major II and a variable-pitch propeller and with a retractable undercarriage, but although it was just ready in time for the race it failed to start owing to last-minute difficulties with retraction, and in the following year its flying days came to an end when it was sent to Farnborough for full-scale wind tunnel testing, a role made possible by its small span.

To turn to the light twin-engined type, progress continued with the useful little Monospar right up to the outbreak of war. On establishing themselves at Hanworth in 1934 the General Aircraft Company had developed the original design into the ST-10 with Pobjoy Niagara engines of 90 h.p., and in due course there followed the ST-11, with retractable undercarriage, and the more powerful ST-12 with two Gipsy Major engines. Few examples of these versions were built, but in the year of King George the Fifth's Jubilee—1935—a special type known as the Monospar Jubilee appeared, essentially an ST-10 with an additional seat at the rear of the cabin for an occasional fifth passenger. The Jubilee, or ST-25, was popular both with private owners and for charter and internal airline duties, and the idea was carried further in 1936 with the introduction of the Monospar de Luxe. Five different versions of this were offered (Standard, de Luxe, Transport, Freighter and Ambulance), and they embodied various refinements including Pobjoy Niagara III engines with electric starters, trimming tabs on elevator and rudder and the unusual feature for the time of a homing radio receiver fitted as standard. It was indeed the policy of the manufacturers to equip their machines comprehensively with instruments and blind-flying equipment, and so the new Monospars represented good value at their prices of £1,750 for the Standard and £1,985 for the de Luxe version. The final Monospar development, known as the Universal, was modified in the interests of good single-engine handling to have twin fins and rudders in place of the single central fin of earlier versions, and twenty-six machines so modified were produced and sold, many of them abroad.

After designing his auxiliary sailplane and a modified version of the

Pou du Ciel known as the Cantilever Pou, Mr L. E. Baynes embarked upon a novel type of two-seater light aeroplane, joining with Sir John Carden at Heston to form the firm of Carden-Baynes for this purpose. The machine, the Baynes Bee, was a twin-engined pusher employing two special 40-h.p. Carden-Ford converted motor-car engines which were supercharged by Centric blowers running at 1·1 times engine speed and were neatly buried in the wings, each being supported aft from the main spar in cantilever fashion and driving its propeller through an extension shaft. The whole structure was of wood, and the wing was attached to the fuselage by two bolts and a swivel pin, so that in place of the conventional wing-folding arrangement it could quickly be unfastened and swung round, engines and all, into a fore-and-aft direction. Pilot and passenger sat side by side in an enclosed cabin in front of the leading edge, with dual control provided by means of a T-shaped control column between the seats. The undercarriage was an echo of the distant days of the Lympne competitions, for like the English Electric Wren and the Avro 558 biplane of 1923 the Bee had its wheels half-buried in the underside of the fuselage, an arrangement which reduces drag at the cost of introducing certain handling difficulties, especially when taxying or landing across wind. The Bee was a most original attempt to produce a small twin-engined aeroplane with a reasonable performance, but the prototype suffered a forced landing on its first flight because of engine overheating, and although Mr Baynes planned to develop it into a three-seater called the B.3 with a tricycle undercarriage and air-cooled Walter Mikron engines this interesting project came to an end with the outbreak of war.

Similar ideas inspired the twin-engined Hordern-Richmond Autoplane, built by the Heston Aircraft Company in 1936 according to the ideas of their test pilot Mr E. G. Hordern and those of the Duke of Richmond and Gordon. The flat-four Continental A-40 engines, each of 40 h.p., were conventionally mounted in nacelles on each wing-root, and in the nose of the fuselage was a cabin for two people side by side with space for luggage or a third person behind, the cabin roof and sides being removable for easy access. Normal wooden construction was used throughout, with folding wings and a simple fixed undercarriage, and the control system was unorthodox in that the rudder bar was dispensed with and the rudder was operated by a wheel at the top of the control column. Like the Bee, however, the Hordern-Richmond achieved no commercial success and only the prototype G-AEOG was built.

The twin-engined de Havilland Dragonfly or D.H.90 biplane closely resembled its larger commercial relative the D.H. Dragon Rapide but deserves inclusion in this book because it was specifically intended as a high-quality machine for the wealthier private owner. Whereas the Rapide was fitted with Gipsy Six engines and was capable of carrying six to eight passengers at a cruising speed of 130 m.p.h., the Dragonfly with its Gipsy Majors naturally offered a lower performance with a maximum of five occupants including the pilot. The seating arrangements were somewhat unusual, being laid out in two side-by-side pairs with the fifth person accommodated on a single seat in the middle of the cabin. From a structural viewpoint the machine embodied a number of new ideas, including a monocoque fuselage made of pre-formed plywood and a lower centre-section of cantilever type with only the outer wing-bay braced, this leaving the lower wing-root clear of obstruction as a step for access to the cabin through a door placed between the wings, rather as in the Heston Phoenix. In spite of its fairly high price (£2,650) the Dragonfly found a considerable number of purchasers and a total of 66 production aeroplanes were built at Hatfield, a large proportion of them for export.

On the whole the very light two-seaters such as the Hillson Praga did not achieve much popularity with British designers in the 1930s, largely perhaps because it was felt that their performance and handling qualities in the rough weather so often experienced in the British Isles would be unsatisfactory for training or touring purposes. Most of these smaller types seen in England, such as the Praga itself and the American Piper Cub, Taylor Cub, Aeronca and others, were of foreign origin and were then manufactured under licence in anticipation of a demand which generally turned out to be somewhat disappointing; but one successful two-seater of foreign design intermediate between the above-mentioned types and the standard club trainer of 100 h.p. and over was the curiously-named Tipsy, so called from the name of its designer E. O. Tips of the Belgian subsidiary of the Fairey Aviation Company. In 1935 M Tips had designed a little single-seater of extremely attractive appearance—the Tipsy S—but although the prototype (registered OO-TIP) was much seen at aviation displays it did not enjoy the commercial success that it appeared to merit. Shortly afterwards M Tips applied the experience gained with the single-seater to the design of a two-seat version with Czechoslovakian Walter Mikron engine of 62 h.p., and this aeroplane, called the Tipsy B, was demonstrated in England in the early summer of 1937 and in due course put into production at Hanworth.

The Tipsy B, a clean low-wing cantilever monoplane built of wood, was unusual in having an open cockpit with side-by-side seating, and to avoid excessive fuselage width the seats were slightly staggered to allow the instructor or passenger, seated on the right, to place his left arm behind the other occupant. A large curved windscreen was fitted to protect both occupants from draughts. The wing was built as a single unit passing below the fuselage and was fitted with split flaps. The Tipsy's docile handling qualities and excellent performance allied with economy—it could cover 100 miles in the hour at cruising speed using only three-and-a-quarter gallons of petrol—gave it a wide appeal for training and touring purposes, and fifteen of the two-seater types were built before September 1939, some being used for Civil Air Guard instructional work. A large proportion survived the war and are still flying in the hands of communal flying groups, private owners and clubs, their numbers having been increased by the addition of a small batch of a two-seater cabin version of post-war design and construction known as the Belfair. The Walter Mikron engine was also chosen for a small cabin two-seater of similar appearance to the Tipsy—the Chrislea Airguard, designed by Mr R. C. Christophorides and Mr B. V. Leak and built at Heston in 1938. This was intended for Civil Air Guard use but only one was built.

One of the many experimental light aeroplanes of the period was the Deekay Knight two-seater monoplane, built at Broxbourne in 1937 to the design of Mr S. C. Hart-Still. This was built of wood to prove the design and it was intended later to build the type in plastic materials, a typical component proposed being a wing spar formed to a bulbous section in plastic and reinforced with metal tubes. These intentions came to nothing, but the single aeroplane built had a four-spar wing with the curious feature of a number of external ribs running in the line of flight, and was fitted with flaps and neatly faired undercarriage legs with braked wheels. The two occupants sat side by side in the cabin, which had a fixed windscreen and a backward-sliding canopy. The original idea had been to fit the aeroplane with the American Aeromarine radial engine, but plans to produce this engine under licence in England were frustrated by lack of capacity due to the current military expansion, and a Cirrus Minor was therefore used, which gave a cruising speed of 105 m.p.h.

What was perhaps the most attractive of the whole pre-war range of light Miles types in appearance, performance and handling qualities owed its existence to a specification laid down by Mr Whitney Straight, who after a career in motor-racing had entered civil aviation in 1934 and was soon operating a chain of aerodromes and flying clubs throughout Great Britain. The Miles M.11 or Whitney Straight, first flown in 1936 and put into production for the uses of the Straight Corporation and for private owners in the following year, followed the Hornet Moth plan of side-by-side seating with ample luggage space behind, but in accordance with Miles practice was a low-wing cantilever aeroplane built of wood and fitted with a Gipsy Major engine. The speed range of from 145 to 38 m.p.h. was excellent, the low stalling speed being due to split flaps which were operated by means of the Theed pneumatic system from the depression in the engine inlet manifold. No operating loads were felt by the pilot with this system, and after total engine failure sufficient reserve vacuum was retained for two complete cycles of operation. A three-seater version of the Whitney Straight which appeared early in 1938 was the Miles Monarch, an equally attractive touring machine which carried a third occupant behind the others on the starboard side with a luggage space to port. The lines and performance of the Monarch were very similar to those of its predecessor, but there were detailed differences: the wings were not arranged to fold, and the pneumatic flaps incorporated a new system of operation known as the Miles Glide Control. With this system the flap and throttle levers, both placed at the pilot's left hand, were interconnected so that a forward movement of the throttle after the flaps had been lowered raised them to a gated position at 25°, allowing much of the drag to be shed without a serious loss of lift. Although only eleven Monarchs were built they had a remarkable record of reliability and freedom from accident; only one was lost on war service, and of the six machines built to British order in 1938 and 1939 three still remain on the British register (Plate 56).

The Whitney Straight and the Monarch represented the best in Miles design for the private pilot in the immediate pre-war years, and were deservedly popular, but the growing pace of R.A.F. expansion compelled attention to be focused largely on the Magister contract, and no other Miles type intended for purely private flying reached the stage of production until after the war. One interesting development of the Hawk to private order deserves mention, however. The M.12, or Mohawk, built in 1936 especially for Colonel Charles Lindbergh, was a tandem two-seater with sliding cabin top, with lines similar to those of the Hawk series but with an American Menasco Buccaneer engine of 250 h.p. which gave it a top speed of almost 200 miles an hour. Lindbergh's requirements included an alternative float undercarriage interchangeable with the pair of single-strut legs fitted for land operation. After receiving its certificate of airworthiness early in 1937 the Mohawk was used by its owner for touring Europe and India, and after a period of war service in England was restored for civilian use in 1946 and used for air racing before being sold abroad a few years later.

The last of the de Havilland light aeroplanes to appear before the war —the D.H.94 Moth Minor—displayed a grace of line which makes it outstanding even among the products of a manufacturer with a particular talent for good-looking aircraft (Plate 58). The reader may have been thinking that the de Havilland Company, in the face of its competitors Miles and Percival, had been somewhat slow to follow the trend towards the low-wing cantilever type of light aeroplane, but in fact this was not the case. The origins of the Moth Minor went back as far as 1931, when its forerunner the D.H.81 Swallow Moth monoplane, fitted with a special

Halford-designed engine of 80 h.p. named the Gipsy IV, first flew at Stag Lane. The aim was to reverse the trend towards higher power and to offer the private owner a simple type which should cost even less to operate than the Moth; but owing to the very success of the Moth itself and that of the Puss and Leopard Moths, the possibility of putting the Swallow Moth into production had to be set aside. Captain de Havilland, however, personally kept the idea alive, and in 1936 he set a small team of young designers to work on a simple two-seater with folding wings based on the D.H.81, while Major Halford's office settled to the task of producing a new 90-h.p. engine which in due course received the name of Gipsy Minor.

The first experimental Moth Minor was flown by Captain de Havilland on a June evening in 1937, and formed the basis for later production. The well-tried plywood box fuselage of Moth type was retained, and a stub wing acted as a support for a neat cantilever undercarriage and contained a 13-gallon fuel tank to port and a space to starboard which could be used for luggage or for a second fuel tank. Fixed to the stub wing and arranged to fold were the outer wing panels of high aspect ratio built up on two wooden box spars, and to steepen the very flat glide a large perforated air-brake was fitted under the centre-section. Although the open cockpit arrangement was more usual, some of the Moth Minors built were of closed type with coupé tops faired in to the rear fuselage somewhat after the fashion of the T.K.2. The Minor's cruising speed of over 100 m.p.h., its economical fuel consumption, simple handling qualities and low price of £595 made it extremely attractive to private owners and to clubs, and brisk production was under way throughout the summer of 1939; but after war broke out, with one hundred and eleven machines already delivered to customers, the production of the Moth Minor was transferred to the de Havilland subsidiary in Australia and the '94 shop' at Hatfield was cleared in readiness for more serious matters. Thus ended the tale of the Moth family, for the Minor was the last of its celebrated line, and although a post-war successor from the Canadian de Havilland Company was built in British factories, no further original light aeroplanes appeared on the drawing boards of Hatfield, to the great regret of the many for whom the words 'light aeroplane' and 'de Havilland' had become almost synonymous.

The Moth Minor was not the only small private aeroplane to be over-whelmed by the war; many designs by less well-known manufacturers which were planned or nearly ready to fly had to be abandoned, including the Hillson Helvellyn and Pennine, the Shapley Kittiwake, the Dart Weasel, the Arpin and Millichamp pushers, the Wicko Windsor and a proposed two-seater development of the attractive little Chilton mono-plane, as well as an advanced twin-engined design from the last-named firm with slots, flaps and retractable undercarriage. Other types which had already shown themselves to be successful had their production career abruptly terminated, and in this category came the tricycle Cygnet, the Mosscraft, the Marendaz trainer and others. The end of private flying in September 1939 brought to a stop a most active and prolific period. Many of the aircraft then made were unsuccessful in the commercial sense and did not go beyond a single prototype, and many of those which were put into production were built in only small numbers, but for sheer variety of design the immediate pre-war years are unlikely ever to be equalled.

⤙ 15 ⤚

The Last Adventurers

1935–39

After the race from Mildenhall to Melbourne in the autumn of 1934, the age of the light biplane with open cockpit was over for the purpose of serious record-breaking. Long-distance solo flying itself was already beginning to lose some of its interest for the public, for the reliability of aircraft and engines hardly needed further demonstration; but in the few years of peace that remained the long routes to Australia, to the Cape and across the Atlantic still carried a small band of solo pilots on their self-imposed task of stretching their personal endurance to its ultimate limits.

It will be remembered that the Yorkshire pilot Mr H. L. Brook had competed in the 'MacRobertson' race in the original Miles Falcon G-ACTM, to which had been fitted the actual Gipsy Major engine which had carried James Mollison safely across both the North and South Atlantic oceans. Mr Brook had, in fact, bought the historic Puss Moth *Heart's Content* as a vehicle for surveying the route to Melbourne, but had been forced down in France by bad weather soon after starting out and had salvaged the engine from the ensuing crash for use in the Falcon. Through various misfortunes in the race itself he failed to reach Australia in time to qualify for any prizes, but after extending his aircraft's range by fitting extra tankage he used it for the return journey some months later. He left Darwin early in the morning of Sunday, 24 March 1935, and landed at Lympne in the afternoon of the following Sunday to set up a new record for the solo flight. The absolute record was by this time no longer held by a solo pilot, having fallen to the green Comet of Cathcart Jones and Waller on their dash back from Melbourne in 6 days and 16 hours carrying newsreel pictures of the race in which they had just taken fourth place. A few months after his arrival Brook made an attempt on the Cape record in the same Falcon but was unsuccessful, ending with a crash at Mersa Matruh.

Brook was soon followed along the route from Australia to England by Miss Jean Batten, who was to become one of the best-known women pilots

58. The last of the Moths: the simple but elegant Moth Minor, the production of which in 1939 was brought to an end by the war

59. The Miles Gemini of 1945. Popular amongst private owners to this day

60. Flight Lieutenant 'Tommy' Rose arriving at Croydon in his Miles Falcon in March 1936 after his flight to the Cape and back

61. Miss Jean Batten with her Percival Gull

of the next few years. When she left Darwin on 12 April 1935 a strong wind from the south-east was lifting a fine red dust off the continent, and Miss Batten therefore climbed to 6,000 ft for the sea crossing in order to take advantage of clearer air and a stronger tail-wind. When she was about 250 miles out from land the Moth's engine suddenly coughed and died, and she was faced with a glide down towards the water. The machine passed through a cloud layer at 3,000 ft, but before the impact the fuel blockage suddenly cleared itself and she was able to climb away again after a terrifying few minutes and continue her journey to Rambang considerably shaken. Undoubtedly the extra height she had in hand had saved her life; in spite of its evil reputation not a single pilot was lost over the Timor Sea in all these years of long-distance flying. Miss Batten eventually reached Croydon without any further alarming incidents, completing the first flight from Australia by a woman pilot in 17 days and 15 hours. Troubles with engine and tyres at Marseilles prevented her from equalling her outward time.

The Percival Gull, which had already performed one fine flight in the hands of Kingsford Smith, was well demonstrated by its designer in June with a non-stop flight from Gravesend to Oran—1,150 miles—at a speed of 160 m.p.h. After taking off at 1.30 a.m. Captain Percival landed at his destination at 8.40, sold one of his aeroplanes during a short stay on the ground and was back in Essex for early dinner the same night. For this flight, which he later capped with one to Stockholm in six hours, Captain Percival received the Johnston Memorial Trophy for navigation. It was at about the same time that the Duchess of Bedford also passed through Oran for a further exploration of North Africa in her Puss Moth, flown by Flight Lieutenant Preston, and on this occasion they made a tour of lonely regions of the Sahara which included visits to the towns of Timbuktu, Niamey and Kano.

The Australian pilot Mr H. F. Broadbent had first appeared in the news in 1931 when he had flown a Gipsy II Avian round Australia in slightly more than seven days; this time was later bettered by Mr C. J. Melrose in a Puss Moth with Gipsy Major engine, and then early in 1935 Broadbent managed to recapture the record in the same machine which Melrose had used by completing the circuit in three days and nine hours. Encouraged by this success he decided to attempt Brook's solo record from Australia to England and set out from Darwin on 10 October, but the flight terminated abruptly with a forced landing in the desert near the R.A.F. station of Shaibah which resulted in damage to an undercarriage leg. Since the Service was unable to offer him adequate help with repairs, Broadbent sold the aeroplane as it stood to one of the officers on the station and completed his journey by Imperial Airways. He remained in

England only long enough to purchase a Percival Gull with 200-h.p. Gipsy Six engine and make preparations for the return flight, and early on 2 November he set out from Croydon in company with Melrose, who was flying a Gull Major. The two pilots reached Karachi together, but the following day came the news of the disappearance of Sir Charles Kingsford Smith over the Bay of Bengal, and Melrose, believing he had seen the exhaust flames of Kingsford Smith's Lockheed Altair above him in the darkness, abandoned his attempt in order to take part in a search. Unhappily it proved fruitless. The fate of the celebrated Australian airman and his navigator remained a mystery for some time, but the eventual discovery of a wheel of his machine led to the supposition that the Altair had struck high ground when flying across the Tenasserim coast from seaward. In the meantime Broadbent in his faster machine carried on successfully to reach Darwin in 6 days 21 hrs 19 mins, or some seven hours faster than the time which had been taken by the missing pilot in his Gull Four two years earlier.

The technically advanced Hendy Heck, with its slots, flaps and retractable undercarriage, was relatively unsuccessful at the air racing and long-distance flying for which it appeared to be so well suited, and the principal claims to fame of the attractive black-and-gold prototype G-ACTC was its return flight from England to the Cape in the hands of Flying Officer David Llewellyn and Mrs Jill Wyndham. The outward journey was not especially successful, but on the return journey they easily beat the time set up by Mrs Mollison almost three years earlier. Naturally the latter still remained valid as a solo record and had the merit of having been achieved in a considerably slower machine.

After the Jubilee celebrations were over, Miss Batten set about planning another long flight and decided to sell her Moth and buy one of the faster and better equipped cabin machines that were now available. She too chose a Percival Gull Six (Plate 61), which with a total fuel capacity of 140 gallons could fly some 2,000 miles without refuelling, and her plan was to follow Mollison's route down the west coast of Africa and thence across to Brazil. Leaving Lympne early one November morning—the very day when the Heck was due to return there from the Cape—she flew across France and crossed the Pyrenees in clear air and bright sunshine at 14,000 ft with the mountains hidden in cloud below. After a landing at Casablanca, 1,350 miles from Lympne and reached in under ten hours, she carried on down the barren Sahara coast and eventually reached Thies aerodrome, 45 miles inland from Dakar, only to find that it was totally lacking in night-flying equipment and that her fuel supplies had been sent to the Dakar aerodrome in error. It had been her original intention to rest for a few days in West Africa before setting out across the ocean, but having made excellent time so far she decided to try and complete the journey in a shorter time than Mollison had done and urged the Commandant to arrange for the fuel tins to be sent to Thies by road. It was 10.30 p.m. the same evening, the second day out from England, when the fuel arrived, and after realising that the take-off would be difficult with a small aerodrome and no wind Miss Batten ruthlessly jettisoned much of the equipment which French safety regulations had compelled her to carry for the flight down the coast; signal pistol, rockets, cartridges and revolver were all left behind, and she took with her only log-books, emergency rations, a thermos flask and a few light personal effects.

After being woken in the dark at 3.30 she at once set to studying the forecast for her route, which offered fair conditions down to latitude 10° north, beyond this the permanent depression well known to the French air-mail pilots, and then better weather continuing to the coast of Brazil. A misty rain was falling as she climbed into the Gull, set her compass with a hand torch and taxied out in the glare of headlights from an assembly of lorries and cars. The Gull took a long run with its heavy load of petrol but eventually climbed away. As she flew out into the Atlantic the overcast weather cleared, only to return again with heavy black clouds and an oily swell, offering the choice of a long detour or a plunge into cloud on instruments; she chose the second alternative and was soon inside the storm at only a thousand feet above the sea. While she was passing through the storm her compass began to behave erratically and finally swung round through 180°, but having no alternative means of ascertaining direction she had to carry on as well as possible until eventually it recovered.

At a point 1,100 miles out from Thies, with 800 miles to go to land, the weather improved as forecast but the south-east wind began to increase, and estimating her drift at 8° she altered course to prevent herself from being drifted away to the north of her intended landfall at Cape San Roque. Soon she sighted a small ship, the only one seen in all that immense distance, and this encouraged her to believe that she was on her track assuming that the ship was bound from Natal to Dakar—though there was the disturbing possibility that it might be from Pernambuco, which would have put her seriously off to the south. Twelve-and-a-half hours after take-off, with no land yet in sight, she turned on to her last tank of fuel—one hour's supply. Shortly afterwards there appeared a low coastline with sand dunes and a lighthouse which she was able to identify as Cape San Roque. She had made an extraordinary accurate landfall with only half a mile of error in nearly 2,000 miles. It was then only a matter of minutes for the Gull to reach the aerodrome of Natal and touch down on Brazilian soil after a crossing lasting thirteen-and-a-quarter hours, having travelled from England to South America in 2 days 13 hrs 15 mins, or almost a whole day faster than Mollison. Miss Batten's subsequent tour to Rio de Janeiro, Buenos Ayres and Montevideo brought her an ecstatic welcome from vast crowds and at Rio she received the Order of the Cruzeiro do Sul from the President of Brazil, Dr Vargas; later, after she had returned to England, she was awarded the C.B.E. in the birthday honours of King Edward VIII.

The year 1936 saw attention concentrated largely on the Cape route. Flight Lieutenant 'Tommy' Rose, chief test pilot to the Miles company, opened the year's record-breaking by a fast run to Cape Town in the Falcon Six with which he had won the King's Cup the previous summer. His first attempt late in January ended in failure when ice drove him down at Abbeville and his aeroplane suffered damage, but then he started again early in February and reached the Cape in 3 days 17 hrs 37 mins, thus at last bettering Amy Mollison's solo time which had remained unapproached since November 1932. His flight was not made simply for the purpose of record-breaking but was in fact a normal business trip to South Africa. At the end of his visit Rose set out for home again and by completing the journey in a little over six days once again improved on Mrs Mollison's time, as well as beating the short-lived record set up by the Heck (Plate 58).

In May, however, Mrs Mollison recaptured both her records with one of the Gipsy Six Percival Gulls of the type which Miss Batten had used so successfully. Carrying a fuel load of 145 gallons in the wings and in the cabin, as well as a Marconi radio set, and following her old route by way of Oran, Gao and Mossamedes, she reached the Cape in three-and-a-quarter days, turned round almost immediately and was back at Croydon less than eight days after her departure.

Some low-powered aeroplanes also made their mark at long-distance flying in 1936. Flying Officer David Llewellyn flew to Johannesburg in a leisurely way in a tiny two-seater Aeronca (Plate 53), and Mr H. L. Brook, flying a Czechoslovak Praga, reached the Cape from Lympne in 16 days. Colonel Sempill, who had recently toured to Australia and back in his Leopard Moth, set up an international distance record for single-seater machines of under 200 kg empty weight with a non-stop flight from Croydon to Berlin in the Kronfeld Super Drone. With its cruising speed of only 60 m.p.h. this 'motor glider', which would have been eligible for the 1923 Lympne trials, took eleven hours for the outward journey but returned in a gale in only nine hours.

In June 1936 came the announcement of another long-distance air race, this time from England to Johannesburg in connection with the Empire Exhibition in the latter city, prizes totalling £10,000 being offered by the South African industrialist Mr I. W. Schlesinger. The race, planned on similar lines to the 'MacRobertson' two years earlier with speed and handicap prizes, attracted an entry list of fourteen aeroplanes, comprising four of the new Vega Gulls, three Mew Gulls, a Miles Sparrowhawk and Hawk Six, a B.A. Eagle, the D.H.92 Dolphin and three twin-engined machines, the Miles Peregrine, B.A. Double Eagle and Airspeed Envoy. Before it began, however, one of the Vega Gulls entered was used in an attempt to match Jean Batten's feat of the previous year with a crossing of the North Atlantic in the hands of a relatively unknown woman pilot, Mrs Beryl Markham. Mrs Markham had been taught to fly in Kenya in 1931 by C. W. A. Scott's co-pilot in the Melbourne race, Mr T. Campbell Black, and had subsequently flown herself to England alone. Continuous head-winds and poor weather delayed her on her crossing, and approaching Newfoundland in fog after twenty hours' flying with fuel running low she was just able to make a landing on Cape Breton Island where the aeroplane tipped on to its nose in boggy ground and was badly damaged.

With the elimination of this Vega Gull, the withdrawal of one other and of the Dolphin, the failure of the Peregrine to be ready in time and the tragic taxying accident to Campbell Black's Mew Gull which resulted in his death, the entry list for the Schlesinger race dwindled to nine, and early in the morning of 29 September these aeroplanes were despatched at one-minute intervals from Portsmouth aerodrome on their way to Johannesburg by way of compulsory check-points at Belgrade and Cairo. The race, however, turned out to be an almost total fiasco, and the winners, C. W. A. Scott and Giles Guthrie, who completed the course in rather less than 53 hours in their Vega Gull G-AEKE, were the only contestants to finish. For the rest the race was a long chapter of misfortunes. The B.A. Eagle of C. G. M. Alington damaged its undercarriage in a forced landing in Bavaria, Major Miller's Mew Gull had to retire at Belgrade, the Double Eagle's undercarriage collapsed at Cairo, Victor Smith's Sparrowhawk withdrew with an oil leak at Khartoum, and smoke from veldt fires was responsible for the crash of both Llewellyn's Vega Gull and the Mew Gull of Captain S. S. Halse. Flying Officer Clouston in the Hawk Six suffered an astonishing series of misfortunes including an almost wrecked engine which was hurriedly repaired with spares belonging to Imperial Airways, a forced landing which damaged a wing and an aileron, and finally an engine failure in total darkness followed by a crash from which he miraculously emerged unhurt. Less fortunate was the Brooklands instructor and former N.F.S. pilot Captain Max Findlay who was killed with one of his crew when the Airspeed Envoy failed to clear some trees taking off from Abercorn. Lack of adequate preparation was widely thought to have been responsible for many of the accidents in the Schlesinger race, and its unfortunate outcome served to show that even

Comparison of Hinkler's flight to Australia in 1928 (Avian) with Jean Batten's flight in 1936 (Gull Six). Night stops, or positions at local midnight, are shown. Only the England–Darwin sections are shown; Hinkler continued to Sydney and Miss Batten to New Zealand

ROUTES

HINKLER

0 Croydon, early departure. 1 Rome. 2 Malta. 3 In desert near Tobruk. 4, 5 Ramleh. 6 Basra. 7 Jask. 8 Karachi. 9 Cawnpore. 10 Calcutta. 11 Rangoon. 12 Victoria Point. 13 Singapore. 14 Bandoeng. 15 Bima, and next day to Darwin.

JEAN BATTEN

0 Lympne, early departure. 1 Brindisi. 2 H3 pumping station. 3 Karachi. 4 Akyab. 5 in air south of Singapore. 6 Koepang (Timor).

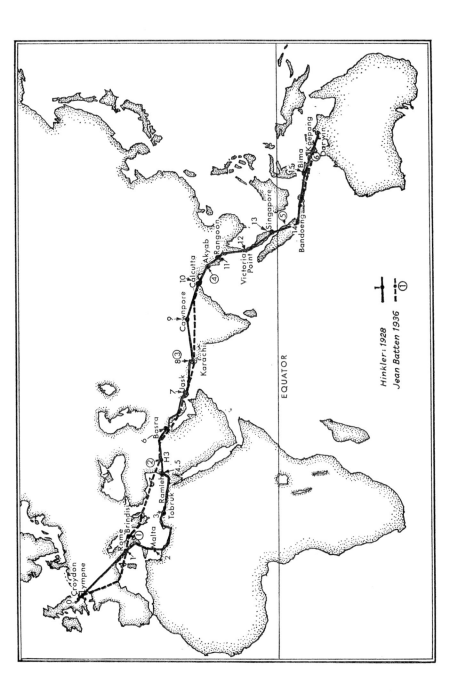

after the great technical advances which had been made over the past few years there was more to successful long-distance flying than mere luck and endurance.

Only a few days after the race Miss Jean Batten set out again in her Gull from Lympne to fulfil a long-standing ambition to fly all the way home to her native New Zealand, an ambition which had been frustrated by the short range of her Gipsy Moth two years earlier. This journey to the Antipodes was a vastly different affair from her earlier flights; the Gull cruised effortlessly at 150 m.p.h. and for much of the way she was able to fly at heights up to 10,000 ft in clear air when the lower levels were obscured by cloud. She reached Karachi in under two-and-a-half days—a remarkable contrast with Amy Johnson's eight-day record only six years before—and after a brief interval for sleep was in the air again for a long day's flight of 1,900 miles, breakfasting at Allahabad and bringing her machine down just at sunset at Akyab in Burma. She rose at 1 a.m. and took off for Alor Star, but as on her previous flight along this part of the route she was beset by furious rainstorms near Victoria Point. The bad weather continued up to her destination, and since the Gull's long range allowed her to do so she passed it by and continued to Georgetown, Penang, landing with the aeroplane's leading edges worn down to the bare wood by the torrential rain through which she had passed. When she reached Koepang, the Gull was manhandled backwards by the local staff, causing the tailwheel tyre to burst. She carried no spare, but the fuel agent ingeniously repaired the puncture by filling the tyre with rubber sponges and she was able to take off for the Timor Sea crossing, reaching Darwin just after midday on 11 October after flying from England in only 5 days 21 hrs, or more than a day faster than Broadbent. When she reached Sydney there was some opposition to her proposed flight across the Tasman, but she was quite determined to fly all the way home and took off from Richmond by the light of a flare path at 4.37 a.m. (local time) on 16 October. Her plan was to fly from Sydney to New Plymouth, near which town the 8,000-ft peak of Mount Egmont would form a good landmark as she came in from seaward, and then to turn northward along the coast to Auckland. The Tasman lived up to its reputation for fierce storms and the journey was not a comfortable one, but again Miss Batten made an astonishingly accurate landfall dead on her track, crossing New Plymouth nine-and-a-half hours out from Australia and landing at Auckland to a warm welcome after flying from England in almost precisely eleven days. A few days after this flight another Gull flown by Mr Ernle Clark, known to the Press as the 'flying farmer', performed the same journey rather less quickly, leaving England on 26 October and landing at Christchurch, N.Z., on 15 November.

Early in January 1937 Mr H. L. Brook and Flying Officer Llewellyn were both preparing Percival Gull machines for the Cape. Brook was first away, leaving Gravesend on the 10th in G-ADZO, the same aircraft which Mrs Mollison had used the year before, but the winter weather defeated him and he had to return. In the following month Llewellyn got away in his Vega *County of Monmouth*, but he too failed in his object, being forced to abandon the flight when a choked oil feed put him down in desert country near the fourth cataract of the Nile, to be succoured by wandering Bedouins with tea flavoured with camels' milk. This was his last attempt at long-distance flying, for in September of the following year he met his death while flying near Lympne aerodrome, where he was chief instructor of the Cinque Ports Flying Club. By 25 April Brook was ready again and left England for Africa; a broken tailwheel at Juba put him out of the running for an attempt on Mrs Mollison's outward record, but by leaving the Cape in the afternoon of May the 2nd and landing at Heston almost precisely four days later he considerably improved upon her homeward time, though not having been officially observed his flight did not strictly speaking constitute a new record.

Meanwhile, in February, Jean Batten had been enjoying a holiday in Australia, where at the Mascot aerodrome at Sydney she met Broadbent and learned of his plans for an attack on the Australia-to-England record established by Brook in the Miles Falcon in 1935. He proposed for this purpose to use a Leopard Moth fitted with a long-range tank in the cabin, and make up by his own powers of endurance what his aeroplane lacked in speed. His first stage took him non-stop over the distance from Darwin to Singapore in 22 hours, and by continuing tirelessly with a good deal of night-flying he reached Lympne on the evening of 3 May, 6 days 8 hrs 25 mins after leaving Australia.

This challenge proved irresistible to Miss Batten and she decided on one more long flight in the Gull which had already carried her to the Argentine and to New Zealand. She was away from Darwin at dawn on 19 October, reached Batavia the same day and took off in darkness for Alor Star to cross the Equator for the fifth time. Apart from the usual problems of weather the flight was comparatively uneventful, but in one tremendous day she flew the 2,150 miles from Rangoon to Karachi, taking off by the light of flares, calling briefly at Allahabad for fuel and to telegraph ahead to Karachi for lights to be put on since a strong head-wind was slowing her down, and then flying on across India at low altitude in scorching heat and violent bumpiness in order to minimise the effects of the wind. In spite of this immensely long day she slept only four hours before taking off again. Poor weather continued to trouble her, with the aerodrome at Cyprus flooded and unusable, furious storms across the

Mediterranean and even a waterspout visible while passing Rhodes. After a few detours she reached Marseilles where she landed briefly for coffee before carrying on to reach Lympne in a time fourteen hours less than Broadbent's. She had actually been quicker than on her previous outward journey, in spite of the fact that the prevailing winds usually ensured shorter times when flying eastward. This was her last long flight, and with it she became the first person to hold the solo record between England and Australia in both directions at the same time. A tumultuous welcome at Croydon was followed by banquets and the award of the gold medal of the Royal Aero Club, as well as the novelty of an appearance on the recently initiated television service of the B.B.C.

The last word on the Australia route fell to Broadbent in April 1938. Shortly after Clouston and Victor Ricketts had completed their fast round trip from England to New Zealand and back in eleven days in the D.H. Comet originally used by Scott and Black, Broadbent set out for home flying alone in his Vega Gull and made a quick journey as far as the Dutch East Indies, but here extreme fatigue forced him down near Sesok on the coast of Flores and the machine went up on its nose after striking a boulder and damaged its propeller. There was nothing to be done on the spot, so Broadbent placed the Vega in charge of some native sentries, arranged for the erection of a screen of palm leaves to protect it from the sun, and left it. He obtained a lift to the nearest stopping place of Q.A.N.T.A.S. in a seaplane of the Dutch Navy and from there went on to Sydney. A cable to de Havillands at Edgware brought a new propeller out by airliner in a very short time and Broadbent, who had returned from Sydney with a D.H. service engineer, set out with it across a seventy-mile strait in a native boat. This journey was unexpectedly protracted owing to lack of wind and the travellers had to subsist for 26 hours on two cups of coffee, but eventually they unloaded the propeller on Flores, fitted it and took off with little margin to spare—down a slope and over a cliff edge in conditions of no wind—to continue the flight to Sydney. Having missed the eastbound solo record, Broadbent decided to attack Miss Batten's time from Australia to England, and left Darwin in the early hours of an April morning. The Vega, with its constant-speed propeller, was a little faster than Miss Batten's fixed-pitch Gull and had a range of almost 3,000 miles, and Broadbent reached Lympne in ten fast stages. His time for the journey, which at the time of writing—over twenty-five years later—still stands as a solo record for the journey, was 5 days 4 hrs 21 mins, equivalent to an overall speed of 77·4 m.p.h. inclusive of all time spent on the ground. It was, he claimed, the least exhausting of the journeys he had done over the route, and he could easily have flown the 2,000 miles from Darwin to Singapore without landing had he not wanted to land at Sourabaya to thank the Shell agent there for the help given him over the propeller incident on the previous journey.

The last of the long-distance solo flights by light aeroplane in the age of record-breaking forms a remarkable illustration of the progress made in the mere dozen or so years since the earliest of the solo pilots set out in their Moths and Avians. The aeroplane used was the tiny Percival Mew Gull G-AEXF which had originally been used by Captain Miller in the Johannesburg race, and the pilot was the young Mr Alex Henshaw, who had already made a name for himself in air racing and had in fact won the 1938 King's Cup at Hatfield in the same machine. His plan was to make a quick dash to the Cape and return, challenging not only the existing solo records for the outward and homeward journeys, but also the very fast double flight of Flying Officer Clouston and Mrs Kirby Green in November 1937 using the all-conquering Comet G-ACSS. To familiarise himself with the west coast route, which he proposed to use, Henshaw had surveyed it in a Vega Gull in the spring of 1938, accompanied by his father, before getting down to the task of preparing the Mew Gull for the journey.

Since space was extremely limited in his little machine, the installation of the extra fuel and other items required for such a flight presented a number of problems, and the aeroplane was extensively remodelled by Essex Aero Limited of Gravesend. In the interests of high speed the cabin top was lowered four inches, further restricting the pilot's cramped space, and to the original pair of 20-gallon wing tanks was added a 40-gallon tank directly in front of the pilot, to provide space for which the instrument board had to be moved to the rear. A fourth tank holding a 7-gallon emergency supply was elaborately shaped to fit in the small space between the pilot's ankles and over the rudder bar, and the total of 87 gallons thus squeezed into the machine was sufficient to give a 2,000-mile range at 225 m.p.h. Behind the pilot in the locker was an emergency radio set to comply with French regulations for the desert route over North Africa, and the problem of food supply was met by two thermos flasks, one of beef-tea and one of egg and milk, clipped to the cockpit wall under each of the pilot's knees, with a supply of nuts, raisins, apples and oranges behind his heels. In take-off condition fully loaded with all equipment, fuel and pilot, the Mew Gull weighed 2,350 lbs, necessitating a special category certificate of airworthiness, though for better performance at this weight the Gipsy Six R engine originally used for racing had now been replaced by the Gipsy Six II with a de Havilland constant-speed airscrew in place of the two-position Ratier. With its fixed undercarriage and stalling speed of 76 m.p.h. the Mew Gull was a very poor proposition for forced landings in restricted spaces, and to deal with this risk Henshaw prudently wore a parachute.

The start was made in foggy conditions at Gravesend at half-past three in the morning of 5 February, and the cloud and ice of the northern winter at first forced Henshaw to fly high. The poor weather continued as far as North Africa and caused him to lose some time in finding his first landing place at Oran, but from here he flew on without delay across the Sahara and by 7 p.m. of the following day, less than forty hours after take-off, he had completed the 6,400 miles of the west coast route and was safely down at Cape Town. After a rest of little more than a day there he was away again for home and completed the return journey with astonishing regularity, taking only eleven minutes longer than he had done for the outward flight. His arrival at Gravesend caused some alarm as both he and the interior of the cockpit were seen to be liberally covered with blood, and he was lifted out with something of the appearance of a badly defeated boxer, but it turned out that he had suffered nothing more serious than a severe attack of nose bleeding just before landing.

Henshaw's fine flight to the Cape and back took only 4 days 10 hrs and his *average* speed of 120 m.p.h.—which included all stops and the day on the ground at Cape Town—was greatly in excess of the *maximum* speed of the Cirrus Moth in which Lieutenant Bentley had made the first light aeroplane flight to the Cape twelve years earlier.

This was the last of the great long-distance flights of the period between the wars. Only a few months afterwards the whole resources of British aviation were turned to purposes of destruction for the second time in history, and when peace came again in 1945 the age of records was over. This is not to say that the light aeroplane has not been used occasionally for this particular sporting purpose in post-war years; but by 1945 aviation had finally come of age and the light-hearted spirit of the years of Hinkler, Mollison and Amy Johnson had gone. The whole outlook of the present day towards such individual enterprises is totally changed. The Second World War brought into being a popular notion, fostered perhaps by the immense expenditure on such vast undertakings as the invasion of Europe and the atom bomb, that any technical goal is capable of achievement in more or less automatic and soulless fashion provided only that the necessary millions of money and man-hours can be allotted to it, and provided also (the cynic may add) that the objective to be achieved is sufficiently inimical to the interests of mankind as a whole. We can only look back with regret on the years when the light aeroplane was still the key to high adventure, when even commercial flying had about it something of the feeling of the pioneering days, and when the military pilot had not yet become primarily the agent of mass destruction on an unimaginable scale. There is today a limitless future for the small aeroplane as a practical

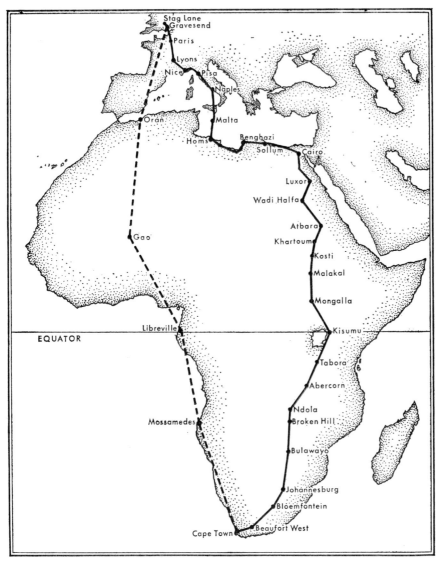

Comparison between the flights of Lieutenant Bentley in 1927 (solid line) and Mr Alex Henshaw in 1939 (broken line) from England to the Cape

ROUTES

BENTLEY

Stag Lane, Paris, Lyons, Nice, Pisa, Naples, Malta, Homs, Benghazi, Sollum, Cairo, Luxor, Wadi Halfa, Atbara, Khartoum, Kosti, Malakal, Mongalla, Kisumu, Tabora, Abercorn, Ndola, Broken Hill, Bulawayo, Johannesburg, Bloemfontein, Beaufort West, Cape Town

HENSHAW

Gravesend, Oran, Gao, Libreville, Mossamedes, Cape Town

vehicle for the business man or the private owner, and for each new generation learning to fly must remain an exhilarating and new experience; but
with the coming of world-wide air traffic organisation, of complex and
costly navigational devices and everyday passenger air travel for millions,
the day of the long-distance solo pilot who did so much to bring these
things to pass seems to be ended for ever.

⤙ 16 ⤚

Postscript

The 3rd of September 1939 saw the end of an age for the light aeroplane movement—an age which had begun almost exactly sixteen years earlier when the motor-gliders had buzzed and spluttered across the turf of Lympne and mounted waveringly up against the Channel wind. This very brief span of time had witnessed the astonishing rise of the Moth, the great solo flights across the world, the multifarious activities of the clubs, the annual sporting events culminating in the spectacle of the King's Cup Race, and against this lively background the steady development of the small aeroplane into a vehicle of world-wide appeal and of extraordinary efficiency and refinement. The 1930s are not years upon which people in this country can look back with much satisfaction, and it is all the more pleasant, therefore, to remember that in the restricted field with which we are dealing they were a golden time indeed. When war began, however, all this was brought to an abrupt end; the busy activity of the clubs and the private owners was cut off as if by a knife, and although (as some argued) training at club aerodromes could with advantage have been allowed to continue for a time, as the work of the flying schools had done after 1914, the official ruling that all flying should cease was firmly imposed. The aircraft in the clubs' possession stood in their hangars until requisitioned ('impressed' was the official term) for communications duty with the Royal Air Force, and the private owner's machine was treated in the same way in spite of his protests that his counterpart, the private motorist, had been allowed to continue on a limited scale with a basic petrol ration. Thus the Hornet Moths, Monarchs and Vega Gulls whose gay colours had given to summer gatherings something of the brilliance of a mediaeval tournament passed into drab war-paint and entered upon a duty from which some, like many of their former owners, did not return.

There had been those, among them the redoubtable Mr C. G. Grey, who had derided the usefulness of many of the members of the flying clubs in time of war, pointing to the futility of training 'women and old gentlemen' to become pilots. This view turned out to be totally mistaken. The 'women and old gentlemen'—the latter being middle-aged amateur pilots of only the modest standard of medical fitness implied by the possession of an 'A' licence—were for the most part quickly absorbed by the A.T.A., an organisation formed by British Airways to assist in the maintenance of communications after air attack but principally used in practice for the duty of ferrying military aircraft between the factories and Service aerodromes. The letters stood for Air Transport Auxiliary, but the unofficial alternative of Ancient and Tattered Airmen indicated that many of the male pilots employed, at any rate, were no longer in their first youth. It soon became commonplace to see the blue-clad figures of these 'amateurs' emerging from Lancasters or Spitfires at the end of a ferry flight of several hundred miles through English winter weather, often after an extremely sketchy introduction to the characteristics of the type of aircraft through a hasty look at the Pilot's Notes. In this way was yet another blow dealt at the myth that flying was a matter for highly-trained supermen, a belief which the coming of the Moth and the light aeroplane movement had already done much to dispel.

Most of the pilots of the light aeroplane clubs who were of military age found their way into one or other of the Services on flying duties, passing through the Flying Training Schools either to go on to operational work or to return to those schools as instructors, and they were to be found in large numbers in every mess or wardroom in the early part of the war. The Fleet Air Arm in particular was exceptionally heavily manned by ex-amateur pilots. One typical club, the Herts and Essex Flying Club of Broxbourne, had trained 400 members to 'A' licence standard in peace-time and then provided 75 candidates for the R.A.F., 17 for the Fleet Air Arm, 18 for Air Transport Auxiliary and 30 for instructional duties. The record of the Portsmouth Aero Club was still more remarkable, with 150 out of a total of 233 amateur pilots in the R.A.F. alone, and the same Service claimed 45% of the 8,000 staff members of the Midland Bank who served in the war—a direct consequence of the Bank's subsidised flying scheme put into operation a few years earlier. The Civil Air Guard made a large contribution, too, for over 7,000 out of 10,600 members who were effective at the outbreak of war were used for flying duties of one kind or another.

In this way the State received a direct return for the money which had been spent on subsidies between 1925 and the beginning of hostilities, a total amounting in round figures to £682,000* if grants to both the light aeroplane and gliding movements are taken together. It is impossible, of course, to assess the value of this return in any precise monetary terms, for to do so it would be necessary to establish how many military aeroplanes were saved from accident by the extra skill, or indefinable 'air sense', or knowledge of England and its weather, of the former club pilots who were

* Some of this money was in fact still being paid up to 1942.

62. The Thruxton Jackaroo, a four-seater adaptation of the Tiger Moth
which first appeared in 1958

63. The most successful British light aeroplane in the decade following the Second
World War: the Auster Autocrat with 90-h.p. Cirrus Minor engine

64. The air way and the motorway: a British-built Turbulent single-seater in flight over the M 1

65. A typical flying-club scene in the 1950s: pre-war aeroplanes, limited money and equipment, but undimmed enthusiasm

flying them; how many small boys who were later to distinguish themselves in air fighting were first drawn to aviation by visiting their local flying club to stare at a Moth; how many instructors, handing on to their
pupils a skill and an enthusiasm which had first been imparted to themselves at Stag Lane or Woodford by pilots of the Great War, thereby
inspired them to extra efforts which may have helped to change the course
of history. No answer can be forthcoming to these questions, and all that
can be said with certainty is that the light aeroplane clubs and the amateur
flying movement as a whole, brought into being by the foresight of Sefton
Brancker and sustained by annual sums which in the aggregate would not
have kept the war going for a single day, were thereby enabled to play a
central part in British aviation throughout fourteen years of peace and so
to influence in countless imponderable ways the six years of war that
followed. In assessing their importance in the long term, too, it is essential
to take the wider view of which the military balance-sheet is only a part.
The flying clubs were set up not for the production of military pilots but
in order to inculcate the elusive quality of 'airmindedness' and so to benefit
aviation as a whole, and this they did to such good purpose that many of
their old members, first drawn to flying by the sheer fun of it all, still
remain widely scattered in various capacities about an aeronautical scene
from which the fun has nearly (but happily not quite) departed. It is hard
to believe that, taken over the years, the nation as a whole did not have the
better part of the bargain.

The war took its course, and the full responsibility of training thousands of pilots *ab initio* fell upon the direct descendants of three civil aeroplanes, the Moth, the Miles Hawk and the Blackburn Bluebird. The bulk
of this work was done by the de Havilland Tiger Moth, which by the
accident of war became one of the most famous of all training aeroplanes,
rivalling the Avro 504 both in numbers made in war-time and in its subsequent long and useful life in peace. Well over 8,000 Tiger Moths were built,
5,000 of them in Britain and the remainder in Australia, Canada and New
Zealand. Second in numbers came the Magister to provide elementary
training in more modern style according to the Miles cantilever monoplane formula, and third the Blackburn B.2, essentially a Bluebird in its
general layout though much modified structurally to provide the robustness desirable for intensive military training. The name of A. V. Roe did
not feature so prominently in the elementary training field as it had done
between 1914 and 1918 although the Avro Tutor, a close contemporary of
the Tiger Moth, performed useful service in the hands of pupil-instructors
at the Central Flying School.

It was only occasionally in those strenuous times that the enthusiast
for light aeroplanes had the opportunity to recapture the spirit of the

flying-club days, unless he happened to be an instructor at one of the Elementary Flying Training Schools, which long retained their pleasantly civilian air without in any way sacrificing their efficiency. In odd places and at odd times would occur the happy conjunction of an 'A' licence holder in uniform and one of the aeroplanes he had known and loved in time of peace, and he would then marvel at being paid to carry out as a duty what had formerly been a somewhat expensive hobby, and exclaim with F. D. Tredrey that 'flying for a living is the very prince of occupations'. Now and then an enterprising commanding officer, who might himself once have been an enthusiastic private pilot, would somehow succeed in appropriating a light aeroplane outside the range of ordinary Service types for his personal use or that of his pilots. A Comper Swift spent part of the war with No. 25 Squadron at Wittering, painted the same matt black as the night-fighters with which it shared quarters and fitted with long-range tanks for extended operations at night, and the Kronfeld Drone owned by a day-fighter squadron was often operated against the local ducks with a forward-firing shotgun aimed with a ring-and-bead sight!

As early as 1943, with the end of the war distantly in sight, those who had been concerned with the light aeroplane movement in more peaceful days began to consider its future, and a memorandum was sent to the Goverment by the Royal Aero Club on the subject of its revival. In June 1945 a deputation called upon the Minister of Civil Aviation, Lord Swinton, to discuss the same matter, and was followed by another in December. In 1946 the General Council of Light Aeroplane Clubs was reconstituted as the Association of British Aero Clubs, and this body co-operated with the Royal Aero Club and the British Gliding Association in the setting up of a committee to explore the requirements for a new generation of British light aeroplanes and gliders. Since it was non-official, though formed with the blessing of the Ministry of Civil Aviation, this body received the name of the Informal Light Aircraft Committee, and its twenty-four members (counting the chairman, Mr P. G. Masefield) numbered among them ten practising pilots of aeroplanes or gliders. They included also a number of persons who had been prominent in the private flying movement before the war, among them Mr Marcus Langley and Mr W. S. Shackleton, whose work in light aeroplane design has been discussed in earlier chapters.

The committee presented its first report in January 1947. Its primary recommendation was that design studies should be made of an all-metal light aeroplane suitable for training and touring and costing not more than £1,000 if built in quantity, and an extremely detailed specification of this machine, the I.L.A.C. Type 1, was laid down for the guidance of designers. Its main features were side-by-side seating with full dual controls, a fixed tricycle undercarriage, good stalling characteristics with inability to spin, and a cruising speed of not less than 110 m.p.h. for five hours with two persons and 60 lbs of luggage. There were further detailed provisions about safety, and the design was to be such that maintenance and overhaul costs would be kept to a minimum. In spite of this, the prospects of individual ownership looked bleak in the austere post-war world, for estimates of the lowest cost of operation based on 100 hours' flying a year were in the region of £600, though it was thought that a club with six such aircraft flying 750 hours a year each would in ideal conditions be able to offer flying at about £3 per hour.

The position of the clubs which had been revived was at this time difficult if not desperate. They were for the most part leading a hole-and-corner existence in derelict aerodrome buildings, unsubsidised and with little or no security of tenure, and their flying rates of £3 an hour or so for the surplus Tiger Moths, Magisters and Austers which had been released to them by the Ministry of Aircraft Production were resulting in a steady loss of money. In July 1947 the Advisory Committee on Private Flying, whose chairman was Mr Whitney Straight, attempted to come to their aid and issued its preliminary report, which made sweeping recommendations for the complete co-ordination of all popular aviation activities on a national scale. It proposed State grants to cover the building of prototype aircraft to the I.L.A.C. specification, an interest-free loan to finance their production in great quantities and a three-year programme of subsidies rising to a maximum payment of £900,000 in the third year to enable the flying clubs to increase in number to 100 and to offer flying to the public at the attractively low rate of £1 an hour.

It is not perhaps surprising that neither the Government of the day nor successive Governments, beset by the economic difficulties which followed the war, were willing to put these recommendations into practice. It is questionable, too, whether even heavily subsidised club flying would have had much popular appeal so soon after the aeroplane had for the second time in history become firmly associated in the public mind with the black-out, high explosive and sudden death. In 1947 it seemed that everyone's brother-in-law had recently been captain of a Lancaster or pilot of a Typhoon, and the jargon surrounding military flying was still on all lips. As in 1918, however, the situation was more that pilots just demobilised wished to continue flying than that the public at large wished to begin it, and these young men, struggling with the problems of new jobs and unfamiliar domesticity, were less well placed than most to find money for aviation as a hobby even with its cost artificially reduced by State aid. The clubs and the light aeroplane movement had made a substantial contribution to the war effort, but the war was now over and the case for further extensive support from public funds was not overwhelming. The Government therefore limited itself to a payment of £50,000 to the clubs to cover its obligations in respect of the cancellation of the Civil Air Guard subsidy agreement and to pay for the aircraft which it had requisitioned.

Although subsidies on the grand scale were out of the question, help for the light aeroplane and gliding movements came from several quarters. In 1947 Lord Kemsley, the newspaper proprietor, put into practice a plan inspired by Lieutenant-Commander Terence Horsley of the Fleet Air Arm (a keen glider pilot and ex-newspaperman), by setting up a fund of £100,000 from which trustees were empowered to make grants and interest-free loans for the support of private and sporting flying. Among the many beneficiaries of the Kemsley Trust were the National Air Races, including the King's Cup Race, which were revived at Elmdon in 1949 for the first time since the war and continued annually thereafter.

In 1950 the Under-Secretary of State for Air, Mr Geoffrey de Freitas, set in motion a scheme of flying scholarships for cadets of the Air Training Corps operated through their local flying clubs, which thus received valuable support at a difficult time. An increase of 9d. in the tax on petrol imposed in the Budget of the same year was remitted to the flying clubs after an appeal had been made to the Chancellor, and successive increments were dealt with in the same way, a useful form of hidden subsidy on each hour flown. These two measures did much to rescue the clubs from their post-war financial difficulties and place them on the road to recovery. Further support was provided by the firms' flying club scheme introduced in 1951, under which the Inland Revenue authorities were induced by the Association of British Aero Clubs to extend tax reliefs to companies in respect of grants subsidising flying by their employees with established flying clubs. In this way popular aviation was brought within the reach of people of comparatively small means who would not otherwise have been able to afford it. In a typical case it was made possible for flying time (limited to an amount sufficient to obtain and keep up a licence) to be purchased for 10s. an hour or about one-seventh of its economic cost, so that a private pilots' licence even to the more exacting post-war standards could be gained for £20 or so. In real terms this was quite as cheap as the Civil Air Guard had been thirteen years before, although of course its application was (and is) limited to a few fortunate individuals whose employers were willing to operate the scheme.

In spite of the enterprising attempts of the Informal Light Aeroplane Committee to lay down a basis for future development, the art of light aeroplane design, in which Great Britain had played such a prominent part in the days before the war, fell into a sorry state of inactivity in the fifteen years after 1945. In a period as long as that separating the English Electric

Wren of 1923 from the Miles Monarch of 1938 few original types were constructed, and it is only recently that there have been encouraging signs of recovery. That taxation should have thinned the ranks of the more affluent private owners in England since the war is not surprising; what is remarkable, however, is that the established aircraft manufacturers, wholly taken up with larger military and commercial types, should have made almost no attempt over these years to explore the very considerable export market for the private and business aeroplane, with the result that the field was left open to the American manufacturers such as Piper, Beech and Cessna.

The mainstay of the revived flying clubs and of what export trade there was in this field was undoubtedly the Auster, descendant of the pre-war Taylorcraft. Many Austers were built during the war for military observation duties and some found their way back into civil life, the most numerous being the Auster V three-seater with American Lycoming horizontally-opposed four-cylinder engine of 130 h.p. Immediately the war ended the British Taylorcraft company put into limited production the two-seat Arrow, a successor to the Plus C of 1939, also fitted with an American engine, the 75-h.p. Continental. At this time, however, import restrictions made the supply of American engines and spares very difficult unless the aircraft to which they were fitted were themselves intended for export, and to ease this situation the Auster company (as it had now become) set about the modification of these two types to take British engines. The result was the J.4, or two-seater Arrow with 90-h.p. Cirrus Minor 1, and the three-seater Autocrat with 100-h.p. Cirrus Minor 2—by far the most numerous of British post-war light aeroplanes with a total production of over four hundred (Plate 63). The Autocrat still remains a popular machine for the private owner and flying club, and in 1956 it was modified into the Alpha by the substitution of a more powerful engine, the Gipsy Major, for the Cirrus; this engine had also been used in the four-seater Autocar of 1949 and the Aiglet of 1950. The Aiglet Trainer of 1951 was a fully aerobatic type with reduced span, capable of carrying four people for normal flying in a fuselage similar to that of the Autocar and having a markedly better performance than its predecessors by reason of its Gipsy Major 10 engine of 145 h.p. in place of the 130-h.p. Gipsy Major 1. The Atlantic four-seater executive tourer shown at the S.B.A.C. Show at Farnborough in 1957 was not proceeded with, but the same theme was continued in the 'D' range of Austers with Lycoming engines introduced in 1960 and quickly followed by the radically modernised and improved Airedale of 1961, the first product of the new Beagle group described below.

The Tiger Moth shared the Auster's popularity as a club and private aeroplane after 1945 and continues to do so at the time of writing, thirty years after its first appearance. For touring purposes its open cockpits, low speed and relative aerodynamic inefficiency render it decidedly out of date, but its excellent handling qualities give it a permanent place in the affections of those who enjoy flying for its own sake. As a sporting and aerobatic machine the 'Tiger' will probably continue for many more years as a reminder of a more heroic age of aviation although it has long been out of production. In its post-war career it has shown a remarkable adaptability, and as well as undergoing various conversions for agricultural duties such as crop-spraying it has appeared in touring form with enclosed cockpits and has even followed the example of the pre-war Fox Moth by becoming a cabin four-seater—the Thruxton Jackaroo (Plate 62). In this machine ingenious modification of the fuselage has enabled two pairs of side-by-side seats to be inserted in place of the original tandem cockpits and although its performance is somewhat reduced from the original the Jackaroo provides another remarkable illustration of the lifting powers of the pre-war light biplane.

The Tiger Moth biplane and the range of Auster types, in spite of their good qualities as club trainers and private owners' aircraft, only represented two strands remaining from the rich fabric of design of the 1930s. The firm of Miles Aircraft Limited, with its long experience of the efficient low-wing cantilever monoplane, continued this theme in 1945 with the four-seater Messenger, a war-time communications machine which continued in civil production when the war ended. It at once became a popular aeroplane for the private owner because of its roomy cabin, good view and excellent low-speed characteristics, helped by the use of flaps of Miles auxiliary-aerofoil type behind the trailing edge of the wing. A twin-engined version of the Messenger, the Gemini, appeared in the same year, fitted originally with two Cirrus Minor engines but later modified to take a variety of more powerful engines for better performance (Plate 59). A development of the Gemini, the Aries of 1951, was fitted with Cirrus Major 3 engines of 155 h.p. each, and was capable of a top speed of over 170 m.p.h. with a good performance on one engine.

The Gemini and Messenger—the former with a retractable undercarriage—represented the most advanced design in the immediate post-war field of British light aeroplanes. For the rest (apart from the Auster and Tiger Moth) the private flying movement carried on with such machines as the Percival Proctor, a civil version of the military communications aircraft of the war years which was itself a development of the Vega Gull, and a variety of older types including the Magister, Hornet Moth, Moth Minor, Monarch, Whitney Straight, B.A. Swallow and many others that have already been described. The average club aerodrome or aviation meeting in the 1950s presented an appearance not greatly different from that of 1938 (Plate 65), and only the rare and exciting appearance of a foreign type served to remind the thoughtful of how much leeway would one day have to be made up. An analysis made in April 1958 by Mr John Blake, editor of the *Royal Aero Club Gazette*, showed that out of over 1,200 aircraft in the class below 10,500 lbs all-up weight (a category embracing such larger machines as the Dove and the Rapide) only 129 were ten years old or less and of this number 98 were Austers. The smaller types included:

> 294 Austers
> 255 Tiger Moths
> 96 Proctors
> 60 Geminis
> 50 Messengers

and there were also 80 Rapides and 66 Doves used for business and light commercial flying. This was a very different situation from pre-war days; a Cirrus Moth of 1925 which was still flying ten years later would then have seemed a very old aeroplane indeed.

There were a few bright spots upon an otherwise depressing canvas. The stream of successful de Havilland light aeroplanes which had ceased with the Moth Minor of 1939 began to move forward again when an all-metal low-wing monoplane trainer, the Chipmunk, was designed and built at the Toronto headquarters of the de Havilland Aircraft Company of Canada in 1946. This new type, intended as a replacement for the Tiger Moth, embodied all the usual de Havilland virtues of excellent handling qualities combined with good looks, and the graceful lines of the tail unit were directly adapted from those of the war-time Mosquito. The Chipmunk was quickly put to use by the Royal Canadian Air Force and its adoption by the Royal Air Force in 1949 justified production being started in England. Some years later a change in Service training methods resulted in a large number of surplus military Chipmunks being offered for sale on the civil market, and when various difficulties over certification had been overcome they began to appear in the hands of the clubs and the private owners. For training and for the enthusiast who enjoys pure flying the type is ideal, but with its unmistakeably military flavour and unsocial tandem seating the Chipmunk is not (and was never designed to be) the perfect aeroplane for the average touring owner-pilot. The same might be said for the ex-R.A.F. Percival Prentice trainer, which from 1957 onwards appeared in various civil conversions carrying up to seven people.

Not long after the war there appeared a small four-seater machine somewhat similar in general lines and in structure to the Auster but with tricycle undercarriage and flat-four Lycoming engine of 125 h.p. The most unusual feature of this aeroplane, the Chrislea Ace, was an attempt at simplification of the orthodox system of flying controls by the use of a handwheel having three degrees of freedom. This system, however, was not popular with pilots, so a second aircraft, the Super Ace with Gipsy Major 10 engine, reverted to the standard arrangement of wheel and rudder-bar, and these controls were retained in a later development with tail-wheel undercarriage known as the Skyjeep, with provision for carrying light freight or a stretcher as an alternative to the normal four seats. The Chrislea series, which like the pre-war Airguard were designed by Mr R. C. Christopherides, found a very limited market at home and abroad but their manufacturers were forced to close down in 1952.

An interesting but abortive development of 1947 was the Newbury Eon, a low-wing cantilever monoplane of wooden stressed-skin construction with tricycle undercarriage, designed to carry four people on the 100 h.p. of a Cirrus Minor engine. The manufacturers were Messrs Elliotts of Newbury, who at this time were engaged on production of the Olympia sailplane, and in its short career the single aeroplane built was extensively used for the launching of gliders by aero-towing. Not surprisingly the engine power proved to be inadequate for the desired carrying capacity, and a Gipsy Major 10 was fitted in place of the Cirrus; this enabled the machine to reach a top speed of 136 m.p.h. and to carry a payload of 600 lbs comprising three passengers and a reasonable supply of luggage. Unfortunately this promising aircraft came to a sudden end in 1950 in a similar way to the last of the Westland Widgeons two years earlier; it was started with throttle open and wrecked after a take-off with no pilot on board.

A stimulus to amateur and professional designers was provided by a Light Aircraft Design Competition announced by the Royal Aero Club early in 1952, with entries to be submitted by the end of the year. There were three categories—touring, aerobatic and racing—with prizes of £100, £50 and £25 to be won in each, and the considerable amount of latent interest in the country was shown by the number and variety of the designs submitted. Perhaps the most original was that which was awarded the first prize in the racing class, a jet-propelled single-seater designed by a team at the Ministry of Supply experimental establishment at Boscombe Down, which among many novel features had a single-wheel undercarriage and a system of bled-off jets operated by sideways movement of the control column to keep the machine laterally level on the ground. Hopes were raised in some breasts of a latter-day Lympne trial at which prototypes would compete one against the other, but regrettably this happy notion came to nothing and the competition hardly proceeded beyond the paper stage, although the winning machine in the touring category was later built in Australia, its designer's country of origin.

Although the Boscombe Down jet racer was not constructed, the range of small gas turbines made by the French Turboméca firm were employed in two little racing aeroplanes built to special order in the 1950's. The first of these to fly, in December 1953, was the Miles M.77 Sparrowjet, a conversion of the prototype pre-war Sparrowhawk for the racing pilot Mr Fred Dunkerley. The original Gipsy Major engine was removed, a single-seat cockpit built into a new nose and two Turboméca Palas jet engines, each of 330 lbs static thrust, were then fitted in the wing-roots. With this modification the Sparrowjet had a top speed comparable with that of the Mew Gull, and after some initial difficulties Mr Dunkerley succeeding in winning the 1957 King's Cup at 228 m.p.h., surprising everyone by flashing across the finishing line well ahead of the rest of the field while a previous item on the programme was still in progress.

The second of the light jet racers came a year or two later. It was the Somers-Kendall S.K.1, designed by Mr Hugh Kendall for another well-known racing pilot of post-war years, Mr J. N. Somers. A clean machine built of wood on stressed-skin principles, and weighing only 685 lbs empty, it was fitted with a single Palas mounted amidships and exhausting between the two sides of a V-tail. It had the remarkable top speed for so small an aeroplane of 332 m.p.h., and its flight tests, carried out by the designer, had much in common with those of full-sized jet aircraft including the appearance of compressibility phenomena in the dive. Unfortunately, its extremely expensive development (put at £25,000) was not repaid by racing successes, and it has been kept in storage since 1957 after being accidentally damaged. Another application of the small gas turbine to light aircraft took place in 1956 when the Miles company at Shoreham used the larger Turboméca Marboré jet engine of 880 lbs static thrust as the basis for a fast two-seater trainer, the Student, which proved capable of a top speed of nearly 300 m.p.h.

In 1955 Captain E. W. Percival reappeared on the scene as an active designer of small aeroplanes with his E.P.9 agricultural and general-purpose machine built at Stapleford Tawney in Essex and flown by him for the first time just before Christmas of that year. The small company set up by him to build this machine was known as Edgar Percival Aircraft Limited, the original concern at Luton having by this time been absorbed into the Hunting Group of aviation interests and being no longer connected with its original founder. The E.P.9 was built in a mixture of steel-tube and light alloy, and large doors were provided at the rear of its capacious fuselage to allow a variety of loads to be carried as alternatives to the tanks of fertiliser or insecticide used for the direct agricultural role.

The necessary low-speed flying qualities were ensured by the use of flaps and drooping ailerons. In 1958 the design passed into the hands of the Lancashire Aircraft Company at Salmesbury aerodrome near Blackburn and the type was modified and renamed the Lancashire Prospector.

In the 'ultra-light' single-seater field activity was somewhat restricted for the first decade after the end of the war. The interests of the amateur aircraft builder were looked after by the Ultra-Light Aircraft Association, now the Popular Flying Association, which did much to overcome official resistance to home building and secured important concessions from the authorities over matters of airworthiness and certification. Some of its work was concerned with the restoration to flying condition of pre-war single-seaters, but it also helped those who wished to build their own aeroplanes either to their own designs or from professionally-designed kits of parts, and continues to do so. A typical successful amateur design of recent years is the Taylor monoplane with Aeronca-J.A.P. engine, first flown in 1959; while one of the best-known types designed especially for the amateur constructor is Mr Latimer-Needham's Luton Minor, originally brought out in 1936. After Luton Aircraft Limited had been reconstituted as Phoenix Aircraft Limited the Minor was brought up to date and in line with post-war airworthiness requirements, and placed on the market in kit form at £104. With engines available at a further £100 each it was thus made possible for the amateur to construct his own aeroplane for some £250, comparable to the cost of building the Pou du Ciel when allowance is made for the change in the value of money since the 1930s. At the time of writing over one hundred Minors are being, or have been, built all over the world. The larger two-seater Luton Major, with Walter Mikron engine, is also available in kit form for about £500.

Towards the end of the 1950s various Continental light aeroplanes began to appear in England, and these included two interesting single-seaters, the Druine Turbulent and the Tipsy Nipper, both fitted with versions of the Volkswagen car engine adapted for aircraft use. A British version of the former (Plate 64), which is a low-wing monoplane of straight-forward wooden construction, began to be built by Rollason Aircraft and Engines Limited at Croydon in 1957, and a considerable number have now appeared, some made by amateurs. The Tiger Club of Redhill operates several Turbulents as well as the famous biplane after which it is named, and is able to offer flying to its members on them at approximately half the cost of standard machines. The club's founder, Mr Norman Jones, who is also managing director of the Rollason company, has been an active pilot since the distant days of the London Aeroplane Club in 1925, when he owned the original de Havilland Moth G-EBKT jointly with Mrs

Elliott-Lynn. Today he regularly flies his own Turbulent to aviation meetings on both sides of the Channel.

The Tipsy Nipper embodies a number of ingenious features including a tricycle undercarriage, a fuselage of steel tube covered with fabric, and a 'shoulder-wing' arrangement carrying the pilot beneath a transparent canopy with the main wing spar running across the cockpit above his knees. The machine is fully aerobatic and caused a sensation on its first arrival in this country by its loops and rolls and ability to manoeuvre briskly on the ground with the aid of disc brakes and nosewheel steering. Both the Turbulent and the Nipper are available ready to fly in this country at prices close to £1,000 new, and represent the most modern expression of the old idea of the 'motor-cycle of the air'.

The influx of new types from the Continent was not confined to single-seaters. The extremely attractive French two-seater Piel Emeraude was built in England in 1958 as the Garland-Bianchi Linnet, modified to meet British airworthiness requirements and constructed by the Garland Aircraft Company of Maidenhead. Another French design to a similar specification, the Jodel D.117, appeared in this country in the same year and was soon followed by the Ambassadeur (three/four seats) and the Mousquetaire (four/five seats), as well as by a host of small foreign aeroplanes of other makes and nationalities—Austrian, Czechoslovakian, West German, Italian, Polish and Swedish.

The lifting in 1959 of the severe restrictions which had lain upon the importation of American aircraft ever since war-time days had an immediate effect. At last modern light aeroplanes especially designed for the private and business pilot and equipped with all refinements such as cabin heaters, soundproofing, engine starters and the radio aids which are essential for practical everyday use were freely available in a country which had been starved of them for two decades, at prices ranging from £3,000 or so for a modern but second-hand machine up to many times that figure for a miniature airliner intended for use by a large business organisation employing a professional pilot. The latter type of user had already been well served by such British designs as the de Havilland Dove, and therefore it was the smaller single-engined machine which formed the really striking contrast with the ageing pre-war aeroplanes which had become so familiar over the years of stagnation. Within a year small American aircraft to the value of over one million pounds had been sold in this country, the majority to firms and individuals intending to use them for business purposes.

This was indeed a depressing commentary on the unwillingness or inability of British manufacturers to cater for an important aviation market over fifteen post-war years; but there soon followed a more cheering event which may one day appear to have been as significant to the progress of the British light aeroplane as the first flight of the Moth thirty-five years earlier. In October 1960 it was announced that through the enterprise of Mr P. G. Masefield an organisation embracing the existing Miles and Auster companies would come into being with extensive backing from the Pressed Steel Company of Oxford under the title of British Executive and General Aviation Limited, abbreviated as 'Beagle'. It was planned first to modernise the Auster range to produce an effective competitor to the American Pipers and Cessnas; second to continue development of Miles types along their traditional low-wing lines; and third, to build a twin-engined business transport aeroplane originated by Mr Masefield himself during his period as managing director of the Bristol Aeroplane Company. In due season a complete range of modern aeroplanes suitable for the flying clubs, the private owner and the business user would be brought into being, and the difficulty caused by the lack of suitable British engines would be overcome by an agreement under which the series of horizontally-opposed engines made by the Continental Motors Corporation of America would be manufactured under licence in England by the Rolls-Royce company. The first of the 'new look' Austers, the Airedale, made its first public appearance at the end of April 1961, only four months after work was begun on the project. In August of the same year the 'executive twin'—the B.206—first flew at Shoreham, and by May 1963 an initial batch of 20 had been ordered for the R.A.F. A new Auster type, the A.61 Terrier, was placed on the market at under £2,000 for the flying clubs and the private owner, and a Gemini replacement—the Beagle-Miles M.218, a light twin-engined type designed, like its predecessor, by Mr G. H. Miles—first took the air in August 1962. It is too early to predict what the outcome of this extremely interesting Beagle development will be, but its advent without doubt injected into British aviation a life and an enthusiasm which had too long been absent.

We have now reached the end of our story, but for those who may wish to take up flying for business or pleasure, a brief summary of the present position of the flying clubs and of private ownership may not be out of place. At the time of writing there are over 100 flying clubs affiliated to the Association of British Aero Clubs and Centres scattered throughout the country and within easy reach of almost every area*. Although the membership of a few of these is limited to certain classes of individual such as the employees of particular firms, the great majority are open to the general public and will readily provide advice and trial flying lessons on request. The cost of flying with these clubs, which are not now directly subsidised

* See Appendix.

by the State, is in the region of £3 10s. to £4 10s. per flying hour, and a
course leading to the private pilot's licence will cost between £100 and
£150. For this sum, equivalent to say £30 to £50 in pre-war terms, the
pupil will receive a very much more thorough training than he received in
earlier days; a minimum of thirty hours' flying, half of it solo, is now
required in contrast to the three hours' solo of the old 'A' licence, and
before qualifying the new pilot will have carried out solo flights across
country with landings at strange aerodromes. Having obtained his licence
he will inevitably be attracted to the idea of becoming a private owner or
of joining a group which operates its own machine, and the cost of this
need not be great. Second-hand light aeroplanes are advertised every week
in the aeronautical journals at prices from £300 upwards, and the strict
maintenance standards imposed by law have the double advantage of
ensuring that little risk is involved in purchase and of helping to reduce
depreciation. Unlike a car, a light aeroplane requires neither a licence nor
insurance, although naturally it is prudent to carry at least third-party
cover. The fixed costs of running a standard type of light aeroplane, comprising hangarage, maintenance and insurance, may amount to some £150
or £200 annually and thereafter fuel costs per mile are comparable with
those of a car. Complete engine overhaul is an expensive item, but in the
case of the popular Gipsy Major engine it is required only after each
1,500 hours' flying, equivalent to about 150,000 miles, and the cost may
therefore be spread over many years.

These figures refer to the older type of standard light aeroplane such
as the Hornet Moth, and it is possible to fly both more cheaply and more
expensively. Solely for pleasure-flying in good weather a group of five or
more qualified pilots may be formed to operate a little single-seater such
as the Rollason Turbulent or the Tipsy Nipper, and they will then be
eligible for the same refund of petrol tax as is granted to the clubs. The
fixed costs of running such a machine are less than half those quoted above,
and when divided among five persons they will be very low indeed. Each
member of the group will then be able to fly when he likes, subject only to
the agreement of his fellow-members, for about 25s. an hour or fourpence
a mile. At the other end of the scale comes the larger light aeroplane of
so-called 'executive' type costing upwards of £5,000 and fully equipped
with radio aids to make it suitable for use into and out of busy aerodromes
in adverse weather conditions. In the nature of things such a machine will
rarely be owned entirely for pleasure-flying on account of its cost, but will
probably spend much of its life on business travel and be used occasionally
for holiday and weekend flying in exactly the same way as many company-
owned motor-cars.

There is little doubt that the great bulk of the personal flying of the future will be for business purposes, and to those who remember the bright early beginnings of the British light aeroplane and the carefree days of Lympne this may appear a somewhat soulless and depressing prospect. In fact, however, the development of this branch of aviation is likely to help rather than to hinder the true amateur pilot. It is not putting the matter too strongly to say that there are interests in this country which would welcome the complete disappearance of the small aeroplane, leaving the air free for the professionally-flown military or commercial machine, and against these powerful interests no individual wishing to use the air merely for pleasure can hope to prevail effectively. A strong private and business flying movement, however, rallied under the banner of 'general aviation' (an expression covering all branches of activity outside Service and regular air line flying) and including a considerable element of important firms with substantial investments in small aeroplanes as part of their normal transport arrangements, is in a position to press effectively for an increased freedom for the personal aeroplane—a freedom which is a marked feature of the American scene and which has hitherto been signally lacking in this country. In the flush of post-war enthusiasm for regular air transport, the authorities have steadily reduced the usefulness of small private aeroplanes by excluding them from certain airports, closing other airports used by them and imposing restrictions upon the use of large portions of the available air space. This tendency is now overdue for reversal. The air is a very large place; the volume of it lying over the British Isles between ground level and 10,000 ft, and which is navigable by aircraft of all types, amounts to 250,000 cubic miles, and although some regions of this immense volume contain many more aeroplanes than others, to speak of 'overcrowding' is not to state a physical fact but to admit a limitation of human powers of organisation. The problems of air traffic control in all weathers are formidable indeed, but their solution must not be allowed to lie in discrimination against one class of user.

The amateur pilot, on his part, will in the future have to submit to a greater measure of discipline than in the past and must accept that the carefree days of the 1920s are gone for good, but this need discourage no one from learning to fly. American experience has shown that the use of radio and blind-flying instruments to the standard necessary for the private pilot is well within the capacity of anyone who is otherwise fit to be in the air, and can readily be introduced into flying training from the beginning. Nothing in flying a modern light aeroplane should present difficulty to the ordinary man or woman, but aviation is not an activity for the chronically careless. It is the keen and knowledgeable motorist or motor-cyclist who is wanted in the air, and to such people the instinctive drills and disciplines which must be part of every pilot's equipment will in no way detract from the pleasure which the air has to offer. The aim must be for personal flying to be made available to as wide a public as possible with all the freedom the air can offer, but at the same time for there to be sanctions for use against those who by deliberate neglect endanger the lives of others.

Perhaps twenty or thirty years hence it will be possible to write a sequel to this book and follow the British light aeroplane through a second great age after its renaissance in the early 1960s. The early days of adventure are over, and the future will be concerned more with utility than with achievements that reach the headlines. If all that is recorded in these pages is not to have happened in vain, it is essential that in the years to come thousands of ordinary people should take to the air and find in personal flying what so many have found before them; a fascinating sport, a swift and convenient means of transport, and something deeper—a wider outlook on the world through a sort of extra dimension in the mind—which even today sets the pilot a little apart from the rest of humanity. The air, like the sea and the mountains, offers to mankind something which cannot adequately be described but is only to be experienced; but one cannot find it by travelling in an aeroplane, in Mignet's words, 'like an ordinary package'; one must fly and not merely be flown.

Appendices

The following appendices, each numbered to correspond with a chapter in the main text, present in tabular form brief details of the aeroplanes and flights dealt with in the book, as well as some particulars of the past activities and present whereabouts of flying clubs in the United Kingdom.

The aircraft dimensions, weights and performance data have largely been taken from *Jane's All the World's Aircraft*, *Flight* and occasionally from other sources listed in the Bibliography. The tables include certain minor types of light aeroplane which are not mentioned in the main text. In the years since 1945 the business or 'executive' aeroplane has come into prominence, and this category includes types which are scarcely 'light' by any definition and which are normally flown by fully qualified professional crews. Since the scope of this book is limited to the personal side of flying, only those aircraft which are likely to be flown by the keen amateur pilot have been included; in practice this tends to set an upper limit to engine power of about 300 h.p.

The dimensions quoted have been rounded off to the nearest inch. For the earlier aeroplanes some details of performance are unobtainable. It must be borne in mind when referring to the tables that all the performance figures are subject to the usual engineering tolerances, and that in earlier days the practice (now universal) of correcting results to standard atmosphere conditions was not always adhered to, especially in the case of light aeroplanes. Since changes in weight affect the performance of aeroplanes, especially the rate of climb and ceiling, all figures should strictly speaking be related to a definite weight. This is not always done in published information, but it may usually be assumed that the figures quoted refer to the normal all-up weight.

Finally, the dates of departure and arrival quoted in the tables of flights are in all cases local dates. The distinction between local and Greenwich times and dates is chiefly of importance in connection with flights between England and Australia.

CHAPTER I

DETAILS OF AIRCRAFT MENTIONED

Year	Type	Engine	Max. B.H.P.	Span	Length	Wing area, sq ft	Weight empty, lbs	Weight loaded, lbs	Max. speed, m.p.h.	Remarks
1919	Austin Whippet	Anzani radial	45	21' 6"	16' 3"		500	730	85	One later had Cirrus engine.
1919	Avro Baby	Green	35	25'	17' 6"	176	607	860	82	Later fitted with 100-h.p. Anzani.
1919	Blackburn Sidecar	A.B.C. Gnat	40	27' 3"	20' 6"		123		83	
1919	Boulton & Paul P.9	R.A.F. 1A	90	27' 6"	24' 5"	285	1244	1770	104	
1919	Bristol Babe	Siddeley Ounce	40	19' 8"	14' 11"		460	683	85	Flown with 35-h.p. Viale radial. Another had 60-h.p. Le Rhône rotary.
1922	Bristol Taxiplane	Bristol Lucifer	100	31' 1"	23' 6"	291	1210	2000	90	
1919	Central Centaur IV	Anzani radial	100	34' 2"	24' 9"		900	1400	75	
1919	Grahame–White Bantam	Le Rhône rotary	80	20'	16' 6"		640	995	100	
1907–09	Santos Dumont Demoiselle	Clément	32	18'	20'	115	242	530		Built in different forms by a number of manufacturers. Details and engines vary.

CHAPTER 2

Entries for the Gliding Competition held at Itford Hill, 16–21 October 1922

No.	Entrant	Pilot	Type	Span	Length	Wing area, sq ft	Weight empty, lbs	loaded, lbs	Wing loading, lbs/sq ft
1.	E. T. Prosser	E. T. Prosser	Biplane	40'	29'		190		
2.	Handasyde Aircraft Co. & F. P. Raynham	F. P. Raynham	Monoplane	36'	16' 7"	157	160	380	2·4
3.	G. W. Cain	G. W. Cain	Monoplane	36'	17' 6"		120		
4.	De Havilland Aircraft Co.	Capt. H. S. Broad	Braced monoplane	50'	26' 6"		250	400	
5.	Charles Christopher	Charles Christopher	Monoplane ornithopter	25'	18'		50		
6.	H. E. Waite	H. E. Waite	Monoplane	54'	15'				
7.	J. M. Hargreaves	J. M. Hargreaves	Biplane	25'	20'				
8.	British Helicopter Company	F. J. W. Purton and P. A. Purton	Monoplane helicopter	15'	10' (body)	200 (approx.)			
9.	J. J. O'Freddy	J. J. O'Freddy	Sail biplane	21'	39'		150		
10.	C. Frobisher	C. Frobisher	Monoplane	30'	15'		100		
11.	A. P. Maxfield	A. P. Maxfield	Biplane	26'	18' 6"		110		
12.	H. S. Dixon	H. S. Dixon	Monoplane ornithopter	30'	13'		60		
13.	George England (1922) Ltd	E. C. Gordon England	Monoplane	28'	17' 6"	120	85	230	1·9
14.	A. H. Knott	A. H. Knott	Monoplane	20'	12' 4"		80		
15.	J. Jeyes	J. Jeyes	Monoplane (Klemperer type)	32'	20' 9"	172	132	280	1·63

No.			Type						
16.	J. H. Robertson	J. H. Robertson	Monoplane	42' 6"	22' 5"	235	190	360	1·5
17.	S/Ldr. M. E. A. Wright, F. T. Courtney and Capt. W. H. Sayers	S/Ldr. M. E. A. Wright and F. T. Courtney	Monoplane						
18.	Capt. F. W. Merriam	Capt. F. W. Merriam	Monoplane	38' 4"	19' 6"		200	360	
19.	A. H. G. Fokker	A. H. G. Fokker and W. G. R. Hinchliffe	2 Biplanes	40' / 26' 3"	22' 9" / 19' 6"	(Two-seater) (Single-seater)			
20.	Lt. Col. C. O. Smeaton	Lt. Col. C. O. Smeaton	Monoplane	23'	16' 6"		140		
21.	W. L. Jennings	W. L. Jennings	Braced monoplane	23'	16' 6" (Nos. 20 and 21 both designed by W. L. Jennings)		140		
22.	L. Peyret	A. Maneyrol	Tandem monoplane	21' 8"	17' 6"	156	147·4		
23.	S. H. G. Brown	S. H. G. Brown	Monoplane	41' 6"	15'	165 (approx.)	114		
24.	Inventions Development Company	R. M. Balston	Monoplane	36'	14'				
25.	Hakim R. Singh	Hakim R. Singh	Monoplane	19'	15'		116		
26.	Dewoitine Co.	G. Barbot	Monoplane	37'	16'		180		
27.	Capt. R. H. Stocken	Capt. R. H. Stocken	Monoplane	45'	21' 3"	124			
28.	A. Jackson	A. Jackson	Monoplane						
29.	N. R. Gordon	N. R. Gordon	Monoplane ornithopter						
30.	P. W. Kingwell & Son	G. Collier	Biplane						
31.	S/Ldr. A. Gray and F/O W. J. Buchanan	S/Ldr. A. Gray	Monoplane						
32.	C. Winchester and E. Brynildsen	C. Winchester and E. Brynildsen	Biplane	As No. 4					
33.	E. D. C. Herne	E. D. C. Herne	Monoplane						
34.	J. G. Lee	J. G. Lee	Biplane						
35.	T. P. Hetherington	T. P. Hetherington	Monoplane						

CHAPTER 3: PART 1

ENTRIES IN MOTOR GLIDER COMPETITIONS HELD AT LYMPNE, 8–13 OCTOBER 1923

No.	Entrant	Pilot	Aircraft	Type	Engine	Drive
1.	Grigg Motor and Engineering Co.			Same as No. 5		
2.	Maj. O. T. Gnosspelius and J. Lankester Parker	J. Lankester Parker	Gull	Monoplane	697 c.c. Blackburne	Chain 1·61:1 pusher
3.	English Electric Co.	S/Ldr. M. E. A. Wright	Wren	Monoplane	398 c.c. A.B.C.	Direct
4.	English Electric Co.	F/Lt. W. H. Longton	Wren	Monoplane	398 c.c. A.B.C.	Direct
5.	A. V. Roe & Co.	H. J. L. Hinkler	Avro 558	Biplane	B. & H. vee twin	Direct
6.	A. V. Roe & Co.	H. J. L. Hinkler	Avro 560	Monoplane	697 c.c. Blackburne	Direct
7.	Gloucestershire Aircraft Co.	L. L. Carter	Gannet	Biplane	Two-stroke Carden	Direct
8.	De Havilland Aircraft Co.	Capt. G. de Havilland and Capt. H. Broad	D.H.53	Monoplane	750 c.c. Douglas	Direct
9.	George Parnall and Co.	Capt. Norman Macmillan	Pixie I	Monoplane	500 c.c. Douglas	Chain 2:1
10.	Vickers Ltd.	Capt. S. F. Cockerell	Viget	Biplane	750 c.c. Douglas	Chain 3:1
11.	G. S. Bush and F/O H. A. Hamersley	F/O H. A. Hamersley	Avro 558	Biplane	500 c.c. Douglas	Chain 2·5:1
12.	A. S. Butler	Maj. H. Hemming	D.H.53	Monoplane	750 c.c. Douglas	Direct
13.	F. P. Raynham	F. P. Raynham	Handasyde	Monoplane	750 c.c. Douglas	Direct
14.	Royal Aircraft Establishment Aero Club	F/Lt. P. W. S. Bulman	Hurricane	Monoplane	600 c.c. Douglas	Chain 2:1
15.	Louis Peyret	A. Maneyrol	Peyret	Monoplane	750 c.c. Sergant	Geared 2·5:1
16.	Jean B. Richard	Baron Georges Kervyn de Lettenhove	Poncelet	Monoplane	750 c.c. Sergant	Geared 2·5:1
17.	The Addlestone Aeronautical Association Ltd.	J. Herbert James	A.N.E.C.	Monoplane	697 c.c. Blackburne	Direct
18.	Hubert Blundell	Maurice W. Piercey	A.N.E.C.	Monoplane	697 c.c. Blackburne	Direct
19.	Maj. O. T. Gnosspelius and J. Lankester Parker	Capt. R. H. Stocken	Gull	Monoplane	697 c.c. Blackburne	Chain 1·61:1 pusher
20.	P. W. Kingwell	H. Sykes	Kingwell	Tandem monoplane	398 c.c. A.B.C.	
21.	Georges A. de Ro	V. Simonet	Poncelet	Monoplane	750 c.c. Sergant	Geared 2·5:1
22.	Louis Peyret	A. Maneyrol	Peyret	Monoplane	500 c.c. Douglas	
23.	A. G. Pointing and J. T. Jeyes	A. G. Pointing and J. T. Jeyes	Sayers-Handley Page	Monoplane	500 c.c. Douglas	Direct
24.	George Parnall and Co.	Capt. Norman Macmillan	Pixie II	Monoplane	750 c.c. Douglas	Chain 2:1
25.	Maj. Vernon A. Bradshaw	C. Barnard	Sayers-H.P.	Monoplane	398 c.c. A.B.C.	Direct
26.	Handley Page	G. P. Olley	Sayers-H.P.	Monoplane	697 c.c. Blackburne	Direct
27.	Percy Salmon		Salmon	Tandem monoplane	3¼ h.p. Bradshaw	
28.	Falcon Aircraft Co.	F/O C. A. Bouchier	Falcon	Monoplane		

CHAPTER 3: PART 2

TECHNICAL DETAILS AND PERFORMANCES OF AIRCRAFT IN MOTOR GLIDER COMPETITIONS

Aircraft	Technical Details							Performance in Competitions			
	H.P. at R.P.M.		Span	Length overall	Wing area, sq.ft	Weight, lbs Empty	Loaded	Speed, m.p.h.	Fuel, m.p.g.	Distance, miles	Altitude, ft
A.N.E.C.	26	3,800	32' 10"	15' 7"	145	290	470	74	87·5	775	14,400
Avro 558 (Douglas)	17	4,000	30'	19' 8"	166	298	483		63·3	50	13,850
Avro 560	15	2,500	36'	21'	110	310	490		59·3	1,000	
D.H.53	15	2,200	30' 1"	19' 8"	120	310	490	57·5		375	
Gannet	13	3,800	18'	16' 8"	108	248	440	(Did not fly—engine trouble)			
Gull	26	2,500	36' 2"	20' 10"	164	360	540	55·25	65·7	37·5	
Handasyde	15	3,000	30' 0"	19' 2"	135	300	500			158·5	
Sayers-H.P.	8		36' 6"	21' 3"	158	274	450	58·5		37·5	
Hurricane	20·5	4,000	23'	16'	80	375	564			25	9,400
Peyret (Sergant)	16	3,200	32' 4"	18' 3"	164	330	515		53·4	125	
Pixie I	13	3,000	29'	18'	100	279	457				
Pixie II	26	5,000	17' 10"	18'	60	279	460	76·1			
Poncelet	15	3,200	36' 6"	21' 6"	247	490	690			75	
Poncelet	15	3,200		21' 6"	210	425	625			50	
Viget	19	3,400	25'	17' 4"	200	390	570	58·1	87·5	362·5	
Wren	7	2,500	37'	24' 3"	145	232	420				

CHAPTER 3: PART 3

NOT ENTERED IN COMPETITIONS

Aircraft	Max. B.H.P.	Span	Length	Wing area, sq.ft	Weight, lbs empty	loaded	Max. speed, m.p.h.	Engine
R.A.E. Zephyr	17	29'		250	400 (approx.)	635	50–55	500 c.c. Douglas, 2:1 chain drive.

No.	Name	Entrant	Pilot	Engine	Drive	B.H.P. Max.	Span
1.	Brownie I	Bristol Aeroplane Co.	C. F. Uwins, T. W. Campbell	Bristol Cherub	Direct	32	36′ 7″
2.	Brownie II	Bristol Aeroplane Co.	F. Barnwell	Bristol Cherub	Direct	32	34′ 7″
3.	Cranwell	Cranwell Light Aeroplane Club	N. Comper, R. P. Mackay	Bristol Cherub	Direct	32	29′ 8″
4.	Wee Bee I	Wm. Beardmore & Co. Ltd.	M. W. Piercey	Bristol Cherub	Direct	32	38′
5.	Wood Pigeon	Westland Aircraft Works	A. J. Winstanley, S. H. Gaskell	Bristol Cherub	Direct	32	22′ 9″
6.	Widgeon	Westland Aircraft Works	A. J. Winstanley, S. H. Gaskell	Blackburne 3-cyl. radial	Direct	30	30′ 8″
7.	A.N.E.C. II	Air Navigation & Eng. Co. Ltd.	J. H. James	Anzani 1100 c.c.	Direct	30	38′
8.	Satellite	Short Bros. Ltd.	J. Lankester Parker	Bristol Cherub	Direct	32	34′
9.	Sparrow	Supermarine Aviation Works Ltd.	H. C. Biard	Blackburne 3 cyl. radial	Direct	30	33 4″
10.	Avis	A. V. Roe & Co. Ltd.	H. J. L. Hinkler	Bristol Cherub	Geared	32	30′
11.	Avis	A. V. Roe & Co. Ltd.	H. J. L. Hinkler	Blackburne 3-cyl radial	Direct	30	30′
12.	Bluebird	Blackburn Aeroplane & Motor Co. Ltd.	A. G. Lotan	Blackburne 3-cyl. radial	Direct	30	28′
13.	Raine	F. E. Raine					38′
14.	Cygnet I	Hawker Engineering Co. Ltd.	W. H. Longton	Anzani 1100 c.c.	Direct	30	28′
15.	Cygnet II	Hawker Engineering Co. Ltd.	F. P. Raynham	A.B.C. Scorpion	Direct	30	28′
16.	Vagabond	Vickers Ltd.	S/Ldr. H. J. Payn	Bristol Cherub	Direct	32	28′
17.	Pixie III	G. Parnall & Co.	W. Sholto Douglas and R. A. de H. Haig	Bristol Cherub	Direct	32	32′ 5″
18.	Pixie IIIA	G. Parnall & Co.	W. Sholto Douglas and R. A. de H. Haig	Bristol Cherub	Direct	32	32′ 5″
19.	Pixie IIIA	G. Parnall & Co.	W. Sholto Douglas and R. A. de H. Haig	Blackburne 3-cyl. radial	Direct	30	32′ 5″

Type	Engine	Max. B.H.P.
Short Cockle light flying-boat	2 Blackburne 696 c.c.	16 each

Part 1

plane Competitions held at Lympne, 4 October 1924

Length overall	Wing area, sq ft	Weight, lbs.		Performance in Competitions					
		Empty	Loaded	High speed, m.p.h.	Low speed, m.p.h.	Get off, yards	Pull up, yards	Distance flown, miles	Total marks
26' 3"	178	500	870	65·19	38·73	215	102·6	512·5	562·32
26' 3"	172	500	870		Eliminated				
23' 3"	223·5	515	890				99·4	762·5	50·6
22' 2"	187	462	837	70·11	39·66	235	124·0	737·5	588·52
19' 6"	155	439	779				125		
21'	145	475	815		Eliminated				
20' 8"	185	387	730		Eliminated				
23' 9"	168	483	850		Eliminated				
22' 8"	256	475	860		Eliminated				
24'	255	565	938		Eliminated				
24'	255	565	938	Scratched (same machine as No. 10 but with different engine)					
21' 8"	243	495	875		Scratched				
21' 9"	176		710		Scratched				
20' 5"	165	373	730		43·95	269	66·7	400	264·3
20' 5"	165	373	780		37·42	250	72·67	475	277·33
21' 10"	235	527	887		Eliminated				
21' 2"	137			Scratched (same machine as No. 18 but flown as a monoplane)					
21' 2"	238			Withdrawn with damaged engine					
21' 2"	238				37·22	301	70·0	450	229·0

Part 2

COMPETITIONS

Span	Length	Wing area, sq ft	Weight loaded, lbs	Max. speed, m.p.h.
36'	24' 8"	196	880	68

No.	Entrant	Pilot	Type	Engine	Max. B.H.P.	Span	Length	Wi Ar sq
1.	Blackburn Aeroplane & Motor Co.	W. H. Longton	Bluebird	Genet	75	28′	21′ 8″	237
2.	De Havilland Aircraft Co.	Capt. H. S. Broad	Moth	Genet	75	29′	23′ 6″	22c
3.	Bristol Aeroplane Co.	C. F. Uwins	Brownie	Cherub III	36	37′ 4″	26′ 3″	18c
4.	R.A.E. Aero Club	F/Lt. J. A. Gray or F/O R. L. Ragg	Cygnet	Cherub III	36	28′	20′ 5″	165
5.	R.A.E. Aero Club	F/O M. Richards or F/O R. L. Ragg	Sirocco	Cherub III	36	33′	21′	15c
6.	T. O. M. Sopwith and F. Sigrist	F/Lt. P. W. S. Bulman	Cygnet II	Cherub III	36	28′	20′ 5″	165
7.	Supermarine Aviation Works	H. C. Biard	Sparrow II	Cherub III	36	34′	23′ 9″	192
8.	Halton Aero Club	F/Lts .C. G.Halliday and F. le Poer Trench	H.A.C.1	Cherub III	36	28′ 6″	22′	195
9.	A. V. Roe & Co. Ltd.	H. J. L. Hinkler	Avian	Genet	75	32′	24′	294
10.	A. V. Roe & Co. Ltd.	W/Cdr. W. Sholto Douglas	Avis	Blackburne Thrush	35	30′	24′	255
11.	Cranwell Light Aeroplane Club		C.L.A.4	Pobjoy P	65	27′ 4″	22′ 3″	164
12.	Cranwell Light Aeroplane Club	F/Lt. N. Comper	C.L.A.4.	Cherub III	36	27′ 4″	22′ 3″	164
13.	H. W. Martin	Lt. Col. G. L. P. Henderson	A.N.E.C. Missel Thrush	Blackburne Thrush	35	28′	21′ 6″	210
14.	Geo. G. Parnall Ltd.	F. T. Courtney	Pixie III	Cherub III	36	32′ 5″	21′ 3″	137
15.	Seven Aero Club	F/O G. E. F. Boyes	Satellite	A.B.C. Scorpion II	42	34′	23′ 9″	168
16.	Seven Aero Club	F/Lt. A. P. Ritchie	Wood Pigeon	A.B.C. Scorpion II	42	22′ 9″	19′ 6″	155

Notes: (i) In the case of machines which actually reached the competition, weights quoted are those at which the eliminating tests were passed and the competition flown. In other cases they are estimates.

Type	Engine	Max. B.H.P.	Span
A.N.E.C. (single-seater)	1100 c.c. Anzani	30	18′ 4″
Cranwell C.L.A.3	Cherub II	32	21′
R.A.E. Hurricane	Cherub II	32	23′

ART I

ITIONS AT LYMPNE, 12–17 SEPTEMBER, 1926

	Weight, lbs			Performance in Competition				
mpty	Fuel and oil	Useful Load	Loaded	Miles flown	Fuel used lbs	Average speed, m.p.h.	Figure of Merit lb-miles per lb	Placings
721	107	472	1300	Eliminated				
735	115	700	1550	1386	592·23	(55·84)	(1641)	(Retired)
623	47	340	1010	1994	402·09	59·71	1687	Third prize
431	57	362	850	1994	398·88	55·68	1808	Second prize
595			900	Scratched (not flown)				
421	49	430	900	1994	388·83	64·98	2203	First prize
605	55	340	1000	Did not complete 1st day's flying				(Retired)
480	60	340	880	Scratched				
695	77	828	1600	1282	507	(72·71)	(2092)	(Retired)
606	104	340	1050	508	108		(1600)	(Retired)
				Scratched				
529	61	340	930	Eliminated				
500	50	340	890	Unable to compete owing to accident				
522	63	340	925	1994	439·87	58·94	1541	Fourth place
697	63	340	1100			Eliminated		
570	75	340	985	1008	334	(48·73)	(1046)	(Retired)

(ii) Figures of merit of machines which did not complete the
course are not strictly comparable with those of machines
which did, since only completed laps counted, but they are
quoted in parentheses to indicate approximate performances.

PART 2

COMPETITIONS

Length	Wing Area, sq ft	Weight, loaded lbs	Max. speed, m.p.h.
15′ 7″	82	530	84
18′ 6″	70	530 (325 empty)	95–100
17′ 8″	80	550 (approx.)	85

CHAPTER 6

DETAILS OF MOTHS UP TO 1928

Year	Engine	Max. B.H.P.	Span	Length	Wing area, sq ft	Weight		Max. speed m.p.h.	Stalling speed, m.p.h.	Initial rate of climb, ft/min	Ceiling, ft	Range, statute miles	Fuel capacity, gallons
						empty lbs	loaded lbs						
1925	Cirrus I	60	30'	23' 8"	243	770	1240(N)	91	38	430	13,000(A)	320	19
1926	Genet	75	30'	24' 3"	243	810	1550	93	41	590	16,000	410	19
1927	Cirrus II	80	30'	23' 8"	243	855	1550(N) 1400(A)	98	41	650	17,000(A)	430	19
1928	Cirrus III	94	30'	23' 8"	243	955	1750	101	44	570	14,600	290	19

(N) = normal (A) = aerobatic (S) = service (A) = absolute

Details of Light Aircraft 1926–29

Year	Type	Engine	Max. B.H.P.	Span	Length	Wing area, sq ft	Weight empty, lbs	Weight loaded, lbs	Max. speed, m.p.h.	Stalling speed, m.p.h.	Initial rate of climb ft/min	Ceiling, ft	Range statute miles	Fuel cap., galls.	Notes
1929	A.B.C. Robin	Scorpion II	40	25' 4"	17' 7"	110	415	680	105	40	750	17,000(S)	340	8	Estimated performance.
1927	Avro Avian II	Cirrus II	80	28'	24' 3"	245	907	1467	98	40	650	15,000	325	20	
	Avro Avian III	Cirrus II	80	28'	24' 3"	245	935	1435	102	40		15,000	400		
1929	Avro Avian IVM	Cirrus-Hermes	115	28'	24' 3"	245	1005	1523	105	40			360	24	Metal fuselage; also fitted Genet Major engine. Kingsford Smith's 'Southern Cross Junior' had Gipsy II.
	Avro Sports Avian	Cirrus-Hermes	115	28'	24' 3"	245	1000	1600	120	45			420	24	
1927–28	Blackburn Bluebird II and III	Genet II	80	28'	22' 6"	238	793	1385	88	35		11,300(A)	300		
1929	Blackburn Bluebird IV	Gipsy I	100	30'	23' 2"	246	1040	1750	103	44	720	13,500(S)	338	23	All-metal version; also fitted with Gipsy II and III, Cirrus III and Cirrus-Hermes engines. Available as seaplane.
1929	Civilian Coupé	Hornet	80	35' 6"	19'	168	918	1500(N) 1300(A)	100	40	670	12,500(S)	360	16	Later fitted with Genet Major engine.
1929	Clarke Cheetah	Blackburn Thrush	35												
1929	Desoutter I	Cirrus-Hermes	115	36'	27'	190	1100	1900	113	45–50	860	17,000	450	20	
1927	D.H.71 Tiger Moth	Experimental D.H. Engine	135	22' 6"	18' 7"	76.5	618	905	203	60 (approx.)		over 19,000			The other machine built had Cirrus II engine.
1928	D.H.60 Gipsy Moth	Gipsy I	100	30'	23' 11"	243	955	1750	103	44	570	14,600(A)	300 (approx.)	19	
	D.H.60 Gipsy Moth	Gipsy II	120	30'	23' 11"	243	980	1750	107	44	830	17,000(A)	300 (approx.)	19	
1929	D.H.60.M Metal Moth	Gipsy I	100	30'	23' 11"	243	990	1750	Performance as wooden Moths above						Metal fuselage; originally called Special Model.
	D.H.60.M Metal Moth	Gipsy II	120	30'	23' 11"	243	1015	1750	Performance as wooden Moths above						
1929	Dudley Watt D.W.2	Cirrus III	95	39' 8"	25' 10"	350	1050	1500	90	25			330		

(N)=normal (A)=aerobatic (A)=absolute (S)=service

DETAILS OF LIGHT AIRCRAFT 1926–29—continued

Year	Type	Engine	Max. B.H.P.	Span	Length	Wing area, sq ft	Weight empty, lbs	Weight loaded, lbs	Max. speed, m.p.h.	Stalling speed, m.p.h.	Initial rate of climb ft/min	Ceiling, ft	Range, statute miles	Fuel cap, galls	Notes
1929–30	Granger Archaeopteryx	Cherub I	32	27' 6"	15'				95						
1929	Glenny Gadfly	Scorpion II	40	25' 10"	17' 10"	108	455	750	91	45	505	13,000			
1928	Halton H.A.C.2 Minus	Cherub III	32	28' 6"		130	450	720	95	40					
1929	Halton H.A.C.3 Meteor	2 Cherub III	32 each	44'		150		722	120 (est.)	25 (est.)					Never flown.
1929	Hendy Hobo	Scorpion II	40	32'	19' 6"			650	100						
1929	Hinkler Ibis	2 Salmson A.D.9	40 each												
1927	Parnall Imp	Genet II	80	25' 6"	21' 2"	176	850	1320(N)	102	40	800	16,000(A)	400	23	
1928	Parnall Elf	Cirrus-Hermes	115	31' 3"	22' 10"	195	1020	1650(N) 1550(A)	108	45					
1928	Simmonds Spartan	Cirrus III	95	28'	23' 11"	240	1000	1680(N) 1400(A)	103	44			320	20	Also fitted with Gipsy I and II and Cirrus-Hermes engines. Three-seat version also built.
1926	Short Mussel I	Cirrus I	60	36'	25'	200	968	1430	80	42	350				Later fitted with Cirrus II engine.
1929	Short Mussel II	Cirrus III	95	37' 3"	24' 11"	214	1061	1640	102	48	620		300 (approx.)	15	
1929	Southern Martlet	Hornet	80	25'	20' 3"	180	630	1040	112	40	1100				Also fitted with Genet Major engine.
	Southern Martlet	Genet II	80	25'	20' 3"	180	705	1030	112	40	1100		280		
	Southern Martlet	Gipsy II	120	25'	20' 3"	156		1105	130	40	1700				
1931	Metal Martlet	Hermes I	115	23' 6"	20' 6"	216	680		130		1400	20,000	400		
1929	Surrey A.L.1	Salmson A.C.7	95	28' 9"	20'			1200	110	45					
1927	Westland Widgeon III	Cirrus II	80	36' 4"	23' 5"	200	852	1400	100	42	560	14,000(S)	400		Also fitted with Cirrus III, Hornet and Gipsy engines.
1929	Westland Widgeon IIIA	Genet II	80	36' 4"	23' 5"	200	775	1325	100	42	560	15,000(S)	315		Also fitted with Cirrus-Hermes engines. Metal fuselage.
		Cirrus III	95	36' 4"	23' 5"	200	945	1650(N) 1450(A)	104	46	600				
		Gipsy I	100	36' 4"	23' 5"	200			108		640	16,000			

CHAPTER 9

SOME LIGHT AEROPLANE FLIGHTS 1926–29

Pilot	Route	Type of aeroplane and registration	Date of Departure	Date of Arrival	Time taken
Capt. T. Neville Stack and B. M. T. S. Leete	England–India	D.H.60 Moths {G-EBMO {G-EBKO	15 Nov. 1926	8 Jan. 1927	54 days
Lt. R. R. Bentley	England–Cape	D.H.60 Moth G-EBSO	1 Sept. 1927	28 Sept. 1927	28 days
Capt. W. N. Lancaster and Mrs Keith Miller	England–Australia	Avro Avian III G-EBTU	14 Oct. 1927	9 Mar. 1928	4 months 24 days
H. J. L. Hinkler	England–Australia	Avro Avian G-EBOV	7 Feb. 1928	22 Feb. 1928	15 days
Lady Heath	Cape–England	Avro Avian III G-EBUG	17 Feb. 1928	17 May 1928	3 months
Lady Bailey	England–Cape / Cape–England	D.H.60 Moth G-EBSF / D.H.60 Moth G-EBTG	9 Mar. 1928 / 21 Sept. 1928	30 Apr. 1928 / 16 Jan. 1929	52 days / 4 months
Lt. P. Murdoch	England–Cape	Avro Avian III G-EBVU	30 July 1928	12 Aug. 1928	13½ days
Vicomte and Vicomtesse de Sibour	World tour	D.H.60G Gipsy Moth G-EBZR	14 Sept. 1928	19 July 1929	10 months
Capt. R. L. Rattray	England–Gold Coast	D.H. Cirrus III Moth G-EBZZ	5 Dec. 1928	15 Jan. 1929	41 days
S/Ldr. L. Slatter	England–Natal	Blackburn Bluebird IV G-AABV	7 Mar. 1929	15 Apr. 1929	39 days

CHA▮

DETAILS OF LIGHT A▮

Year	Type	Engine	Max. B.H.P.	Span	Length	Wing area, sq ft	Weight empty, lbs	loaded lbs
1931	Arrow Active I	Cirrus-Hermes IIB	115	24'	18' 7"	120	853	1210
1932	Arrow Active II	Gipsy III	120	24'	18' 7"	120	925	1325(
1930	Avro 621 Tutor	Lynx IV	215	34'	26' 6"	300	1791	2448
1931	Avro 631 Cadet	Genet Major	135	30'	24' 9"	262	1270	1860
1932	Avro Club Cadet	Genet Major	135	30' 2"	24' 9"	262	1222	1757
1934	Avro Commodore	Lynx IV	215	37' 4"	27' 3"	307	2325	3500
1933–4	B.K. Swallow	Salmson A.D.9R	75	42' 8"	26' 3"	220	960	1500
	B.K. Swallow	Cataract II	85	42' 8"	26' 3"	220	930	1500
1934	B.K. Eagle	Gipsy Major	130	39' 3"	26'	200	1350	2300
	B.K. Eagle	Gipsy Six	200	39' 3"	26'	200	1510	2400
1932–3	B.A.C. Drone	Douglas 750 c.c.	23	39' 8"	21' 10"	172	390	640
1932	Blackburn B.2	Cirrus-Hermes IVA	120	30' 2"	24' 3"	246	1175	1850(1770(
	Blackburn B.2	Gipsy III	120	30' 2"	24' 3"	246	1122	1850(1675(
1933	Cierva C.30 autogiro	Genet Major 1A	140	Rotor dia. 37'	19' 8"	Blade area (total) 47	1250	1800
1930	Comper Swift	Scorpion II	40	24'	18' 4"	90	331	600
1931	Comper Swift	Pobjoy R	85	24'	17' 8"	90	530	850(780(
1932	Comper Swift	Gipsy III	120	24'	17' 8"	90	730	1130
1932	Comper Swift	Gipsy Major	130	24'	17' 8"	90	730	1130
1934	Comper Mouse	Gipsy Major	130	37' 6"	25' 1"	172	1300	2215(2000(
1934	Comper Streak	Special Gipsy Major	146	23' 6"	18'	80	880	1500
1934	Comper Kite	Pobjoy Niagara	90	23' 6"	19' 3"	80	750	1350
1934	de Bruyne Snark	Gipsy Major	130	42' 6"	24' 7"	216	1180	2200
1930	D.H.80 Puss Moth	Gipsy III	120	36' 9"	25'	222	1180–1210	2050
1931	D.H.60T Moth Trainer	Gipsy II	120	30'	23' 11"	243		1820(1604(
1932	D.H.60 Moth	Gipsy III	120	30'	23' 11"	243	1005	1750
1934	D.H.60 Moth	Gipsy Major	130	30'	23' 11"	243	1040	1750
1931–2	D.H.82A Tiger Moth	Gipsy Major	130	29' 4"	23' 11"	239	1095	1825(1750(
1932	D.H.83 Fox Moth	Gipsy III	120	30' 10"	25" 9'	247	1100	2070
1932	D.H.83 Fox Moth	Gipsy Major	130	30' 10"	25' 9"	247		2100
1933	D.H.85 Leopard Moth	Gipsy Major	130	37' 6"	24' 6"	206	1335	2225
1930	Desoutter II	Gipsy III	120	35' 8"	26'	183	1200	2000
1930	Hawker Tomtit	Mongoose IIIA	155	28' 6"	23' 5"	238	1100	1750
1930	Hendy 302	Cirrus-Hermes	115	35'	22' 10"	178	1045	1900
1934	Hendy Heck	Gipsy Six	200	31' 6"	26' 2"	105	1811	2600
1932	Miles Satyr	Pobjoy R	85	21'	18'	117	594	900
1933	Miles Hawk	Cirrus IIIA	95	33'	24'	169	1014	1800
1934	Miles Hawk Major	Gipsy Major	130	33'	24'	169	1070	1800
1931	Monospar ST-3	2 Salmson A.D.9	50 each	38'	22'	183	1057	1800
1932	(G.A.)*Monospar ST-4	2 Pobjoy R	85 each	40' 2"	26' 4"	219	1480	2550
1933	(G.A.) Monospar ST-6	2 Pobjoy R	85 each	40' 2"	26' 4"	219	1500	2600
1934	(G.A.) Monospar ST-10	2 Niagara I	90 each	40' 2"	26' 4"	219	1470	2750

* (G.A.) indicates General Aircraft.   (N) = normal   (A) = aerobatic

10

RAFT TYPES 1930–34

Max. speed, m.p.h.	Stalling speed, m.p.h.	Initial rate of climb, ft/min	Ceiling ft	Range, statute miles	Fuel capacity, gallons	Notes
140	50		20,000	345		
144	50			420		
122	50	950	16,000(S)	250		Prototype had Mongoose engine. Type 621 developed into Type 626.
113		750	13,000(S)	350		
115						Also fitted with Hermes IV and Gipsy Major engines.
125	55	650	11,500(S)	470	100	
102	32	750	16,000	420	19	
110	32	800	17,000	420	19	
148	45	700	16,000	650	40	
170	48	950	19,000	600	40	This engine fitted for racing only.
70	22	380	12,500(S)	300		
112	46	620		320	22	
112	46	620		320	22	Prototype had this engine.
112	under 20	700	12,000(S)	250	23	
105	35	700		350		Early Swifts also had Salmson A.D.9 engine.
135	35	1400	22,000(S)			
165	50	1400	20,000(S)			
170	50	1400	20,000(S)			
cruise 130				600	33	
over 170					46	
155						
120	40	600	15,500	500	32	
127	44	630	17,500(A)		35	Also fitted with Gipsy Major engine.
106	45	730	13,800(S)	230	19	Developed into Tiger Moth.
109	42	780	18,750(A)	230	19	
113	42	892	20,000	300	19	Known as Moth Major.
109	45	673	13,600(S)	300	19	Originally had Gipsy III engine.
109	51	492	10,000(S)	438	25	
114	52	576	11,500(S)	410		
140	42	600	14,000(S)	715	35	
128	45–50	1000	17–20,000	540	30	
124	45	1000	19,500	350		Many other engines fitted.
132	44	850	16,000(S)	750	41	Later had Hermes IV engine.
170	40			620	40	Later became Parnall Heck.
122	44	1400				
115	42	860	16,000(S)	450	20	Also fitted Gipsy III, Hermes IV engines.
150	42	1300	20,000			
110	39	950	18,000		26	
128	48	815	16,000(A)	500	40	
135	48	850	16,000(S)	550		Also fitted with Pobjoy Niagara engines.
142	48	900	16,000(S)	585		

(S) = service   (A) = absolute

Chapter

Year	Type	Engine	Max. B.H.P.	Span	Length	Wing area, sq ft	Weight empty, lbs	Weig loade lbs
1931–2	P.B. Scarab	Cherub III	32	30′	21′	127		650
1932	Percival Gull Four	Cirrus-Hermes IV	130	36′	24′ 8″	169	1170	2050
	Percival Gull Four	Javelin III	160	36′	24′ 8″	169	1170	2250
	Percival Gull Four	Gipsy Major	130	36′	24′ 8″	169	1290	2300
1934	Percival Gull Six	Gipsy Six	200	36′	25′	169	1500	2450
1934	Percival Mew Gull	Javelin IA	165	24′	18′ 3″	88	996	1460
	Percival Mew Gull	Gipsy Six	200	24′	18′ 3″	88	1040	1545
1930	Robinson Redwing I	Hornet	75	30′ 6″	22′ 3″	250	860	1325
	Robinson Redwing II	Genet IIA	88	30′ 6″	22′ 3″	250	870	1450
1930	Segrave Meteor (Blackburn Segrave)	2 Gipsy III	120 each	39′ 6″	28′ 6″	230	2240	3300
1933	Shackleton-Murray S.M.1	Hirth H.M.60	70	40′	25′ 7″	210	880	1450
1930	Spartan Arrow	Gipsy I	100	30′ 7″	25′	251	950	1750 1560
	Spartan Arrow	Gipsy II	120	30′ 7″	25′	251	965	1750 1560
	Spartan Arrow	Cirrus-Hermes II	115	30′ 7″	25′	251	975	1750 1560
1932	Spartan Clipper	Pobjoy R	85	34′	28′ 2″	150	770	1300
1934	T.K.1	Gipsy III	120	27′	23′ 2″	184	940	1450
1931	Wheeler Slymph	Tomtit	24	22′	14′ 9″			530

(N) = normal   (A) = aerobatic

ontinued

Max. speed, m.p.h.	Stalling speed, m.p.h.	Initial rate of climb, ft/min	Ceiling ft	Range, statute miles	Fuel capacity, gallons	Notes
78	32	600				
147	42	850	16,000(S)	700	40	
165				700	40	
155				745		
178			20,000	640		
195	65			550		
204	65	1400		540		
92	30	650				Only the first aircraft had this engine.
95	30	800		250	16	Redwing III (1933) had reduced span (24′) and area (154 sq ft).
138	59	800	14,000	340 (450)	42 (52)	One aircraft had tubular-spar wing and Gipsy Major engines.
90	38	580	14,000(S)	250	13	
99	41	530			22 or 34	
104	41	700			22 or 34	
102	41	630			22 or 34	Also fitted with Cirrus III engine.
110		800			15	Later fitted with Pobjoy Niagara III engine.
118	46	920	19,700(A)		12	
						Single-seater monoplane designed and built by F/Lt. (now Air Commodore) A. H. Wheeler. Never flown.

(S) = service   (A) = absolute

Chapter 12

Some Light Aeroplane Flights 1930–34

Pilot	Route	Type	Departure	Arrival	Time taken
F. C. Chichester	England–Australia	D.H. Gipsy Moth G-AAKK	20 Dec. 1929	25 Jan. 1930* (Darwin)	5 weeks
F/O H. L. Piper and F/O C. E. Kay	England–Australia	Desoutter G-AATI	9 Feb. 1930	23 Mar. 1930	6 weeks
Aspy Merman Engineer	England–India	D.H. Gipsy Moth	25 Apr. 1930	11 May 1930	17 days
Miss Amy Johnson	England–Australia	D.H. Gipsy Moth G-AAAH	5 May 1930	24 May 1930	19 days
Capt. F. R. Matthews	England–Australia	D.H. Puss Moth G-ABDW	16 Sept. 1930	18 Oct. 1930	32 days
Mrs Victor Bruce	World tour	Blackburn Bluebird IV G-ABDS	25 Sept. 1930	20 Feb. 1931	5 months
W/Cdr. C. Kingsford Smith	England–Australia	Avro Avian IVA G-ABCF	9 Oct. 1930	19 Oct. 1930	9½ days
O. Garden	England–Australia	D.H. Gipsy Moth G-AASA	17 Oct. 1930	4 Nov 1930	18 days
F. C. Chichester	Tasman Sea crossing New Zealand–Australia	D.H. Gipsy Moth ZK-AKK	28 Mar. 1931	Early June 1931	10 weeks
C. W. A. Scott	England–Australia	D.H. Gipsy Moth G-ABHY	1 Apr. 1931	10 Apr. 1931	9 days 4 hrs
J. A. Mollison	Australia–England	D.H. Gipsy Moth VH-UQA	26 May 1931	5 June 1931	10 days 23 hrs
Lt. R. F. Caspareuthus	Australia–England	D.H. Gipsy Moth VH-UFT	29 July 1931	6 Aug. 1931	8 days 19 hrs
Miss P. Salaman and A. G. Store	England–Cape	D.H. Puss Moth	5 Oct. 1931	13 Oct. 1931	8 days
C. A. Butler	England–Australia	Comper Swift G-ABRE	30 Oct. 1931	5 Nov. 1931	5 days 6 hrs
S/Ldr. H. J. L. Hinkler	South Atlantic crossing West to East	D.H. Puss Moth CF-APK	31 Oct. 1931	5 Nov. 1931	9 days 2 hrs
			25 Nov. 1931	26 Nov. 1931	22 hrs
J. A. Mollison	England–Cape	D.H. Puss Moth G-ABKG	24 Mar. 1932	28 Mar. 1932	4 days 17 hrs
C. W. A. Scott	England–Australia	D.H. Gipsy Moth G-ACOA	19 Apr. 1932	28 Apr. 1932	8 days 20 hrs
J. A. Mollison	Atlantic crossing East to West	D.H. Puss Moth G-ABXY	18 Aug. 1932	19 Aug. 1932	31 hrs 20 mins
Mrs Amy Mollison	England–Cape	D.H. Puss Moth G-ACAB	14 Nov. 1932	18 Nov. 1932	4 days 7 hrs
	Cape–England	D.H. Puss Moth G-ACAB	11 Dec. 1932	18 Dec. 1932	7 days 7 hrs
J. A. Mollison	South Atlantic crossing East to West	D.H. Puss Moth G-ABXY	9 Feb. 1933	9 Feb. 1933	17 hrs 40 mins
Sir C. Kingsford Smith	England–Australia	Percival Gull Four G-ACJV	4 Oct. 1933	11 Oct. 1933	7 days 4 hrs
B. Rubin and K. H. F. Waller	Australia–England	D.H. Leopard Moth G-ACLX	23 Apr. 1934	1 May 1934	8 days 12 hrs
Miss J. Batten	England–Australia	D.H. Gipsy Moth G-AARB	8 May 1934	23 May 1934	14 days 23 hrs
J. Grierson	England–Canada by northern route	D.H. Fox Moth G-ACRK	20 July 1934	30 Aug. 1934	6 weeks (includes crash at Reykjavik)
C. J. Melrose	Australia–England	D.H. Puss Moth VH-UQO	20 Sept. 1934	28 Sept. 1934	8 days 9 hrs

*Reached Sydney 30 January.

CHAPTER 13

The State-subsidised Light Aeroplane Clubs in Great Britain 1925–38*

Year	No. of clubs on 31 Dec.	No. of flying members on 31 Dec.	Total No. of members on 31 Dec.	No. of 'A' licences gained in year	No. of members holding 'A' licences on 31 Dec.	Hours flown by members in year, dual and solo	Total hours flown by club aircraft
1925	5	489	780	5	10	633	727
1926	6	616	1,058	57	89	3,842	4,358
1927	10	1,245	2,187	82	210	5,274	6,158
1928	13	1,769	3,288	219	434	10,383	12,201
1929	13	2,664	4,505	334	717	16,391	18,722
1930	19	3,704	7,041	481	1,270	25,555	29,888
1931	22	3,384	6,585	372	1,526	24,277	28,686
1932	22	2,011	4,239	287	1,083	20,754	23,962
1933	18	2,709	5,090	354	1,569	22,937	25,255
1934	30	4,683	7,780	441	1,823	28,341	31,286
1935	41	5,968	10,541	644	2,489	44,840	49,219
1936	48	7,025	12,141	880	3,287	59,181	64,981
1937	53	7,157	12,871	744	3,418	56,455	61,836
1938	64	13,243	20,230	937	4,352	77,162	82,591
		(5,882)	(6,655)	(330)	(1,281)	(22,545)	(22,748)

Notes: (i) In addition to the 'A' licences shown, a few members went on to obtain 'B' licences to enable them to fly professionally; on the average, however, their numbers did not exceed one or two per club per year. Many of those intending to take up flying as a profession took instruction at the unsubsidised flying schools.

(ii) The figures shown in brackets for the year 1938 relate to members of the Civil Air Guard. They are included in the total given in the line above.

* Abstracted from the *Reports on the Progress of Civil Aviation 1926-37* and from the *Statistical and Technical Review of Civil Aviation 1938-39* and reproduced by permission of the Controller of H.M. Stationery Office.

Details of Light

Year	Type	Engine	Max. B.H.P.	Span	Length	Wing area, sq ft
1935	Aeronca C.3	Aeronca	40	36′	20′	142
1938	Arpin	Salmson A.D.9R	68	31′ 6″	23′ 2″	165
1935	B.A. Swallow 2	Cataract III	90	42′ 8″	27′	215
	B.A. Swallow 2	Cirrus Minor I	90	42′ 8″	27′	215
1935	B.A. Eagle 2	Gipsy Major	130	39′ 3″	26′	200
1935	B.A. Cupid	Gipsy Major	130	35′	23′ 4″	
1938	Barnwell B.S.W.1	Scott Squirrel	34	25′		
1936	Broughton-Blayney Brawny	Carden-Ford	30	25′ 6″	15′ 6″	
1935	Carden-Baynes Auxiliary	Villiers 2-stroke	9	45′ 6″	20′	120
1936	Carden-Baynes Bee	2 Carden-Ford supercharged	40 each	29′ 10″	23′	141
1937	Chilton	Carden Ford	32	24′	17′ 6″	78
	Chilton	Train 4T	44	24′	17′ 6″	
1938	Chrislea Airguard	Walter Mikron 2	62	36′	21′ 6″	
1936	C.L.W. Curlew	Niagara III	95	26′ 6″	21′ 6″	
1936	C.W. Cygnet	Cirrus Minor	90	34′ 6″	24′ 3″	165
	C.W. Cygnet	Gipsy Major	130	34′ 6″	24′ 3″	165
	(G.A.) Cygnet	Cirrus Major II	150	34′ 6″	23′ 3″	179
1937	Currie Wot	Aeronca-J.A.P.	40	22′ 1″	18′ 2″	
1936	Dart Pup	Ava 4a-oo	27	29′ 7″	19′ 8″	113
1936	Dart Kitten	Ava 4a-oo	27	31′ 9″	21′ 4″	129
1936	Dart Flittermouse	Scott Squirrel	34	40′ 6″	22′ 6″	
1936–7	de Bruyne Ladybird	Scott Squirrel	34	32′	20′	
1937	Deekay Knight	Cirrus Minor	90	31′ 6″	22′ 10″	140
1934–5	D.H. 87 Hornet Moth	Gipsy Major	130	31′ 11″	24′ 11″	245
1935	D.H. 90 Dragonfly	2 Gipsy Major	130 each	43′	31′ 8″	288
1937–9	D.H. 94 Moth Minor	Gipsy Minor	90	36′ 7″	24′ 5″	162
1936	Foster, Wikner Wicko	Wicko F (Ford V8)	85	34′ 6″	23′ 3″	153
	Foster, Wikner Wicko	Cirrus Minor	90	34′ 6″	23′ 3″	153
	Foster, Wikner Wicko	Gipsy Major	130	34′ 6″	23′ 3″	153
1935	G.A. Monospar ST-12	2 Gipsy Major	130 each	40′ 2″	26′ 4″	217
1935	G.A. Monospar ST-25	2 Niagara II	90 each	40′ 2″	26′ 4″	217
1936	G.A. Monospar Universal	2 Niagara III	95 each	40′ 2″	25′ 4″	217
1937	Gordon Dove	Douglas Sprite	28	27′ 3″	18′ 3″	112
1938	Helmy Aerogypt	3 Sprites	28 each	26′ 4″	19′ 0″	
1935	Heston Phoenix	Gipsy Six, Series I	200	40′ 4″	30′ 2″	272
	Heston Phoenix	Gipsy Six, Series II	205	40′ 4″	30′ 2″	272
1936	Hillson Praga	Praga B	36	36′	21′ 6″	152
	Hillson Praga	Aeronca-J.A.P.	40	36′	21′ 6″	152
1939	Hillson Helvellyn	Cirrus Minor	90	33′	22′	

TER 14
AIRCRAFT 1935–39

Weight empty, lbs	Weight loaded, lbs	Max. speed, m.p.h.	Stalling speed, m.p.h.	Initial rate of climb, ft/min	Ceiling, ft	Range, statute miles	Fuel capacity, gallons	Notes
569	1005	95	30 approx.	450	12,000	200		Later had British-made Aeronca-J.A.P. engine of same power, becoming Aeronca 100.
740	1261	108	38	680		475		Pusher monoplane; later fitted Cirrus Minor I. Tricycle undercarriage.
990	1500	104	30	800	17,000	355	19¼	
1000	1500	104	30	700	16,500	390	19¼	
1450	2400	148 135	45	700	16,000	650	40	One only built.
	750							Single-seater designed by Captain Barnwell. Killed in it in 1938.
		80				200		Originally Perman Grasshopper.
310	500	35–40	25				½ hr fuel	
880	1350	110	40	700		300		
398	700	112	35	650		500	8	
370	650	125	35	1000		400	8	
810	1300(N) 1250(A)	118	37	550	14,000(S)	375		2-seater cabin monoplane.
970	1500	127						
1050	1600	125				500		Prototype.
1200	1900	130		700	14,000(S)	650	27	
1475	2200	135		800		445		
405	575	77						
485	705	75						Later fitted with Cherub III engine.
510	752	95	30–35	600	19,700(A)	340		
640		64						
420	800	95						Later fitted with Cherub III engine.
850	1450(N) 1300(A)	125	39	800	17,500(S)		20	2-seater cabin monoplane intended for production using plastics. Only one built.
1255	2000	124	40	690	14,300(S)	623	35	Square-tipped version.
2550	4000	144–147		775	15,700(S)	885	87	
970	1550(N) 1450(A)	118	43	620	16,600(S)	300	13	Tankage for 26 gallons could be fitted.
1170	1700	115	55		10,000(S)	250		
938	1500							
1255	2000	140	45		20,000(S)	500		Also had Cirrus Major engine.
1840	2875	158	54	1233	19,400(S)	410		
1680	2875	142	52	800	14,000(S)	585		
1818	2875	131		710	15,300	419		
382	600	95	30	600		400	8	Single-seat monoplane resembling Chilton. 4-seater cabin monoplane; fitted with Continental A-65 engines after the war.
2120	3300	148	55	700	15,500	500		
2140	3300	150	55	700	15,500	500		
584	1080	93		350		280		
900	1500	120 (approx.)						2-seater open-cockpit monoplane; one only built.

(N)=normal   (A)=aerobatic   (A)=absolute   (S)=service

Year	Type	Engine	Max. B.H.P.	Span	Length	Wing area, sq ft
1936	Hordern-Richmond	2 Continental A-40	40 each	43′ 3″	24′ 6″	215
1936	Kronfeld Super Drone	Douglas Sprite	23	39′ 8″	21′ 2″	172
	Kronfeld Drone de Luxe	Carden-Ford	30	39′ 8″	21′ 2″	172
1937	Kronfeld Monoplane	Carden-Ford	30	39′ 8″	21′ 2″	172
1936–7	Luton Buzzard 1 and 2	Anzani	35	35′ 6″	21′ 6″	
	Luton Minor	Anzani	35	25′	20′	
1939	Luton Major	Mikron 2	62	35′ 2″	23′ 9″	
1937–8	Marendaz Mk. III	Gipsy Six	200	31′	26′	131
1939	Marendaz Trainer	Cirrus Minor I	90	34′	22′ 4″	
1937	Martin Monoplane	Cherub III	32			
1934–5	Miles Falcon	Gipsy Major	130	35′	25′	174
1935	Miles Falcon	Gipsy Six	200	35′	25′	174
1935	Miles Merlin	Gipsy Six	200	37′	25′ 10″	196
1935	Miles Nighthawk	Gipsy Six	200	35′	25′	
1935	Miles Hawcon	Gipsy Six				
1935–6	Miles Hawk Trainer	Gipsy Major	130	34′	24′	176
1935	Miles Hawk Speed Six	Gipsy Six	200	33′	24′	169
1937	Miles Magister	Gipsy Major	130	33′ 10″	25′ 3″	172
1938	Miles M.18	Gipsy Major	130	31′	24′ 10″	
		Cirrus Major II	150	31′	24′ 10″	
1935	Miles Sparrowhawk	Gipsy Major h.c.	146	28′	23′ 6″	138
1937	Miles Hobby	Gipsy Major II	145	21′ 6″	22′	80
1936	Miles Whitney Straight	Gipsy Major	130	35′ 8″	25′	
1937	Miles Monarch	Gipsy Major	130	35′ 8″	26′	180
1936	Miles Mohawk	Menasco Buccaneer	270	35′	25′ 6″	183
1937	Moss M.A.1	Niagara III	95	34′	23′ 3″	154
1939	Moss M.A.2	Cirrus Minor	90	34′	23′ 3″	154
1936	Percival Vega Gull	Gipsy Six, Series I	200	39′ 6″	25′ 4″	197
	Percival Vega Gull	Gipsy Six, Series II	205	39′ 6″	25′ 4″	197
1935–7	Percival Mew Gull	Gipsy Six, Series I	200	24′ 9″	20′ 3″	88
	Percival Mew Gull	Gipsy Six, Series II	205	24′ 9″	20′ 3″	88
1936	Perman Parasol	Perman Ford	30	25′ 6″	15′ 6″	
1935 (in England)	Pou du Ciel	Various 22–38 h.p.		22′	13′	137
1937	Shapley Kittiwake	Continental A-50	50	20′ 3″	20′ 3″	
1938	Shapley Kittiwake	Niagara III	90	32′	20′ 10″	
1938	Taylorcraft A	Continental A-40	40	36′	22′ 10″	167
1939	Taylorcraft Plus C	Lycoming O-145	55	36′	22′ 10″	167
1939	Taylorcraft D	Cirrus Minor I	90	36′	22′ 10″	167
1935	T.K.2	Gipsy Major Ic	140	32′	22′ 3″	125
	T.K.2	Gipsy Major II	140	28′	22′ 5″	
1937	T.K.4	Gipsy Major II	140	19′ 8″	15′ 6″	57
1936–7	Tipsy S	Douglas Sprite	28	24′ 6″	18′ 9″	100
1937	Tipsy B	Mikron 2	62	32′ 2″	21′ 8″	129
1938	Watkinson Dingbat	Carden-Ford	30	28′	16′	

continued

Weight empty, lbs	loaded, lbs	Max. speed, m.p.h.	Stalling speed, m.p.h.	Initial rate of climb, ft/min	Ceiling, ft	Range, statute miles	Fuel capacity, gallons	Notes
1125	1750	98	35	450		200		
390	450	70	28–30	380	12,500	300		Firm became Kronfeld Ltd in 1936.
640	720	73	33 (approx.)	480	12,500	340		
390	640	73						Data for Buzzard II.
400	600	95						Pre-war version also fitted with Scorpion engine.
380	600	85						
600	1030	105						4-seater cabin monoplane; never flown.
960	1500	124						2-seater open-cockpit monoplane.
		80						
1300	1950 (2200 max.)	145	44	750	15,000(S)	615		
1550	2350	180		1000		560		
1600	3000	155	50					Fitted Gipsy Six, Series II, post-war.
1650	2400	175						Experimental type built for Air Ministry.
1210	1720			1300	18,000	400		Developed into R.A.F. Magister (see below).
1355	1900	185	45	1500	20,000	406		
1240	1825	145	45		18,000(S)			
1180	1800							
1306	1925	130						
1080	1750	180	42			415		Also fitted Gipsy Major I and II.
1140	1527	over 200						
1250	2000	145	38	850		570	30 (or 44)	
1360	2150	145	40	850	17,400(S)	600	30 (or 45)	
1605	2700	190–195	44			450		2-seater cabin monoplanes; later rebuilt with open cockpits.
950	1400	130	38					Similar to above.
950	1400	125	38			450		
1660	3000	170			18,000	630		
1740	3250	174			18,000	660		
1080	1850	225		1400		750		Modified in various ways for racing, to max. of 256 m.p.h.
1150	2125	230	60	1700	21,000	860		
	600	80						
350	550	70		300		200		Built in various forms. Data given is for Abbott Pou (30-h.p. Carden-Ford).
630	1000	116						Open cockpit two-seater monoplane.
901	1600	120						Cabin version of above.
586	1050	91		390	14,000	230		Also had 50-h.p. Continental.
720	1200	110		550		275		
890	1450	120		1000		325		Civil version of R.A.F. Taylorcraft Auster.
1078	1600	174						
1135	1650	182						1938 racing version.
900	1300							
287	532	80	40					Also had Sarolea Epervier engine.
618	1074	112	37	600	19,000			
460	700	90						Single-seater monoplane; one only built.

(N)=normal   (A)=aerobatic   (A)=absolute   (S)=service

CHAPTER 15

SOME LIGHT AEROPLANE FLIGHTS 1935–39

Pilot	Route	Type of Aeroplane and registration	Date of departure	Date of arrival	Time taken	Notes
H. L. Brook	Australia–England	Miles Falcon G-ACTM	24 Mar. 1935	31 Mar. 1935	7 days 19 hrs 50 mins	
Miss Jean Batten	Australia–England	D.H. Moth G-AARB	12 Apr. 1935	29 Apr. 1935	17 days 15 hrs 15 mins	
H. F. Broadbent	England–Australia	Percival Gull Six	2 Nov. 1935	9 Nov. 1935	6 days 21 hrs 19 mins	
F/O D. Llewellyn and Mrs Jill Wyndham	Cape–England	Hendy Heck G-ACTC	4 Nov. 1935	11 Nov. 1935	6 days 21 hrs 19 mins	
Miss Jean Batten	South Atlantic crossing, East to West	Percival Gull Six G-ADPR	13 Nov. 1935	13 Nov. 1935	13 hrs 15 mins	Part of flight England–Brazil in 2 days 13 hrs 15 mins.
F/Lt. T. Rose	England–Cape	Miles Falcon Six G-ADLC	6 Feb. 1936	10 Feb. 1936	3 days 17 hrs 37 mins	
	Cape–England		3 Mar. 1936	9 Mar. 1936	6 days 6 hrs 57 mins	
F/O D. Llewellyn	England–Johannesburg	Aeronca G-AEAC	7 Feb. 1936	1 Mar. 1936	23 days	
Mrs Amy Mollison	England–Cape	Percival Gull Six G-ADZO	4 May 1936	7 May 1936	3 days 6 hrs 26 mins	
	Cape–England		8 May 1936	12 May 1936	4 days 16 hrs 17 mins	
H. L. Brook	England–Cape.	Praga G-ADXL	6 May 1936	22 May 1936	16 days 4½ hrs	
Mrs Beryl Markham	North Atlantic crossing, East to West	Percival Vega Gull	4 Sept. 1936	5 Sept. 1936	20 hrs	
C. W. A. Scott and G. Guthrie	England–Johannesburg (Schlesinger race)	Percival Vega Gull G-AEKE	29 Sept. 1936	1 Oct. 1936	2 days 4 hrs 57 mins	
Miss Jean Batten	England–Australia	Percival Gull Six G-ADPR	5 Oct. 1936	11 Oct. 1936	5 days 21 hrs 2 mins	Continued to New Zealand in 11 days 1 hr 25 mins.
H. F. Broadbent	Australia–England	D.H. Leopard Moth VH-AHB	27 Apr. 1937	3 May 1937	6 days 8 hrs 25 mins	

H. L. Brook	Cape–England	Percival Gull Six G-ADZO	1 May 1937	5 May 1937	4 days 20 mins
Miss Jean Batten	Australia–England	Percival Gull Six G-ADPR	19 Oct. 1937	24 Oct. 1937	5 days 18 hrs 15 mins
H. F. Broadbent	Australia–England	Percival Vega Gull	17 Apr. 1938	22 Apr. 1938	5 days 4 hrs 21 mins
A. Henshaw	England–Cape	Percival Mew Gull G-AEXF	5 Feb. 1939	6 Feb. 1939	1 day 15 hrs 25 mins
	Cape–England		8 Feb. 1939	9 Feb. 1939	1 day 15 hrs 36 mins

DETAILS OF LIGH\[

Year	Type	Engine	Max. B.H.P.	Span	Length	Wing area, sq ft	Weight empty, lbs	loaded, lbs
1945	Auster V	Lycoming O-290	130	36′	22′ 5″	167	1100	1990
1946	Auster Autocrat	Cirrus Minor II	100	36′	23′ 5″	185	1052	1850
1946	Auster Arrow	Continental C-75	75	36′	22′ 9″	185	872	1450
1946	Auster J.4	Cirrus Minor I	90	36′	22′ 6″	185	955	1600
1949	Auster Autocar	Gipsy Major 1	130	36′	23′ 4″	185	1413	2400
1950-2	Auster Autocar	Cirrus Major 3	155	36′	23′ 2″	185	1367	2450
1950	Auster Aiglet	Gipsy Major 1	130	36′	23′ 8″	185	1215	2000
1951	Auster Aiglet Trainer	Gipsy Major 1	130	32′	23′ 2″	164	1323	2200(N 1950(A
1955	Auster Alpine	Gipsy Major 10	145	36′	23′ 6″	185	1464	2250
1955	Auster Agricola	Continental O-470-M	240	42′	27′ 6″	255	1900	Up to 3810
1956	Auster Alpha	Gipsy Major 1	130	36′	23′ 8″	185	1219	2000
1957	Auster Atlantic	Continental E.185-10	185	36′	23′ 10″			2700
1958	Auster Workmaster	Lycoming O-360-A	180	36′	23′ 7″	185		2550
1960	Auster D.4	Lycoming O-235	108	36′	23′ 4″	185	1232	1900
1960	Auster D.5	Lycoming O-320	160	36′	23′ 4″	185	1361	2200
1960	Auster D.6	Lycoming O-320	160	36′	23′ 4″	185	1423	2450
1961	Beagle-Auster Terrier	Gipsy Major 10, Mk. 2	145	36′	23′ 3″	184	1636	2350
1961	Beagle-Auster Airedale	Lycoming O-360-A	180	36′ 4″	26′ 4″	190	1630	2750
1962	Beagle-Miles M.218	2 Continental O-300	145 each	37′	25′ 3″	170	2164	3200
1961-2	Beagle-Wallis Autogiro	McCulloch	65	Rotor dia. 20′ 2″	9′ 6″			580
1950	Britten-Norman BN-1F	Aeronca-J.A.P.	40	23′	16′ 7″		408	630
1946	Chrislea Ace	Lycoming O-290	125	34′	21′	165	1040	1950
1948	Chrislea Super Ace	Gipsy Major 10	145	36′	21′ 6″	177	1350	2350
1949	Chrislea Skyjeep	Cirrus Major 3	155	36′	22′ 2″	177	1623	2550
1958	Currie Wot	Aeronca-J.A.P.	35	22′ 1″	18′ 9″	146	530	790
	Currie Wot	Walter Mikron	62	22′ 1″	18′ 9″	146	530	790
Civil use 1956	D.H. Chipmunk, Mk. 21	Gipsy Major 10, Mk. 2	145	34′ 4″	25′ 5″	172	1425	2014
1955-6	Edgar Percival E.P.9	Lycoming GO-480	270	43′ 6″	30′	228	2010	3500(N
1948	Essex Aero Sprite	Flat four	100	30′	24′ 7″		879	1548
1948	Fairey Primer	Gipsy Major 10	145	32′ 10″	27′ 6″	155	1572	2170
1958	Garland Linnet	Continental C-90	90	26′ 4″	20′ 9″		802	1400
1961-2	Hampshire Halcyon	2 Walter Minor	105 each	30′	23′ 7″		1090	2000

(N)=normal   (A)=aerobatic

PART I

AIRCRAFT AFTER 1945

Max. speed, m.p.h.	Stalling speed, m.p.h.	Initial rate of climb, ft/min	Ceiling, ft	Range, statute miles	Fuel capacity, gallons	Notes
130		950	15,000	250		Followed military I, II, III and IV; VD had Gipsy Major engine.
120	30	568	14,000	320	15	
98	36	430	10,000(S)	320	15	
108	37	746	12,500(S)	320	15	Similar to Arrow except for engine.
116	34	525	11,000(S)	500	32	4-seater.
127	36	710	14,000(S)	485	32	
126	28	900	18,000	220	15	Principally used for crop-spraying.
132	29	705	12,500	275(545)	16(32)	Fully aerobatic, 4-seater. Reduced span.
128	31	1025	22,000	460	32	Aiglet Trainer with Autocar wings.
136	53	790	15,300(S)	260	25	Low-wing agricultural monoplane; only two built.
126	30	710	15,000	200	15	Similar to Autocrat but higher power.
Cruise 135	50–55	800–1150		440		4-seater; prototype only.
104		650			32	
112	29	540	8,800(S)	250	16	2-seater. 'D' series had metal wing spars.
127	35	750	12,600(S)	460	32	3-seater.
125	36	580	10,000(S)	450	32	4-seater, otherwise as D.5.
123	33	530	10,000(S)	320	22	
148	52	730	14,900(S)	650(1050)	32(52)	Other Auster designs include the military Marks 6, 7, 9 and 11.
185	58	1370	21,700(S)	578 (with max. payload)	70	
80	12	Over 1000				Originally developed from U.S. Bensen Gyro-Copter.
84						
127	45	720	16,000	290	16·5	
126	38	800	16,000	400	25	
126	48	550	12,000(S)	500	36	
82	38	350	3,000(S)	228	7	Built post-war.
98	38	700	over 10,000(S)	350	12	Built post-war.
138		840	15,800(S)	380	18	
146	37 (light)	1140	17,500	580 (max.)	56	Later became Lancashire Prospector.
140	44	680		760		All-magnesium 2-seater cabin monoplane. Construction abandoned.
140		790	16,000(S)	400	21·5	Developed from Tipsy M.
130			11,500	700	28	French design, built in England.
160 (est.)	40	1400	18,000(S)	900	54	4-seater monoplane. Prototype only to date.

(A)=absolute   (S)=service

Year	Type	Engine	Max. B.H.P.	Span	Length	Wing area, sq ft	Weight empty, lbs	loaded lbs
1949–53	Hants & Sussex Herald	Aeronca-J.A.P.	40	29'	21' 6"		580	800
(Civil) 1945	Miles Messenger	Cirrus Major 3	155	36' 2"	24'	191	1450	2400
1945	Miles Gemini	2 Cirrus Minor 2	100 each	36' 2"	22' 3"	191	1910	3000
1951	Miles Aries	2 Cirrus Major 3	155 each	36' 2"	22' 5"	191	2462	3475
1953	Miles Sparrowjet	2 Turboméca Palas	330 lb*	28' 8"	27' 7"	156	1450	2400
1957	Miles Student	2 Turboméca Marboré	880 lb*	29' 2"	30' 9"	144	2300	3600
1947	Newbury Eon	Cirrus Minor 2	100	37'	25'	173		1950
1948	Newbury Eon	Gipsy Major 10	145	37'	25'	173		2150
(Civil) 1946	Percival Proctor I, II, III, IV	Gipsy Queen 2	210	39' 6"	25' 10"	197	1875	3250
1946	Percival Proctor V	Gipsy Queen 2	210	39' 6"	28' 2"	202	2450	3500
(Civil) 1956	Percival Prentice	Gipsy Queen 30	250	46' 0"	31' 3"	305	3080	4650
1958	Phoenix L.A.4a Minor	Aeronca-J.A.P.	37	25'	20' 9"	125	390	627
1958	Phoenix L.A.5 Major	Walter Mikron 2	62	35' 2"	23' 9"	163	600	1030
1948	Planet Satellite	Gipsy Queen 30	250	33' 6"	26' 3"	153	1600	2905
1947	Portsmouth Aerocar	2 Cirrus Major III	155 each	42'	26' 3"	255	2800	4200
1958	Rollason (Druine) Turbulent	Ardem 4	30	21' 5"	17' 4"		341	606
	Rollason (Druine) Condor	Continental A-75	75	30' 2"	21' 6"	135	820	1367
1948	Slingsby Motor Tutor	Aeronca-J.A.P.	37	43' 4"	20' 10"	170	570	807
1954–5	Somers-Kendall S.K.1	Turboméca Palas	330 lb*	22' 9"	20' 10"		685	1500
1960	Tawney Owl	Porsche	75	24'	19' 6"	120	800	1200
1958–9	Taylor Monoplane	Aeronca-J.A.P.	38	21'	15'	72	400	610
1958 (In England)	Thruxton Jackaroo	Gipsy Major 1	130	30' 4"	25' 9"	247	1360	2180
1957	Tipsy Belfair	Walter Mikron 2	62	31' 2"	21' 8"	130	540	1100
	Tipsy Junior	Walter Mikron 2	62	22' 8"	18' 7"	113	440	770
1947–8	Tipsy M	Gipsy Major 10	145	32' 10"	27' 6"		1572	1960
1958–60	Tipsy Nipper	Stark Stamo	45	19' 8"	15'	81	412	660

* Figure refers to static thrust per engine.

ntinued

Max. speed, m.p.h.	Stalling speed, m.p.h.	Initial rate of climb, ft/min	Ceiling, ft	Range, statute miles	Fuel capacity, gallons	Notes
92						Single-seater. Little flown, abandoned 1954.
135	25	950	16,000(S)	460	36	Developed from war-time M-28, originally conceived as replacement for Whitney Straight and Monarch. Also fitted with Gipsy Major ID and 10 engines.
145	35 (I.A.S.)	650	13,500	555(1015)	36(60)	Twin-engined Messenger, also fitted with Gipsy Major, Lycoming and Continental engines.
172		1300	20,000	675	60	Development of Gemini.
220		2100		270	80	Converted Sparrowhawk.
290	69	2050		476	100	Jet trainer. Prototype only to date.
112	43	525	10,000(S)	350	18	
136	50	675	13,400(S)	350	18	
165		1020	17,000	660		Wartime versions of Vega Gull, passed into civil use later.
157	55	680	14,000(S)	500	40	First civil Proctor. Mk. 6 later had 250-h.p. Gipsy Queen 30 engine.
150	56	700	15,000(S)	485	40	2/3 seater. Also short-range 7-seater conversion by Aviation Traders.
85	28	450		180	6·5	Pre-war design brought up to date.
105	35	700		300	11	Pre-war design brought up to date.
208	62	1450	22,000(A)	1000	56	All-magnesium 4/5 seater pusher monoplane. Never flew.
176		1300	19,500(S)	627	120	6-seater. Smaller version with Cirrus Minor engine not completed.
87	28	492		190	8·8	French design built in England.
101 cruise	34	698		300	10	French design built in England.
70	34	410	16,500(S)	246	9·5	Slingsby Tutor glider fitted with engine.
332						2-seater jet racer. Only one built.
120 (est.)	40	800	12,000(S)	over 500	18	2-seater pusher monoplane. Prototype only to date.
104	38	1400		230	6	Amateur-built single-seater.
104	37	600		250	19	
110	37	500	19,700	465	13	Post-war cabin version of Tipsy two-seater.
112	34		18,000	340		
134						
101	35	630	13,100(S)	200	7·5	Designed and built by Avions Fairey of Belgium. Earlier version had Pollmann 40-h.p. engine.

(A)=absolute   (S)=service

CHAPTER 16: PART 2

FLYING CLUBS AND GROUPS IN THE UNITED KINGDOM COM-
PILED FROM THE MEMBERSHIP LISTS OF THE ASSOCIATION OF
BRITISH AERO CLUBS AND CENTRES AND OF THE POPULAR
FLYING ASSOCIATION

A.B.A.C. Clubs and Air Centres

Name of Club or Air Centre	*Aerodrome*
Bedfordshire Air Centre	Cranfield
Blackbushe Aero Club	Blackbushe
Blackpool and Fylde Aero Club	Squires Gate
Bournemouth Flying Club	Hurn
Bristol and Wessex Aeroplane Club	Lulsgate
Caithness Flying Club	Wick
Cambridge Aero Club	Cambridge
Cessna Flying Club	Staverton
Channel Islands Aero Club	Jersey
Colchester Flying Club	Boxted
Cotswold Aero Club	Staverton
Coventry Aeroplane Club	Baginton
Cumberland Flying Club	Carlisle
Derby Air Centre	Burnaston
East Anglian Flying Club	Ipswich
East Yorkshire Aero Club	—
Edinburgh Flying Club	Turnhouse
Elstree Flying Club	Elstree
Exeter Aero Club	Exeter
Fair Oaks Aero Club	Fair Oaks (Woking)
Flairavia Flying Club	Biggin Hill
Glamorgan Flying Club	Rhoose
Halfpenny Green Flying Club	Halfpenny Green (nr. Wolverhampton)
Hampshire Aeroplane Club	Eastleigh (Southampton)
Herefordshire Aero Club	Shobdon
Herts and Essex Aero Club	Stapleford Tawney
Isle of Wight Air Centre and Flying Club	Sandown
Lancashire Aero Club	Barton
Leeds/Bradford Air Centre	Yeadon
Leicestershire Aero Club	Leicester East
Liverpool Flying Club	Speke
Luton Flying Club	Luton
Midland Aero Club	Elmdon
Newcastle-upon-Tyne Aero Club	Woolsington
Norfolk and Norwich Aero Club	Swanton Morley
Northamptonshire Aero Club	Sywell
Northern School of Aviation Flying Club	Squires Gate
Oxford Aeroplane Club	Oxford (Kidlington)
Plymouth Aero Club	Plymouth
Portsmouth Aero Club	Portsmouth
Rochester Flying Club	Rochester
Scottish Aero Club	Perth
Scottish Air Centre	Perth

Shaftesbury Flying Club	Private field
Sherwood Flying Club	Tollerton
Shropshire Flying Group	Sleap
Skegness Aero Club	Ingoldmells
Southend-on-Sea Municipal Air Centre and Flying School	Southend (Rochford)
Southern Aero Club	Shoreham
Surrey and Kent Flying Club	Biggin Hill
Swansea and District Flying School and Club	Fairwood Common
Turnhouse Air Centre	Turnhouse (Edinburgh)
Ulster Flying Club	Newtownards
Warwickshire Aero Club	Elmdon
West London Aero Club	White Waltham
Wiltshire Flying Club	Thruxton
Wolverhampton Aero Club	Wolverhampton

A.B.A.C. Community Operated Clubs

Alouette Flying Club	Biggin Hill
Experimental Flying Group	Biggin Hill
Isle of Man Flying Club	Ronaldsway

A.B.A.C. Groups

Air Touring Club	Biggin Hill
Allied Flying Group	Woolsington
Alpha Mike Flying Group	Thruxton
Banbury Flying Group	Edgehill
Bircher Flying Group	Wolverhampton
Bustard Flying Group	Old Sarum
Caribbean Flying Group	Elstree
Clifton Flying Group	Lulsgate
Denham Auster Group	Denham
Desford Flying Club	Hurn
Dispatchers Flying Group	—
Dove Flying Group	Blackbushe
Easy King Flying Group	Sywell
Executive and Sporting Aero Club	—
Eyre Flying Club	Elstree
Falcon Group	—
Gafir Flying Club	Luton
Gledhill Flying Group	Speke
Highfield Flying Group	Wolverhampton
High Wycombe Flying Group	Booker
Hilton Flying Group	Wolverhampton
Holland Park Flying Group	Elstree
Hornet Moth Flying Group	Denham
Knight Flying Group	Staverton
Magister Flying Group	Denham
Maitland Drewery Flying Group	Biggin Hill
Middlesex Flying Group	Elstree
Mona Flying Club	—
Nipper Flying Group	Elstree
Northumbrian Flying Group	Woolsington
North Waltham Flying Group	Thruxton
North West Flying Group	Limavady

Nottingham Air Touring Group	Tollerton
Ongar Flying Club	Fyfield
Panda Flying Group	Luton
Paris Flying Group	Luton
Plymouth Magister Flying Group	Plymouth
Rhoose Flying Club	Rhoose
Roberts Eagle Flying Group	Elstree
St Edward's Flying Group	Kidlington
Severn Lamb Flying Group	Edgehill
Shirley Flying Group	Elmdon
Southdown Flying Group	Wellcross Grange Fields (nr. Horsham, Sussex)
South Western Flying Club	—
Spartan Flying Group	Denham
Stoke-on-Trent Flying Club	Meir
Streatham Flying Club	Denham
Thirty-Two Group	Wolverhampton
Tibbenham Tiger Group	Tibbenham
Tiger Club	Redhill
Tiger Moth Flying Group	Poddington
Turnhouse Tiger Group	Turnhouse
Variety Artists and Civil Flying Club	Biggin Hill
Waveney Flying Group	Seething
Willie Jig Flying Group	Lulsgate
Worcester Aero Group	Halfpenny Green

P. F. A. Co-Ownership Groups and Clubs

Air Touring Group	Luton
Arden Flying Group	Kidlington, Elstree and Yeadon
Armada Flying Group	Plymouth
Armstrong Whitworth Flying Group	Baginton
Bristol Siddeley Flying Club	Baginton
Biggin Hill Flying Club	Biggin Hill
Biggleswade Flying Group	Panshanger
Birmingham Airport Flying Group	Elmdon
Blackpool and Fylde Aero Club	Squires Gate
Bolton Flying Group	Barton
Bourne and District Flying Club	Folkingham
Bournemouth Flying Group	Christchurch
Bristol Channel Flying Group	Swansea
Brooklands Flying Group	Barton
Cambridge Private Flying Club	Cambridge
Cardiff Ultra-Light Aeroplane Club	Rhoose
Coningsby Flying Group	Coningsby
Double-Alpha Flying Group	Speke
East London Flying Group	Stapleford Tawney
Chesterfield Air Touring Group	Leicester East
Felthorpe Flying Group	Fakenham
Garke Group	White Waltham
G.E.C. (Coventry) Flying Group	Baginton
Glamorgan Flying Group	Rhoose
Gower Flying Club	Rhoose
Great Easton Flying Group	Stansted

Hadrian Group	Woolsington
Herriard Flying Group	Lasham
Hornet Private Flying Group	Luton
Humber Flying Group	Skegness
K.K. P.F.A. Group	White Waltham
Lincoln Aero Club	Kirton Lindsey
Lotus Flying Group	Panshanger
Marwood Flying Group	Barton
McAully Flying Group	Little Snoring
Mill Hill Group	Elstree
Montgomeryshire Ultra-Light Flying Club	Heldre Hill, Welshpool
M.P.M. Flying Group	Elstree
Old Warden Flying Group	Biggleswade
Perseus Flying Group	—
P.F.A. Group 100	White Waltham
Proctor Group	Baginton
R.A.F. Syerston Flying Club	Syerston
R.A.F. Waddington Flying Group	Waddington
Rollason Flying Group	Biggin Hill
Rutherglen Group	Rutherglen
Silverline Flying Group	Eastleigh
600 Sqdn. (City of London) Flying Club	Biggin Hill
615 Sqdn. Flying Group	Biggin Hill
Southampton Group	Eastleigh
Southport Aero Club	Hesketh Park
Southwell Air Touring Club	Tollerton
Stapleford Flying Group	Stapleford Tawney
Swallow Flying Group	Elstree
Tiger Club	Redhill and Fair Oaks
Tipsy Flying Group	Baginton
T.K. Flying Group	Hatfield
Thruxton Flying Group	Thruxton
Ulster Aero Group	Sydenham
Warwickshire Flying Club	Elmdon
Welwyn Flying Group	Panshanger
West Lancs Flying Group	Speke
Winkfield Flying Group	White Waltham
Woking Flying Club	Redhill
Worcester Aero Group	—
Yorkshire Flying Group	Sherburn-in-Elmet
Yorkshire Territorial Flying Group	Yeadon
Kingfisher Flying Group	—
Firwood Flying Group	—
Hertfordshire Experimental Group	—
Maghaberry Flying Group	—
Corvex Group	—
Luton Wildcats	Luton
Calleva Group	Thruxton
Frilford Flying Group	Kidlington
Farnborough Popular Flying Group	—
North Downs Flying Group	—
Wolverhampton Ultra-Light Flying Group	—

Bibliography

ALI, Alban, *The Scarlet Angel* (Duckworth, 1934).

BANNER, Hubert S., *Amy Johnson* (Rich and Cowan, 1933).

BATTEN, Jean, *My Life* (G. G. Harrap & Co., 1938).

BENNETT, Benjamin, *Down Africa's Skyways* (Hutchinson, 1932).

BIARD, H. C., *Wings* (Hurst & Blackett, 1934).

BRETT, R. Dallas, *History of British Aviation 1908–1914* (John Hamilton, 1934).

BROAD, H. S., *Flying Wisdom* (Sampson Low, 1939).

BRUCE, Hon. Mrs. Victor, *The Bluebird's Flight* (Chapman & Hall, 1931).

CHICHESTER, F. C., *Solo to Sydney* (John Hamilton, 1930).

CHICHESTER, F. C., *Seaplane Solo* (Faber & Faber, 1933). 2nd ed. *Alone Across the Tasman Sea* (Allen & Unwin, 1945).

CHICHESTER, F. C., *Ride on the Wind* (Hamish Hamilton, 1936).

CLARKE, Basil, *Atlantic Adventure* (Allen & Wingate, 1958).

CLOUSTON, A. E., *The Dangerous Skies* (Cassell & Co., 1954).

DE HAVILLAND, Sir Geoffrey, *Sky Fever* (Hamish Hamilton, 1961).

DORMAN, Geoffrey, *Fifty Years Fly Past* (Forbes Robertson, 1951).

ELLISON, Norman F., *Flying Matilda* (Angus & Robertson (Sydney), 1957).

FAWCETT, Edward Douglas, *From Heston to the High Alps* (Macmillan, 1936).

GANDAR DOWER, K. C., *Amateur Adventure* (Rich & Cowan, 1934).

GARNETT, David, *A Rabbit in the Air* (Chatto & Windus, 1932. Reprinted 1951).

GIBBS-SMITH, Charles H., *The Aeroplane* (H.M.S.O., 1960).

GORE, John F. (ed.), *Mary, Duchess of Bedford 1865–1937* (John Murray, 1938). (Diaries.)

GRAHAME-WHITE, Claude and HARPER, Harry, *The Story of the Aeroplane* (T. Werner Laurie, 1911).

GRIERSON, John, *Through Russia by Air* (G. T. Foulis & Co., 1934).

GRIERSON, John, *High Failure* (Wm. Hodge & Co., 1936).

HEATH, Lady and MURRAY, Stella Wolfe, *Woman and Flying* (John Long, 1929).

HUMBLE, Richard, *Cape Town to Clyde* (Longmans, Green & Co., 1932).

HURREN, B. J., *Fellowship of the Air* (Iliffe & Sons, 1951).

JACKSON, A. J., *British Civil Aircraft 1919–59* (Putnam, 1959–60).

Jane's All the World's Aircraft (Sampson Low, Marston and Co. Ltd).

LEEMING, John F., *Airdays* (G. G. Harrap & Co., 1936).

LUKINS, A. H. (ed. Russell, D. A.), *The Book of Westland Aircraft* (Harborough Pub. Co., 1944).

LUKINS, A. H. (ed. Russell, D. A.), *The Book of Miles Aircraft* (Harborough Pub. Co., 1945).

LUKINS, A. H. (ed. Russell, D. A.), *The Book of Bristol Aircraft* (Harborough Pub. Co., 1946).

MACMILLAN, Norman, *Sir Sefton Brancker* (Wm. Heinemann, 1935).

MACMILLAN, Norman, *Great Airmen* (G. Bell & Sons, 1955).

MACMILLAN, Norman, *Great Aircraft* (G. Bell & Sons, 1960).

MARKHAM, Beryl, *West with the Night* (G. G. Harrap & Co., 1943).

MERRIAM, F. Warren, *First Through the Clouds* (Batsford, 1954).

MIGNET, Henri, *Le Sport de l'Air* (Imp. A. Taffin-Lefort, Paris), transl. as *The Flying Flea* (Sampson Low, 1935).

MOLLISON, J. A., *Death Cometh Soon or Late* (Hutchinson, 1932).

MOLLISON, J. A., *Playboy of the Air* (Michael Joseph, 1937).

PENROSE, Harald, *I Flew with the Birds* (Country Life, 1949).

POUND, Reginald and HARMSWORTH, Geoffrey, *Northcliffe* (Cassell, 1959).

PRESTON, R. L., *How to Become an Air Pilot* (Sampson Low, 1930).

SCOTT, C. W. A., *Scott's Book* (Hodder & Stoughton, 1934).

SEMPILL, Col. the Master of, *The Air and the Plain Man* (Elkin, Matthews & Marrot, 1931).

SHARP, C. Martin, *DH—An Outline of de Havilland History* (Faber & Faber, 1961).

SHEPHERD, E. Colston, *Great Flights* (Adam & Charles Black, 1939).

SIBOUR, Violette de, *Flying Gipsies* (G. P. Putnam's Sons, 1930).

SMITH, Sir Charles E. Kingsford, *My Flying Life* (Andrew Melrose, 1937).

STEWART, Oliver, *First Flights* (Routledge & Kegan Paul, 1957).

SUTHERLAND, Duke of, *Looking Back* (Odhams, 1957).

TREDREY, Frank D., *Pilot's Summer* (Duckworth, 1939).

TURNER, C. C., *The Old Flying Days* (Sampson Low & Co., 1927).

WHITE, T. H., *England Have my Bones* (Collins, 1936).

YOUNG, A. B. Filson, *Growing Wings* (Michael Joseph, 1936).

Unfortunately most of the books published before the war are now out of print. Those who wish to capture the atmosphere of learning to fly with the light aeroplane clubs of the 1920s and 1930s should not fail to read John Leeming, David Garnett, T. H. White, Douglas Fawcett and Filson Young. Gandar Dower and Alban Ali are not referred to in the text since their flights must be regarded as minor ones, but their books are not the less interesting for this and should certainly be read by those wishing to study the period. There are hardly any books dealing with the Lympne trials, but *Great Aircraft* offers a detailed account of the Parnall Pixie by its pilot Captain Norman Macmillan.

Index